# 50% OFF

## Online NYSTCE ATAS Prep Course!

Dear Customer,

Thank you for your purchase of this NYSTCE ATAS Study Guide. Included with your purchase is **discounted access to our online NYSTCE ATAS Online Course.** Many NYSTCE courses are needlessly expensive and don't deliver enough value. Our course provides the best NYSTCE ATAS prep material, and with discounted access, **you only pay half price**.

**We have structured our online course to perfectly complement your printed study guide**. The NYSTCE ATAS Online Course contains **in-depth lessons** that cover all the most important topics, **180+ video reviews** that explain difficult concepts, **500 practice questions** to ensure you feel prepared, and more than **520 digital flashcards**, so you can study while you're on the go.

***Online NYSTCE ATAS Prep Course***

**Topics Covered:**

- Reading
  - Vocabulary and Word Relationships
  - Main Ideas & Author's Purpose
- Writing
  - Subjects and Predicates
  - The Writing Process
- Mathematics
  - Fractions and Decimals
  - Proportions and Ratios
- Instructional Support
  - Developmental Literacy
  - Behavior Management

**Course Features:**

- NYSTCE ATAS Study Guide
  - Get content that complements our best-selling study guide.
- Full-Length Practice Tests
  - With 500 practice questions, you can test yourself again and again.
- Mobile Friendly
  - If you need to study on the go, the course is easily accessible from your mobile device.
- NYSTCE ATAS Flashcards
  - Our course includes a flashcards mode with over 520 content cards for you to study.

To lock in your discounted access, visit mometrix.com/university/nystce-atas or simply scan this QR code with your smartphone. At the checkout page, enter the discount code: **atas50off**

If you have any questions or concerns, please contact us at support@mometrix.com.

# Access Your Online Resources

**Don't miss out on the Online Resources included with your purchase!**

Your purchase of this product unlocks access to our Online Resources page. Elevate your study experience with our **interactive practice test interface**, along with all of the additional resources that we couldn't include in this book.

**Flip to the Online Resources section at the end of this book to find the link and a QR code to get started!**

# NYSTCE®

## Assessment of Teaching Assistant Skills (ATAS) (095) Secrets Study Guide

NYSTCE® ATAS Exam Preparation Book

5 Full-Length Practice Tests

175+ Online Video Tutorials

**3rd Edition**

Written and edited by Matthew Bowling

Printed in the United States of America

This paper meets the requirements of ANSI/NISO Z39.48-1992 (Permanence of Paper).



Paperback
ISBN 13: 978-1-5167-2909-8
ISBN 10: 1-5167-2909-9

# DEAR FUTURE EXAM SUCCESS STORY

First of all, **THANK YOU** for purchasing Mometrix study materials!

Second, congratulations! You are one of the few determined test-takers who are committed to doing whatever it takes to excel on your exam. **You have come to the right place.** We developed these study materials with one goal in mind: to deliver you the information you need in a format that's concise and easy to use.

In addition to optimizing your guide for the content of the test, we've outlined our recommended steps for breaking down the preparation process into small, attainable goals so you can make sure you stay on track.

We've also analyzed the entire test-taking process, identifying the most common pitfalls and showing how you can overcome them and be ready for any curveball the test throws you.

Standardized testing is one of the biggest obstacles on your road to success, which only increases the importance of doing well in the high-pressure, high-stakes environment of test day. Your results on this test could have a significant impact on your future, and this guide provides the information and practical advice to help you achieve your full potential on test day.

**Your success is our success**

**We would love to hear from you!** If you would like to share the story of your exam success or if you have any questions or comments in regard to our products, please contact us at **800-673-8175** or **support@mometrix.com**.

Thanks again for your business and we wish you continued success!

Sincerely,
The Mometrix Test Preparation Team

# Table of Contents

# Introduction

**Thank you for purchasing this resource**! You have made the choice to prepare yourself for a test that could have a huge impact on your future, and this guide is designed to help you be fully ready for test day. Obviously, it's important to have a solid understanding of the test material, but you also need to be prepared for the unique environment and stressors of the test, so that you can perform to the best of your abilities.

For this purpose, the first section that appears in this guide is the **Secret Keys**. We've devoted countless hours to meticulously researching what works and what doesn't, and we've boiled down our findings to the five most impactful steps you can take to improve your performance on the test. We start at the beginning with study planning and move through the preparation process, all the way to the testing strategies that will help you get the most out of what you know when you're finally sitting in front of the test.

We recommend that you start preparing for your test as far in advance as possible. However, if you've bought this guide as a last-minute study resource and only have a few days before your test, we recommend that you skip over the first two Secret Keys since they address a long-term study plan.

If you struggle with **test anxiety**, we strongly encourage you to check out our recommendations for how you can overcome it. Test anxiety is a formidable foe, but it can be beaten, and we want to make sure you have the tools you need to defeat it.

# Secret Key #1 – Plan Big, Study Small

There's a lot riding on your performance. If you want to ace this test, you're going to need to keep your skills sharp and the material fresh in your mind. You need a plan that lets you review everything you need to know while still fitting in your schedule. We'll break this strategy down into three categories.

## Information Organization

Start with the information you already have: the official test outline. From this, you can make a complete list of all the concepts you need to cover before the test. Organize these concepts into groups that can be studied together, and create a list of any related vocabulary you need to learn so you can brush up on any difficult terms. You'll want to keep this vocabulary list handy once you actually start studying since you may need to add to it along the way.

## Time Management

Once you have your set of study concepts, decide how to spread them out over the time you have left before the test. Break your study plan into small, clear goals so you have a manageable task for each day and know exactly what you're doing. Then just focus on one small step at a time. When you manage your time this way, you don't need to spend hours at a time studying. Studying a small block of content for a short period each day helps you retain information better and avoid stressing over how much you have left to do. You can relax knowing that you have a plan to cover everything in time. In order for this strategy to be effective though, you have to start studying early and stick to your schedule. Avoid the exhaustion and futility that comes from last-minute cramming!

## Study Environment

The environment you study in has a big impact on your learning. Studying in a coffee shop, while probably more enjoyable, is not likely to be as fruitful as studying in a quiet room. It's important to keep distractions to a minimum. You're only planning to study for a short block of time, so make the most of it. Don't pause to check your phone or get up to find a snack. It's also important to **avoid multitasking**. Research has consistently shown that multitasking will make your studying dramatically less effective. Your study area should also be comfortable and well-lit so you don't have the distraction of straining your eyes or sitting on an uncomfortable chair.

The time of day you study is also important. You want to be rested and alert. Don't wait until just before bedtime. Study when you'll be most likely to comprehend and remember. Even better, if you know what time of day your test will be, set that time aside for study. That way your brain will be used to working on that subject at that specific time and you'll have a better chance of recalling information.

Finally, it can be helpful to team up with others who are studying for the same test. Your actual studying should be done in as isolated an environment as possible, but the work of organizing the information and setting up the study plan can be divided up. In between study sessions, you can discuss with your teammates the concepts that you're all studying and quiz each other on the details. Just be sure that your teammates are as serious about the test as you are. If you find that your study time is being replaced with social time, you might need to find a new team.

# Secret Key #2 – Make Your Studying Count

You're devoting a lot of time and effort to preparing for this test, so you want to be absolutely certain it will pay off. This means doing more than just reading the content and hoping you can remember it on test day. It's important to make every minute of study count. There are two main areas you can focus on to make your studying count.

## Retention

It doesn't matter how much time you study if you can't remember the material. You need to make sure you are retaining the concepts. To check your retention of the information you're learning, try recalling it at later times with minimal prompting. Try carrying around flashcards and glance at one or two from time to time or ask a friend who's also studying for the test to quiz you.

To enhance your retention, look for ways to put the information into practice so that you can apply it rather than simply recalling it. If you're using the information in practical ways, it will be much easier to remember. Similarly, it helps to solidify a concept in your mind if you're not only reading it to yourself but also explaining it to someone else. Ask a friend to let you teach them about a concept you're a little shaky on (or speak aloud to an imaginary audience if necessary). As you try to summarize, define, give examples, and answer your friend's questions, you'll understand the concepts better and they will stay with you longer. Finally, step back for a big picture view and ask yourself how each piece of information fits with the whole subject. When you link the different concepts together and see them working together as a whole, it's easier to remember the individual components.

Finally, practice showing your work on any multi-step problems, even if you're just studying. Writing out each step you take to solve a problem will help solidify the process in your mind, and you'll be more likely to remember it during the test.

## Modality

*Modality* simply refers to the means or method by which you study. Choosing a study modality that fits your own individual learning style is crucial. No two people learn best in exactly the same way, so it's important to know your strengths and use them to your advantage.

For example, if you learn best by visualization, focus on visualizing a concept in your mind and draw an image or a diagram. Try color-coding your notes, illustrating them, or creating symbols that will trigger your mind to recall a learned concept. If you learn best by hearing or discussing information, find a study partner who learns the same way or read aloud to yourself. Think about how to put the information in your own words. Imagine that you are giving a lecture on the topic and record yourself so you can listen to it later.

For any learning style, flashcards can be helpful. Organize the information so you can take advantage of spare moments to review. Underline key words or phrases. Use different colors for different categories. Mnemonic devices (such as creating a short list in which every item starts with the same letter) can also help with retention. Find what works best for you and use it to store the information in your mind most effectively and easily.

# Secret Key #3 – Practice the Right Way

Your success on test day depends not only on how many hours you put into preparing, but also on whether you prepared the right way. It's good to check along the way to see if your studying is paying off. One of the most effective ways to do this is by taking practice tests to evaluate your progress. Practice tests are useful because they show exactly where you need to improve. Every time you take a practice test, pay special attention to these three groups of questions:

- The questions you got wrong
- The questions you had to guess on, even if you guessed right
- The questions you found difficult or slow to work through

This will show you exactly what your weak areas are, and where you need to devote more study time. Ask yourself why each of these questions gave you trouble. Was it because you didn't understand the material? Was it because you didn't remember the vocabulary? Do you need more repetitions on this type of question to build speed and confidence? Dig into those questions and figure out how you can strengthen your weak areas as you go back to review the material.

Additionally, many practice tests have a section explaining the answer choices. It can be tempting to read the explanation and think that you now have a good understanding of the concept. However, an explanation likely only covers part of the question's broader context. Even if the explanation makes perfect sense, **go back and investigate** every concept related to the question until you're positive you have a thorough understanding.

As you go along, keep in mind that the practice test is just that: practice. Memorizing these questions and answers will not be very helpful on the actual test because it is unlikely to have any of the same exact questions. If you only know the right answers to the sample questions, you won't be prepared for the real thing. **Study the concepts** until you understand them fully, and then you'll be able to answer any question that shows up on the test.

It's important to wait on the practice tests until you're ready. If you take a test on your first day of study, you may be overwhelmed by the amount of material covered and how much you need to learn. Work up to it gradually.

On test day, you'll need to be prepared for answering questions, managing your time, and using the test-taking strategies you've learned. It's a lot to balance, like a mental marathon that will have a big impact on your future. Like training for a marathon, you'll need to start slowly and work your way up. When test day arrives, you'll be ready.

Start with the strategies you've read in the first two Secret Keys—plan your course and study in the way that works best for you. If you have time, consider using multiple study resources to get different approaches to the same concepts. It can be helpful to see difficult concepts from more than one angle. Then find a good source for practice tests. Many times, the test website will suggest potential study resources or provide sample tests.

## Practice Test Strategy

If you're able to find at least three practice tests, we recommend this strategy:

### UNTIMED AND OPEN-BOOK PRACTICE

Take the first test with no time constraints and with your notes and study guide handy. Take your time and focus on applying the strategies you've learned.

### TIMED AND OPEN-BOOK PRACTICE

Take the second practice test open-book as well, but set a timer and practice pacing yourself to finish in time.

### TIMED AND CLOSED-BOOK PRACTICE

Take any other practice tests as if it were test day. Set a timer and put away your study materials. Sit at a table or desk in a quiet room, imagine yourself at the testing center, and answer questions as quickly and accurately as possible.

Keep repeating timed and closed-book tests on a regular basis until you run out of practice tests or it's time for the actual test. Your mind will be ready for the schedule and stress of test day, and you'll be able to focus on recalling the material you've learned.

# Secret Key #4 – Pace Yourself

Once you're fully prepared for the material on the test, your biggest challenge on test day will be managing your time. Just knowing that the clock is ticking can make you panic even if you have plenty of time left. Work on pacing yourself so you can build confidence against the time constraints of the exam. Pacing is a difficult skill to master, especially in a high-pressure environment, so **practice is vital**.

Set time expectations for your pace based on how much time is available. For example, if a section has 60 questions and the time limit is 30 minutes, you know you have to average 30 seconds or less per question in order to answer them all. Although 30 seconds is the hard limit, set 25 seconds per question as your goal, so you reserve extra time to spend on harder questions. When you budget extra time for the harder questions, you no longer have any reason to stress when those questions take longer to answer.

Don't let this time expectation distract you from working through the test at a calm, steady pace, but keep it in mind so you don't spend too much time on any one question. Recognize that taking extra time on one question you don't understand may keep you from answering two that you do understand later in the test. If your time limit for a question is up and you're still not sure of the answer, mark it and move on, and come back to it later if the time and the test format allow. If the testing format doesn't allow you to return to earlier questions, just make an educated guess; then put it out of your mind and move on.

On the easier questions, be careful not to rush. It may seem wise to hurry through them so you have more time for the challenging ones, but it's not worth missing one if you know the concept and just didn't take the time to read the question fully. Work efficiently but make sure you understand the question and have looked at all of the answer choices, since more than one may seem right at first.

Even if you're paying attention to the time, you may find yourself a little behind at some point. You should speed up to get back on track, but do so wisely. Don't panic; just take a few seconds less on each question until you're caught up. Don't guess without thinking, but do look through the answer choices and eliminate any you know are wrong. If you can get down to two choices, it is often worthwhile to guess from those. Once you've chosen an answer, move on and don't dwell on any that you skipped or had to hurry through. If a question was taking too long, chances are it was one of the harder ones, so you weren't as likely to get it right anyway.

On the other hand, if you find yourself getting ahead of schedule, it may be beneficial to slow down a little. The more quickly you work, the more likely you are to make a careless mistake that will affect your score. You've budgeted time for each question, so don't be afraid to spend that time. Practice an efficient but careful pace to get the most out of the time you have.

# Secret Key #5 – Have a Plan for Guessing

When you're taking the test, you may find yourself stuck on a question. Some of the answer choices seem better than others, but you don't see the one answer choice that is obviously correct. What do you do?

The scenario described above is very common, yet most test takers have not effectively prepared for it. Developing and practicing a plan for guessing may be one of the single most effective uses of your time as you get ready for the exam.

In developing your plan for guessing, there are three questions to address:

- When should you start the guessing process?
- How should you narrow down the choices?
- Which answer should you choose?

## When to Start the Guessing Process

Unless your plan for guessing is to select C every time (which, despite its merits, is not what we recommend), you need to leave yourself enough time to apply your answer elimination strategies. Since you have a limited amount of time for each question, that means that if you're going to give yourself the best shot at guessing correctly, you have to decide quickly whether or not you will guess.

Of course, the best-case scenario is that you don't have to guess at all, so first, see if you can answer the question based on your knowledge of the subject and basic reasoning skills. Focus on the key words in the question and try to jog your memory of related topics. Give yourself a chance to bring the knowledge to mind, but once you realize that you don't have (or you can't access) the knowledge you need to answer the question, it's time to start the guessing process.

It's almost always better to start the guessing process too early than too late. It only takes a few seconds to remember something and answer the question from knowledge. Carefully eliminating wrong answer choices takes longer. Plus, going through the process of eliminating answer choices can actually help jog your memory.

**Summary**: Start the guessing process as soon as you decide that you can't answer the question based on your knowledge.

## How to Narrow Down the Choices

The next chapter in this book (**Test-Taking Strategies**) includes a wide range of strategies for how to approach questions and how to look for answer choices to eliminate. You will definitely want to read those carefully, practice them, and figure out which ones work best for you. Here though, we're going to address a mindset rather than a particular strategy.

Your odds of guessing an answer correctly depend on how many options you are choosing from.

| **Number of options left** | 5 | 4 | 3 | 2 | 1 |
|---|---|---|---|---|---|
| **Odds of guessing correctly** | 20% | 25% | 33% | 50% | 100% |

You can see from this chart just how valuable it is to be able to eliminate incorrect answers and make an educated guess, but there are two things that many test takers do that cause them to miss out on the benefits of guessing:

- Accidentally eliminating the correct answer
- Selecting an answer based on an impression

We'll look at the first one here, and the second one in the next section.

To avoid accidentally eliminating the correct answer, we recommend a thought exercise called **the $5 challenge**. In this challenge, you only eliminate an answer choice from contention if you are willing to bet $5 on it being wrong. Why $5? Five dollars is a small but not insignificant amount of money. It's an amount you could afford to lose but wouldn't want to throw away. And while losing $5 once might not hurt too much, doing it twenty times will set you back $100. In the same way, each small decision you make—eliminating a choice here, guessing on a question there—won't by itself impact your score very much, but when you put them all together, they can make a big difference. By holding each answer choice elimination decision to a higher standard, you can reduce the risk of accidentally eliminating the correct answer.

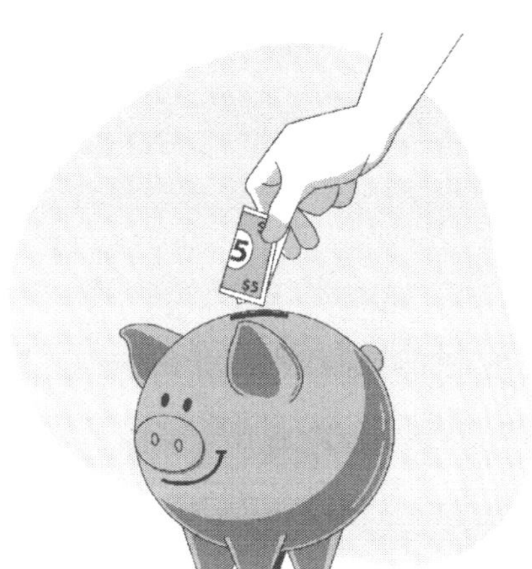

The $5 challenge can also be applied in a positive sense: If you are willing to bet $5 that an answer choice *is* correct, go ahead and mark it as correct.

**Summary**: Only eliminate an answer choice if you are willing to bet $5 that it is wrong.

## Which Answer to Choose

You're taking the test. You've run into a hard question and decided you'll have to guess. You've eliminated all the answer choices you're willing to bet $5 on. Now you have to pick an answer. Why do we even need to talk about this? Why can't you just pick whichever one you feel like when the time comes?

The answer to these questions is that if you don't come into the test with a plan, you'll rely on your impression to select an answer choice, and if you do that, you risk falling into a trap. The test writers know that everyone who takes their test will be guessing on some of the questions, so they intentionally write wrong answer choices to seem plausible. You still have to pick an answer though, and if the wrong answer choices are designed to look right, how can you ever be sure that you're not falling for their trap? The best solution we've found to this dilemma is to take the decision out of your hands entirely. Here is the process we recommend:

**Once you've eliminated any choices that you are confident (willing to bet $5) are wrong, select the first remaining choice as your answer.**

Whether you choose to select the first remaining choice, the second, or the last, the important thing is that you use some preselected standard. Using this approach guarantees that you will not be enticed into selecting an answer choice that looks right, because you are not basing your decision on how the answer choices look.

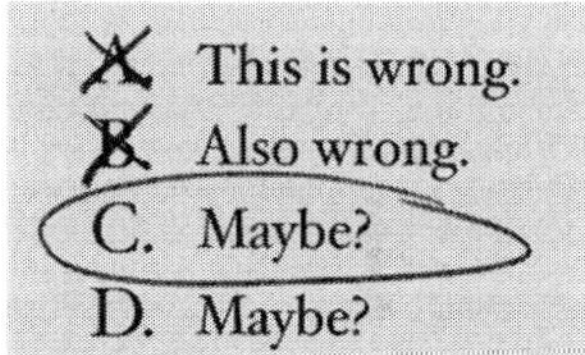


This is not meant to make you question your knowledge. Instead, it is to help you recognize the difference between your knowledge and your impressions. There's a huge difference between thinking an answer is right because of what you know, and thinking an answer is right because it looks or sounds like it should be right.

**Summary**: To ensure that your selection is appropriately random, make a predetermined selection from among all answer choices you have not eliminated.

# Test-Taking Strategies

This section contains a list of test-taking strategies that you may find helpful as you work through the test. By taking what you know and applying logical thought, you can maximize your chances of answering any question correctly!

It is very important to realize that every question is different and every person is different: no single strategy will work on every question, and no single strategy will work for every person. That's why we've included all of them here, so you can try them out and determine which ones work best for different types of questions and which ones work best for you.

## Question Strategies

### ⊘ Read Carefully

Read the question and the answer choices carefully. Don't miss the question because you misread the terms. You have plenty of time to read each question thoroughly and make sure you understand what is being asked. Yet a happy medium must be attained, so don't waste too much time. You must read carefully and efficiently.

### ⊘ Contextual Clues

Look for contextual clues. If the question includes a word you are not familiar with, look at the immediate context for some indication of what the word might mean. Contextual clues can often give you all the information you need to decipher the meaning of an unfamiliar word. Even if you can't determine the meaning, you may be able to narrow down the possibilities enough to make a solid guess at the answer to the question.

### ⊘ Prefixes

If you're having trouble with a word in the question or answer choices, try dissecting it. Take advantage of every clue that the word might include. Prefixes can be a huge help. Usually, they allow you to determine a basic meaning. *Pre-* means before, *post-* means after, *pro-* is positive, *de-* is negative. From prefixes, you can get an idea of the general meaning of the word and try to put it into context.

### ⊘ Hedge Words

Watch out for critical hedge words, such as *likely, may, can, often, almost, mostly, usually, generally, rarely,* and *sometimes.* Question writers insert these hedge phrases to cover every possibility. Often an answer choice will be wrong simply because it leaves no room for exception. Be on guard for answer choices that have definitive words such as *exactly* and *always.*

### ⊘ Switchback Words

Stay alert for *switchbacks.* These are the words and phrases frequently used to alert you to shifts in thought. The most common switchback words are *but, although,* and *however.* Others include *nevertheless, on the other hand, even though, while, in spite of, despite,* and *regardless of.* Switchback words are important to catch because they can change the direction of the question or an answer choice.

### ✓ Face Value

When in doubt, use common sense. Accept the situation in the problem at face value. Don't read too much into it. These problems will not require you to make wild assumptions. If you have to go beyond creativity and warp time or space in order to have an answer choice fit the question, then you should move on and consider the other answer choices. These are normal problems rooted in reality. The applicable relationship or explanation may not be readily apparent, but it is there for you to figure out. Use your common sense to interpret anything that isn't clear.

## Answer Choice Strategies

### ✓ Answer Selection

The most thorough way to pick an answer choice is to identify and eliminate wrong answers until only one is left, then confirm it is the correct answer. Sometimes an answer choice may immediately seem right, but be careful. The test writers will usually put more than one reasonable answer choice on each question, so take a second to read all of them and make sure that the other choices are not equally obvious. As long as you have time left, it is better to read every answer choice than to pick the first one that looks right without checking the others.

### ✓ Answer Choice Families

An answer choice family consists of two (in rare cases, three) answer choices that are very similar in construction and cannot all be true at the same time. If you see two answer choices that are direct opposites or parallels, one of them is usually the correct answer. For instance, if one answer choice says that quantity *x* increases and another either says that quantity *x* decreases (opposite) or says that quantity *y* increases (parallel), then those answer choices would fall into the same family. An answer choice that doesn't match the construction of the answer choice family is more likely to be incorrect. Most questions will not have answer choice families, but when they do appear, you should be prepared to recognize them.

### ✓ Eliminate Answers

Eliminate answer choices as soon as you realize they are wrong, but make sure you consider all possibilities. If you are eliminating answer choices and realize that the last one you are left with is also wrong, don't panic. Start over and consider each choice again. There may be something you missed the first time that you will realize on the second pass.

### ✓ Avoid Fact Traps

Don't be distracted by an answer choice that is factually true but doesn't answer the question. You are looking for the choice that answers the question. Stay focused on what the question is asking for so you don't accidentally pick an answer that is true but incorrect. Always go back to the question and make sure the answer choice you've selected actually answers the question and is not merely a true statement.

### ✓ Extreme Statements

In general, you should avoid answers that put forth extreme actions as standard practice or proclaim controversial ideas as established fact. An answer choice that states the "process should be used in certain situations, if..." is much more likely to be correct than one that states the "process should be discontinued completely." The first is a calm rational statement and doesn't even make a definitive, uncompromising stance, using a hedge word *if* to provide wiggle room, whereas the second choice is far more extreme.

### ⊘ Benchmark

As you read through the answer choices and you come across one that seems to answer the question well, mentally select that answer choice. This is not your final answer, but it's the one that will help you evaluate the other answer choices. The one that you selected is your benchmark or standard for judging each of the other answer choices. Every other answer choice must be compared to your benchmark. That choice is correct until proven otherwise by another answer choice beating it. If you find a better answer, then that one becomes your new benchmark. Once you've decided that no other choice answers the question as well as your benchmark, you have your final answer.

### ⊘ Predict the Answer

Before you even start looking at the answer choices, it is often best to try to predict the answer. When you come up with the answer on your own, it is easier to avoid distractions and traps because you will know exactly what to look for. The right answer choice is unlikely to be word-for-word what you came up with, but it should be a close match. Even if you are confident that you have the right answer, you should still take the time to read each option before moving on.

## General Strategies

### ⊘ Tough Questions

If you are stumped on a problem or it appears too hard or too difficult, don't waste time. Move on! Remember though, if you can quickly check for obviously incorrect answer choices, your chances of guessing correctly are greatly improved. Before you completely give up, at least try to knock out a couple of possible answers. Eliminate what you can and then guess at the remaining answer choices before moving on.

### ⊘ Check Your Work

Since you will probably not know every term listed and the answer to every question, it is important that you get credit for the ones that you do know. Don't miss any questions through careless mistakes. If at all possible, try to take a second to look back over your answer selection and make sure you've selected the correct answer choice and haven't made a costly careless mistake (such as marking an answer choice that you didn't mean to mark). This quick double check should more than pay for itself in caught mistakes for the time it costs.

### ⊘ Pace Yourself

It's easy to be overwhelmed when you're looking at a page full of questions; your mind is confused and full of random thoughts, and the clock is ticking down faster than you would like. Calm down and maintain the pace that you have set for yourself. Especially as you get down to the last few minutes of the test, don't let the small numbers on the clock make you panic. As long as you are on track by monitoring your pace, you are guaranteed to have time for each question.

### ⊘ Don't Rush

It is very easy to make errors when you are in a hurry. Maintaining a fast pace in answering questions is pointless if it makes you miss questions that you would have gotten right otherwise. Test writers like to include distracting information and wrong answers that seem right. Taking a little extra time to avoid careless mistakes can make all the difference in your test score. Find a pace that allows you to be confident in the answers that you select.

### ⊘ Keep Moving

Panicking will not help you pass the test, so do your best to stay calm and keep moving. Taking deep breaths and going through the answer elimination steps you practiced can help to break through a stress barrier and keep your pace.

## Final Notes

The combination of a solid foundation of content knowledge and the confidence that comes from practicing your plan for applying that knowledge is the key to maximizing your performance on test day. As your foundation of content knowledge is built up and strengthened, you'll find that the strategies included in this chapter become more and more effective in helping you quickly sift through the distractions and traps of the test to isolate the correct answer.

Now that you're preparing to move forward into the test content chapters of this book, be sure to keep your goal in mind. As you read, think about how you will be able to apply this information on the test. If you've already seen sample questions for the test and you have an idea of the question format and style, try to come up with questions of your own that you can answer based on what you're reading. This will give you valuable practice applying your knowledge in the same ways you can expect to on test day.

**Good luck and good studying!**

# Five-Week NYSTCE Assessment of Teaching Assistant Skills (095) Test Study Plan

On the next few pages, we've provided an optional study plan to help you use this study guide to its fullest potential over the course of five weeks. If you have ten weeks available and want to spread it out more, spend two weeks on each section of the plan.

Below is a quick summary of the subjects covered in each week of the plan.

- Week 1: Reading
- Week 2: Writing
- Week 3: Mathematics
- Week 4: Instructional Support
- Week 5: Practice Tests

Please note that not all subjects will take the same amount of time to work through.

Five full-length practice tests are included in this study guide. We recommend saving any additional tests for after you've completed the study plan. Take these practice tests without any reference materials a day or two before the real thing as practice runs to get yourself in the mode of answering questions at a good pace.

# Week 1: Reading

## Instructional Content

First, read carefully through the Reading chapter in this book, checking off your progress as you go:

- ❑ Meaning of General Vocabulary Words
- ❑ Main Idea of a Reading Passage
- ❑ Sequence of Ideas
- ❑ Textual and Graphic Information
- ❑ Other Reading Comprehension Skills

As you read, do the following:

- Highlight any sections, terms, or concepts you think are important
- Draw an asterisk (*) next to any areas you are struggling with
- Watch the review videos to gain more understanding of a particular topic
- Take notes in your notebook or in the margins of this book

After you've read through everything, go back and review any sections that you highlighted or that you drew an asterisk next to, referencing your notes along the way.

# Week 2: Writing

## Instructional Content

First, read carefully through the Writing chapter in this book, checking off your progress as you go:

- ❑ Parts of Speech
- ❑ Agreement and Sentence Structure
- ❑ Punctuation
- ❑ Common Usage Mistakes
- ❑ The Writing Process
- ❑ Outlining and Organizing Ideas
- ❑ Coherence in Writing
- ❑ Writing Style and Form
- ❑ Formality in Writing

As you read, do the following:

- Highlight any sections, terms, or concepts you think are important
- Draw an asterisk (*) next to any areas you are struggling with
- Watch the review videos to gain more understanding of a particular topic
- Take notes in your notebook or in the margins of this book

After you've read through everything, go back and review any sections that you highlighted or that you drew an asterisk next to, referencing your notes along the way.

# Week 3: Mathematics

## Instructional Content

First, read carefully through the Mathematics chapter in this book, checking off your progress as you go:

- ❑ Number Basics
- ❑ Number Lines
- ❑ Absolute Value
- ❑ Operations
- ❑ Subtraction with Regrouping
- ❑ Order of Operations
- ❑ Properties of Exponents
- ❑ Factors and Multiples
- ❑ Rational Numbers
- ❑ Fractions, Decimals, and Percentages
- ❑ Proportions and Ratios
- ❑ Linear Expressions
- ❑ Slope
- ❑ Linear Equations
- ❑ Solving Equations
- ❑ Cross Multiplication
- ❑ Rounding and Estimation
- ❑ Scientific Notation
- ❑ Precision, Accuracy, and Error
- ❑ Metric and Customary Measurements

As you read, do the following:

- Highlight any sections, terms, or concepts you think are important
- Draw an asterisk (*) next to any areas you are struggling with
- Watch the review videos to gain more understanding of a particular topic
- Take notes in your notebook or in the margins of this book

After you've read through everything, go back and review any sections that you highlighted or that you drew an asterisk next to, referencing your notes along the way.

# Week 4: Instructional Support

## INSTRUCTIONAL CONTENT

First, read carefully through the Instructional Support chapter in this book, checking off your progress as you go:

❑ General Pedagogy
❑ Instruction Related to Reading and Writing
❑ Instruction Related to Mathematics

As you read, do the following:

- Highlight any sections, terms, or concepts you think are important
- Draw an asterisk (*) next to any areas you are struggling with
- Watch the review videos to gain more understanding of a particular topic
- Take notes in your notebook or in the margins of this book

After you've read through everything, go back and review any sections that you highlighted or that you drew an asterisk next to, referencing your notes along the way.

# Week 5: Practice Tests

Your success on test day depends not only on how many hours you put into preparing, but also on whether you prepared the right way. It's good to check along the way to see if your studying is paying off. One of the most effective ways to do this is by taking practice tests to evaluate your progress. Practice tests are useful because they show exactly where you need to improve. Every time you take a practice test, pay special attention to these three groups of questions:

- The questions you got wrong
- The questions you had to guess on, even if you guessed right
- The questions you found difficult or slow to work through

This will show you exactly what your weak areas are, and where you need to devote more study time. Ask yourself why each of these questions gave you trouble. Was it because you didn't understand the material? Was it because you didn't remember the vocabulary? Do you need more repetitions on this type of question to build speed and confidence? Dig into those questions and figure out how you can strengthen your weak areas as you go back to review the material.

## Practice Test #1

Now that you've read over the instructional content, it's time to take a practice test. Complete Practice Test #1. Take this test with **no time constraints**, and feel free to reference the applicable sections of this guide as you go. Once you've finished, check your answers against the provided answer key. For any questions you answered incorrectly, review the answer rationale, and then **go back and review** the applicable sections of the book. The goal in this stage is to understand why you answered the question incorrectly, and make sure that the next time you see a similar question, you will get it right.

## Practice Tests #2 and #3

Next, complete Practice Tests #2 and #3. For each test, give yourself **3 hours** to complete all of the questions. You should again feel free to reference the guide and your notes, but be mindful of the clock. If you run out of time before you finish all of the questions, mark where you were when time expired, but go ahead and finish taking the practice test. Once you've finished, check your answers against the provided answer key, and as before, review the answer rationale for any that you answered incorrectly and then go back and review the associated instructional content. Your goal is still to increase understanding of the content but also to get used to the time constraints you will face on the test.

## Practice Tests #4 and #5

Finally, complete Practice Tests #4 and #5. For each test, give yourself **3 hours** to complete all of the questions. This time, take the test without referencing the guide or your notes. Once you've finished, check your answers, review the answer rationale for any questions that you answered incorrectly, and then review the associated instructional content. Your goal is to get used to the constraints of the real test while ensuring that you understand the content.

As you go along, keep in mind that the practice test is just that: practice. Memorizing these questions and answers will not be very helpful on the actual test because it is unlikely to have any of the same exact questions. If you only know the right answers to the sample questions, you won't be prepared for the real thing. **Study the concepts** until you understand them fully, and then you'll be able to answer any question that shows up on the test.

# Reading

Transform passive reading into active learning! After immersing yourself in this chapter, put your comprehension to the test by taking a quiz. The insights you gained will stay with you longer this way. Scan the QR code to go directly to the chapter quiz interface for this study guide. If you're using a computer, simply visit the online resources page at **mometrix.com/resources719/nystceatas-29098** and click the Chapter Quizzes link.

## Meaning of General Vocabulary Words

### Word Roots and Prefixes and Suffixes

#### *Affixes*

Affixes in the English language are morphemes that are added to words to create related but different words. Derivational affixes form new words based on and related to the original words. For example, the affix *-ness* added to the end of the adjective *happy* forms the noun *happiness.* Inflectional affixes form different grammatical versions of words. For example, the plural affix *-s* changes the singular noun *book* to the plural noun *books*, and the past tense affix *-ed* changes the present tense verb *look* to the past tense *looked.* Prefixes are affixes placed in front of words. For example, *heat* means to make hot; *preheat* means to heat in advance. Suffixes are affixes placed at the ends of words. The *happiness* example above contains the suffix *-ness.* Circumfixes add parts both before and after words, such as how *light* becomes *enlighten* with the prefix *en-* and the suffix *-en.* Interfixes create compound words via central affixes: *speed* and *meter* become *speedometer* via the interfix *-o-*.

**Review Video: Affixes**
Visit mometrix.com/academy and enter code: 782422

#### *Word Roots, Prefixes, and Suffixes to Help Determine Meanings of Words*

Many English words were formed from combining multiple sources. For example, the Latin *habēre* means "to have," and the prefixes *in-* and *im-* mean a lack or prevention of something, as in *insufficient* and *imperfect.* Latin combined *in-* with *habēre* to form *inhibēre,* whose past participle was *inhibitus*. This is the origin of the English word *inhibit,* meaning to prevent from having. Hence by knowing the meanings of both the prefix and the root, one can decipher the word meaning. In Greek, the root *enkephalo-* refers to the brain. Many medical terms are based on this root, such as encephalitis and hydrocephalus. Understanding the prefix and suffix meanings (*-itis* means inflammation; *hydro-* means water) allows a person to deduce that encephalitis refers to brain inflammation and hydrocephalus refers to water (or other fluid) in the brain.

**Review Video: Root Words in English**
Visit mometrix.com/academy and enter code: 896380

**Review Video: Determining Word Meanings**
Visit mometrix.com/academy and enter code: 894894

### Prefixes

Knowing common prefixes is helpful for all readers as they try to determining meanings or definitions of unfamiliar words. For example, a common word used when cooking is *preheat.* Knowing that *pre-* means in advance can also inform them that *presume* means to assume in advance, that *prejudice* means advance judgment, and that this understanding can be applied to many other words beginning with *pre-*. Knowing that the prefix *dis-* indicates opposition informs the meanings of words like *disbar, disagree, disestablish,* and many more. Knowing *dys-* means bad, impaired, abnormal, or difficult informs *dyslogistic, dysfunctional, dysphagia,* and *dysplasia.*

### Suffixes

In English, certain suffixes generally indicate both that a word is a noun, and that the noun represents a state of being or quality. For example, *-ness* is commonly used to change an adjective into its noun form, as with *happy* and *happiness, nice* and *niceness,* and so on. The suffix *–tion* is commonly used to transform a verb into its noun form, as with *converse* and *conversation or move* and *motion*. Thus, if readers are unfamiliar with the second form of a word, knowing the meaning of the transforming suffix can help them determine meaning.

### Prefixes for Numbers

| Prefix | Definition | Examples |
|---|---|---|
| **bi-** | two | bisect, biennial |
| **mono-** | one, single | monogamy, monologue |
| **poly-** | many | polymorphous, polygamous |
| **semi-** | half, partly | semicircle, semicolon |
| **uni-** | one | uniform, unity |

### Prefixes for Time, Direction, and Space

| Prefix | Definition | Examples |
|---|---|---|
| **a-** | in, on, of, up, to | abed, afoot |
| **ab-** | from, away, off | abdicate, abjure |
| **ad-** | to, toward | advance, adventure |
| **ante-** | before, previous | antecedent, antedate |
| **anti-** | against, opposing | antipathy, antidote |
| **cata-** | down, away, thoroughly | catastrophe, cataclysm |
| **circum-** | around | circumspect, circumference |
| **com-** | with, together, very | commotion, complicate |
| **contra-** | against, opposing | contradict, contravene |
| **de-** | from | depart |
| **dia-** | through, across, apart | diameter, diagnose |
| **dis-** | away, off, down, not | dissent, disappear |
| **epi-** | upon | epilogue |
| **ex-** | out | extract, excerpt |
| **hypo-** | under, beneath | hypodermic, hypothesis |
| **inter-** | among, between | intercede, interrupt |
| **intra-** | within | intramural, intrastate |
| **ob-** | against, opposing | objection |
| **per-** | through | perceive, permit |
| **peri-** | around | periscope, perimeter |
| **post-** | after, following | postpone, postscript |
| **pre-** | before, previous | prevent, preclude |

| Prefix | Definition | Examples |
| --- | --- | --- |
| **pro-** | forward, in place of | propel, pronoun |
| **retro-** | back, backward | retrospect, retrograde |
| **sub-** | under, beneath | subjugate, substitute |
| **super-** | above, extra | supersede, supernumerary |
| **trans-** | across, beyond, over | transact, transport |
| **ultra-** | beyond, excessively | ultramodern, ultrasonic |



NEGATIVE PREFIXES

| Prefix | Definition | Examples |
| --- | --- | --- |
| **a-** | without, lacking | atheist, agnostic |
| **in-** | not, opposing | incapable, ineligible |
| **non-** | not | nonentity, nonsense |
| **un-** | not, reverse of | unhappy, unlock |

EXTRA PREFIXES

| Prefix | Definition | Examples |
| --- | --- | --- |
| **for-** | away, off, from | forget, forswear |
| **fore-** | previous | foretell, forefathers |
| **homo-** | same, equal | homogenized, homonym |
| **hyper-** | excessive, over | hypercritical, hypertension |
| **in-** | in, into | intrude, invade |
| **mal-** | bad, poorly, not | malfunction, malpractice |
| **mis-** | bad, poorly, not | misspell, misfire |
| **neo-** | new | Neolithic, neoconservative |
| **omni-** | all, everywhere | omniscient, omnivore |
| **ortho-** | right, straight | orthogonal, orthodox |
| **over-** | above | overbearing, oversight |
| **pan-** | all, entire | panorama, pandemonium |
| **para-** | beside, beyond | parallel, paradox |
| **re-** | backward, again | revoke, recur |
| **sym-** | with, together | sympathy, symphony |

Below is a list of common suffixes and their meanings:

ADJECTIVE SUFFIXES

| Suffix | Definition | Examples |
| --- | --- | --- |
| **-able (-ible)** | capable of being | toler*able*, ed*ible* |
| **-esque** | in the style of, like | picturesque, grotesque |
| **-ful** | filled with, marked by | thankful, zestful |
| **-ific** | make, cause | terrific, beatific |
| **-ish** | suggesting, like | churlish, childish |
| **-less** | lacking, without | hopeless, countless |
| **-ous** | marked by, given to | religious, riotous |

NOUN SUFFIXES

| Suffix | Definition | Examples |
| --- | --- | --- |
| **-acy** | state, condition | accuracy, privacy |
| **-ance** | act, condition, fact | acceptance, vigilance |
| **-ard** | one that does excessively | drunkard, sluggard |

| Suffix | Definition | Examples |
|---|---|---|
| **-ation** | action, state, result | occupation, starvation |
| **-dom** | state, rank, condition | serfdom, wisdom |
| **-er (-or)** | office, action | teach*er*, elevat*or*, hon*or* |
| **-ess** | feminine | waitress, duchess |
| **-hood** | state, condition | manhood, statehood |
| **-ion** | action, result, state | union, fusion |
| **-ism** | act, manner, doctrine | barbarism, socialism |
| **-ist** | worker, follower | monopolist, socialist |
| **-ity (-ty)** | state, quality, condition | acid*ity*, civil*ity*, twen*ty* |
| **-ment** | result, action | Refreshment |
| **-ness** | quality, state | greatness, tallness |
| **-ship** | position | internship, statesmanship |
| **-sion (-tion)** | state, result | revi*sion*, expedi*tion* |
| **-th** | act, state, quality | warmth, width |
| **-tude** | quality, state, result | magnitude, fortitude |

#### VERB SUFFIXES

| Suffix | Definition | Examples |
|---|---|---|
| **-ate** | having, showing | separate, desolate |
| **-en** | cause to be, become | deepen, strengthen |
| **-fy** | make, cause to have | glorify, fortify |
| **-ize** | cause to be, treat with | sterilize, mechanize |

## NUANCE AND WORD MEANINGS

### *SYNONYMS AND ANTONYMS*

When you understand how words relate to each other, you will discover more in a passage. This is explained by understanding **synonyms** (e.g., words that mean the same thing) and **antonyms** (e.g., words that mean the opposite of one another). As an example, *dry* and *arid* are synonyms, and *dry* and *wet* are antonyms.

There are many pairs of words in English that can be considered synonyms, despite having slightly different definitions. For instance, the words *friendly* and *collegial* can both be used to describe a warm interpersonal relationship, and one would be correct to call them synonyms. However, *collegial* (kin to *colleague*) is often used in reference to professional or academic relationships, and *friendly* has no such connotation.

If the difference between the two words is too great, then they should not be called synonyms. *Hot* and *warm* are not synonyms because their meanings are too distinct. A good way to determine whether two words are synonyms is to substitute one word for the other word and verify that the meaning of the sentence has not changed. Substituting *warm* for *hot* in a sentence would convey a different meaning. Although warm and hot may seem close in meaning, warm generally means that the temperature is moderate, and hot generally means that the temperature is excessively high.

Antonyms are words with opposite meanings. *Light* and *dark*, *up* and *down*, *right* and *left*, *good* and *bad*: these are all sets of antonyms. Be careful to distinguish between antonyms and pairs of words that are simply different. *Black* and *gray*, for instance, are not antonyms because gray is not the opposite of black. *Black* and *white*, on the other hand, are antonyms.

Not every word has an antonym. For instance, many nouns do not. What would be the antonym of *chair*? During your exam, the questions related to antonyms are more likely to concern adjectives. You will recall that adjectives are words that describe a noun. Some common adjectives include *purple*, *fast*, *skinny*, and *sweet*. From those four adjectives, *purple* is the item that lacks a group of obvious antonyms.

**Review Video: Synonyms and Antonyms**
Visit mometrix.com/academy and enter code: 105612

### *Denotative vs. Connotative Meaning*

The **denotative** meaning of a word is the literal meaning. The **connotative** meaning goes beyond the denotative meaning to include the emotional reaction that a word may invoke. The connotative meaning often takes the denotative meaning a step further due to associations the reader makes with the denotative meaning. Readers can differentiate between the denotative and connotative meanings by first recognizing how authors use each meaning. Most non-fiction, for example, is fact-based and authors do not use flowery, figurative language. The reader can assume that the writer is using the denotative meaning of words. In fiction, the author may use the connotative meaning. Readers can determine whether the author is using the denotative or connotative meaning of a word by implementing context clues.

**Review Video: Connotation and Denotation**
Visit mometrix.com/academy and enter code: 310092

### *Nuances of Word Meaning*

A word's denotation is simply its objective dictionary definition. However, its connotation refers to the subjective associations, often emotional, that specific words evoke in listeners and readers. Two or more words can have the same dictionary meaning, but very different connotations. Writers use diction (word choice) to convey various nuances of thought and emotion by selecting synonyms for other words that best communicate the associations they want to trigger for readers. For example, a car engine is naturally greasy; in this sense, "greasy" is a neutral term. But when a person's smile, appearance, or clothing is described as "greasy," it has a negative connotation. Some words have even gained additional or different meanings over time. For example, *awful* used to be used to describe things that evoked a sense of awe. When *awful* is separated into its root word, awe, and suffix, -ful, it can be understood to mean "full of awe." However, the word is now commonly used to describe things that evoke repulsion, terror, or another intense, negative reaction.

**Review Video: Word Usage in Sentences**
Visit mometrix.com/academy and enter code: 197863

## Using Context to Determine Meaning

### Context Clues

Readers of all levels will encounter words that they have either never seen or have encountered only on a limited basis. The best way to define a word in **context** is to look for nearby words that can assist in revealing the meaning of the word. For instance, unfamiliar nouns are often accompanied by examples that provide a definition. Consider the following sentence: *Dave arrived at the party in hilarious garb: a leopard-print shirt, buckskin trousers, and bright green sneakers.* If a reader was unfamiliar with the meaning of garb, he or she could read the examples (i.e., a leopard-print shirt, buckskin trousers, and bright green sneakers) and quickly determine that the word means *clothing*. Examples will not always be this obvious. Consider this sentence: *Parsley, lemon, and flowers were just a few of the items he used as garnishes.* Here, the word *garnishes* is exemplified by parsley, lemon, and flowers. Readers who have eaten in a variety of restaurants will probably be able to identify a garnish as something used to decorate a plate.

**Review Video: Reading Comprehension: Using Context Clues**
Visit mometrix.com/academy and enter code: 613660

#### Using Contrast in Context Clues

In addition to looking at the context of a passage, readers can use contrast to define an unfamiliar word in context. In many sentences, the author will not describe the unfamiliar word directly; instead, he or she will describe the opposite of the unfamiliar word. Thus, you are provided with some information that will bring you closer to defining the word. Consider the following example: *Despite his intelligence, Hector's low brow and bad posture made him look obtuse.* The author writes that Hector's appearance does not convey intelligence. Therefore, *obtuse* must mean unintelligent. Here is another example: *Despite the horrible weather, we were beatific about our trip to Alaska*. The word *despite* indicates that the speaker's feelings were at odds with the weather. Since the weather is described as *horrible*, then *beatific* must mean something positive.

#### Substitution to Find Meaning

In some cases, there will be very few contextual clues to help a reader define the meaning of an unfamiliar word. When this happens, one strategy that readers may employ is **substitution**. A good reader will brainstorm some possible synonyms for the given word, and he or she will substitute these words into the sentence. If the sentence and the surrounding passage continue to make sense, then the substitution has revealed at least some information about the unfamiliar word. Consider the sentence: *Frank's admonition rang in her ears as she climbed the mountain.* A reader unfamiliar with *admonition* might come up with some substitutions like *vow, promise, advice, complaint*, or *compliment.* All of these words make general sense of the sentence, though their meanings are diverse. However, this process has suggested that an admonition is some sort of message. The substitution strategy is rarely able to pinpoint a precise definition, but this process can be effective as a last resort.

Occasionally, you will be able to define an unfamiliar word by looking at the descriptive words in the context. Consider the following sentence: *Fred dragged the recalcitrant boy kicking and screaming up the stairs.* The words *dragged, kicking*, and *screaming* all suggest that the boy does not want to go up the stairs. The reader may assume that *recalcitrant* means something like unwilling or protesting. In this example, an unfamiliar adjective was identified.

Additionally, using description to define an unfamiliar noun is a common practice compared to unfamiliar adjectives, as in this sentence: *Don's wrinkled frown and constantly shaking fist identified him as a curmudgeon of the first order.* Don is described as having a *wrinkled frown and constantly shaking fist*, suggesting that a *curmudgeon* must be a grumpy person. Contrasts do not always provide detailed information about the unfamiliar word, but they at least give the reader some clues.

#### WORDS WITH MULTIPLE MEANINGS

When a word has more than one meaning, readers can have difficulty determining how the word is being used in a given sentence. For instance, the verb *cleave*, can mean either *join* or *separate*. When readers come upon this word, they will have to select the definition that makes the most sense. Consider the following sentence: *Hermione's knife cleaved the bread cleanly*. Since a knife cannot join bread together, the word must indicate separation. A slightly more difficult example would be the sentence: *The birds cleaved to one another as they flew from the oak tree.* Immediately, the presence of the words *to one another* should suggest that in this sentence *cleave* is being used to mean *join*. Discovering the intent of a word with multiple meanings requires the same tricks as defining an unknown word: look for contextual clues and evaluate the substituted words.

### *CONTEXT CLUES TO HELP DETERMINE MEANINGS OF WORDS*

If readers simply bypass unknown words, they can reach unclear conclusions about what they read. However, looking for the definition of every unfamiliar word in the dictionary can slow their reading progress. Moreover, the dictionary may list multiple definitions for a word, so readers must search the word's context for meaning. Hence context is important to new vocabulary regardless of reader methods. Four types of context clues are examples, definitions, descriptive words, and opposites. Authors may use a certain word, and then follow it with several different examples of what it describes. Sometimes authors actually supply a definition of a word they use, which is especially true in informational and technical texts. Authors may use descriptive words that elaborate upon a vocabulary word they just used. Authors may also use opposites with negation that help define meaning.

#### EXAMPLES AND DEFINITIONS

An author may use a word and then give examples that illustrate its meaning. Consider this text: "Teachers who do not know how to use sign language can help students who are deaf or hard of hearing understand certain instructions by using gestures instead, like pointing their fingers to indicate which direction to look or go; holding up a hand, palm outward, to indicate stopping; holding the hands flat, palms up, curling a finger toward oneself in a beckoning motion to indicate 'come here'; or curling all fingers toward oneself repeatedly to indicate 'come on', 'more', or 'continue.'" The author of this text has used the word "gestures" and then followed it with examples, so a reader unfamiliar with the word could deduce from the examples that "gestures" means "hand motions." Readers can find examples by looking for signal words "for example," "for instance," "like," "such as," and "e.g."

While readers sometimes have to look for definitions of unfamiliar words in a dictionary or do some work to determine a word's meaning from its surrounding context, at other times an author may make it easier for readers by defining certain words. For example, an author may write, "The company did not have sufficient capital, that is, available money, to continue operations." The author defined "capital" as "available money," and heralded the definition with the phrase "that is." Another way that authors supply word definitions is with appositives. Rather than being introduced by a signal phrase like "that is," "namely," or "meaning," an appositive comes after the vocabulary word it defines and is enclosed within two commas. For example, an author may write, "The Indians introduced the Pilgrims to pemmican, cakes they made of lean meat dried and mixed with fat, which proved greatly beneficial to keep settlers from starving while trapping." In this example, the appositive phrase following "pemmican" and preceding "which" defines the word "pemmican."

### Descriptions

When readers encounter a word they do not recognize in a text, the author may expand on that word to illustrate it better. While the author may do this to make the prose more picturesque and vivid, the reader can also take advantage of this description to provide context clues to the meaning of the unfamiliar word. For example, an author may write, "The man sitting next to me on the airplane was obese. His shirt stretched across his vast expanse of flesh, strained almost to bursting." The descriptive second sentence elaborates on and helps to define the previous sentence's word "obese" to mean extremely fat. A reader unfamiliar with the word "repugnant" can decipher its meaning through an author's accompanying description: "The way the child grimaced and shuddered as he swallowed the medicine showed that its taste was particularly repugnant."

### Opposites

Text authors sometimes introduce a contrasting or opposing idea before or after a concept they present. They may do this to emphasize or heighten the idea they present by contrasting it with something that is the reverse. However, readers can also use these context clues to understand familiar words. For example, an author may write, "Our conversation was not cheery. We sat and talked very solemnly about his experience and a number of similar events." The reader who is not familiar with the word "solemnly" can deduce by the author's preceding use of "not cheery" that "solemn" means the opposite of cheery or happy, so it must mean serious or sad. Or if someone writes, "Don't condemn his entire project because you couldn't find anything good to say about it," readers unfamiliar with "condemn" can understand from the sentence structure that it means the opposite of saying anything good, so it must mean reject, dismiss, or disapprove. "Entire" adds another context clue, meaning total or complete rejection.

### *Syntax to Determine Part of Speech and Meanings of Words*

Syntax refers to sentence structure and word order. Suppose that a reader encounters an unfamiliar word when reading a text. To illustrate, consider an invented word like "splunch." If this word is used in a sentence like "Please splunch that ball to me," the reader can assume from syntactic context that "splunch" is a verb. We would not use a noun, adjective, adverb, or preposition with the object "that ball," and the prepositional phrase "to me" further indicates "splunch" represents an action. However, in the sentence, "Please hand that splunch to me," the reader can assume that "splunch" is a noun. Demonstrative adjectives like "that" modify nouns. Also, we hand someone some*thing*—a thing being a noun; we do not hand someone a verb, adjective, or adverb. Some sentences contain further clues. For example, from the sentence, "The princess wore the glittering splunch on her head," the reader can deduce that it is a crown, tiara, or something similar from the syntactic context, without knowing the word.

### *Syntax to Indicate Different Meanings of Similar Sentences*

The syntax, or structure, of a sentence affords grammatical cues that aid readers in comprehending the meanings of words, phrases, and sentences in the texts that they read. Seemingly minor differences in how the words or phrases in a sentence are ordered can make major differences in meaning. For example, two sentences can use exactly the same words but have different meanings based on the word order:

- "The man with a broken arm sat in a chair."
- "The man sat in a chair with a broken arm."

While both sentences indicate that a man sat in a chair, differing syntax indicates whether the man's or chair's arm was broken.

**Review Video: Syntax**
Visit mometrix.com/academy and enter code: 242280

### *Determining Meaning of Phrases and Paragraphs*

Like unknown words, the meanings of phrases, paragraphs, and entire works can also be difficult to discern. Each of these can be better understood with added context. However, for larger groups of words, more context is needed. Unclear phrases are similar to unclear words, and the same methods can be used to understand their meaning. However, it is also important to consider how the individual words in the phrase work together. Paragraphs are a bit more complicated. Just as words must be compared to other words in a sentence, paragraphs must be compared to other paragraphs in a composition or a section.

### *Determining Meaning in Various Types of Compositions*

To understand the meaning of an entire composition, the type of composition must be considered. **Expository writing** is generally organized so that each paragraph focuses on explaining one idea, or part of an idea, and its relevance. **Persuasive writing** uses paragraphs for different purposes to organize the parts of the argument. **Unclear paragraphs** must be read in the context of the paragraphs around them for their meaning to be fully understood. The meaning of full texts can also be unclear at times. The purpose of composition is also important for understanding the meaning of a text. To quickly understand the broad meaning of a text, look to the introductory and concluding paragraphs. Fictional texts are different. Some fictional works have implicit meanings, but some do not. The target audience must be considered for understanding texts that do have an implicit meaning, as most children's fiction will clearly state any lessons or morals. For other fiction, the application of literary theories and criticism may be helpful for understanding the text.

## Resources for Determining Word Meaning and Usage

While these strategies are useful for determining the meaning of unknown words and phrases, sometimes additional resources are needed to properly use the terms in different contexts. Some words have multiple definitions, and some words are inappropriate in particular contexts or modes of writing. The following tools are helpful for understanding all meanings and proper uses for words and phrases.

- **Dictionaries** provide the meaning of a multitude of words in a language. Many dictionaries include additional information about each word, such as its etymology, its synonyms, or variations of the word.
- **Glossaries** are similar to dictionaries, as they provide the meanings of a variety of terms. However, while dictionaries typically feature an extensive list of words and comprise an entire publication, glossaries are often included at the end of a text and only include terms and definitions that are relevant to the text they follow.
- **Spell Checkers** are used to detect spelling errors in typed text. Some spell checkers may also detect the misuse of plural or singular nouns, verb tenses, or capitalization. While spell checkers are a helpful tool, they are not always reliable or attuned to the author's intent, so it is important to review the spell checker's suggestions before accepting them.
- **Style Manuals** are guidelines on the preferred punctuation, format, and grammar usage according to different fields or organizations. For example, the Associated Press Stylebook is a style guide often used for media writing. The guidelines within a style guide are not

always applicable across different contexts and usages, as the guidelines often cover grammatical or formatting situations that are not objectively correct or incorrect.

# Main Idea of a Reading Passage

## MAIN IDEAS AND SUPPORTING DETAILS

### *IDENTIFYING TOPICS AND MAIN IDEAS*

One of the most important skills in reading comprehension is the identification of **topics** and **main ideas**. There is a subtle difference between these two features. The topic is the subject of a text (i.e., what the text is all about). The main idea, on the other hand, is the most important point being made by the author. The topic is usually expressed in a few words at the most while the main idea often needs a full sentence to be completely defined. As an example, a short passage might be written on the topic of penguins, and the main idea could be written as *Penguins are different from other birds in many ways*. In most nonfiction writing, the topic and the main idea will be **stated directly** and often appear in a sentence at the very beginning or end of the text. When being tested on an understanding of the author's topic, you may be able to skim the passage for the general idea by reading only the first sentence of each paragraph. A body paragraph's first sentence is often—but not always—the main **topic sentence** which gives you a summary of the content in the paragraph.

However, there are cases in which the reader must figure out an **unstated** topic or main idea. In these instances, you must read every sentence of the text and try to come up with an overarching idea that is supported by each of those sentences.

Note: The main idea should not be confused with the thesis statement. While the main idea gives a brief, general summary of a text, the thesis statement provides a **specific perspective** on an issue that the author supports with evidence.

**Review Video: Topics and Main Ideas**
Visit mometrix.com/academy and enter code: 407801

### *SUPPORTING DETAILS*

**Supporting details** are smaller pieces of evidence that provide backing for the main point. In order to show that a main idea is correct or valid, an author must add details that prove their point. All texts contain details, but they are only classified as supporting details when they serve to reinforce some larger point. Supporting details are most commonly found in informative and persuasive texts. In some cases, they will be clearly indicated with terms like *for example* or *for instance*, or they will be enumerated with terms like *first*, *second*, and *last*. However, you need to be prepared for texts that do not contain those indicators. As a reader, you should consider whether the author's supporting details really back up his or her main point. Details can be factual and correct, yet they may not be **relevant** to the author's point. Conversely, details can be relevant, but be ineffective because they are based on opinion or assertions that cannot be proven.

**Review Video: Supporting Details**
Visit mometrix.com/academy and enter code: 396297

## Author's Purpose

### Author's Purpose

Usually, identifying the author's **purpose** is easier than identifying his or her **position**. In most cases, the author has no interest in hiding his or her purpose. A text that is meant to entertain, for instance, should be written to please the reader. Most narratives, or stories, are written to entertain, though they may also inform or persuade. Informative texts are easy to identify, while the most difficult purpose of a text to identify is persuasion because the author has an interest in making this purpose hard to detect. When a reader discovers that the author is trying to persuade, he or she should be skeptical of the argument. For this reason, persuasive texts often try to establish an entertaining tone and hope to amuse the reader into agreement. On the other hand, an informative tone may be implemented to create an appearance of authority and objectivity.



An author's purpose is evident often in the **organization** of the text (e.g., section headings in bold font points to an informative text). However, you may not have such organization available to you in your exam. Instead, if the author makes his or her main idea clear from the beginning, then the likely purpose of the text is to **inform**. If the author begins by making a claim and provides various arguments to support that claim, then the purpose is probably to **persuade**. If the author tells a story or wants to gain the reader's attention more than to push a particular point or deliver information, then his or her purpose is most likely to **entertain**. As a reader, you must judge authors on how well they accomplish their purpose. In other words, you need to consider the type of passage (e.g., technical, persuasive, etc.) that the author has written and if the author has followed the requirements of the passage type.

**Review Video: Understanding the Author's Intent**
Visit mometrix.com/academy and enter code: 511819

#### Informational Texts

An **informational text** is written to educate and enlighten readers. Informational texts are almost always nonfiction and are rarely structured as a story. The intention of an informational text is to deliver information in the most comprehensible way. So, look for the structure of the text to be very clear. In an informational text, the thesis statement is one or two sentences that normally appears at the end of the first paragraph. The author may use some colorful language, but he or she is likely to put more emphasis on clarity and precision. Informational essays do not typically appeal to the emotions. They often contain facts and figures and rarely include the opinion of the author; however, readers should remain aware of the possibility for bias as those facts are presented. Sometimes a persuasive essay can resemble an informative essay, especially if the author maintains an even tone and presents his or her views as if they were established fact.

**Review Video: Informational Text**
Visit mometrix.com/academy and enter code: 924964

#### Persuasive Writing

In a persuasive essay, the author is attempting to change the reader's mind or **convince** him or her of something that he or she did not believe previously. There are several identifying characteristics of **persuasive writing**. One is **opinion presented as fact**. When authors attempt to persuade readers, they often present their opinions as if they were fact. Readers must be on guard for statements that sound factual but which cannot be subjected to research, observation, or experiment. Another characteristic of persuasive writing is **emotional language**. An author will often try to play on the emotions of readers by appealing to their sympathy or sense of morality. When an author uses colorful or evocative language with the intent of arousing the reader's passions, then the author may be attempting to persuade. Finally, in many cases, a persuasive text will give an **unfair explanation of opposing positions**, if these positions are mentioned at all.

### Entertaining Texts

The success or failure of an author's intent to **entertain** is determined by those who read the author's work. Entertaining texts may be either fiction or nonfiction, and they may describe real or imagined people, places, and events. Entertaining texts are often narratives or poems. A text that is written to entertain is likely to contain **colorful language** that engages the imagination and the emotions. Such writing often features a great deal of figurative language, which typically enlivens the subject matter with images and analogies.

Though an entertaining text is not usually written to persuade or inform, authors may accomplish both of these tasks in their work. An entertaining text may *appeal to the reader's emotions* and cause him or her to think differently about a particular subject. In any case, entertaining texts tend to showcase the personality of the author more than other types of writing.

### Descriptive Text

In a sense, almost all writing is descriptive, insofar as an author seeks to describe events, ideas, or people to the reader. Some texts, however, are primarily concerned with **description**. A descriptive text focuses on a particular subject and attempts to depict the subject in a way that will be clear to readers. Descriptive texts contain many adjectives and adverbs (i.e., words that give shades of meaning and create a more detailed mental picture for the reader). A descriptive text fails when it is unclear to the reader. A descriptive text will certainly be informative and may be persuasive and entertaining as well.

**Review Video: Descriptive Texts**
Visit mometrix.com/academy and enter code: 174903

### Expression of Feelings

When an author intends to **express feelings**, he or she may use **expressive and bold language**. An author may write with emotion for any number of reasons. Sometimes, authors will express feelings because they are describing a personal situation of great pain or happiness. In other situations, authors will attempt to persuade the reader and will use emotion to stir up the passions. This kind of expression is easy to identify when the writer uses phrases like *I felt* and *I sense*. However, readers may find that the author will simply describe feelings without introducing them. As a reader, you must know the importance of recognizing when an author is expressing emotion and not to become overwhelmed by sympathy or passion. Readers should maintain some **detachment** so that they can still evaluate the strength of the author's argument or the quality of the writing.

**Review Video: Emotional Language in Literature**
Visit mometrix.com/academy and enter code: 759390

### Expository Passage

An **expository** passage aims to **inform** and enlighten readers. Expository passages are nonfiction and usually center around a simple, easily defined topic. Since the goal of exposition is to teach, such a passage should be as clear as possible. Often, an expository passage contains helpful organizing words, like *first*, *next*, *for example*, and *therefore*. These words keep the reader **oriented** in the text. Although expository passages do not need to feature colorful language and artful writing, they are often more effective with these features. For a reader, the challenge of expository passages is to maintain steady attention. Expository passages are not always about subjects that will naturally interest a reader, so the writer is often more concerned with **clarity** and **comprehensibility** than with engaging the reader. By reading actively, you can ensure a good habit of focus when reading an expository passage.

**Review Video: Expository Passages**
Visit mometrix.com/academy and enter code: 256515

#### NARRATIVE PASSAGE

A **narrative** passage is a story that can be fiction or nonfiction. However, there are a few elements that a text must have in order to be classified as a narrative. First, the text must have a **plot** (i.e., a series of events). Narratives often proceed in a clear sequence, but this is not a requirement. If the narrative is good, then these events will be interesting to readers. Second, a narrative has **characters**. These characters could be people, animals, or even inanimate objects—so long as they participate in the plot. Third, a narrative passage often contains **figurative language** which is meant to stimulate the imagination of readers by making comparisons and observations. For instance, a *metaphor*, a common piece of figurative language, is a description of one thing in terms of another. *The moon was a frosty snowball* is an example of a metaphor. In the literal sense this is obviously untrue, but the comparison suggests a certain mood for the reader.

#### TECHNICAL PASSAGE

A **technical** passage is written to *describe* a complex object or process. Technical writing is common in medical and technological fields, in which complex ideas of mathematics, science, and engineering need to be explained *simply* and *clearly*. To ease comprehension, a technical passage usually proceeds in a very logical order. Technical passages often have clear headings and subheadings, which are used to keep the reader oriented in the text. Additionally, you will find that these passages divide sections up with numbers or letters. Many technical passages look more like an outline than a piece of prose. The amount of **jargon** or difficult vocabulary will vary in a technical passage depending on the intended audience. As much as possible, technical passages try to avoid language that the reader will have to research in order to understand the message, yet readers will find that jargon cannot always be avoided.

**Review Video: Technical Passages**
Visit mometrix.com/academy and enter code: 478923

# Sequence of Ideas

## COMMON ORGANIZATIONS OF TEXTS

### *ORGANIZATION OF THE TEXT*

The way a text is organized can help readers understand the author's intent and his or her conclusions. There are various ways to organize a text, and each one has a purpose and use. Usually, authors will organize information logically in a passage so the reader can follow and locate the information within the text. However, since not all passages are written with the same logical structure, you need to be familiar with several different types of passage structure.

**Review Video: Sequence of Events in a Story**
Visit mometrix.com/academy and enter code: 807512

### Chronological

When using **chronological** order, the author presents information in the order that it happened. For example, biographies are typically written in chronological order. The subject's birth and childhood are presented first, followed by their adult life, and lastly the events leading up to the person's death.

### Cause and Effect

One of the most common text structures is **cause and effect**. A **cause** is an act or event that makes something happen, and an **effect** is the thing that happens as a result of the cause. A cause-and-effect relationship is not always explicit, but there are some terms in English that signal causes, such as *since*, *because*, and *due to*. Furthermore, terms that signal effects include *consequently, therefore, this leads to*. As an example, consider the sentence *Because the sky was clear, Ron did not bring an umbrella*. The cause is the clear sky, and the effect is that Ron did not bring an umbrella. However, readers may find that sometimes the cause-and-effect relationship will not be clearly noted. For instance, the sentence *He was late and missed the meeting* does not contain any signaling words, but the sentence still contains a cause (he was late) and an effect (he missed the meeting).

**Review Video: Cause and Effect**
Visit mometrix.com/academy and enter code: 868099

**Review Video: Rhetorical Strategy of Cause and Effect Analysis**
Visit mometrix.com/academy and enter code: 725944

### Multiple Effects

Be aware of the possibility for a single cause to have **multiple effects.** (e.g., *Single cause*: Because you left your homework on the table, your dog engulfed the assignment. *Multiple effects*: As a result, you receive a failing grade, your parents do not allow you to go out with your friends, you miss out on the new movie, and one of your classmates spoils it for you before you have another chance to watch it).

### Multiple Causes

Also, there is the possibility for a single effect to have **multiple causes.** (e.g., *Single effect*: Alan has a fever. *Multiple causes*: An unexpected cold front came through the area, and Alan forgot to take his multi-vitamin to avoid getting sick.) Additionally, an effect can in turn be the cause of another effect, in what is known as a cause-and-effect chain. (e.g., As a result of her disdain for procrastination, Lynn prepared for her exam. This led to her passing her test with high marks. Hence, her resume was accepted and her application was approved.)

### Cause and Effect in Persuasive Essays

**Persuasive essays**, in which an author tries to make a convincing argument and change the minds of readers, usually include cause-and-effect relationships. However, these relationships should not always be taken at face value. Frequently, an author will assume a cause or take an effect for granted. To read a persuasive essay effectively, readers need to judge the cause-and-effect relationships that the author is presenting. For instance, imagine an author wrote the following: *The parking deck has been unprofitable because people would prefer to ride their bikes.* The relationship is clear: the cause is that people prefer to ride their bikes, and the effect is that the parking deck has been unprofitable. However, readers should consider whether this argument is conclusive. Perhaps there are other reasons for the failure of the parking deck: a down economy, excessive fees, etc. Too often, authors present causal relationships as if they are fact rather than opinion. Readers should be on the alert for these dubious claims.

### Problem-Solution

Some nonfiction texts are organized to **present a problem** followed by a solution. For this type of text, the problem is often explained before the solution is offered. In some cases, as when the problem is well known, the solution may be introduced briefly at the beginning. Other passages may focus on the solution, and the problem will be referenced only occasionally. Some texts will outline multiple solutions to a problem, leaving readers to choose among them. If the author has an interest or an allegiance to one solution, he or she may fail to mention or describe accurately some of the other solutions. Readers should be careful of the author's agenda when reading a problem-solution text. Only by understanding the author's perspective and interests can one develop a proper judgment of the proposed solution.

### Compare and Contrast

Many texts follow the **compare-and-contrast** model in which the similarities and differences between two ideas or things are explored. Analysis of the similarities between ideas is called **comparison**. In an ideal comparison, the author places ideas or things in an equivalent structure, i.e., the author presents the ideas in the same way. If an author wants to show the similarities between cricket and baseball, then he or she may do so by summarizing the equipment and rules for each game. Be mindful of the similarities as they appear in the passage and take note of any differences that are mentioned. Often, these small differences will only reinforce the more general similarity.

**Review Video: Compare and Contrast**
Visit mometrix.com/academy and enter code: 798319

Thinking critically about ideas and conclusions can seem like a daunting task. One way to ease this task is to understand the basic elements of ideas and writing techniques. Looking at the ways different ideas relate to each other can be a good way for readers to begin their analysis. For instance, sometimes authors will write about two ideas that are in opposition to each other. Or, one author will provide his or her ideas on a topic, and another author may respond in opposition. The analysis of these opposing ideas is known as **contrast**. Contrast is often marred by the author's obvious partiality to one of the ideas. A discerning reader will be put off by an author who does not engage in a fair fight. In an analysis of opposing ideas, both ideas should be presented in clear and reasonable terms. If the author does prefer a side, you need to read carefully to determine the areas where the author shows or avoids this preference. In an analysis of opposing ideas, you should proceed through the passage by marking the major differences point by point with an eye that is looking for an explanation of each side's view. For instance, in an analysis of capitalism and communism, there is an importance in outlining each side's view on labor, markets, prices, personal responsibility, etc. Additionally, as you read through the passages, you should note whether the opposing views present each side in a similar manner.

### Sequence

Readers must be able to identify a text's **sequence**, or the order in which things happen. Often, when the sequence is very important to the author, the text is indicated with signal words like *first*, *then*, *next*, and *last*. However, a sequence can be merely implied and must be noted by the reader. Consider the sentence *He walked through the garden and gave water and fertilizer to the plants.* Clearly, the man did not walk through the garden before he collected water and fertilizer for the plants. So, the implied sequence is that he first collected water, then he collected fertilizer, next he walked through the garden, and last he gave water or fertilizer as necessary to the plants. Texts do not always proceed in an orderly sequence from first to last. Sometimes they begin at the end and start over at the beginning. As a reader, you can enhance your understanding of the passage by taking brief notes to clarify the sequence.

**Review Video: Sequence**
Visit mometrix.com/academy and enter code: 489027

## Making and Evaluating Predictions

### *Making Predictions*

When we read literature, **making predictions** about what will happen in the writing reinforces our purpose for reading and prepares us mentally. A **prediction** is a guess about what will happen next. Readers constantly make predictions based on what they have read and what they already know. We can make predictions before we begin reading and during our reading. Consider the following sentence: *Staring at the computer screen in shock, Kim blindly reached over for the brimming glass of water on the shelf to her side.* The sentence suggests that Kim is distracted, and that she is not looking at the glass that she is going to pick up. So, a reader might predict that Kim is going to knock over the glass. Of course, not every prediction will be accurate: perhaps Kim will pick the glass up cleanly. Nevertheless, the author has certainly created the expectation that the water might be spilled.

As we read on, we can test the accuracy of our predictions, revise them in light of additional reading, and confirm or refute our predictions. Predictions are always subject to revision as the reader acquires more information. A reader can make predictions by observing the title and illustrations; noting the structure, characters, and subject; drawing on existing knowledge relative to the subject; and asking "why" and "who" questions. Connecting reading to what we already know enables us to learn new information and construct meaning. For example, before third-graders read a book about Johnny Appleseed, they may start a KWL chart—a list of what they *Know*, what they *Want* to know or learn, and what they have *Learned* after reading. Activating existing background knowledge and thinking about the text before reading improves comprehension.

**Review Video: Predictive Reading**
Visit mometrix.com/academy and enter code: 437248

***Test-taking tip***: To respond to questions requiring future predictions, your answers should be based on evidence of past or present behavior and events.

### *Evaluating Predictions*

When making predictions, readers should be able to explain how they developed their prediction. One way readers can defend their thought process is by citing textual evidence. Textual evidence to evaluate reader predictions about literature includes specific synopses of the work, paraphrases of the work or parts of it, and direct quotations from the work. These references to the text must support the prediction by indicating, clearly or unclearly, what will happen later in the story. A text may provide these indications through literary devices such as foreshadowing. Foreshadowing is anything in a text that gives the reader a hint about what is to come by emphasizing the likelihood of an event or development. Foreshadowing can occur through descriptions, exposition, and dialogue. Foreshadowing in dialogue usually occurs when a character gives a warning or expresses a strong feeling that a certain event will occur. Foreshadowing can also occur through irony. However, unlike other forms of foreshadowing, the events that seem the most likely are the opposite of what actually happens. Instances of foreshadowing and irony can be summarized, paraphrased, or quoted to defend a reader's prediction.

**Review Video: Textual Evidence for Predictions**
Visit mometrix.com/academy and enter code: 261070



## Making Inferences and Drawing Conclusions

**Inferences** are logical conclusions that readers make based on their observations and previous knowledge. An inference is based on both what is found in a passage or a story and what is known from personal experience. For instance, a story may say that a character is frightened and can hear howling in the distance. Based on both what is in the text and personal knowledge, it is a logical conclusion that the character is frightened because he hears the sound of wolves. A good inference is supported by the information in a passage.

### Implicit and Explicit Information

By inferring, readers construct meanings from text that are personally relevant. By combining their own schemas or concepts and their background information pertinent to the text with what they read, readers interpret it according to both what the author has conveyed and their own unique perspectives. Inferences are different from **explicit information**, which is clearly stated in a passage. Authors do not always explicitly spell out every meaning in what they write; many meanings are implicit. Through inference, readers can comprehend implied meanings in the text, and also derive personal significance from it, making the text meaningful and memorable to them. Inference is a natural process in everyday life. When readers infer, they can draw conclusions about what the author is saying, predict what may reasonably follow, amend these predictions as they continue to read, interpret the import of themes, and analyze the characters' feelings and motivations through their actions.

### Example of Drawing Conclusions from Inferences

*Read the excerpt and decide why Jana finally relaxed.*

> Jana loved her job, but the work was very demanding. She had trouble relaxing. She called a friend, but she still thought about work. She ordered a pizza, but eating it did not help. Then, her kitten jumped on her lap and began to purr. Jana leaned back and began to hum a little tune. She felt better.

You can draw the conclusion that Jana relaxed because her kitten jumped on her lap. The kitten purred, and Jana leaned back and hummed a tune. Then she felt better. The excerpt does not explicitly say that this is the reason why she was able to relax. The text leaves the matter unclear, but the reader can infer or make a "best guess" that this is the reason she is relaxing. This is a logical conclusion based on the information in the passage. It is the best conclusion a reader can make based on the information he or she has read. Inferences are based on the information in a passage, but they are not directly stated in the passage.

***Test-taking tip***: While being tested on your ability to make correct inferences, you must look for **contextual clues**. An answer can be true, but not the best or most correct answer. The contextual clues will help you find the answer that is the **best answer** out of the given choices. Be careful in your reading to understand the context in which a phrase is stated. When asked for the implied meaning of a statement made in the passage, you should immediately locate the statement and read the **context** in which the statement was made. Also, look for an answer choice that has a similar phrase to the statement in question.

> **Review Video: <u>Inference</u>**
> Visit mometrix.com/academy and enter code: 379203
>
> **Review Video: <u>How to Support a Conclusion</u>**
> Visit mometrix.com/academy and enter code: 281653

## Plot and Story Structure

### *Plot and Story Structure*

The **plot** includes the events that happen in a story and the order in which they are told to the reader. There are several types of plot structures, as stories can be told in many ways. The most common plot structure is the chronological plot, which presents the events to the reader in the same order they occur for the characters in the story. Chronological plots usually have five main parts, the **exposition**, **rising action**, the **climax**, **falling action**, and the **resolution**. This type of plot structure guides the reader through the story's events as the characters experience them and is the easiest structure to understand and identify. While this is the most common plot structure, many stories are nonlinear, which means the plot does not sequence events in the same order the characters experience them. Such stories might include elements like flashbacks that cause the story to be nonlinear.

> **Review Video: <u>How to Make a Story Map</u>**
> Visit mometrix.com/academy and enter code: 261719

#### <u>Exposition</u>

The **exposition** is at the beginning of the story and generally takes place before the rising action begins. The purpose of the exposition is to give the reader context for the story, which the author may do by introducing one or more characters, describing the setting or world, or explaining the events leading up to the point where the story begins. The exposition may still include events that contribute to the plot, but the **rising action** and main conflict of the story are not part of the exposition. Some narratives skip the exposition and begin the story with the beginning of the rising action, which causes the reader to learn the context as the story intensifies.

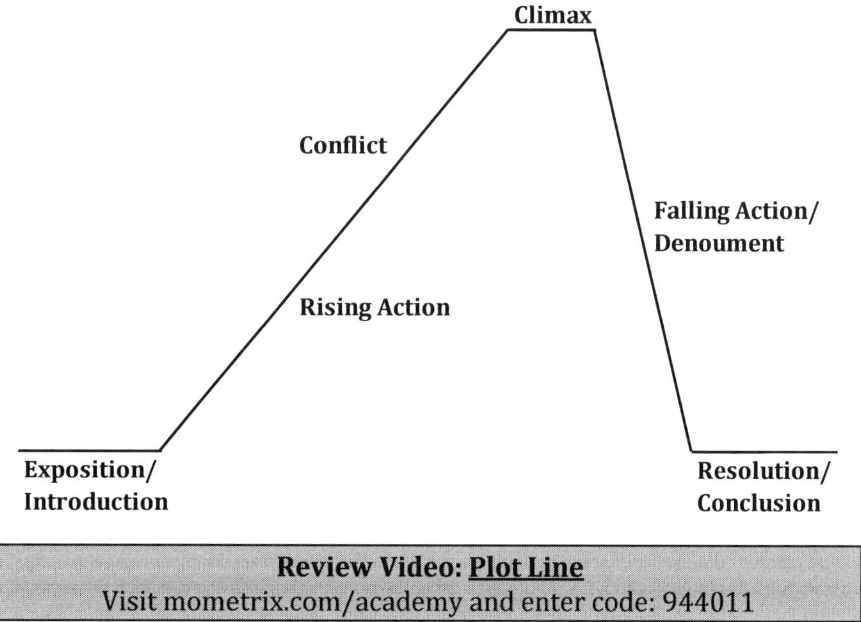


**Review Video: Plot Line**
Visit mometrix.com/academy and enter code: 944011

## CONFLICT

A **conflict** is a problem to be solved. Literary plots typically include one conflict or more. Characters' attempts to resolve conflicts drive the narrative's forward movement. **Conflict resolution** is often the protagonist's primary occupation. Physical conflicts like exploring, wars, and escapes tend to make plots most suspenseful and exciting. Emotional, mental, or moral conflicts tend to make stories more personally gratifying or rewarding for many audiences. Conflicts can be external or internal. A major type of internal conflict is some inner personal battle, or **man versus self**. Major types of external conflicts include **man versus nature**, **man versus man**, and **man versus society**. Readers can identify conflicts in literary plots by identifying the protagonist and antagonist and asking why they conflict, what events develop the conflict, where the climax occurs, and how they identify with the characters.

*Read the following paragraph and discuss the type of conflict present:*

> Timothy was shocked out of sleep by the appearance of a bear just outside his tent. After panicking for a moment, he remembered some advice he had read in preparation for this trip: he should make noise so the bear would not be startled. As Timothy started to hum and sing, the bear wandered away.

There are three main types of conflict in literature: **man versus man**, **man versus nature**, and **man versus self**. This paragraph is an example of man versus nature. Timothy is in conflict with the bear. Even though no physical conflict like an attack exists, Timothy is pitted against the bear.

Timothy uses his knowledge to "defeat" the bear and keep himself safe. The solution to the conflict is that Timothy makes noise, the bear wanders away, and Timothy is safe.

**Review Video: Conflict**
Visit mometrix.com/academy and enter code: 559550

**Review Video: Determining Relationships in a Story**
Visit mometrix.com/academy and enter code: 929925

### Rising Action

The **rising action** is the part of the story where conflict **intensifies**. The rising action begins with an event that prompts the main conflict of the story. This may also be called the **inciting incident**. The main conflict generally occurs between the protagonist and an antagonist, but this is not the only type of conflict that may occur in a narrative. After this event, the protagonist works to resolve the main conflict by preparing for an altercation, pursuing a goal, fleeing an antagonist, or doing some other action that will end the conflict. The rising action is composed of several additional events that increase the story's tension. Most often, other developments will occur alongside the growth of the main conflict, such as character development or the development of minor conflicts. The rising action ends with the **climax**, which is the point of highest tension in the story.

### Climax

The **climax** is the event in the narrative that marks the height of the story's conflict or tension. The event that takes place at the story's climax will end the rising action and bring about the results of the main conflict. If the conflict was between a good protagonist and an evil antagonist, the climax may be a final battle between the two characters. If the conflict is an adventurer looking for heavily guarded treasure, the climax may be the adventurer's encounter with the final obstacle that protects the treasure. The climax may be made of multiple scenes, but can usually be summarized as one event. Once the conflict and climax are complete, the **falling action** begins.

### Falling Action

The **falling action** shows what happens in the story between the climax and the resolution. The falling action often composes a much smaller portion of the story than the rising action does. While the climax includes the end of the main conflict, the falling action may show the results of any minor conflicts in the story. For example, if the protagonist encountered a troll on the way to find some treasure, and the troll demanded the protagonist share the treasure after retrieving it, the falling action would include the protagonist returning to share the treasure with the troll. Similarly, any unexplained major events are usually made clear during the falling action. Once all significant elements of the story are resolved or addressed, the story's resolution will occur. The **resolution** is the end of the story, which shows the final result of the plot's events and shows what life is like for the main characters once they are no longer experiencing the story's conflicts.

### Resolution

The way the conflict is **resolved** depends on the type of conflict. The plot of any book starts with the lead up to the conflict, then the conflict itself, and finally the solution, or **resolution**, to the conflict. In **man versus man** conflicts, the conflict is often resolved by two parties coming to some sort of agreement or by one party triumphing over the other party. In **man versus nature** conflicts, the conflict is often resolved by man coming to some realization about some aspect of nature. In

**man versus self** conflicts, the conflict is often resolved by the character growing or coming to an understanding about part of himself.

### *THEME*

A **theme** is a central idea demonstrated by a passage. Often, a theme is a lesson or moral contained in the text, but it does not have to be. It also is a unifying idea that is used throughout the text; it can take the form of a common setting, idea, symbol, design, or recurring event. A passage can have two or more themes that convey its overall idea. The theme or themes of a passage are often based on **universal themes**. They can frequently be expressed using well-known sayings about life, society, or human nature, such as "Hard work pays off" or "Good triumphs over evil." Themes are not usually stated **explicitly**. The reader must figure them out by carefully reading the passage. Themes are created through descriptive language or events in the plot. The events of a story help shape the themes of a passage.

#### EXAMPLE

*Explain why "if you care about something, you need to take care of it" accurately describes the theme of the following excerpt.*

> Luca collected baseball cards, but he wasn't very careful with them. He left them around the house. His dog liked to chew. One day, Luca and his friend Bart were looking at his collection. Then they went outside. When Luca got home, he saw his dog chewing on his cards. They were ruined.

This excerpt tells the story of a boy who is careless with his baseball cards and leaves them lying around. His dog ends up chewing them and ruining them. The lesson is that if you care about something, you need to take care of it. This is the theme, or point, of the story. Some stories have more than one theme, but this is not really true of this excerpt. The reader needs to figure out the theme based on what happens in the story. Sometimes, as in the case of fables, the theme is stated directly in the text. However, this is not usually the case.

**Review Video: Themes in Literature**
Visit mometrix.com/academy and enter code: 732074

## Textual and Graphic Information

### CRITICAL READING SKILLS

### *OPINIONS, FACTS, AND FALLACIES*

Critical thinking skills are mastered through understanding various types of writing and the different purposes authors can have for writing different passages. Every author writes for a purpose. When you understand their purpose and how they accomplish their goal, you will be able to analyze their writing and determine whether or not you agree with their conclusions.

Readers must always be aware of the difference between fact and opinion. A **fact** can be subjected to analysis and proven to be true. An **opinion**, on the other hand, is the author's personal thoughts or feelings and may not be altered by research or evidence. If the author writes that the distance from New York City to Boston is about two hundred miles, then he or she is stating a fact. If the author writes that New York City is too crowded, then he or she is giving an opinion because there is no objective standard for overpopulation. Opinions are often supported by facts. For instance, an author might use a comparison between the population density of New York City and that of other major American cities as evidence of an overcrowded population. An opinion supported by facts tends to be more convincing. On the other hand, when authors support their opinions with other opinions, readers should employ critical thinking and approach the argument with skepticism.

**Review Video: Distinguishing Fact and Opinion**
Visit mometrix.com/academy and enter code: 870899

### Reliable Sources

When you read an argumentative passage, you need to be sure that facts are presented to the reader from **reliable sources**. An opinion is what the author thinks about a given topic. An opinion is not common knowledge or proven by expert sources, instead the information is the personal beliefs and thoughts of the author. To distinguish between fact and opinion, a reader needs to consider the type of source that is presenting information, the information that backs-up a claim, and the author's motivation to have a certain point-of-view on a given topic. For example, if a panel of scientists has conducted multiple studies on the effectiveness of taking a certain vitamin, then the results are more likely to be factual than those of a company that is selling a vitamin and simply claims that taking the vitamin can produce positive effects. The company is motivated to sell their product, and the scientists are using the scientific method to prove a theory. Remember, if you find sentences that contain phrases such as "I think...", then the statement is an opinion.

### Biases

In their attempts to persuade, writers often make mistakes in their thought processes and writing choices. These processes and choices are important to understand so you can make an informed decision about the author's credibility. Every author has a point of view, but authors demonstrate a **bias** when they ignore reasonable counterarguments or distort opposing viewpoints. A bias is evident whenever the author's claims are presented in a way that is unfair or inaccurate. Bias can be intentional or unintentional, but readers should be skeptical of the author's argument in either case. Remember that a biased author may still be correct. However, the author will be correct in spite of, not because of, his or her bias.

A **stereotype** is a bias applied specifically to a group of people or a place. Stereotyping is considered to be particularly abhorrent because it promotes negative, misleading generalizations about people. Readers should be very cautious of authors who use stereotypes in their writing. These faulty assumptions typically reveal the author's ignorance and lack of curiosity.

**Review Video: Bias and Stereotype**
Visit mometrix.com/academy and enter code: 644829

## Reading Informational Texts

### *Language Use*

#### Literal and Figurative Language

As in fictional literature, informational text also uses both **literal language**, which means just what it says, and **figurative language**, which imparts more than literal meaning. For example, an informational text author might use a simile or direct comparison, such as writing that a racehorse "ran like the wind." Informational text authors also use metaphors or implied comparisons, such as "the cloud of the Great Depression." Imagery may also appear in informational texts to increase the reader's understanding of ideas and concepts discussed in the text.

**Review Video: Figurative Language**
Visit mometrix.com/academy and enter code: 584902

### *Explicit and Implicit Information*

When informational text states something explicitly, the reader is told by the author exactly what is meant, which can include the author's interpretation or perspective of events. For example, a professor writes, "I have seen students go into an absolute panic just because they weren't able to complete the exam in the time they were allotted." This explicitly tells the reader that the students were afraid, and by using the words "just because," the writer indicates their fear was exaggerated out of proportion relative to what happened. However, another professor writes, "I have had students come to me, their faces drained of all color, saying 'We weren't able to finish the exam.'" This is an example of implicit meaning: the second writer did not state explicitly that the students were panicked. Instead, he wrote a description of their faces being "drained of all color." From this description, the reader can infer that the students were so frightened that their faces paled.

**Review Video: Explicit and Implicit Information**
Visit mometrix.com/academy and enter code: 735771

### *Making Inferences About Informational Text*

With informational text, reader comprehension depends not only on recalling important statements and details, but also on reader inferences based on examples and details. Readers add information from the text to what they already know to draw inferences about the text. These inferences help the readers to fill in the information that the text does not explicitly state, enabling them to understand the text better. When reading a nonfictional autobiography or biography, for example, the most appropriate inferences might concern the events in the book, the actions of the subject of the autobiography or biography, and the message the author means to convey. When reading a nonfictional expository (informational) text, the reader would best draw inferences about problems and their solutions, and causes and their effects. When reading a nonfictional persuasive text, the reader will want to infer ideas supporting the author's message and intent.

### *Structures or Organizational Patterns in Informational Texts*

Informational text can be **descriptive**, appealing to the five senses and answering the questions what, who, when, where, and why. Another method of structuring informational text is sequence and order. **Chronological** texts relate events in the sequence that they occurred, from start to finish, while how-to texts organize information into a series of instructions in the sequence in which the steps should be followed. **Comparison-contrast** structures of informational text describe various ideas to their readers by pointing out how things or ideas are similar and how they are different. **Cause and effect** structures of informational text describe events that occurred and identify the causes or reasons that those events occurred. **Problem and solution** structures of informational texts introduce and describe problems and offer one or more solutions for each problem described.

### *Determining an Informational Author's Purpose*

Informational authors' purposes are why they write texts. Readers must determine authors' motivations and goals. Readers gain greater insight into a text by considering the author's motivation. This develops critical reading skills. Readers perceive writing as a person's voice, not simply printed words. Uncovering author motivations and purposes empowers readers to know what to expect from the text, read for relevant details, evaluate authors and their work critically, and respond effectively to the motivations and persuasions of the text. The main idea of a text is what the reader is supposed to understand from reading it; the purpose of the text is why the author has written it and what the author wants readers to do with its information. Authors state some purposes clearly, while other purposes may be unstated but equally significant. When stated purposes contradict other parts of a text, the author may have a hidden agenda. Readers can better evaluate a text's effectiveness, whether they agree or disagree with it, and why they agree or disagree through identifying unstated author purposes.

### IDENTIFYING AUTHOR'S POINT OF VIEW OR PURPOSE

In some informational texts, readers find it easy to identify the author's point of view and purpose, such as when the author explicitly states his or her position and reason for writing. But other texts are more difficult, either because of the content or because the authors give neutral or balanced viewpoints. This is particularly true in scientific texts, in which authors may state the purpose of their research in the report, but never state their point of view except by interpreting evidence or data.

To analyze text and identify point of view or purpose, readers should ask themselves the following four questions:

1. With what main point or idea does this author want to persuade readers to agree?
2. How does this author's word choice affect the way that readers consider this subject?
3. How do this author's choices of examples and facts affect the way that readers consider this subject?
4. What is it that this author wants to accomplish by writing this text?

**Review Video: Understanding the Author's Intent**
Visit mometrix.com/academy and enter code: 511819

**Review Video: Author's Position**
Visit mometrix.com/academy and enter code: 827954

### EVALUATING ARGUMENTS MADE BY INFORMATIONAL TEXT WRITERS

When evaluating an informational text, the first step is to identify the argument's conclusion. Then identify the author's premises that support the conclusion. Try to paraphrase premises for clarification and make the conclusion and premises fit. List all premises first, sequentially numbered, then finish with the conclusion. Identify any premises or assumptions not stated by the author but required for the stated premises to support the conclusion. Read word assumptions sympathetically, as the author might. Evaluate whether premises reasonably support the conclusion. For inductive reasoning, the reader should ask if the premises are true, if they support the conclusion, and if so, how strongly. For deductive reasoning, the reader should ask if the argument is valid or invalid. If all premises are true, then the argument is valid unless the conclusion can be false. If it can, then the argument is invalid. An invalid argument can be made valid through alterations such as the addition of needed premises.

### USE OF RHETORIC IN INFORMATIONAL TEXTS

There are many ways authors can support their claims, arguments, beliefs, ideas, and reasons for writing in informational texts. For example, authors can appeal to readers' sense of **logic** by communicating their reasoning through a carefully sequenced series of logical steps to help "prove" the points made. Authors can appeal to readers' **emotions** by using descriptions and words that evoke feelings of sympathy, sadness, anger, righteous indignation, hope, happiness, or any other emotion to reinforce what they express and share with their audience. Authors may appeal to the **moral** or **ethical values** of readers by using words and descriptions that can convince readers that something is right or wrong. By relating personal anecdotes, authors can supply readers with more accessible, realistic examples of points they make, as well as appealing to their emotions. They can provide supporting evidence by reporting case studies. They can also illustrate their points by making analogies to which readers can better relate.

## Technical Language

### *Technical Language*

Technical language is more impersonal than literary and vernacular language. Passive voice makes the tone impersonal. For example, instead of writing, "We found this a central component of protein metabolism," scientists write, "This was found a central component of protein metabolism." While science professors have traditionally instructed students to avoid active voice because it leads to first-person ("I" and "we") usage, science editors today find passive voice dull and weak. Many journal articles combine both. Tone in technical science writing should be detached, concise, and professional. While one may normally write, "This chemical has to be available for proteins to be digested," professionals write technically, "The presence of this chemical is required for the enzyme to break the covalent bonds of proteins." The use of technical language appeals to both technical and non-technical audiences by displaying the author or speaker's understanding of the subject and suggesting their credibility regarding the message they are communicating.

### *Technical Material for Non-Technical Readers*

Writing about **technical subjects** for **non-technical readers** differs from writing for colleagues because authors place more importance on delivering a critical message than on imparting the maximum technical content possible. Technical authors also must assume that non-technical audiences do not have the expertise to comprehend extremely scientific or technical messages, concepts, and terminology. They must resist the temptation to impress audiences with their scientific knowledge and expertise and remember that their primary purpose is to communicate a message that non-technical readers will understand, feel, and respond to. Non-technical and technical styles include similarities. Both should formally cite any references or other authors' work utilized in the text. Both must follow intellectual property and copyright regulations. This includes the author's protecting his or her own rights, or a public domain statement, as he or she chooses.

**Review Video: Technical Passages**
Visit mometrix.com/academy and enter code: 478923

#### Non-Technical Audiences

Writers of technical or scientific material may need to write for many non-technical audiences. Some readers have no technical or scientific background, and those who do may not be in the same field as the authors. Government and corporate policymakers and budget managers need technical information they can understand for decision-making. Citizens affected by technology or science are a different audience. Non-governmental organizations can encompass many of the preceding groups. Elementary and secondary school programs also need non-technical language for presenting technical subject matter. Additionally, technical authors will need to use non-technical language when collecting consumer responses to surveys, presenting scientific or para-scientific material to the public, writing about the history of science, and writing about science and technology in developing countries.

#### Use of Everyday Language

Authors of technical information sometimes must write using non-technical language that readers outside their disciplinary fields can comprehend. They should use not only non-technical terms, but also normal, everyday language to accommodate readers whose native language is different than the language the text is written in. For example, instead of writing that "eustatic changes like thermal expansion are causing hazardous conditions in the littoral zone," an author would do better to write that "a rising sea level is threatening the coast." When technical terms cannot be avoided, authors should also define or explain them using non-technical language. Although authors must cite references and acknowledge their use of others' work, they should avoid the kinds of references or citations that they would use in scientific journals—unless they reinforce author messages. They should not use endnotes, footnotes, or any other complicated referential techniques because non-technical journal publishers usually do not accept them. Including high-resolution illustrations, photos, maps, or satellite images and incorporating multimedia into digital publications will enhance non-technical writing about technical subjects. Technical authors may publish using non-technical language in e-journals, trade journals, specialty newsletters, and daily newspapers.

## Types of Technical Writing

### *Types of Printed Communication*

#### Memo

A memo (short for *memorandum*) is a common form of written communication. There is a standard format for these documents. It is typical for there to be a **heading** at the top indicating the author, date, and recipient. In some cases, this heading will also include the author's title and the name of his or her institution. Below this information will be the **body** of the memo. These documents are typically written by and for members of the same organization. They usually contain a plan of action, a request for information on a specific topic, or a response to such a request. Memos are considered to be official documents, so they are usually written in a **formal** style. Many memos are organized with numbers or bullet points, which make it easier for the reader to identify key ideas.

#### Posted Announcement

People post **announcements** for all sorts of occasions. Many people are familiar with notices for lost pets, yard sales, and landscaping services. In order to be effective, these announcements need to *contain all of the information* the reader requires to act on the message. For instance, a lost pet announcement needs to include a good description of the animal and a contact number for the owner. A yard sale notice should include the address, date, and hours of the sale, as well as a brief description of the products that will be available there. When composing an announcement, it is important to consider the perspective of the **audience**—what will they need to know in order to respond to the message? Although a posted announcement can have color and decoration to attract the eye of the passerby, it must also convey the necessary information clearly.

#### Classified Advertisement

Classified advertisements, or **ads**, are used to sell or buy goods, to attract business, to make romantic connections, and to do countless other things. They are an inexpensive, and sometimes free, way to make a brief **pitch**. Classified ads used to be found only in newspapers or special advertising circulars, but there are now online listings as well. The style of these ads has remained basically the same. An ad usually begins with a word or phrase indicating what is being **sold** or **sought**. Then, the listing will give a brief **description** of the product or service. Because space is limited and costly in newspapers, classified ads there will often contain abbreviations for common attributes. For instance, two common abbreviations are *bk* for *black*, and *obo* for *or best offer*. Classified ads will then usually conclude by listing the **price** (or the amount the seeker is willing to pay), followed by **contact information** like a telephone number or email address.

#### Scale Readings of Standard Measurement Instruments

The scales used on **standard measurement instruments** are fairly easy to read with a little practice. Take the **ruler** as an example. A typical ruler has different units along each long edge. One side measures inches, and the other measures centimeters. The units are specified close to the zero reading for the ruler. Note that the ruler does not begin measuring from its outermost edge. The zero reading is a black line a tiny distance inside of the edge. On the inches side, each inch is indicated with a long black line and a number. Each half-inch is noted with a slightly shorter line. Quarter-inches are noted with still shorter lines, eighth-inches are noted with even shorter lines, and sixteenth-inches are noted with the shortest lines of all. On the centimeter side, the second-largest black lines indicate half-centimeters, and the smaller lines indicate tenths of centimeters, otherwise known as millimeters.



## VISUAL INFORMATION IN INFORMATIONAL TEXTS

### *CHARTS, GRAPHS, AND VISUALS*

#### TABLES

Tables are presented in a standard format so they will be easy to read and understand. A title is at the top, a short phrase indicating the information the table or graph intends to convey. The title of a table could be something like "Median Income for Various Education Levels" or "Price of Milk Compared to Demand." A table is composed of information laid out in vertical columns and horizontal rows. Typically, each column will have a label. If "Median Income for Various Education Levels" was placed in a table format, the two columns could be labeled "Education Level" and "Median Annual Salary." Each location on the table is called a cell, which holds a piece of information. Cells are defined by their column and row (e.g., second column, fifth row).

**Median Annual Salary for Various Education Levels**

| Education Level | Median Annual Salary |
|---|---|
| Associate degree | $52,260 |
| Bachelor's degree | $74,464 |
| Master's degree | $86,372 |
| Professional degree | $108,160 |
| Doctoral degree | $108,316 |

#### GRAPHS

Like a table, a graph typically has a title at the top. This title may simply state the identities of the two axes: e.g., "Income vs. Education." However, the title may also be something more descriptive, like "A comparison of average income with level of education." In any case, bar and line graphs are laid out along two perpendicular lines, or axes. The vertical axis is called the *y*-axis, and the horizontal axis is called the *x*-axis. It is typical for the *x*-axis to be the independent variable and the *y*-axis to be the dependent variable. The independent variable is the one manipulated by the researcher or creator of the graph. In the above example, the independent variable would be "education level," since the maker of the graph will define these values (associate degree, bachelor's degree, master's degree, etc.). The dependent value is not controlled by the researcher.

When selecting a graph format, it is important to consider the intention and the structure of the presentation. A bar graph is appropriate for displaying the relations between a series of distinct quantities that are on the same scale. For instance, if one wanted to display the amount of money spent on groceries during the months of a year, a bar graph would be appropriate. The vertical axis would represent values of money, and the horizontal axis would identify each month. A line graph also requires data expressed in common units, but it is better for demonstrating the general trend in that data. If the grocery expenses were plotted on a line graph instead of a bar graph, there would be more emphasis on whether the amount of money spent rose or fell over the course of the year.

Whereas a bar graph is good for showing the relationships between the different values plotted, the line graph is good for showing whether the values tended to increase, decrease, or remain stable.

## Pie Chart

A pie chart, also known as a circle graph, is useful for depicting how a single unit or category is divided. The standard pie chart is a circle with designated wedges. Each wedge is **proportional** in size to a part of the whole. For instance, consider Shawna, a student at City College, who uses a pie chart to represent her budget. If she spends half of her money on rent, then the pie chart will represent that amount with a line through the center of the pie. If she spends a quarter of her money on food, there will be a line extending from the edge of the circle to the center at a right angle to the line depicting rent. This illustration would make it clear that the student spends twice the amount of money on rent as she does on food.

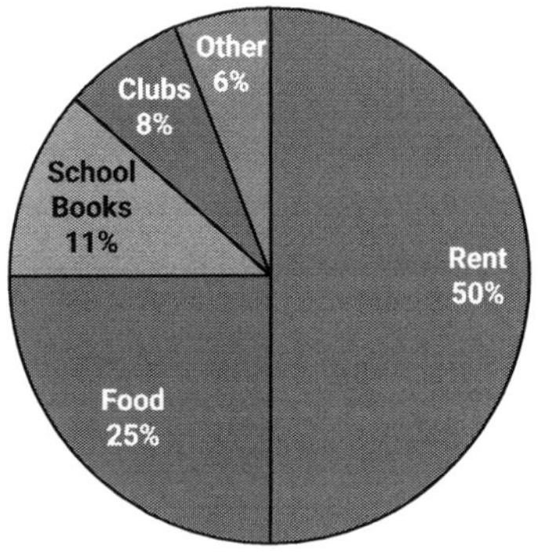


A pie chart is effective at showing how a single entity is divided into parts. They are not effective at demonstrating the relationships between parts of different wholes. For example, an unhelpful use of a pie chart would be to compare the respective amounts of state and federal spending devoted to infrastructure since these values are only meaningful in the context of the entire budget.

## Bar Graph

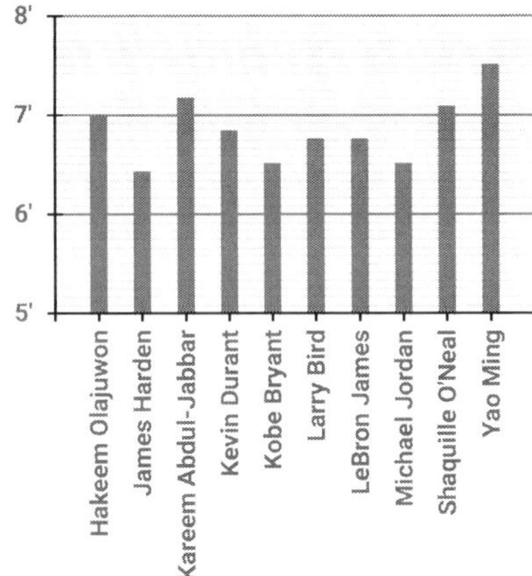


The bar graph is one of the most common visual representations of information. **Bar graphs** are used to illustrate sets of numerical **data**. The graph has a vertical axis (along which numbers are listed) and a horizontal axis (along which categories, words, or some other indicators are placed). One example of a bar graph is a depiction of the respective heights of famous basketball players: the vertical axis would contain numbers ranging from five to eight feet, and the horizontal axis would contain the names of the players. The length of the bar above the player's name would illustrate his height, and the top of the bar would stop perpendicular to the height listed along the left side. In this representation, one would see that Yao Ming is taller than Michael Jordan because Yao's bar would be higher.

### Line Graph

A line graph is a type of graph that is typically used for measuring trends over time. The graph is set up along a vertical and a horizontal **axis**. The variables being measured are listed along the left side and the bottom side of the axes. Points are then plotted along the graph as they correspond with their values for each variable. For instance, consider a line graph measuring a person's income for each month of the year. If the person earned $1500 in January, there should be a point directly above January (perpendicular to the horizontal axis) and directly to the right of $1500 (perpendicular to the vertical axis). Once all of the lines are plotted, they are connected with a line from left to right. This line provides a nice visual illustration of the general **trends** of the data, if they exist. For instance, using the earlier example, if the line sloped up, then one would see that the person's income had increased over the course of the year.

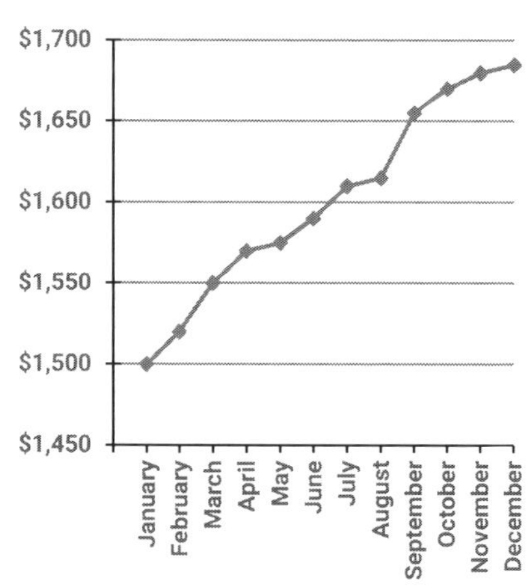


### Pictographs

A **pictograph** is a graph, generally in the horizontal orientation, that uses pictures or symbols to represent the data. Each pictograph must have a key that defines the picture or symbol and gives the quantity each picture or symbol represents. Pictures or symbols on a pictograph are not always shown as whole elements. In this case, the fraction of the picture or symbol shown represents the same fraction of the quantity a whole picture or symbol stands for.

> **Review Video: Pictographs**
> Visit mometrix.com/academy and enter code: 147860

# Other Reading Comprehension Skills

## Persuasion and Rhetoric

### *Persuasive Techniques*

To **appeal using reason**, writers present logical arguments, such as using "If... then... because" statements. To **appeal to emotions**, authors may ask readers how they would feel about something or to put themselves in another's place, present their argument as one that will make the audience feel good, or tell readers how they should feel. To **appeal to character**, **morality**, or **ethics**, authors present their points to readers as the right or most moral choices. Authors cite expert opinions to show readers that someone very knowledgeable about the subject or viewpoint agrees with the author's claims. **Testimonials**, usually via anecdotes or quotations regarding the author's subject, help build the audience's trust in an author's message through positive support from ordinary people. **Bandwagon appeals** claim that everybody else agrees with the author's argument and persuade readers to conform and agree, also. Authors **appeal to greed** by presenting their choice as cheaper, free, or more valuable for less cost. They **appeal to laziness** by presenting their views as more convenient, easy, or relaxing. Authors also anticipate potential objections and argue against them before audiences think of them, thereby depicting those objections as weak.

Authors can use **comparisons** like analogies, similes, and metaphors to persuade audiences. For example, a writer might represent excessive expenses as "hemorrhaging" money, which the author's recommended solution will stop. Authors can use negative word connotations to make some choices unappealing to readers, and positive word connotations to make others more appealing. Using **humor** can relax readers and garner their agreement. However, writers must take care: ridiculing opponents can be a successful strategy for appealing to readers who already agree with the author, but can backfire by angering other readers. **Rhetorical questions** need no answer, but create effect that can force agreement, such as asking the question, "Wouldn't you rather be paid more than less?" **Generalizations** persuade readers by being impossible to disagree with. Writers can easily make generalizations that appear to support their viewpoints, like saying, "We all want peace, not war" regarding more specific political arguments. **Transfer** and **association** persuade by example: if advertisements show attractive actors enjoying their products, audiences imagine they will experience the same. **Repetition** can also sometimes effectively persuade audiences.

**Review Video: Using Rhetorical Strategies for Persuasion**
Visit mometrix.com/academy and enter code: 302658

### *Classical Author Appeals*

In his *On Rhetoric,* ancient Greek philosopher Aristotle defined three basic types of appeal used in writing, which he called *pathos, ethos,* and *logos.* ***Pathos*** means suffering or experience and refers to appeals to the emotions (the English word *pathetic* comes from this root). Writing that is meant to entertain audiences, by making them either happy, as with comedy, or sad, as with tragedy, uses *pathos.* Aristotle's *Poetics* states that evoking the emotions of terror and pity is one of the criteria for writing tragedy. ***Ethos*** means character and connotes ideology (the English word *ethics* comes from this root). Writing that appeals to credibility, based on academic, professional, or personal merit, uses *ethos.* ***Logos*** means "I say" and refers to a plea, opinion, expectation, word or speech, account, opinion, or reason (the English word *logic* comes from this root.) Aristotle used it to mean persuasion that appeals to the audience through reasoning and logic to influence their opinions.

#### Rhetorical Devices

- An **anecdote** is a brief story authors may relate to their argument, which can illustrate their points in a more real and relatable way.
- **Aphorisms** concisely state common beliefs and may rhyme. For example, Benjamin Franklin's "Early to bed and early to rise / Makes a man healthy, wealthy, and wise" is an aphorism.
- **Allusions** refer to literary or historical figures to impart symbolism to a thing or person and to create reader resonance. In John Steinbeck's *Of Mice and Men,* protagonist George's last name is Milton. This alludes to John Milton, who wrote *Paradise Lost*, and symbolizes George's eventual loss of his dream.
- **Satire** exaggerates, ridicules, or pokes fun at human flaws or ideas, as in the works of Jonathan Swift and Mark Twain.
- A **parody** is a form of satire that imitates another work to ridicule its topic or style.
- A **paradox** is a statement that is true despite appearing contradictory.
- **Hyperbole** is overstatement using exaggerated language.
- An **oxymoron** combines seeming contradictions, such as "deafening silence."
- **Analogies** compare two things that share common elements.
- **Similes** (stated comparisons using the words *like* or *as*) and **metaphors** (stated comparisons that do not use *like* or *as*) are considered forms of analogy.
- When using logic to reason with audiences, **syllogism** refers either to deductive reasoning or a deceptive, very sophisticated, or subtle argument.
- **Deductive reasoning** moves from general to specific, **inductive reasoning** from specific to general.

- **Diction** is author word choice that establishes tone and effect.
- **Understatement** achieves effects like contrast or irony by downplaying or describing something more subtly than warranted.
- **Chiasmus** uses parallel clauses, the second reversing the order of the first. Examples include T. S. Eliot's "Has the Church failed mankind, or has mankind failed the Church?" and John F. Kennedy's "Ask not what your country can do for you; ask what you can do for your country."
- **Anaphora** regularly repeats a word or phrase at the beginnings of consecutive clauses or phrases to add emphasis to an idea. A classic example of anaphora was Winston Churchill's emphasis of determination: "[W]e shall fight on the beaches, we shall fight on the landing grounds, we shall fight in the fields and in the streets, we shall fight in the hills; we shall never surrender..."



## Reading Comprehension and Connecting with Texts

### *Comparing Two Stories*

When presented with two different stories, there will be **similarities** and **differences** between the two. A reader needs to make a list, or other graphic organizer, of the points presented in each story. Once the reader has written down the main point and supporting points for each story, the two sets of ideas can be compared. The reader can then present each idea and show how it is the same or different in the other story. This is called **comparing and contrasting ideas**.

The reader can compare ideas by stating, for example: "In Story 1, the author believes that humankind will one day land on Mars, whereas in Story 2, the author believes that Mars is too far away for humans to ever step foot on." Note that the two viewpoints are different in each story that the reader is comparing. A reader may state that: "Both stories discussed the likelihood of humankind landing on Mars." This statement shows how the viewpoint presented in both stories is based on the same topic, rather than how each viewpoint is different. The reader will complete a comparison of two stories with a conclusion.

**Review Video: How to Compare and Contrast**
Visit mometrix.com/academy and enter code: 833765

### *Outlining a Passage*

As an aid to drawing conclusions, **outlining** the information contained in the passage should be a familiar skill to readers. An effective outline will reveal the structure of the passage and will lead to solid conclusions. An effective outline will have a title that refers to the basic subject of the text, though the title does not need to restate the main idea. In most outlines, the main idea will be the first major section. Each major idea in the passage will be established as the head of a category. For instance, the most common outline format calls for the main ideas of the passage to be indicated with Roman numerals. In an effective outline of this kind, each of the main ideas will be represented by a Roman numeral and none of the Roman numerals will designate minor details or secondary ideas. Moreover, all supporting ideas and details should be placed in the appropriate place on the outline. An outline does not need to include every detail listed in the text, but it should feature all of those that are central to the argument or message. Each of these details should be listed under the corresponding main idea.

**Review Video: Outlining as an Aid to Drawing Conclusions**
Visit mometrix.com/academy and enter code: 584445

### *Using Graphic Organizers*

Ideas from a text can also be organized using **graphic organizers**. A graphic organizer is a way to simplify information and take key points from the text. A graphic organizer such as a timeline may have an event listed for a corresponding date on the timeline, while an outline may have an event listed under a key point that occurs in the text. Each reader needs to create the type of graphic organizer that works the best for him or her in terms of being able to recall information from a story. Examples include a spider-map, which takes a main idea from the story and places it in a bubble with supporting points branching off the main idea. An outline is useful for diagramming the main and supporting points of the entire story, and a Venn diagram compares and contrasts characteristics of two or more ideas.

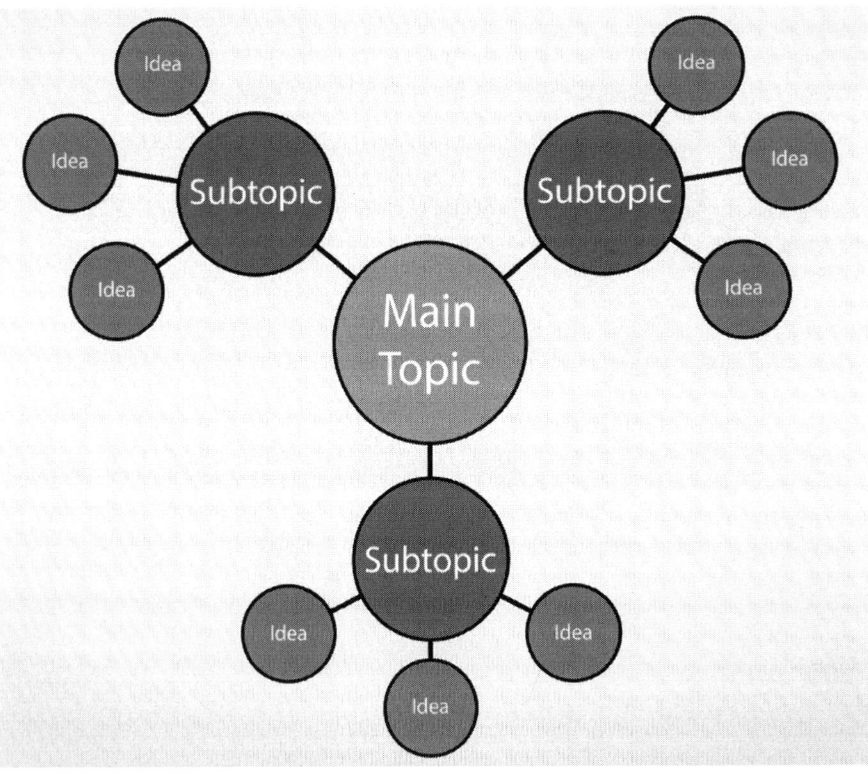


**Review Video: Graphic Organizers**
Visit mometrix.com/academy and enter code: 665513

### *Making Logical Conclusions about a Passage*

A reader should always be drawing conclusions from the text. Sometimes conclusions are **implied** from written information, and other times the information is **stated directly** within the passage. One should always aim to draw conclusions from information stated within a passage, rather than to draw them from mere implications. At times an author may provide some information and then describe a counterargument. Readers should be alert for direct statements that are subsequently rejected or weakened by the author. Furthermore, you should always read through the entire passage before drawing conclusions. Many readers are trained to expect the author's conclusions at either the beginning or the end of the passage, but many texts do not adhere to this format.

Drawing conclusions from information implied within a passage requires confidence on the part of the reader. **Implications** are things that the author does not state directly, but readers can assume based on what the author does say. Consider the following passage: *I stepped outside and opened my* *umbrella. By the time I got to work, the cuffs of my pants were soaked.* The author never states that it is raining, but this fact is clearly implied. Conclusions based on implication must be well supported by the text. In order to draw a solid conclusion, readers should have **multiple pieces of evidence**. If readers have only one piece, they must be assured that there is no other possible explanation than their conclusion. A good reader will be able to draw many conclusions from information implied by the text, which will be a great help on the exam.



### *Drawing Conclusions*

A common type of inference that a reader has to make is **drawing a conclusion**. The reader makes this conclusion based on the information provided within a text. Certain facts are included to help a reader come to a specific conclusion. For example, a story may open with a man trudging through the snow on a cold winter day, dragging a sled behind him. The reader can logically **infer** from the setting of the story that the man is wearing heavy winter clothes in order to stay warm. Information is implied based on the setting of a story, which is why **setting** is an important element of the text. If the same man in the example was trudging down a beach on a hot summer day, dragging a surf board behind him, the reader would assume that the man is not wearing heavy clothes. The reader makes inferences based on their own experiences and the information presented to them in the story.

***Test-taking tip***: When asked to identify a conclusion that may be drawn, look for critical "hedge" phrases, such as *likely*, *may*, *can*, and *will often*, among many others. When you are being tested on this knowledge, remember the question that writers insert into these hedge phrases to cover every possibility. Often an answer will be wrong simply because there is no room for exception. Extreme positive or negative answers (such as always or never) are usually not correct. When answering these questions, the reader **should not** use any outside knowledge that is not gathered directly or reasonably inferred from the passage. Correct answers can be derived straight from the passage.

#### Example

Read the following sentence from *Little Women* by Louisa May Alcott and draw a conclusion based upon the information presented:

> *You know the reason Mother proposed not having any presents this Christmas was because it is going to be a hard winter for everyone; and she thinks we ought not to spend money for pleasure, when our men are suffering so in the army.*

Based on the information in the sentence, the reader can conclude, or **infer**, that the men are away at war while the women are still at home. The pronoun *our* gives a clue to the reader that the character is speaking about men she knows. In addition, the reader can assume that the character is speaking to a brother or sister, since the term "Mother" is used by the character while speaking to another person. The reader can also come to the conclusion that the characters celebrate Christmas, since it is mentioned in the **context** of the sentence. In the sentence, the mother is presented as an unselfish character who is opinionated and thinks about the wellbeing of other people.

### *Summarizing*

A helpful tool is the ability to **summarize** the information that you have read in a paragraph or passage format. This process is similar to creating an effective outline. First, a summary should accurately define the main idea of the passage, though the summary does not need to explain this main idea in exhaustive detail. The summary should continue by laying out the most important supporting details or arguments from the passage. All of the significant supporting details should be included, and none of the details included should be irrelevant or insignificant. Also, the summary should accurately report all of these details. Too often, the desire for brevity in a summary leads to the sacrifice of clarity or accuracy. Summaries are often difficult to read because they omit all of the graceful language, digressions, and asides that distinguish great writing. However, an effective summary should communicate the same overall message as the original text.

**Review Video: Summarizing Text**
Visit mometrix.com/academy and enter code: 172903

### Paraphrasing

**Paraphrasing** is another method that the reader can use to aid in comprehension. When paraphrasing, one puts what they have read into their own words by rephrasing what the author has written, or one "translates" all of what the author shared into their own words by including as many details as they can.

### Evaluating a Passage

It is important to understand the logical conclusion of the ideas presented in an informational text. **Identifying a logical conclusion** can help you determine whether you agree with the writer or not. Coming to this conclusion is much like making an inference: the approach requires you to combine the information given by the text with what you already know and make a logical conclusion. If the author intended for the reader to draw a certain conclusion, then you can expect the author's argumentation and detail to be leading in that direction.

One way to approach the task of drawing conclusions is to make brief **notes** of all the points made by the author. When the notes are arranged on paper, they may clarify the logical conclusion. Another way to approach conclusions is to consider whether the reasoning of the author raises any pertinent questions. Sometimes you will be able to draw several conclusions from a passage. On occasion these will be conclusions that were never imagined by the author. Therefore, be aware that these conclusions must be **supported directly by the text**.

### Evaluation of Summaries

A summary of a literary passage is a condensation in the reader's own words of the passage's main points. Several guidelines can be used in evaluating a summary. The summary should be complete yet concise. It should be accurate, balanced, fair, neutral, and objective, excluding the reader's own opinions or reactions. It should reflect in similar proportion how much each point summarized was covered in the original passage. Summary writers should include tags of attribution, like "Macaulay argues that" to reference the original author whose ideas are represented in the summary. Summary writers should not overuse quotations; they should only quote central concepts or phrases they cannot precisely convey in words other than those of the original author. Another aspect of evaluating a summary is considering whether it can stand alone as a coherent, unified composition. In addition, evaluation of a summary should include whether its writer has cited the original source of the passage they have summarized so that readers can find it.

### Making Connections to Enhance Comprehension

Reading involves thinking. For good comprehension, readers make **text-to-self**, **text-to-text**, and **text-to-world connections**. Making connections helps readers understand text better and predict what might occur next based on what they already know, such as how characters in the story feel or what happened in another text. Text-to-self connections with the reader's life and experiences make literature more personally relevant and meaningful to readers. Readers can make connections before, during, and after reading—including whenever the text reminds them of something similar they have encountered in life or other texts. The genre, setting, characters, plot elements, literary structure and devices, and themes an author uses allow a reader to make connections to other works of literature or to people and events in their own lives. Venn diagrams and other graphic organizers help visualize connections. Readers can also make double-entry notes: key content, ideas, events, words, and quotations on one side, and the connections with these on the other.



## READING ARGUMENTATIVE WRITING

### *AUTHOR'S ARGUMENT IN ARGUMENTATIVE WRITING*

In argumentative writing, the argument is a belief, position, or opinion that the author wants to convince readers to believe as well. For the first step, readers should identify the **issue**. Some issues are controversial, meaning people disagree about them. Gun control, foreign policy, and the death penalty are all controversial issues. The next step is to determine the **author's position** on the issue. That position or viewpoint constitutes the author's argument. Readers should then identify the **author's assumptions**: things he or she accepts, believes, or takes for granted without needing proof. Inaccurate or illogical assumptions produce flawed arguments and can mislead readers. Readers should identify what kinds of **supporting evidence** the author offers, such as research results, personal observations or experiences, case studies, facts, examples, expert testimony and opinions, and comparisons. Readers should decide how relevant this support is to the argument.

**Review Video: Argumentative Writing**
Visit mometrix.com/academy and enter code: 561544

#### EVALUATING AN AUTHOR'S ARGUMENT

The first three reader steps to **evaluate an author's argument** are to identify the **author's assumptions**, identify the **supporting evidence**, and decide **whether the evidence is relevant**. For example, if an author is not an expert on a particular topic, then that author's personal experience or opinion might not be relevant. The fourth step is to assess the **author's objectivity**. For example, consider whether the author introduces clear, understandable supporting evidence and facts to support the argument. The fifth step is evaluating whether the author's **argument is complete**. When authors give sufficient support for their arguments and also anticipate and respond effectively to opposing arguments or objections to their points, their arguments are complete. However, some authors omit information that could detract from their arguments. If instead they stated this information and refuted it, it would strengthen their arguments. The sixth step in evaluating an author's argumentative writing is to assess whether the **argument is valid**. Providing clear, logical reasoning makes an author's argument valid. Readers should ask themselves whether the author's points follow a sequence that makes sense, and whether each point leads to the next. The seventh step is to determine whether the author's **argument is credible**, meaning that it is convincing and believable. Arguments that are not valid are not credible, so step seven depends on step six. Readers should be mindful of their own biases as they evaluate and should not expect authors to conclusively prove their arguments, but rather to provide effective support and reason.

#### EVALUATING AN AUTHOR'S METHOD OF APPEAL

To evaluate the effectiveness of an appeal, it is important to consider the author's purpose for writing. Any appeals an author uses in their argument must be relevant to the argument's goal. For example, a writer that argues for the reclassification of Pluto, but primarily uses appeals to emotion, will not have an effective argument. This writer should focus on using appeals to logic and support their argument with provable facts. While most arguments should include appeals to logic, emotion, and credibility, some arguments only call for one or two of these types of appeal. Evidence can support an appeal, but the evidence must be relevant to truly strengthen the appeal's effectiveness. If the writer arguing for Pluto's reclassification uses the reasons for Jupiter's classification as evidence, their argument would be weak. This information may seem relevant because it is related to the classification of planets. However, this classification is highly dependent on the size of the celestial object, and Jupiter is significantly bigger than Pluto. This use of evidence is illogical and does not support the appeal. Even when appropriate evidence and appeals are used, appeals and arguments lose their effectiveness when they create logical fallacies.

### EVIDENCE

The term **text evidence** refers to information that supports a main point or minor points and can help lead the reader to a conclusion about the text's credibility. Information used as text evidence is precise, descriptive, and factual. A main point is often followed by supporting details that provide evidence to back up a claim. For example, a passage may include the claim that winter occurs during opposite months in the Northern and Southern hemispheres. Text evidence for this claim may include examples of countries where winter occurs in opposite months. Stating that the tilt of the Earth as it rotates around the sun causes winter to occur at different times in separate hemispheres is another example of text evidence. Text evidence can come from common knowledge, but it is also valuable to include text evidence from credible, relevant outside sources.

**Review Video: Textual Evidence**
Visit mometrix.com/academy and enter code: 486236

Evidence that supports the thesis and additional arguments needs to be provided. Most arguments must be supported by facts or statistics. A fact is something that is known with certainty, has been verified by several independent individuals, and can be proven to be true. In addition to facts, examples and illustrations can support an argument by adding an emotional component. With this component, you persuade readers in ways that facts and statistics cannot. The emotional component is effective when used alongside objective information that can be confirmed.

### CREDIBILITY

The text used to support an argument can be the argument's downfall if the text is not credible. A text is **credible**, or believable, when its author is knowledgeable and objective, or unbiased. The author's motivations for writing the text play a critical role in determining the credibility of the text and must be evaluated when assessing that credibility. Reports written about the ozone layer by an environmental scientist and a hairdresser will have a different level of credibility.

**Review Video: Author Credibility**
Visit mometrix.com/academy and enter code: 827257

### APPEAL TO EMOTION

Sometimes, authors will appeal to the reader's emotion in an attempt to persuade or to distract the reader from the weakness of the argument. For instance, the author may try to inspire the pity of the reader by delivering a heart-rending story. An author also might use the bandwagon approach, in which he suggests that his opinion is correct because it is held by the majority. Some authors resort to name-calling, in which insults and harsh words are delivered to the opponent in an attempt to distract. In advertising, a common appeal is the celebrity testimonial, in which a famous person endorses a product. Of course, the fact that a famous person likes something should not really mean anything to the reader. These and other emotional appeals are usually evidence of poor reasoning and a weak argument.

**Review Video: Emotional Language in Literature**
Visit mometrix.com/academy and enter code: 759390

### Counter Arguments

When authors give both sides to the argument, they build trust with their readers. As a reader, you should start with an undecided or neutral position. If an author presents only his or her side to the argument, then they are not exhibiting credibility and are weakening their argument.

Building common ground with readers can be effective for persuading neutral, skeptical, or opposed readers. Sharing values with undecided readers can allow people to switch positions without giving up what they feel is important. People who may oppose a position need to feel that they can change their minds without betraying who they are as a person. This appeal to having an open mind can be a powerful tool in arguing a position without antagonizing other views. Objections can be countered on a point-by-point basis or in a summary paragraph. Be mindful of how an author points out flaws in counter arguments. If they are unfair to the other side of the argument, then you should lose trust with the author.

## Chapter Quiz

Ready to see how well you retained what you just read? Scan the QR code to go directly to the chapter quiz interface for this study guide. If you're using a computer, simply visit the online resources page at **mometrix.com/resources719/nystceatas-29098** and click the Chapter Quizzes link.

# Writing

Transform passive reading into active learning! After immersing yourself in this chapter, put your comprehension to the test by taking a quiz. The insights you gained will stay with you longer this way. Scan the QR code to go directly to the chapter quiz interface for this study guide. If you're using a computer, simply visit the online resources page at **mometrix.com/resources719/nystceatas-29098** and click the Chapter Quizzes link.

## Parts of Speech

### Nouns

A noun is a person, place, thing, or idea. The two main types of nouns are **common** and **proper** nouns. Nouns can also be categorized as abstract (i.e., general) or concrete (i.e., specific).

#### *Common Nouns*

**Common nouns** are generic names for people, places, and things. Common nouns are not usually capitalized.

Examples of common nouns:

*People*: boy, girl, worker, manager

*Places*: school, bank, library, home

*Things*: dog, cat, truck, car

**Review Video: Nouns**
Visit mometrix.com/academy and enter code: 344028

#### *Proper Nouns*

**Proper nouns** name specific people, places, or things. All proper nouns are capitalized.

Examples of proper nouns:

*People*: Abraham Lincoln, George Washington, Martin Luther King, Jr.

*Places*: Los Angeles, California; New York; Asia

*Things*: Statue of Liberty, Earth, Lincoln Memorial

Note: Some nouns can be either common or proper depending on their use. For example, when referring to the planet that we live on, *Earth* is a proper noun and is capitalized. When referring to the dirt, rocks, or land on our planet, *earth* is a common noun and is not capitalized.

### General and Specific Nouns

**General nouns** are the names of conditions or ideas. **Specific nouns** name people, places, and things that are understood by using your senses.

General nouns:

*Condition*: beauty, strength

*Idea*: truth, peace

Specific nouns:

*People*: baby, friend, father

*Places*: town, park, city hall

*Things*: rainbow, cough, apple, silk, gasoline

### Collective Nouns

**Collective nouns** are the names for a group of people, places, or things that may act as a whole. The following are examples of collective nouns: *class, company, dozen, group, herd, team,* and *public.* Collective nouns usually require an article, which denotes the noun as being a single unit. For instance, a choir is a group of singers. Even though there are many singers in a choir, the word choir is grammatically treated as a single unit. If we refer to the members of the group, and not the group itself, it is no longer a collective noun.

Incorrect: The *choir are* going to compete nationally this year.

Correct: The *choir is* going to compete nationally this year.

Incorrect: The *members* of the choir *is* competing nationally this year.

Correct: The *members* of the choir *are* competing nationally this year.

## Pronouns

Pronouns are words that are used to stand in for nouns. A pronoun may be classified as personal, intensive, relative, interrogative, demonstrative, indefinite, and reciprocal.

**Personal**: *Nominative* is the case for nouns and pronouns that are the subject of a sentence. *Objective* is the case for nouns and pronouns that are an object in a sentence. *Possessive* is the case for nouns and pronouns that show possession or ownership.

*Singular*

| | Nominative | Objective | Possessive |
|---|---|---|---|
| **First Person** | I | me | my, mine |
| **Second Person** | you | you | your, yours |
| **Third Person** | he, she, it | him, her, it | his, her, hers, its |

Writing

*Plural*

| | Nominative | Objective | Possessive |
|---|---|---|---|
| **First Person** | we | us | our, ours |
| **Second Person** | you | you | your, yours |
| **Third Person** | they | them | their, theirs |

**Intensive**: I myself, you yourself, he himself, she herself, the (thing) itself, we ourselves, you yourselves, they themselves

**Relative**: which, who, whom, whose

**Interrogative**: what, which, who, whom, whose

**Demonstrative**: this, that, these, those

**Indefinite**: all, any, each, everyone, either/neither, one, some, several

**Reciprocal**: each other, one another

**Review Video: Nouns and Pronouns**
Visit mometrix.com/academy and enter code: 312073

## Verbs

A verb is a word or group of words that indicates action or being. In other words, the verb shows something's action or state of being or the action that has been done to something. If you want to write a sentence, then you need a verb. Without a verb, you have no sentence.

### Transitive and Intransitive Verbs

A **transitive verb** is a verb whose action indicates a receiver. **Intransitive verbs** do not indicate a receiver of an action. In other words, the action of the verb does not point to an object.

**Transitive**: He drives a car. | She feeds the dog.

**Intransitive**: He runs every day. | She voted in the last election.

A dictionary will tell you whether a verb is transitive or intransitive. Some verbs can be transitive or intransitive.

### Action Verbs and Linking Verbs

**Action verbs** show what the subject is doing. In other words, an action verb shows action. Unlike most types of words, a single action verb, in the right context, can be an entire sentence. **Linking verbs** link the subject of a sentence to a noun or pronoun, or they link a subject with an adjective. You always need a verb if you want a complete sentence. However, linking verbs on their own cannot be a complete sentence.

Common linking verbs include *appear, be, become, feel, grow, look, seem, smell, sound,* and *taste.* However, any verb that shows a condition and connects to a noun, pronoun, or adjective that describes the subject of a sentence is a linking verb.

**Action**: He sings. | Run! | Go! | I talk with him every day. | She reads.

**Linking**:

Incorrect: I am.

Correct: I am John. | The roses smell lovely. | I feel tired.

Note: Some verbs are followed by words that look like prepositions, but they are a part of the verb and a part of the verb's meaning. These are known as phrasal verbs, and examples include *call off*, *look up*, and *drop off*.

**Review Video: Action Verbs and Linking Verbs**
Visit mometrix.com/academy and enter code: 743142

### Voice

Transitive verbs may be in active voice or passive voice. The difference between active voice and passive voice is whether the subject is acting or being acted upon. When the subject of the sentence is doing the action, the verb is in **active voice**. When the subject is being acted upon, the verb is in **passive voice**.

**Active**: Jon drew the picture. (The subject *Jon* is doing the action of *drawing a picture*.)

**Passive**: The picture is drawn by Jon. (The subject *picture* is receiving the action from Jon.)

### Verb Tenses

Verb **tense** is a property of a verb that indicates when the action being described takes place (past, present, or future) and whether or not the action is completed (simple or perfect). Describing an action taking place in the present (*I talk*) requires a different verb tense than describing an action that took place in the past (*I talked*). Some verb tenses require an auxiliary (helping) verb. These helping verbs include *am, are, is* | *have, has, had* | *was, were, will* (or *shall*).

| | |
|---|---|
| Present: I talk | Present perfect: I have talked |
| Past: I talked | Past perfect: I had talked |
| Future: I will talk | Future perfect: I will have talked |

**Present**: The action is happening at the current time.

Example: He *walks* to the store every morning.

To show that something is happening right now, use the progressive present tense: I *am walking*.

**Past**: The action happened in the past.

Example: She *walked* to the store an hour ago.

**Future**: The action will happen later.

Example: I *will walk* to the store tomorrow.

**Present perfect**: The action started in the past and continues into the present or took place previously at an unspecified time.

Example: I *have walked* to the store three times today.

Writing

**Past perfect**: The action was completed at some point in the past. This tense is usually used to describe an action that was completed before some other reference time or event.

Example: I *had eaten* already before they arrived.

**Future perfect**: The action will be completed before some point in the future. This tense may be used to describe an action that has already begun or has yet to begin.

Example: The project *will have been completed* by the deadline.

**Review Video: Present Perfect, Past Perfect, and Future Perfect Verb Tenses**
Visit mometrix.com/academy and enter code: 269472

### *CONJUGATING VERBS*

When you need to change the form of a verb, you are **conjugating** a verb. The key forms of a verb are present tense (sing/sings), past tense (sang), present participle (singing), and past participle (sung). By combining these forms with helping verbs, you can make almost any verb tense. The following table demonstrate some of the different ways to conjugate a verb:

| Tense | First Person | Second Person | Third Person Singular | Third Person Plural |
|---|---|---|---|---|
| **Simple Present** | I sing | You sing | He, she, it sings | They sing |
| **Simple Past** | I sang | You sang | He, she, it sang | They sang |
| **Simple Future** | I will sing | You will sing | He, she, it will sing | They will sing |
| **Present Progressive** | I am singing | You are singing | He, she, it is singing | They are singing |
| **Past Progressive** | I was singing | You were singing | He, she, it was singing | They were singing |
| **Present Perfect** | I have sung | You have sung | He, she, it has sung | They have sung |
| **Past Perfect** | I had sung | You had sung | He, she, it had sung | They had sung |

### *MOOD*

There are three **moods** in English: the indicative, the imperative, and the subjunctive.

The **indicative mood** is used for facts, opinions, and questions.

Fact: You can do this.

Opinion: I think that you can do this.

Question: Do you know that you can do this?

The **imperative** is used for orders or requests.

Order: You are going to do this!

Request: Will you do this for me?

The **subjunctive mood** is for wishes and statements that go against fact.

Wish: I wish that I were famous.

Statement against fact: If I were you, I would do this. (This goes against fact because I am not you. You have the chance to do this, and I do not have the chance.)

## ADJECTIVES

An **adjective** is a word that is used to modify a noun or pronoun. An adjective answers a question: *Which one? What kind?* or *How many?* Usually, adjectives come before the words that they modify, but they may also come after a linking verb.

Which one? The *third* suit is my favorite.

What kind? This suit is *navy blue.*

How many? I am going to buy *four* pairs of socks to match the suit.

**Review Video: Descriptive Text**
Visit mometrix.com/academy and enter code: 174903



### *ARTICLES*

**Articles** are adjectives that are used to distinguish nouns as definite or indefinite. *A*, *an*, and *the* are the only articles. **Definite** nouns are preceded by *the* and indicate a specific person, place, thing, or idea. **Indefinite** nouns are preceded by *a* or *an* and do not indicate a specific person, place, thing, or idea.

Note: *An* comes before words that start with a vowel sound. For example, "Are you going to get an **u**mbrella?"

**Definite**: I lost *the* bottle that belongs to me.

**Indefinite**: Does anyone have *a* bottle to share?

**Review Video: Function of Articles in a Sentence**
Visit mometrix.com/academy and enter code: 449383

### *COMPARISON WITH ADJECTIVES*

Some adjectives are relative and other adjectives are absolute. Adjectives that are **relative** can show the comparison between things. **Absolute** adjectives can also show comparison, but they do so in a different way. Let's say that you are reading two books. You think that one book is perfect, and the other book is not exactly perfect. It is not possible for one book to be more perfect than the other. Either you think that the book is perfect, or you think that the book is imperfect. In this case, perfect and imperfect are absolute adjectives.

Relative adjectives will show the different **degrees** of something or someone to something else or someone else. The three degrees of adjectives include positive, comparative, and superlative.

The **positive** degree is the normal form of an adjective.

Example: This work is *difficult.* | She is *smart.*

The **comparative** degree compares one person or thing to another person or thing.

Example: This work is *more difficult* than your work. | She is *smarter* than me.

The **superlative** degree compares more than two people or things.

Example: This is the *most difficult* work of my life. | She is the *smartest* lady in school.

**Review Video: Adjectives**
Visit mometrix.com/academy and enter code: 470154

## Adverbs

An **adverb** is a word that is used to **modify** a verb, an adjective, or another adverb. Usually, adverbs answer one of these questions: *When? Where? How?* and *Why?* The negatives *not* and *never* are considered adverbs. Adverbs that modify adjectives or other adverbs **strengthen** or **weaken** the words that they modify.

Examples:

He walks *quickly* through the crowd.

The water flows *smoothly* on the rocks.

Note: Adverbs are usually indicated by the morpheme *-ly*, which has been added to the root word. For instance, *quick* can be made into an adverb by adding *-ly* to construct *quickly*. Some words that end in *-ly* do not follow this rule and can behave as other parts of speech. Examples of adjectives ending in *-ly* include: *early, friendly, holy, lonely, silly*, and *ugly*. To know if a word that ends in *-ly* is an adjective or adverb, check your dictionary. Also, while many adverbs end in *-ly*, you need to remember that not all adverbs end in *-ly*.

Examples:

He is *never* angry.

You are *too* irresponsible to travel alone.

**Review Video: Adverbs**
Visit mometrix.com/academy and enter code: 713951

**Review Video: Adverbs that Modify Adjectives**
Visit mometrix.com/academy and enter code: 122570

### *Comparison with Adverbs*

The rules for comparing adverbs are the same as the rules for adjectives.

The **positive** degree is the standard form of an adverb.

Example: He arrives *soon*. | She speaks *softly* to her friends.

The **comparative** degree compares one person or thing to another person or thing.

Example: He arrives *sooner* than Sarah. | She speaks *more softly* than him.

The **superlative** degree compares more than two people or things.

Example: He arrives *soonest* of the group. | She speaks the *most softly* of any of her friends.

## PREPOSITIONS

A **preposition** is a word placed before a noun or pronoun that shows the relationship between that noun or pronoun and another word in the sentence.

*Common prepositions*:

| | | | | |
|---|---|---|---|---|
| about | before | during | on | under |
| after | beneath | for | over | until |
| against | between | from | past | up |
| among | beyond | in | through | with |
| around | by | of | to | within |
| at | down | off | toward | without |

Examples:

The napkin is *in* the drawer.

The Earth rotates *around* the Sun.

The needle is *beneath* the haystack.

Can you find "me" *among* the words?

**Review Video: Prepositions**
Visit mometrix.com/academy and enter code: 946763

## CONJUNCTIONS

**Conjunctions** join words, phrases, or clauses and they show the connection between the joined pieces. **Coordinating conjunctions** connect equal parts of sentences. **Correlative conjunctions** show the connection between pairs. **Subordinating conjunctions** join subordinate (i.e., dependent) clauses with independent clauses.

### *COORDINATING CONJUNCTIONS*

The **coordinating conjunctions** include: *and, but, yet, or, nor, for,* and *so*

Examples:

The rock was small, *but* it was heavy.

She drove in the night, *and* he drove in the day.

Writing

#### *Correlative Conjunctions*

The **correlative conjunctions** are: *either...or* | *neither...nor* | *not only...but also*

Examples:

> *Either* you are coming *or* you are staying.
>
> He *not only* ran three miles *but also* swam 200 yards.

**Review Video: Coordinating and Correlative Conjunctions**
Visit mometrix.com/academy and enter code: 390329

**Review Video: Adverb Equal Comparisons**
Visit mometrix.com/academy and enter code: 231291

#### *Subordinating Conjunctions*

Common **subordinating conjunctions** include:

| | | |
|---|---|---|
| after | since | whenever |
| although | so that | where |
| because | unless | wherever |
| before | until | whether |
| in order that | when | while |

Examples:

> I am hungry *because* I did not eat breakfast.
>
> He went home *when* everyone left.

**Review Video: Subordinating Conjunctions**
Visit mometrix.com/academy and enter code: 958913

### Interjections

**Interjections** are words of exclamation (i.e., audible expression of great feeling) that are used alone or as a part of a sentence. Often, they are used at the beginning of a sentence for an introduction. Sometimes, they can be used in the middle of a sentence to show a change in thought or attitude.

> Common Interjections: Hey! | Oh, | Ouch! | Please! | Wow!

## Agreement and Sentence Structure

### Subjects and Predicates

#### *Subjects*

The **subject** of a sentence names who or what the sentence is about. The subject may be directly stated in a sentence, or the subject may be the implied *you*. The **complete subject** includes the simple subject and all of its modifiers. To find the complete subject, ask *Who* or *What* and insert the verb to complete the question. The answer, including any modifiers (adjectives, prepositional phrases, etc.), is the complete subject. To find the **simple subject**, remove all of the modifiers in the complete subject. Being able to locate the subject of a sentence helps with many problems, such as those involving sentence fragments and subject-verb agreement.

Examples:

The small, red car is the one that he wants for Christmas.
(simple subject: car; complete subject: The small, red car)

The young artist is coming over for dinner.
(simple subject: artist; complete subject: The young artist)

**Review Video: Subjects in English**
Visit mometrix.com/academy and enter code: 444771

In **imperative** sentences, the verb's subject is understood (e.g., [You] Run to the store), but is not actually present in the sentence. Normally, the subject comes before the verb. However, the subject comes after the verb in sentences that begin with *There are* or *There was*.

Direct:

| | | |
|---|---|---|
| John knows the way to the park. | Who knows the way to the park? | John |
| The cookies need ten more minutes. | What needs ten minutes? | The cookies |
| By five o'clock, Bill will need to leave. | Who needs to leave? | Bill |
| There are five letters on the table for him. | What is on the table? | Five letters |
| There were coffee and doughnuts in the house. | What was in the house? | Coffee and doughnuts |

Implied:

| | | |
|---|---|---|
| Go to the post office for me. | Who is going to the post office? | You |
| Come and sit with me, please? | Who needs to come and sit? | You |

### PREDICATES

In a sentence, you always have a predicate and a subject. The subject tells who or what the sentence is about, and the **predicate** explains or describes the subject. The predicate includes the verb or verb phrase and any direct or indirect objects of the verb, as well as any words or phrases modifying these.

Writing

Think about the sentence *He sings*. In this sentence, we have a subject (He) and a predicate (sings). This is all that is needed for a sentence to be complete. Most sentences contain more information, but if this is all the information that you are given, then you have a complete sentence.

Now, let's look at another sentence: *John and Jane sing on Tuesday nights at the dance hall.*

subject: John and Jane | predicate: sing on Tuesday nights at the dance hall.

> **Review Video: Complete Predicate**
> Visit mometrix.com/academy and enter code: 293942

## SUBJECT-VERB AGREEMENT

Verbs must **agree** with their subjects in number and in person. To agree in number, singular subjects need singular verbs and plural subjects need plural verbs. A **singular** noun refers to **one** person, place, or thing. A **plural** noun refers to **more than one** person, place, or thing. To agree in person, the correct verb form must be chosen to match the first, second, or third person subject. The present tense ending *-s* or *-es* is used on a verb if its subject is third person singular; otherwise, the verb's ending is not modified.

> **Review Video: Subject-Verb Agreement**
> Visit mometrix.com/academy and enter code: 479190

### *NUMBER AGREEMENT EXAMPLES:*

Single Subject and Verb: Dan (singular subject) calls (singular verb) home.

Dan is one person. So, the singular verb *calls* is needed.

Plural Subject and Verb: Dan and Bob (plural subject) call (plural verb) home.

More than one person needs the plural verb *call*.

### *PERSON AGREEMENT EXAMPLES:*

First Person: I *am* walking.

Second Person: You *are* walking.

Third Person: He *is* walking.

## COMPLICATIONS WITH SUBJECT-VERB AGREEMENT

### *WORDS BETWEEN SUBJECT AND VERB*

Words that come between the simple subject and the verb have no bearing on subject-verb agreement.

Examples:

The joy (singular subject) of my life returns (singular verb) home tonight.

The phrase *of my life* does not influence the verb *returns*.

The question (singular subject) that still remains unanswered is (singular verb) "Who are you?"

Don't let the phrase "*that still remains*..." trouble you. The subject *question* goes with *is*.

### Compound Subjects

A compound subject is formed when two or more nouns joined by *and*, *or*, or *nor* jointly act as the subject of the sentence.

#### Joined by And

When a compound subject is joined by *and*, it is treated as a plural subject and requires a plural verb.

Examples:

You and Jon (plural subject) are (plural verb) invited to come to my house.

The pencil and paper (plural subject) belong (plural verb) to me.

#### Joined by Or/Nor

For a compound subject joined by *or* or *nor*, the verb must agree in number with the part of the subject that is closest to the verb (italicized in the examples below).

Examples:

Today or tomorrow (subject) is (verb) the day.

Stan or Phil (subject) wants (verb) to read the book.

Neither the pen nor the book (subject) is (verb) on the desk.

Either the blanket or pillows (subject) arrive (verb) this afternoon.

### Indefinite Pronouns as Subject

An indefinite pronoun is a pronoun that does not refer to a specific noun. Some indefinite pronouns function as only singular, some function as only plural, and some can function as either singular or plural depending on how they are used.

### Always Singular

Pronouns such as *each*, *either*, *everybody*, *anybody*, *somebody*, and *nobody* are always singular.

Examples:

Each (singular subject) of the runners has (singular verb) a different bib number.

Is (singular verb) either (singular subject) of you ready for the game?

Note: The words *each* and *either* can also be used as adjectives (e.g., *each* person is unique). When one of these adjectives modifies the subject of a sentence, it is always a singular subject.

Everybody (singular subject) grows (singular verb) a day older every day.

Anybody (singular subject) is (singular verb) welcome to bring a tent.

### Always Plural

Pronouns such as *both*, *several*, and *many* are always plural.

Examples:

Both (plural subject) of the siblings were (plural verb) too tired to argue.

Many (plural subject) have tried (plural verb), but none have succeeded.

### Depend on Context

Pronouns such as *some*, *any*, *all*, *none*, *more*, and *most* can be either singular or plural depending on what they are representing in the context of the sentence.

Examples:

All (singular subject) of my dog's food was (singular verb) still there in his bowl.

By the end of the night, all (plural subject) of my guests were (plural verb) already excited about coming to my next party.

### *Other Cases Involving Plural or Irregular Form*

Some nouns are **singular in meaning but plural in form**: news, mathematics, physics, and economics.

The *news is* coming on now.

*Mathematics is* my favorite class.

Some nouns are plural in form and meaning, and have **no singular equivalent**: scissors and pants.

Do these *pants come* with a shirt?

The *scissors are* for my project.

Mathematical operations are **irregular** in their construction, but are normally considered to be **singular in meaning**.

*One plus one is* two.

*Three times three is* nine.

Note: Look to your **dictionary** for help when you aren't sure whether a noun with a plural form has a singular or plural meaning.



## Complements

A complement is a noun, pronoun, or adjective that is used to give more information about the subject or object in the sentence.

### *Direct Objects*

A direct object is a noun or pronoun that tells who or what **receives** the action of the verb. A sentence will only include a direct object if the verb is a transitive verb. If the verb is an intransitive verb or a linking verb, there will be no direct object. When you are looking for a direct object, find the verb and ask *who* or *what.*

Examples:

I took *the blanket.*

Jane read *books.*

### *Indirect Objects*

An indirect object is a noun or pronoun that indicates what or whom the action had an **influence** on. If there is an indirect object in a sentence, then there will also be a direct object. When you are looking for the indirect object, find the verb and ask *to/for whom or what.*

Examples:

We taught the old dog (indirect object) a new trick (direct object).

I gave them (indirect object) a math lesson (direct object).

**Review Video: Direct and Indirect Objects**
Visit mometrix.com/academy and enter code: 817385

### *Predicate Nominatives and Predicate Adjectives*

As we looked at previously, verbs may be classified as either action verbs or linking verbs. A linking verb is so named because it links the subject to words in the predicate that describe or define the subject. These words are called predicate nominatives (if nouns or pronouns) or predicate adjectives (if adjectives).

Examples:

My father (subject) is a lawyer (predicate nominative).

Your mother (subject) is patient (predicate adjective).

## Pronoun Usage

The **antecedent** is the noun that has been replaced by a pronoun. A pronoun and its antecedent **agree** when they have the same number (singular or plural) and gender (male, female, or neutral).

Examples:

**Singular agreement**: John (antecedent) came into town, and he (pronoun) played for us.

**Plural agreement**: John and Rick (antecedent) came into town, and they (pronoun) played for us.

To determine which is the correct pronoun to use in a compound subject or object, try each pronoun **alone** in place of the compound in the sentence. Your knowledge of pronouns will tell you which one is correct.

Example:

Bob and (I, me) will be going.

Test: (1) *I will be going* or (2) *Me will be going*. The second choice cannot be correct because *me* cannot be used as the subject of a sentence. Instead, *me* is used as an object.

**Answer**: Bob and I will be going.

When a pronoun is used with a noun immediately following (as in "we boys"), try the sentence **without the added noun**.

Example:

(We/Us) boys played football last year.

Test: (1) *We played football last ye*ar or (2) *Us played football last year*. Again, the second choice cannot be correct because *us* cannot be used as a subject of a sentence. Instead, *us* is used as an object.

**Answer**: We boys played football last year.

**Review Video: Pronoun Usage**
Visit mometrix.com/academy and enter code: 666500

**Review Video: Pronoun-Antecedent Agreement**
Visit mometrix.com/academy and enter code: 919704



A pronoun should point clearly to the **antecedent**. Here is how a pronoun reference can be unhelpful if it is puzzling or not directly stated.

antecedent (Ron and Jim); pronoun (he)

**Unhelpful**: Ron and Jim went to the store, and he bought soda.

Who bought soda? Ron or Jim?

antecedent (Jim); pronoun (he)

**Helpful**: Jim went to the store, and he bought soda.

The sentence is clear. Jim bought the soda.

Some pronouns change their form by their placement in a sentence. A pronoun that is a **subject** in a sentence comes in the **subjective case**. Pronouns that serve as **objects** appear in the **objective case**. Finally, the pronouns that are used as **possessives** appear in the **possessive case**.

Examples:

**Subjective case**: *He* is coming to the show.

The pronoun *He* is the subject of the sentence.

**Objective case**: Josh drove *him* to the airport.

The pronoun *him* is the object of the sentence.

**Possessive case**: The flowers are *mine*.

The pronoun *mine* shows ownership of the flowers.

The word *who* is a subjective-case pronoun that can be used as a **subject**. The word *whom* is an objective-case pronoun that can be used as an **object**. The words *who* and *whom* are common in subordinate clauses or in questions.

Examples:

He knows who (subject) wants (verb) to come.

He knows the man whom (object) we want (verb) at the party.

## Clauses

A clause is a group of words that contains both a subject and a predicate (verb). There are two types of clauses: independent and dependent. An **independent clause** contains a complete thought, while a **dependent (or subordinate) clause** does not. A dependent clause includes a subject and a verb, and may also contain objects or complements, but it cannot stand as a complete thought without being joined to an independent clause. Dependent clauses function within sentences as adjectives, adverbs, or nouns.

Example:

I am running (independent clause) because I want to stay in shape. (dependent clause)

The clause *I am running* is an independent clause: it has a subject and a verb, and it gives a complete thought. The clause *because I want to stay in shape* is a dependent clause: it has a subject and a verb, but it does not express a complete thought. It adds detail to the independent clause to which it is attached.

**Review Video: Clauses**
Visit mometrix.com/academy and enter code: 940170

**Review Video: Independent and Dependent Clauses**
Visit mometrix.com/academy and enter code: 556903

### *Types of Dependent Clauses*

#### Adjective Clauses

An **adjective clause** is a dependent clause that modifies a noun or a pronoun. Adjective clauses begin with a relative pronoun (*who, whose, whom, which,* and *that*) or a relative adverb (*where, when,* and *why*).

Also, adjective clauses usually come immediately after the noun that the clause needs to explain or rename. This is done to ensure that it is clear which noun or pronoun the clause is modifying.

Examples:

independent clause: I learned the reason / adjective clause: why I won the award.

independent clause: This is the place / adjective clause: where I started my first job.

An adjective clause can be an essential or nonessential clause. An essential clause is very important to the sentence. **Essential clauses** explain or define a person or thing. **Nonessential clauses** give more information about a person or thing but are not necessary to define them. Nonessential clauses are set off with commas while essential clauses are not.

Examples:

A person (essential clause: who works hard at first) can often rest later in life.

Neil Armstrong, (nonessential clause: who walked on the moon,) is my hero.

**Review Video: Adjective Clauses and Phrases**
Visit mometrix.com/academy and enter code: 520888

## Adverb Clauses

An **adverb clause** is a dependent clause that modifies a verb, adjective, or adverb. In sentences with multiple dependent clauses, adverb clauses are usually placed immediately before or after the independent clause. An adverb clause is introduced with words such as *after, although, as, before, because, if, since, so, unless, when, where*, and *while*.

Examples:

(adverb clause: When you walked outside,) I called the manager.

I will go with you (adverb clause: unless you want to stay.)

## Noun Clauses

A **noun clause** is a dependent clause that can be used as a subject, object, or complement. Noun clauses begin with words such as *how, that, what, whether, which, who,* and *why*. These words can also come with an adjective clause. Unless the noun clause is being used as the subject of the sentence, it should come after the verb of the independent clause.

Examples:

The real mystery is how you avoided serious injury. (noun clause: how you avoided serious injury)

What you learn from each other depends on your honesty with others. (noun clause: What you learn from each other)

### *Subordination*

When two related ideas are not of equal importance, the ideal way to combine them is to make the more important idea an independent clause and the less important idea a dependent or subordinate clause. This is called **subordination**.

Example:

**Separate ideas**: The team had a perfect regular season. The team lost the championship.

**Subordinated**: Despite having a perfect regular season, *the team lost the championship*.

## Phrases

A phrase is a group of words that functions as a single part of speech, usually a noun, adjective, or adverb. A **phrase** is not a complete thought and does not contain a subject and predicate, but it adds detail or explanation to a sentence, or renames something within the sentence.

### *Prepositional Phrases*

One of the most common types of phrases is the prepositional phrase. A **prepositional phrase** begins with a preposition and ends with a noun or pronoun that is the object of the preposition. Normally, the prepositional phrase functions as an **adjective** or an **adverb** within the sentence.

Examples:

The picnic is on the blanket. (prepositional phrase: on the blanket)

I am sick with a fever today. (prepositional phrase: with a fever)

Among the many flowers, John found a four-leaf clover. (prepositional phrase: Among the many flowers,)

### *Verbal Phrases*

A **verbal** is a word or phrase that is formed from a verb but does not function as a verb. Depending on its particular form, it may be used as a noun, adjective, or adverb. A verbal does **not** replace a verb in a sentence.

Examples:

Correct: Walk a mile daily. (verb: Walk)

This is a complete sentence with the implied subject *you*.

Incorrect: To walk (verbal) a mile.

This is not a sentence since there is no functional verb.

There are three types of verbal: **participles**, **gerunds**, and **infinitives**. Each type of verbal has a corresponding **phrase** that consists of the verbal itself along with any complements or modifiers.

## PARTICIPLES

A **participle** is a type of verbal that always functions as an adjective. The present participle always ends with *-ing*. Past participles end with *-d, -ed, -n,* or *-t*. Participles are combined with helping verbs to form certain verb tenses, but a participle by itself cannot function as a verb.

Examples: dance (verb) | dancing (present participle) | danced (past participle)

**Participial phrases** most often come right before or right after the noun or pronoun that they modify.

Examples:

Shipwrecked on an island, (participial phrase) the boys started to fish for food.

Having been seated for five hours, (participial phrase) we got out of the car to stretch our legs.

Praised for their work, (participial phrase) the group accepted the first-place trophy.

## GERUNDS

A **gerund** is a type of verbal that always functions as a **noun**. Like present participles, gerunds always end with *-ing*, but they can be easily distinguished from participles by the part of speech they represent (participles always function as adjectives). Since a gerund or gerund phrase always functions as a noun, it can be used as the subject of a sentence, the predicate nominative, or the object of a verb or preposition.

Examples:

We want to be known for teaching (gerund) the poor (teaching the poor: object of preposition).

Coaching (gerund) this team (Coaching this team: subject) is the best job of my life.

We like practicing (gerund) our songs (practicing our songs: object of verb) in the basement.

Writing

### INFINITIVES

An **infinitive** is a type of verbal that can function as a noun, an adjective, or an adverb. An infinitive is made of the word *to* and the basic form of the verb. As with all other types of verbal phrases, an infinitive phrase includes the verbal itself and all of its complements or modifiers.

Examples:

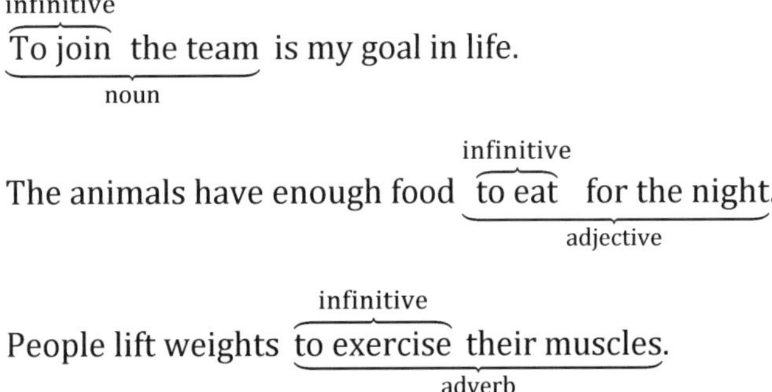


**Review Video: Verbals**
Visit mometrix.com/academy and enter code: 915480

### *APPOSITIVE PHRASES*

An **appositive** is a word or phrase that is used to explain or rename nouns or pronouns. Noun phrases, gerund phrases, and infinitive phrases can all be used as appositives.

Examples:

appositive
Terriers, hunters at heart, have been dressed up to look like lap dogs.

The noun phrase *hunters at heart* renames the noun *terriers*.

appositive
His plan, to save and invest his money, was proven as a safe approach.

The infinitive phrase explains what the plan is.

Appositive phrases can be **essential** or **nonessential**. An appositive phrase is essential if the person, place, or thing being described or renamed is too general for its meaning to be understood without the appositive.

Examples:

essential
Two of America's Founding Fathers, George Washington and Thomas Jefferson, served as presidents.

nonessential
George Washington and Thomas Jefferson, two Founding Fathers, served as presidents.

### *Absolute Phrases*

An absolute phrase is a phrase that consists of **a noun followed by a participle**. An absolute phrase provides **context** to what is being described in the sentence, but it does not modify or explain any particular word; it is essentially independent.

Examples:

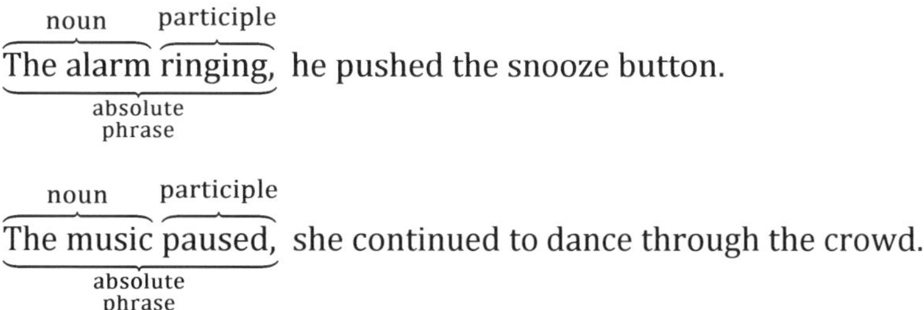


## Parallelism

When multiple items or ideas are presented in a sentence in series, such as in a list, the items or ideas must be stated in grammatically equivalent ways. For example, if two ideas are listed in parallel and the first is stated in gerund form, the second cannot be stated in infinitive form. (e.g., *I enjoy reading and to study.* [incorrect]) An infinitive and a gerund are not grammatically equivalent. Instead, you should write *I enjoy reading and studying* OR *I like to read and to study*. In lists of more than two, all items must be parallel.

Example:

> **Incorrect**: He stopped at the office, grocery store, and the pharmacy before heading home.
>
> The first and third items in the list of places include the article *the*, so the second item needs it as well.
>
> **Correct**: He stopped at the office, *the* grocery store, and the pharmacy before heading home.

Example:

> **Incorrect**: While vacationing in Europe, she went biking, skiing, and climbed mountains.
>
> The first and second items in the list are gerunds, so the third item must be as well.
>
> **Correct**: While vacationing in Europe, she went biking, skiing, and *mountain climbing*.

**Review Video: Parallel Sentence Construction**
Visit mometrix.com/academy and enter code: 831988

## Sentence Purpose

There are four types of sentences: declarative, imperative, interrogative, and exclamatory.

A **declarative** sentence states a fact and ends with a period.

> *The football game starts at seven o'clock.*

An **imperative** sentence tells someone to do something and generally ends with a period. An urgent command might end with an exclamation point instead.

*Don't forget to buy your ticket.*

An **interrogative** sentence asks a question and ends with a question mark.

*Are you going to the game on Friday?*

An **exclamatory** sentence shows strong emotion and ends with an exclamation point.

*I can't believe we won the game!*

## Sentence Structure

Sentences are classified by structure based on the type and number of clauses present. The four classifications of sentence structure are the following:

**Simple**: A simple sentence has one independent clause with no dependent clauses. A simple sentence may have **compound elements** (i.e., compound subject or verb).

Examples:

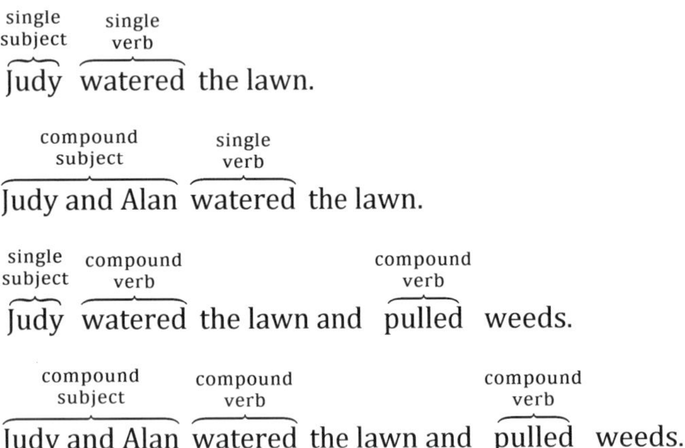


**Compound**: A compound sentence has two or more independent clauses with no dependent clauses. Usually, the independent clauses are joined with a comma and a coordinating conjunction or with a semicolon.

Examples:

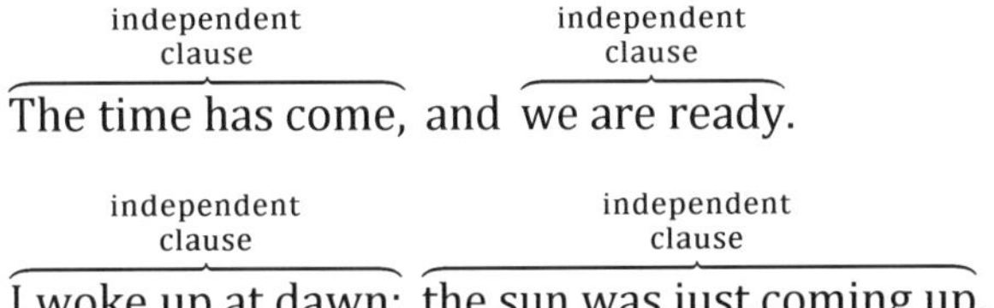

**Complex**: A complex sentence has one independent clause and at least one dependent clause.

Examples:

Although he had the flu, (dependent clause) Harry went to work. (independent clause)

Marcia got married, (independent clause) after she finished college. (dependent clause)

**Compound-Complex**: A compound-complex sentence has at least two independent clauses and at least one dependent clause.

Examples:

John is my friend (independent clause) who went to India, (dependent clause) and he brought back souvenirs. (independent clause)

You may not realize this, (independent clause) but we heard the music (independent clause) that you played last night. (dependent clause)

**Review Video: Sentence Structure**
Visit mometrix.com/academy and enter code: 700478

**Sentence variety** is important to consider when writing an essay or speech. A variety of sentence lengths and types creates rhythm, makes a passage more engaging, and gives writers an opportunity to demonstrate their writing style. Writing that uses the same length or type of sentence without variation can be boring or difficult to read. To evaluate a passage for effective sentence variety, it is helpful to note whether the passage contains diverse sentence structures and lengths. It is also important to pay attention to the way each sentence starts and avoid beginning with the same words or phrases.

## SENTENCE FRAGMENTS

Recall that a group of words must contain at least one **independent clause** in order to be considered a sentence. If it doesn't contain even one independent clause, it is called a **sentence fragment**.

The appropriate process for **repairing** a sentence fragment depends on what type of fragment it is. If the fragment is a dependent clause, it can sometimes be as simple as removing a subordinating word (e.g., when, because, if) from the beginning of the fragment. Alternatively, a dependent clause can be incorporated into a closely related neighboring sentence. If the fragment is missing some required part, like a subject or a verb, the fix might be as simple as adding the missing part.

Examples:

**Fragment**: Because he wanted to sail the Mediterranean.

**Removed subordinating word**: He wanted to sail the Mediterranean.

**Combined with another sentence**: Because he wanted to sail the Mediterranean, he booked a Greek island cruise.

## Run-on Sentences

Run-on sentences consist of multiple independent clauses that have not been joined together properly. Run-on sentences can be corrected in several different ways:

**Join clauses properly**: This can be done with a comma and coordinating conjunction, with a semicolon, or with a colon or dash if the second clause is explaining something in the first.

Example:

> **Incorrect**: I went on the trip, we visited lots of castles.
>
> **Corrected**: I went on the trip, and we visited lots of castles.

**Split into separate sentences**: This correction is most effective when the independent clauses are very long or when they are not closely related.

Example:

> **Incorrect**: The drive to New York takes ten hours, my uncle lives in Boston.
>
> **Corrected**: The drive to New York takes ten hours. My uncle lives in Boston.

**Make one clause dependent**: This is the easiest way to make the sentence correct and more interesting at the same time. It's often as simple as adding a subordinating word between the two clauses or before the first clause.

Example:

> **Incorrect**: I finally made it to the store and I bought some eggs.
>
> **Corrected**: When I finally made it to the store, I bought some eggs.

**Reduce to one clause with a compound verb**: If both clauses have the same subject, remove the subject from the second clause, and you now have just one clause with a compound verb.

Example:

> **Incorrect**: The drive to New York takes ten hours, it makes me very tired.
>
> **Corrected**: The drive to New York takes ten hours and makes me very tired.

Note: While these are the simplest ways to correct a run-on sentence, often the best way is to completely reorganize the thoughts in the sentence and rewrite it.

**Review Video: Fragments and Run-on Sentences**
Visit mometrix.com/academy and enter code: 541989

## Dangling and Misplaced Modifiers

### Dangling Modifiers

A dangling modifier is a dependent clause or verbal phrase that does not have a clear logical connection to a word in the sentence.

Example:

dangling modifier

**Incorrect**: Reading each magazine article, the stories caught my attention.

The word *stories* cannot be modified by *Reading each magazine article*. People can read, but stories cannot read. Therefore, the subject of the sentence must be a person.

gerund phrase

**Corrected**: Reading each magazine article, I was entertained by the stories.

Example:

dangling modifier

**Incorrect**: Ever since childhood, my grandparents have visited me for Christmas.

The speaker in this sentence can't have been visited by her grandparents when *they* were children, since she wouldn't have been born yet. Either the modifier should be clarified or the sentence should be rearranged to specify whose childhood is being referenced.

dependent clause

**Clarified**: Ever since I was a child, my grandparents have visited for Christmas.

adverb phrase

**Rearranged**: Ever since childhood, I have enjoyed my grandparents visiting for Christmas.

### Misplaced Modifiers

Because modifiers are grammatically versatile, they can be put in many different places within the structure of a sentence. The danger of this versatility is that a modifier can accidentally be placed where it is modifying the wrong word or where it is not clear which word it is modifying.

Example:

modifier

**Incorrect**: She read the book to a crowd that was filled with beautiful pictures.

The book was filled with beautiful pictures, not the crowd.

modifier

**Corrected**: She read the book that was filled with beautiful pictures to a crowd.

Example:

modifier

**Ambiguous**: Derek saw a bus nearly hit a man on his way to work.

Was Derek on his way to work or was the other man?

modifier

**Derek**: On his way to work, Derek saw a bus nearly hit a man.

modifier

**The other man**: Derek saw a bus nearly hit a man who was on his way to work.

### *SPLIT INFINITIVES*

A split infinitive occurs when a modifying word comes between the word *to* and the verb that pairs with *to*.

Example: To *clearly* explain vs. *To explain* clearly | To *softly* sing vs. *To sing* softly

Though considered improper by some, split infinitives may provide better clarity and simplicity in some cases than the alternatives. As such, avoiding them should not be considered a universal rule.

### DOUBLE NEGATIVES

Standard English allows **two negatives** only when a **positive** meaning is intended. (e.g., The team was *not displeased* with their performance.) Double negatives to emphasize negation are not used in standard English.

**Negative modifiers** (e.g., never, no, and not) should not be paired with other negative modifiers or negative words (e.g., none, nobody, nothing, or neither). The modifiers *hardly, barely*, and *scarcely* are also considered negatives in standard English, so they should not be used with other negatives.

## Punctuation

### END PUNCTUATION

#### *PERIODS*

Use a period to end all sentences except direct questions and exclamations. Periods are also used for abbreviations.

Examples: 3 p.m. | 2 a.m. | Mr. Jones | Mrs. Stevens | Dr. Smith | Bill, Jr. | Pennsylvania Ave.

Note: An abbreviation is a shortened form of a word or phrase.

### QUESTION MARKS

Question marks should be used following a **direct question**. A polite request can be followed by a period instead of a question mark.

**Direct Question**: What is for lunch today? | How are you? | Why is that the answer?

**Polite Requests**: Can you please send me the item tomorrow. | Will you please walk with me on the track.

**Review Video: Question Marks**
Visit mometrix.com/academy and enter code: 118471

### EXCLAMATION MARKS

Exclamation marks are used after a word group or sentence that shows much feeling or has special importance. Exclamation marks should not be overused. They are saved for proper **exclamatory interjections**.

Example: We're going to the finals! | You have a beautiful car! | "That's crazy!" she yelled.

**Review Video: Exclamation Points**
Visit mometrix.com/academy and enter code: 199367

## COMMAS

The comma is a punctuation mark that can help you understand connections in a sentence. Not every sentence needs a comma. However, if a sentence needs a comma, you need to put it in the right place. A comma in the wrong place (or an absent comma) will make a sentence's meaning unclear.

These are some of the rules for commas:

| Use Case | Example |
|---|---|
| Before a **coordinating conjunction** joining independent clauses | Bob caught three fish, and I caught two fish. |
| After an **introductory phrase** | After the final out, we went to a restaurant to celebrate. |
| After an **adverbial clause** | Studying the stars, I was awed by the beauty of the sky. |
| Between **items in a series** | I will bring the turkey, the pie, and the coffee. |
| For **interjections** | Wow, you know how to play this game. |
| After ***yes*** **and** ***no*** **responses** | No, I cannot come tomorrow. |
| Separate **nonessential modifiers** | John Frank, who coaches the team, was promoted today. |
| Separate **nonessential appositives** | Thomas Edison, an American inventor, was born in Ohio. |
| Separate **nouns of direct address** | You, John, are my only hope in this moment. |
| Separate **interrogative tags** | This is the last time, correct? |
| Separate **contrasts** | You are my friend, not my enemy. |
| Writing **dates** | July 4, 1776, is an important date to remember. |
| Writing **addresses** | He is meeting me at 456 Delaware Avenue, Washington, D.C., tomorrow morning. |
| Writing **geographical names** | Paris, France, is my favorite city. |
| Writing **titles** | John Smith, PhD, will be visiting your class today. |
| Separate **expressions like** ***he said*** | "You can start," she said, "with an apology." |

A comma is also used **between coordinate adjectives** not joined with *and*. However, not all adjectives are coordinate (i.e., equal or parallel). To determine if your adjectives are coordinate, try connecting them with *and* or reversing their order. If it still sounds right, they are coordinate.

**Incorrect**: The kind, brown dog followed me home.

**Correct**: The kind, loyal dog followed me home.

> **Review Video: When to Use a Comma**
> Visit mometrix.com/academy and enter code: 786797

## Semicolons

The semicolon is used to join closely related independent clauses without the need for a coordinating conjunction. Semicolons are also used in place of commas to separate list elements that have internal commas. Some rules for semicolons include:

| Use Case | Example |
|---|---|
| Between closely connected independent clauses **not connected with a coordinating conjunction** | You are right; we should go with your plan. |
| Between independent clauses **linked with a transitional word** | I think that we can agree on this; however, I am not sure about my friends. |
| Between items in a **series that has internal punctuation** | I have visited New York, New York; Augusta, Maine; and Baltimore, Maryland. |

> **Review Video: How to Use Semicolons**
> Visit mometrix.com/academy and enter code: 370605

## Colons

The colon is used to call attention to the words that follow it. When used in a sentence, a colon should only come at the **end** of a **complete sentence**. The rules for colons are as follows:

| Use Case | Example |
|---|---|
| After an independent clause to **make a list** | I want to learn many languages: Spanish, German, and Italian. |
| For **explanations** | There is one thing that stands out on your resume: responsibility. |
| To give a **quote** | He started with an idea: "We are able to do more than we imagine." |
| After the **greeting in a formal letter** | To Whom It May Concern: |
| Show **hours and minutes** | It is 3:14 p.m. |
| Separate a **title and subtitle** | The essay is titled "America: A Short Introduction to a Modern Country." |

> **Review Video: Using Colons**
> Visit mometrix.com/academy and enter code: 868673

## PARENTHESES

Parentheses are used for additional information. Also, they can be used to put labels for letters or numbers in a series. Parentheses should be not be used very often. If they are overused, parentheses can be a distraction instead of a help.

Examples:

**Extra Information**: The rattlesnake (see Image 2) is a dangerous snake of North and South America.

**Series**: Include in the email (1) your name, (2) your address, and (3) your question for the author.

**Review Video: Parentheses**
Visit mometrix.com/academy and enter code: 947743

## QUOTATION MARKS

Use quotation marks to close off **direct quotations** of a person's spoken or written words. Do not use quotation marks around indirect quotations. An indirect quotation gives someone's message without using the person's exact words. Use **single quotation marks** to close off a quotation inside a quotation.

**Direct Quote**: Nancy said, "I am waiting for Henry to arrive."

**Indirect Quote**: Henry said that he is going to be late to the meeting.

**Quote inside a Quote**: The teacher asked, "Has everyone read 'The Gift of the Magi'?"

Quotation marks should be used around the titles of **short works**: newspaper and magazine articles, poems, short stories, songs, television episodes, radio programs, and subdivisions of books or websites.

Examples:

"Rip Van Winkle" (short story by Washington Irving)

"O Captain! My Captain!" (poem by Walt Whitman)

Although it is not standard usage, quotation marks are sometimes used to highlight **irony** or the use of words to mean something other than their dictionary definition. This type of usage should be employed sparingly, if at all.

Examples:

| | |
|---|---|
| The boss warned Frank that he was walking on "thin ice." | Frank is not walking on real ice. Instead, he is being warned to avoid mistakes. |
| The teacher thanked the young man for his "honesty." | The quotation marks around *honesty* show that the teacher does not believe the young man's explanation. |

**Review Video: Quotation Marks**
Visit mometrix.com/academy and enter code: 884918

Writing

Periods and commas are put **inside** quotation marks. Colons and semicolons are put **outside** the quotation marks. Question marks and exclamation points are placed inside quotation marks when they are part of a quote. When the question or exclamation mark goes with the whole sentence, the mark is left outside of the quotation marks.

Examples:

| | |
|---|---|
| Period and comma | We read "The Gift of the Magi," "The Skylight Room," and "The Cactus." |
| Semicolon | They watched "The Nutcracker"; then, they went home. |
| Exclamation mark that is a part of a quote | The crowd cheered, "Victory!" |
| Question mark that goes with the whole sentence | Is your favorite short story "The Tell-Tale Heart"? |

## Apostrophes

An apostrophe is used to show **possession** or the **deletion of letters in contractions**. An apostrophe is not needed with the possessive pronouns *his, hers, its, ours, theirs, whose*, and *yours*.

**Singular Nouns**: David's car | a book's theme | my brother's board game

**Plural Nouns that end with *-s***: the scissors' handle | boys' basketball

**Plural Nouns that end without *-s***: Men's department | the people's adventure

**Review Video: When to Use an Apostrophe**
Visit mometrix.com/academy and enter code: 213068

**Review Video: Punctuation Errors in Possessive Pronouns**
Visit mometrix.com/academy and enter code: 221438

## Hyphens

Hyphens are used to **separate compound words**. Use hyphens in the following cases:

| Use Case | Example |
|---|---|
| **Compound numbers** from 21 to 99 when written out in words | This team needs twenty-five points to win the game. |
| **Written-out fractions** that are used as adjectives | The recipe says that we need a three-fourths cup of butter. |
| Compound adjectives that come before a noun | The well-fed dog took a nap. |
| **Unusual compound words** that would be hard to read or easily confused with other words | This is the best anti-itch cream on the market. |

Note: This is not a complete set of the rules for hyphens. A dictionary is the best tool for knowing if a compound word needs a hyphen.

**Review Video: Hyphens**
Visit mometrix.com/academy and enter code: 981632

## Dashes

Dashes are used to show a **break** or a **change in thought** in a sentence or to act as parentheses in a sentence. When typing, use two hyphens to make a dash. Do not put a space before or after the dash. The following are the functions of dashes:

| Use Case | Example |
|---|---|
| Set off parenthetical statements or an **appositive with internal punctuation** | The three trees—oak, pine, and magnolia—are coming on a truck tomorrow. |
| Show a **break or change in tone or thought** | The first question—how silly of me—does not have a correct answer. |

## Ellipsis Marks

The ellipsis mark has **three** periods (...) to show when **words have been removed** from a quotation. If a **full sentence or more** is removed from a quoted passage, you need to use **four** periods to show the removed text and the end punctuation mark. The ellipsis mark should not be used at the beginning of a quotation. The ellipsis mark should also not be used at the end of a quotation unless some words have been deleted from the end of the final quoted sentence.

Example:

> "Then he picked up the groceries...paid for them...later he went home."

## Brackets

There are two main reasons to use brackets:

| Use Case | Example |
|---|---|
| Placing **parentheses inside of parentheses** | The hero of this story, Paul Revere (a silversmith and industrialist [see Ch. 4]), rode through towns of Massachusetts to warn of advancing British troops. |
| Adding **clarification or detail to a quotation** that is not part of the quotation | The father explained, "My children are planning to attend my alma mater [State University]." |

**Review Video: Brackets**
Visit mometrix.com/academy and enter code: 727546

Writing

# Common Usage Mistakes

## Commonly Confused Words

### *Which, That, and Who*

The words *which*, *that*, and *who* can act as **relative pronouns** to help clarify or describe a noun.

*Which* is used for things only.

Example: Andrew's car, *which is old and rusty,* broke down last week.

*That* is used for people or things. *That* is usually informal when used to describe people.

Example: Is this the only book *that Louis L'Amour wrote?*

Example: Is Louis L'Amour the author *that wrote Western novels?*

*Who* is used for people or for animals that have an identity or personality.

Example: Mozart was the composer *who wrote those operas.*

Example: John's dog, *who is called Max,* is large and fierce.

### *Then and Than*

*Then* is an adverb that indicates sequence or order:

Example: I'm going to run to the library and then come home.

*Than* is special-purpose word used only for comparisons:

Example: Susie likes chips more than candy.

### *Saw and Seen*

*Saw* is the past-tense form of *see.*

Example: I saw a turtle on my walk this morning.

*Seen* is the past participle of *see.*

Example: I have seen this movie before.

### *Affect and Effect*

There are two main reasons that *affect* and *effect* are so often confused: 1) both words can be used as either a noun or a verb, and 2) unlike most homophones, their usage and meanings are closely related to each other. Here is a quick rundown of the four usage options:

**Affect (n)**: feeling, emotion, or mood that is displayed

Example: The patient had a flat *affect.* (i.e., his face showed little or no emotion)

**Affect (v)**: to alter, to change, to influence

Example: The sunshine *affects* the plant's growth.

**Effect (n)**: a result, a consequence

Example: What *effect* will this weather have on our schedule?

**Effect (v)**: to bring about, to cause to be

Example: These new rules will *effect* order in the office.

The noun form of *affect* is rarely used outside of technical medical descriptions, so if a noun form is needed on the test, you can safely select *effect*. The verb form of *effect* is not as rare as the noun form of *affect*, but it's still not all that likely to show up on your test. If you need a verb and you can't decide which to use based on the definitions, choosing *affect* is your best bet.

## HOMOPHONES

**Homophones** are words that sound alike (or similar) but have different **spellings** and **definitions**. A homophone is a type of **homonym**, which is a pair or group of words that are pronounced or spelled the same, but do not mean the same thing.

### *TO, TOO, AND TWO*

*To* can be an adverb or a preposition for showing direction, purpose, and relationship. See your dictionary for the many other ways to use *to* in a sentence.

Examples: I went to the store. | I want to go with you.

*Too* is an adverb that means *also, as well, very,* or *in excess*.

Examples: I can walk a mile too. | You have eaten too much.

*Two* is a number.

Example: You have two minutes left.

### *THERE, THEIR, AND THEY'RE*

*There* can be an adjective, adverb, or pronoun. Often, *there* is used to show a place or to start a sentence.

Examples: I went there yesterday. | There is something in his pocket.

*Their* is a pronoun that is used to show ownership.

Examples: He is their father. | This is their fourth apology this week.

*They're* is a contraction of *they are.*

Example: Did you know that they're in town?

### *KNEW AND NEW*

*Knew* is the past tense of *know*.

Example: I knew the answer.

*New* is an adjective that means something is current, has not been used, or is modern.

Example: This is my new phone.

### *ITS AND IT'S*

*Its* is a pronoun that shows ownership.

Example: The guitar is in its case.

*It's* is a contraction of *it is*.

Example: It's an honor and a privilege to meet you.

Note: The *h* in honor is silent, so *honor* starts with the vowel sound *o*, which must have the article *an*.

### *YOUR AND YOU'RE*

*Your* is a pronoun that shows ownership.

Example: This is your moment to shine.

*You're* is a contraction of *you are*.

Example: Yes, you're correct.

## HOMOGRAPHS

**Homographs** are words that share the same spelling, but have different meanings and sometimes different pronunciations. To figure out which meaning is being used, you should be looking for context clues. The context clues give hints to the meaning of the word. For example, the word *spot* has many meanings. It can mean "a place" or "a stain or blot." In the sentence "After my lunch, I saw a spot on my shirt," the word *spot* means "a stain or blot." The context clues of "After my lunch" and "on my shirt" guide you to this decision. A homograph is another type of homonym.

### *BANK*

(noun): an establishment where money is held for savings or lending

(verb): to collect or pile up

### *CONTENT*

(noun): the topics that will be addressed within a book

(adjective): pleased or satisfied

(verb): to make someone pleased or satisfied

### *FINE*

(noun): an amount of money that acts a penalty for an offense

(adjective): very small or thin

(adverb): in an acceptable way

(verb): to make someone pay money as a punishment

### Incense

(noun): a material that is burned in religious settings and makes a pleasant aroma

(verb): to frustrate or anger

### Lead

(noun): the first or highest position

(noun): a heavy metallic element

(verb): to direct a person or group of followers

(adjective): containing lead

### Object

(noun): a lifeless item that can be held and observed

(verb): to disagree

### Produce

(noun): fruits and vegetables

(verb): to make or create something

### Refuse

(noun): garbage or debris that has been thrown away

(verb): to not allow

### Subject

(noun): an area of study

(verb): to force or subdue

### Tear

(noun): a fluid secreted by the eyes

(verb): to separate or pull apart

## Commonly Misused Words and Phrases

### A Lot

The phrase *a lot* should always be written as two words; never as *alot.*

**Correct**: That's a lot of chocolate!

**Incorrect**: He does that alot.

### Can

The word *can* is used to describe things that are possible occurrences; the word *may* is used to described things that are allowed to happen.

> **Correct**: May I have another piece of pie?
>
> **Correct**: I can lift three of these bags of mulch at a time.
>
> **Incorrect**: Mom said we can stay up thirty minutes later tonight.

### Could Have

The phrase *could of* is often incorrectly substituted for the phrase *could have*. Similarly, *could of*, *may of*, and *might of* are sometimes used in place of the correct phrases *could have*, *may have*, and *might have*.

> **Correct**: If I had known, I would have helped out.
>
> **Incorrect**: Well, that could of gone much worse than it did.

### Myself

The word *myself* is a reflexive pronoun, often incorrectly used in place of *I* or *me*.

> **Correct**: He let me do it myself.
>
> **Incorrect**: The job was given to Dave and myself.

### Off

The phrase *off of* is a redundant expression that should be avoided. In most cases, it can be corrected simply by removing *of*.

> **Correct**: My dog chased the squirrel off its perch on the fence.
>
> **Incorrect**: He finally moved his plate off of the table.

### Supposed To

The phrase *suppose to* is sometimes used incorrectly in place of the phrase *supposed to*.

> **Correct**: I was supposed to go to the store this afternoon.
>
> **Incorrect**: When are we suppose to get our grades?

### Try To

The phrase *try and* is often used in informal writing and conversation to replace the correct phrase *try to*.

> **Correct**: It's a good policy to try to satisfy every customer who walks in the door.
>
> **Incorrect**: Don't try and do too much.

# The Writing Process

## Prewriting

The **prewriting stage** is the part of the process in which the writer focuses on **generating ideas** and developing a broad plan for what he or she wants to accomplish. **Brainstorming** is the process of thinking about a topic and writing down every thought that comes to mind. Brainstorming may also take the form of asking questions that need to be answered by the composition. **Free writing** has a similar goal of writing about a topic in a continuous flow for a short span of time (e.g., 2 to 3 minutes). The goal of these exercises is not to produce high-quality, polished thoughts, but to generate leads to follow when the more structured writing happens later in the process. In research writing, the prewriting stage may also include doing a literature review and **collecting information** to use as evidence in arguments later on. When collecting information, it is important to take clear notes of where an idea was originally found so it can be cited later on. Another key aspect of the prewriting process is **planning phase**. This entails deciding on the overall topic, purpose, tone, and general organization for the rest of the composition. The planning process may involve using aids like outlines, Venn diagrams, flowcharts, and other visual models to help collect and organize information. The planning process does not set the whole composition in stone, but it does help structure the ideas to be written in the drafting phase.



## Drafting

The **drafting stage** of the writing process involves taking the plan for the composition and filling out all of the main ideas for the composition. Some writers prefer to start by writing the introduction and write their whole composition from start to finish, while others may prefer writing the main body paragraphs first and then coming back to the introduction and conclusion. In any case, the drafting process is a first attempt at writing the whole composition from start to finish. A writer may succeed in communicating what he or she wants in the first draft, but it often takes writing **several drafts** before the ideas and arguments take their final form. By the end of the drafting stage, the composition should be close to its final organization with its arguments clearly identified, but it will still need organizational, grammatical, and formatting improvements to be called complete.

## Revising

The **revision stage** is when the writer reads back through his or her work and looks for big-picture issues that affect **clarity** and **cohesion**. These can include organizational issues or flaws in logical flow. Writers should look back through their work to find any assertions or arguments that may be misplaced or lacking in support. They should look also through their work to find any information that does not contribute to the main idea or goal of the composition. Beginning writers may find it difficult to clearly communicate more than two or three main points in their arguments. If this is the case, these writers should eliminate information that detracts from those main points. In this stage, clarity is often more important than comprehensiveness.

## Editing/Proofreading

The **editing or proofreading stage** is focused specifically on improving the grammar and punctuation of the composition. The writer should read each paragraph closely and slowly to identify and fix any grammatical, spelling, or punctuation errors. Some of the worst offenders include subject-verb agreement in complex sentences, changes in tense throughout the document, and changes in perspective (first, second, or third person) or tone (professional, casual, opinionated, etc.). When writing at home, it is often helpful to have a friend or family member look for errors as well. Finally, this phase involves looking for very small errors, so multiple passes should be taken to catch as many problems as possible. One good rule of thumb is to keep reading through the whole document until a full read-through can be accomplished without finding any more errors.

### Publishing

The **publishing stage** refers to putting the document into its final format and delivering it to the audience. This involves formatting the document for presentation. In research writing, the final document may need to conform to a specific publishing standard, such as MLA or APA. In literal publishing, this would also take the form of presenting the document to the final audience, which may involve physical printing or digital publication. Note that once a composition has been published, it is often difficult to change or retract. Before reaching the publishing stage, the writer should have looped through the drafting, revision, and editing process a few times to ensure the writer says exactly what he or she wants before putting it before the final audience.

### Recursive Writing Process

However you approach writing, you may find comfort in knowing that the revision process can occur in any order. The **recursive writing process** is not as difficult as the phrase may make it seem. Simply put, the recursive writing process means that you may need to revisit steps after completing other steps. It also implies that the steps are not required to take place in any certain order. Indeed, you may find that planning, drafting, and revising can all take place at about the same time. The writing process involves moving back and forth between planning, drafting, and revising, followed by more planning, more drafting, and more revising until the writing is satisfactory.

**Review Video: Recursive Writing Process**
Visit mometrix.com/academy and enter code: 951611

## Outlining and Organizing Ideas

### Essays

Essays usually focus on one topic, subject, or goal. There are several types of essays, including informative, persuasive, and narrative. An essay's structure and level of formality depend on the type of essay and its goal. While narrative essays typically do not include outside sources, other types of essays often require some research and the integration of primary and secondary sources.

The basic format of an essay typically has three major parts: the introduction, the body, and the conclusion. The body is further divided into the writer's main points. Short and simple essays may have three main points, while essays covering broader ranges and going into more depth can have almost any number of main points, depending on length.

An essay's introduction should answer three questions:

1. What is the **subject** of the essay?

   If a student writes an essay about a book, the answer would include the title and author of the book and any additional information needed—such as the subject or argument of the book.

2. How does the essay **address** the subject?

   To answer this, the writer identifies the essay's organization by briefly summarizing main points and the evidence supporting them.

3. What will the essay **prove**?

This is the thesis statement, usually the opening paragraph's last sentence, clearly stating the writer's message.

The body elaborates on all the main points related to the thesis, introducing one main point at a time, and includes supporting evidence with each main point. Each body paragraph should state the point in a topic sentence, which is usually the first sentence in the paragraph. The paragraph should then explain the point's meaning, support it with quotations or other evidence, and then explain how this point and the evidence are related to the thesis. The writer should then repeat this procedure in a new paragraph for each additional main point.

The conclusion reiterates the content of the introduction, including the thesis, to remind the reader of the essay's main argument or subject. The essay writer may also summarize the highlights of the argument or description contained in the body of the essay, following the same sequence originally used in the body. For example, a conclusion might look like: Point 1 + Point 2 + Point 3 = Thesis, or Point 1 → Point 2 → Point 3 → Thesis Proof. Good organization makes essays easier for writers to compose and provides a guide for readers to follow. Well-organized essays hold attention better and are more likely to get readers to accept their theses as valid.



## Main Ideas, Supporting Details, and Outlining a Topic

A writer often begins the first paragraph of a paper by stating the **main idea** or point, also known as the **topic sentence**. The rest of the paragraph supplies particular details that develop and support the main point. One way to visualize the relationship between the main point and supporting information is by considering a table: the tabletop is the main point, and each of the table's legs is a supporting detail or group of details. Both professional authors and students can benefit from planning their writing by first making an outline of the topic. Outlines facilitate quick identification of the main point and supporting details without having to wade through the additional language that will exist in the fully developed essay, article, or paper. Outlining can also help readers to analyze a piece of existing writing for the same reason. The outline first summarizes the main idea in one sentence. Then, below that, it summarizes the supporting details in a numbered list. Writing the paper then consists of filling in the outline with detail, writing a paragraph for each supporting point, and adding an introduction and conclusion.

## Introduction

The purpose of the introduction is to capture the reader's attention and announce the essay's main idea. Normally, the introduction contains 50-80 words, or 3-5 sentences. An introduction can begin with an interesting quote, a question, or a strong opinion—something that will **engage** the reader's interest and prompt them to keep reading. If you are writing your essay to a specific prompt, your introduction should include a **restatement or summarization** of the prompt so that the reader will have some context for your essay. Finally, your introduction should briefly state your **thesis or main idea**: the primary thing you hope to communicate to the reader through your essay. Don't try to include all of the details and nuances of your thesis, or all of your reasons for it, in the introduction. That's what the rest of the essay is for!

**Review Video: Introduction**
Visit mometrix.com/academy and enter code: 961328

### *Thesis Statement*

The thesis is the main idea of the essay. A temporary thesis, or working thesis, should be established early in the writing process because it will serve to keep the writer focused as ideas develop. This temporary thesis is subject to change as you continue to write.

The temporary thesis has two parts: a **topic** (i.e., the focus of your essay based on the prompt) and a **comment**. The comment makes an important point about the topic. A temporary thesis should be interesting and specific. Also, you need to limit the topic to a manageable scope. These three questions are useful tools to measure the effectiveness of any temporary thesis:

- Does the focus of my essay have enough interest to hold an audience?
- Is the focus of my essay specific enough to generate interest?
- Is the focus of my essay manageable for the time limit? Too broad? Too narrow?

The thesis should be a generalization rather than a fact because the thesis prepares readers for facts and details that support the thesis. The process of bringing the thesis into sharp focus may help in outlining major sections of the work. Once the thesis and introduction are complete, you can address the body of the work.

**Review Video: Thesis Statements**
Visit mometrix.com/academy and enter code: 691033

### *Supporting the Thesis*

Throughout your essay, the thesis should be **explained clearly and supported** adequately by additional arguments. The thesis sentence needs to contain a clear statement of the purpose of your essay and a comment about the thesis. With the thesis statement, you have an opportunity to state what is noteworthy of this particular treatment of the prompt. Each sentence and paragraph should build on and support the thesis.

When you respond to the prompt, use parts of the passage to support your argument or defend your position. Using supporting evidence from the passage strengths your argument because readers can see your attention to the entire passage and your response to the details and facts within the passage. You can use facts, details, statistics, and direct quotations from the passage to uphold your position. Be sure to point out which information comes from the original passage and base your argument around that evidence.

## Body

In an essay's introduction, the writer establishes the thesis and may indicate how the rest of the piece will be structured. In the body of the piece, the writer **elaborates** upon, **illustrates**, and **explains** the **thesis statement**. How writers arrange supporting details and their choices of paragraph types are development techniques. Writers may give examples of the concept introduced in the thesis statement. If the subject includes a cause-and-effect relationship, the author may explain its causality. A writer will explain or analyze the main idea of the piece throughout the body, often by presenting arguments for the veracity or credibility of the thesis statement. Writers may use development to define or clarify ambiguous terms. Paragraphs within the body may be organized using natural sequences, like space and time. Writers may employ **inductive reasoning**, using multiple details to establish a generalization or causal relationship, or **deductive reasoning**, proving a generalized hypothesis or proposition through a specific example or case.

**Review Video: Drafting Body Paragraphs**
Visit mometrix.com/academy and enter code: 724590

## Paragraphs

After the introduction of a passage, a series of body paragraphs will carry a message through to the conclusion. Each paragraph should be **unified around a main point**. Normally, a good topic sentence summarizes the paragraph's main point. A topic sentence is a general sentence that gives an introduction to the paragraph.

The sentences that follow support the topic sentence. However, though it is usually the first sentence, the topic sentence can come as the final sentence to the paragraph if the earlier sentences give a clear explanation of the paragraph's topic. This allows the topic sentence to function as a concluding sentence. Overall, the paragraphs need to stay true to the main point. This means that any unnecessary sentences that do not advance the main point should be removed.

The main point of a paragraph requires adequate development (i.e., a substantial paragraph that covers the main point). A paragraph of two or three sentences does not cover a main point. This is especially true when the main point of the paragraph gives strong support to the argument of the thesis. An occasional short paragraph is fine as a transitional device. However, a well-developed argument will have paragraphs with more than a few sentences.

### *Methods of Developing Paragraphs*

Common methods of adding substance to paragraphs include examples, illustrations, analogies, and cause and effect.

- **Examples** are supporting details to the main idea of a paragraph or a passage. When authors write about something that their audience may not understand, they can provide an example to show their point. When authors write about something that is not easily accepted, they can give examples to prove their point.
- **Illustrations** are extended examples that require several sentences. Well-selected illustrations can be a great way for authors to develop a point that may not be familiar to their audience.
- **Analogies** make comparisons between items that appear to have nothing in common. Analogies are employed by writers to provoke fresh thoughts about a subject. These comparisons may be used to explain the unfamiliar, to clarify an abstract point, or to argue a point. Although analogies are effective literary devices, they should be used carefully in arguments. Two things may be alike in some respects but completely different in others.
- **Cause and effect** is an excellent device to explain the connection between an action or situation and a particular result. One way that authors can use cause and effect is to state the effect in the topic sentence of a paragraph and add the causes in the body of the paragraph. This method can give an author's paragraphs structure, which always strengthens writing.

### *Types of Paragraphs*

- A **paragraph of narration** tells a story or a part of a story. Normally, the sentences are arranged in chronological order (i.e., the order that the events happened). However, flashbacks (i.e., an anecdote from an earlier time) can be included.
- A **descriptive paragraph** makes a verbal portrait of a person, place, or thing. When specific details are used that appeal to one or more of the senses (i.e., sight, sound, smell, taste, and touch), authors give readers a sense of being present in the moment.
- A **process paragraph** is related to time order (i.e., First, you open the bottle. Second, you pour the liquid, etc.). Usually, this describes a process or teaches readers how to perform a process.

- **Comparing two things** draws attention to their similarities and indicates a number of differences. When authors contrast, they focus only on differences. Both comparing and contrasting may be done point-by-point, noting both the similarities and differences of each point, or in sequential paragraphs, where you discuss all the similarities and then all the differences, or vice versa.

### *Breaking Text into Paragraphs*

For most forms of writing, you will need to use multiple paragraphs. As such, determining when to start a new paragraph is very important. Reasons for starting a new paragraph include:

- To mark off the introduction and concluding paragraphs
- To signal a shift to a new idea or topic
- To indicate an important shift in time or place
- To explain a point in additional detail
- To highlight a comparison, contrast, or cause and effect relationship

## Paragraph Length

Most readers find that their comfort level for a paragraph is between 100 and 200 words. Shorter paragraphs cause too much starting and stopping and give a choppy effect. Paragraphs that are too long often test the attention span of readers. Two notable exceptions to this rule exist. In scientific or scholarly papers, longer paragraphs suggest seriousness and depth. In journalistic writing, constraints are placed on paragraph size by the narrow columns in a newspaper format.

The first and last paragraphs of a text will usually be the introduction and conclusion. These special-purpose paragraphs are likely to be shorter than paragraphs in the body of the work. Paragraphs in the body of the essay follow the subject's outline (e.g., one paragraph per point in short essays and a group of paragraphs per point in longer works). Some ideas require more development than others, so it is good for a writer to remain flexible. A paragraph of excessive length may be divided, and shorter ones may be combined.

## Conclusion

Two important principles to consider when writing a conclusion are strength and closure. A strong conclusion gives the reader a sense that the author's main points are meaningful and important, and that the supporting facts and arguments are convincing, solid, and well developed. When a conclusion achieves closure, it gives the impression that the writer has stated all necessary information and points and completed the work, rather than simply stopping after a specified length. Some things to avoid when writing concluding paragraphs include:

- Introducing a completely new idea
- Beginning with obvious or unoriginal phrases like "In conclusion" or "To summarize"
- Apologizing for one's opinions or writing
- Repeating the thesis word for word rather than rephrasing it
- Believing that the conclusion must always summarize the piece

# Coherence in Writing

## Coherent Paragraphs

A smooth flow of sentences and paragraphs without gaps, shifts, or bumps will lead to paragraph **coherence**. Ties between old and new information can be smoothed using several methods:

- **Linking ideas clearly**, from the topic sentence to the body of the paragraph, is essential for a smooth transition. The topic sentence states the main point, and this should be followed by specific details, examples, and illustrations that support the topic sentence. The support may be direct or indirect. In **indirect support**, the illustrations and examples may support a sentence that in turn supports the topic directly.
- The **repetition of key words** adds coherence to a paragraph. To avoid dull language, variations of the key words may be used.
- **Parallel structures** are often used within sentences to emphasize the similarity of ideas and connect sentences giving similar information.
- Maintaining a **consistent verb tense** throughout the paragraph helps. Shifting tenses affects the smooth flow of words and can disrupt the coherence of the paragraph.

**Review Video: How to Write a Good Paragraph**
Visit mometrix.com/academy and enter code: 682127

## Sequence Words and Phrases

When a paragraph opens with the topic sentence, the second sentence may begin with a phrase like *first of all*, introducing the first supporting detail or example. The writer may introduce the second supporting item with words or phrases like *also*, *in addition*, and *besides*. The writer might introduce succeeding pieces of support with wording like, *another thing*, *moreover*, *furthermore*, or *not only that, but*. The writer may introduce the last piece of support with *lastly*, *finally*, or *last but not least*. Writers get off the point by presenting off-target items not supporting the main point. For example, a main point *my dog is not smart* is supported by the statement, *he's six years old and still doesn't answer to his name*. But *he cries when I leave for school* is not supportive, as it does not indicate lack of intelligence. Writers stay on point by presenting only supportive statements that are directly relevant to and illustrative of their main point.

**Review Video: Sequence**
Visit mometrix.com/academy and enter code: 489027

## Transitions

Transitions between sentences and paragraphs guide readers from idea to idea and indicate relationships between sentences and paragraphs. Writers should be judicious in their use of transitions, inserting them sparingly. They should also be selected to fit the author's purpose—transitions can indicate time, comparison, and conclusion, among other purposes. Tone is also important to consider when using transitional phrases, varying the tone for different audiences. For example, in a scholarly essay, *in summary* would be preferable to the more informal *in short*.

When working with transitional words and phrases, writers usually find a natural flow that indicates when a transition is needed. In reading a draft of the text, it should become apparent where the flow is disrupted. At this point, the writer can add transitional elements during the revision process. Revising can also afford an opportunity to delete transitional devices that seem heavy handed or unnecessary.

**Review Video: Transitions in Writing**
Visit mometrix.com/academy and enter code: 233246

### Types of Transitional Words

| | |
|---|---|
| **Time** | afterward, immediately, earlier, meanwhile, recently, lately, now, since, soon, when, then, until, before, etc. |
| **Sequence** | too, first, second, further, moreover, also, again, and, next, still, besides, finally |
| **Comparison** | similarly, in the same way, likewise, also, again, once more |
| **Contrasting** | but, although, despite, however, instead, nevertheless, on the one hand... on the other hand, regardless, yet, in contrast |
| **Cause and Effect** | because, consequently, thus, therefore, then, to this end, since, so, as a result, if... then, accordingly |
| **Examples** | for example, for instance, such as, to illustrate, indeed, in fact, specifically |
| **Place** | near, far, here, there, to the left/right, next to, above, below, beyond, opposite, beside |
| **Concession** | granted that, naturally, of course, it may appear, although it is true that |
| **Repetition, Summary, or Conclusion** | as mentioned earlier, as noted, in other words, in short, on the whole, to summarize, therefore, as a result, to conclude, in conclusion |
| **Addition** | and, also, furthermore, moreover |
| **Generalization** | in broad terms, broadly speaking, in general |

**Review Video: Transition Words**
Visit mometrix.com/academy and enter code: 707563

**Review Video: How to Effectively Connect Sentences**
Visit mometrix.com/academy and enter code: 948325

## Writing Style and Form

### Writing Style and Linguistic Form

**Linguistic form** encodes the literal meanings of words and sentences. It comes from the phonological, morphological, syntactic, and semantic parts of a language. **Writing style** consists of different ways of encoding the meaning and indicating figurative and stylistic meanings. An author's writing style can also be referred to as his or her **voice**.

Writers' stylistic choices accomplish three basic effects on their audiences:

- They **communicate meanings** beyond linguistically dictated meanings,
- They communicate the **author's attitude**, such as persuasive or argumentative effects accomplished through style, and
- They communicate or **express feelings**.

Within style, component areas include:

- Narrative structure
- Viewpoint
- Focus

- Sound patterns
- Meter and rhythm
- Lexical and syntactic repetition and parallelism
- Writing genre
- Representational, realistic, and mimetic effects
- Representation of thought and speech
- Meta-representation (representing representation)
- Irony
- Metaphor and other indirect meanings
- Representation and use of historical and dialectal variations
- Gender-specific and other group-specific speech styles, both real and fictitious
- Analysis of the processes for inferring meaning from writing

## TONE

Tone may be defined as the writer's **attitude** toward the topic, and to the audience. This attitude is reflected in the language used in the writing. The tone of a work should be **appropriate to the topic** and to the intended audience. While it may be fine to use slang or jargon in some pieces, other texts should not contain such terms. Tone can range from humorous to serious and any level in between. It may be more or less formal, depending on the purpose of the writing and its intended audience. All these nuances in tone can flavor the entire writing and should be kept in mind as the work evolves.

**Review Video: Style, Tone, and Mood**
Visit mometrix.com/academy and enter code: 416961



## WORD SELECTION

A writer's choice of words is a signature of their style. Careful thought about the use of words can improve a piece of writing. A passage can be an exciting piece to read when attention is given to the use of vivid or specific nouns rather than general ones.

Example:

General: His kindness will never be forgotten.

Specific: His thoughtful gifts and bear hugs will never be forgotten.

### *ACTIVE AND PASSIVE LANGUAGE*

Attention should also be given to the kind of verbs that are used in sentences. Active verbs (e.g., run, swim) are about an action. Whenever possible, an **active verb should replace a linking verb** to provide clear examples for arguments and to strengthen a passage overall. When using an active verb, one should be sure that the verb is used in the active voice instead of the passive voice. Verbs are in the active voice when the subject is the one doing the action. A verb is in the passive voice when the subject is the recipient of an action.

Example:

Passive: The winners were called to the stage by the judges.

Active: The judges called the winners to the stage.

> **Review Video: Word Usage In Sentences**
> Visit mometrix.com/academy and enter code: 197863

### CONCISENESS

**Conciseness** is writing that communicates a message in the fewest words possible. Writing concisely is valuable because short, uncluttered messages allow the reader to understand the author's message more easily and efficiently. Planning is important in writing concise messages. If you have in mind what you need to write beforehand, it will be easier to make a message short and to the point. Do not state the obvious.

Revising is also important. After the message is written, make sure you have effective, pithy sentences that efficiently get your point across. When reviewing the information, imagine a conversation taking place, and concise writing will likely result.

### APPROPRIATE KINDS OF WRITING FOR DIFFERENT TASKS, PURPOSES, AND AUDIENCES

When preparing to write a composition, consider the audience and purpose to choose the best type of writing. Four common types of writing are persuasive, expository, and narrative. **Persuasive**, or argumentative writing, is used to convince the audience to take action or agree with the author's claims. **Expository** writing is meant to inform the audience of the author's observations or research on a topic. **Narrative** writing is used to tell the audience a story and often allows more room for creativity. **Descriptive** writing is when a writer provides a substantial amount of detail to the reader so he or she can visualize the topic. While task, purpose, and audience inform a writer's mode of writing, these factors also impact elements such as tone, vocabulary, and formality.

For example, students who are writing to persuade their parents to grant them some additional privilege, such as permission for a more independent activity, should use more sophisticated vocabulary and diction that sounds more mature and serious to appeal to the parental audience. However, students who are writing for younger children should use simpler vocabulary and sentence structure, as well as choose words that are more vivid and entertaining. They should treat their topics more lightly, and include humor when appropriate. Students who are writing for their classmates may use language that is more informal, as well as age-appropriate.

> **Review Video: Writing Purpose and Audience**
> Visit mometrix.com/academy and enter code: 146627

## Formality in Writing

### LEVEL OF FORMALITY

The relationship between writer and reader is important in choosing a **level of formality** as most writing requires some degree of formality. **Formal writing** is for addressing a superior in a school or work environment. Business letters, textbooks, and newspapers use a moderate to high level of formality. **Informal writing** is appropriate for private letters, personal emails, and business correspondence between close associates.

For your exam, you will want to be aware of informal and formal writing. One way that this can be accomplished is to watch for shifts in point of view in the essay. For example, unless writers are using a personal example, they will rarely refer to themselves (e.g., "*I* think that *my* point is very clear.") to avoid being informal when they need to be formal.

Also, be mindful of an author who addresses his or her audience **directly** in their writing (e.g., "Readers, *like you*, will understand this argument.") as this can be a sign of informal writing. Good writers understand the need to be consistent with their level of formality. Shifts in levels of formality or point of view can confuse readers and cause them to discount the message.

### CLICHÉS

Clichés are phrases that have been **overused** to the point that the phrase has no importance or has lost the original meaning. These phrases have no originality and add very little to a passage. Therefore, most writers will avoid the use of clichés. Another option is to make changes to a cliché so that it is not predictable and empty of meaning.

Examples:

> When life gives you lemons, make lemonade.
>
> Every cloud has a silver lining.

### JARGON

Jargon is **specialized vocabulary** that is used among members of a certain trade or profession. Since jargon is understood by only a small audience, writers will use jargon in passages that will only be read by a specialized audience. For example, medical jargon should be used in a medical journal but not in a New York Times article. Jargon includes exaggerated language that tries to impress rather than inform. Sentences filled with jargon are not precise and are difficult to understand.

Examples:

> "He is going to *toenail* these frames for us." (Toenail is construction jargon for nailing at an angle.)
>
> "They brought in a *kip* of material today." (Kip refers to 1000 pounds in architecture and engineering.)

### SLANG

Slang is an **informal** and sometimes private language that is understood by some individuals. Slang terms have some usefulness, but they can have a small audience. So, most formal writing will not include this kind of language.

Examples:

> "Yes, the event was a blast!" (In this sentence, *blast* means that the event was a great experience.)
>
> "That attempt was an epic fail." (By *epic fail*, the speaker means that his or her attempt was not a success.)

### COLLOQUIALISM

A colloquialism is a word or phrase that is found in informal writing. Unlike slang, **colloquial language** will be familiar to a greater range of people. However, colloquialisms are still considered inappropriate for formal writing. Colloquial language can include some slang, but these are limited to contractions for the most part.

Examples:

> "Can *y'all* come back another time?" (Y'all is a contraction of "you all.")
>
> "Will you stop him from building this *castle in the air*?" (A "castle in the air" is an improbable or unlikely event.)

### ACADEMIC LANGUAGE

In educational settings, students are often expected to use academic language in their schoolwork. Academic language is also commonly found in dissertations and theses, texts published by academic journals, and other forms of academic research. Academic language conventions may vary between fields, but general academic language is free of slang, regional terminology, and noticeable grammatical errors. Specific terms may also be used in academic language, and it is important to understand their proper usage. A writer's command of academic language impacts their ability to communicate in an academic or professional context. While it is acceptable to use colloquialisms, slang, improper grammar, or other forms of informal speech in social settings or at home, it is inappropriate to practice non-academic language in academic contexts.

## Chapter Quiz

Ready to see how well you retained what you just read? Scan the QR code to go directly to the chapter quiz interface for this study guide. If you're using a computer, simply visit the online resources page at **mometrix.com/resources719/nystceatas-29098** and click the Chapter Quizzes link.

# Mathematics

Transform passive reading into active learning! After immersing yourself in this chapter, put your comprehension to the test by taking a quiz. The insights you gained will stay with you longer this way. Scan the QR code to go directly to the chapter quiz interface for this study guide. If you're using a computer, simply visit the online resources page at **mometrix.com/resources719/nystceatas-29098** and click the Chapter Quizzes link.

## Number Basics

### Classifications of Numbers

**Numbers** are the basic building blocks of mathematics. Specific features of numbers are identified by the following terms:

**Integer** – any positive or negative whole number, including zero. Integers do not include fractions $\left(\frac{1}{3}\right)$, decimals (0.56), or mixed numbers $\left(7\frac{3}{4}\right)$.

**Prime number** – any whole number greater than 1 that has only two factors, itself and 1; that is, a number that can be divided evenly only by 1 and itself.

**Composite number** – any whole number greater than 1 that has more than two different factors; in other words, any whole number that is not a prime number. For example: The composite number 8 has the factors of 1, 2, 4, and 8.

**Even number** – any integer that can be divided by 2 without leaving a remainder. For example: 2, 4, 6, 8, and so on.

**Odd number** – any integer that cannot be divided evenly by 2. For example: 3, 5, 7, 9, and so on.

**Decimal number** – any number that uses a decimal point to show the part of the number that is less than one. Example: 1.234.

**Decimal point** – a symbol used to separate the ones place from the tenths place in decimals or dollars from cents in currency.

**Decimal place** – the position of a number to the right of the decimal point. In the decimal 0.123, the 1 is in the first place to the right of the decimal point, indicating tenths; the 2 is in the second place, indicating hundredths; and the 3 is in the third place, indicating thousandths.

The **decimal**, or base 10, system is a number system that uses ten different digits (0, 1, 2, 3, 4, 5, 6, 7, 8, 9). An example of a number system that uses something other than ten digits is the **binary**, or base 2, number system, used by computers, which uses only the numbers 0 and 1. It is thought that the decimal system originated because people had only their 10 fingers for counting.

**Rational numbers** include all integers, decimals, and fractions. Any terminating or repeating decimal number is a rational number.

**Irrational numbers** cannot be written as fractions or decimals because the number of decimal places is infinite and there is no recurring pattern of digits within the number. For example, pi (π) begins with 3.141592 and continues without terminating or repeating, so pi is an irrational number.

**Real numbers** are the set of all rational and irrational numbers.

**Review Video: Classification of Numbers**
Visit mometrix.com/academy and enter code: 461071

**Review Video: Prime and Composite Numbers**
Visit mometrix.com/academy and enter code: 565581

### Numbers in Word Form and Place Value

When writing numbers out in word form or translating word form to numbers, it is essential to understand how a place value system works. In the decimal or base-10 system, each digit of a number represents how many of the corresponding place value—a specific factor of 10—are contained in the number being represented. To make reading numbers easier, every three digits to the left of the decimal place is preceded by a comma. The following table demonstrates some of the place values:

| **Power of 10** | $10^3$ | $10^2$ | $10^1$ | $10^0$ | $10^{-1}$ | $10^{-2}$ | $10^{-3}$ |
|---|---|---|---|---|---|---|---|
| **Value** | 1,000 | 100 | 10 | 1 | 0.1 | 0.01 | 0.001 |
| **Place** | thousands | hundreds | tens | ones | tenths | hundredths | thousandths |

For example, consider the number 4,546.09, which can be separated into each place value like this:

4: thousands
5: hundreds
4: tens
6: ones
0: tenths
9: hundredths

This number in word form would be *four thousand five hundred forty-six and nine hundredths.*

**Review Video: Place Value**
Visit mometrix.com/academy and enter code: 205433

## Number Lines

A number line is a graph to see the distance between numbers. Basically, this graph shows the relationship between numbers. So a number line may have a point for zero and may show negative numbers on the left side of the line. Any positive numbers are placed on the right side of the line. For example, consider the points labeled on the following number line:

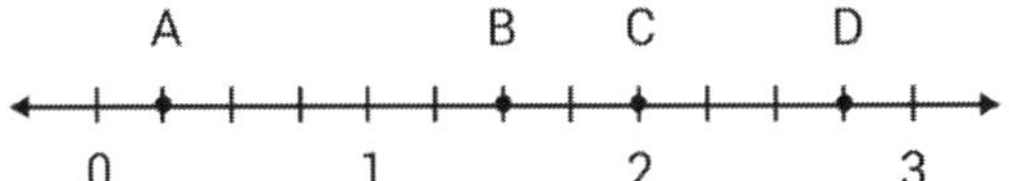

We can use the dashed lines on the number line to identify each point. Each dashed line between two whole numbers is $\frac{1}{4}$. The line halfway between two numbers is $\frac{1}{2}$.

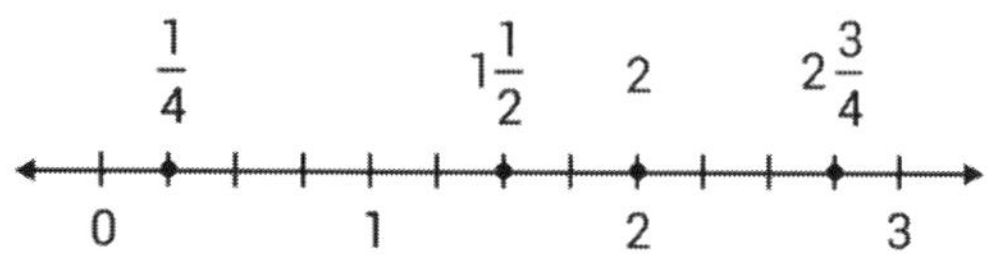


**Review Video: The Number Line**
Visit mometrix.com/academy and enter code: 816439

## Comparing Numbers

### Inequality Notation

The symbols $<$ and $>$ mean "is less than" and "is greater than," respectively. For instance, $3 < 5$ means "3 is less than 5," and $7 > 4$ means "7 is greater than 4." Statements like $3 < 5$ and $7 > 4$ are **inequalities**, and the symbols $<$ and $>$ are **inequality symbols**.

### Whole Numbers and Decimal Numbers

To compare whole or decimal numbers, we look at the most significant place (the leftmost digit) at which they differ. The number with the larger digit in that place is larger. For instance, $0.3\underline{8}74$ and $0.3\underline{9}$ differ in the hundredths place (underlined). Since 8 is smaller than 9, we see $0.3874 < 0.39$. This is clearer if we make the decimals equal in length by writing extra zeroes: $0.3874 < 0.3900$. Similarly, $2\underline{3}.984 < 2\underline{5}.112$ because 3 is smaller than 5, or 23 is smaller than 25.

### Fractions

If fractions have the same denominator, the fraction with the larger numerator is larger. For instance, $\frac{2}{7} < \frac{5}{7}$ since $2 < 5$. We compare fractions with different denominators by finding a common denominator. When comparing the fractions with a common denominator we only compare the numerator, so as a shortcut, we can multiply each numerator by the denominator of the other fraction. The numerator that produces the larger product belongs to the larger fraction. For example, to compare $\frac{7}{8}$ and $\frac{5}{6}$, we note that $7 \cdot 6 = 42$ is larger than $5 \cdot 8 = 40$. Since the numerator 7 produces the larger product, we see $\frac{7}{8} > \frac{5}{6}$. We can also compare fractions by converting them to decimals. For instance, since $\frac{3}{4} = 0.75$ and $\frac{4}{5} = 0.8$ and $0.75 < 0.8$, we conclude $\frac{3}{4} < \frac{4}{5}$.

### Mixed Numbers

To compare mixed numbers we compare their whole number parts. If those are equal, then we compare their fractional parts. For instance, $5\frac{3}{8} > 4\frac{7}{8}$ because $5 > 4$, but $3\frac{5}{9} < 3\frac{8}{9}$ because $\frac{5}{9} < \frac{8}{9}$.

### Square Roots

To compare square roots, we convert it to a decimal, usually with a calculator. To compare two square roots, we compare their radicands. For instance, $\sqrt{11} < \sqrt{14}$ because $11 < 14$.

### NEGATIVE NUMBERS

A negative number is always less than a positive number. Two negative numbers compare in the reverse order of their opposites. For instance, $-6 < -2$ (that is, -6 is smaller, more negative, than -2) because $6 > 2$.

## Absolute Value

A precursor to working with negative numbers is understanding what **absolute values** are. A number's absolute value is simply the distance away from zero a number is on the number line. The absolute value of a number is always positive and is written $|x|$. For example, the absolute value of 3, written as $|3|$, is 3 because the distance between 0 and 3 on a number line is three units. Likewise, the absolute value of -3, written as $|-3|$, is 3 because the distance between 0 and -3 on a number line is three units. So $|3| = |-3|$.

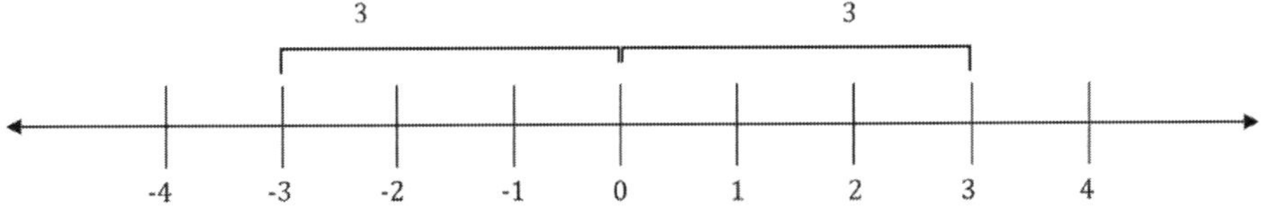


**Review Video: Absolute Value**
Visit mometrix.com/academy and enter code: 314669

## Operations

An **operation** is simply a mathematical process that takes some value(s) as input(s) and produces an output. Elementary operations are often written in the following form: *value operation value*. For instance, in the expression $1 + 2$ the values are 1 and 2 and the operation is addition. Performing the operation gives the output of 3. In this way we can say that $1 + 2$ and 3 are equal, or $1 + 2 = 3$.

### *ADDITION*

**Addition** increases the value of one quantity by the value of another quantity (both called **addends**). Example: $2 + 4 = 6$ or $8 + 9 = 17$. The result is called the **sum**. With addition, the order does not matter, $4 + 2 = 2 + 4$.

When adding signed numbers, if the signs are the same simply add the absolute values of the addends and apply the original sign to the sum. For example, $(+4) + (+8) = +12$ and $(-4) + (-8) = -12$. When the original signs are different, take the absolute values of the addends and subtract the smaller value from the larger value, then apply the original sign of the larger value to the difference. Example: $(+4) + (-8) = -4$ and $(-4) + (+8) = +4$.

### *SUBTRACTION*

**Subtraction** is the opposite operation to addition; it decreases the value of one quantity (the **minuend**) by the value of another quantity (the **subtrahend**). For example, $6 - 4 = 2$ or $17 - 8 = 9$. The result is called the **difference**. Note that with subtraction, the order does matter, $6 - 4 \neq 4 - 6$.

For subtracting signed numbers, change the sign of the subtrahend and then follow the same rules used for addition. Example: $(+4) - (+8) = (+4) + (-8) = -4$

### Multiplication

**Multiplication** can be thought of as repeated addition. One number (the **multiplier**) indicates how many times to add the other number (the **multiplicand**) to itself. Example: $3 \times 2 = 2 + 2 + 2 = 6$. With multiplication, the order does not matter, $2 \times 3 = 3 \times 2$ or $3 + 3 = 2 + 2 + 2$, either way the result (the **product**) is the same.

If the signs are the same, the product is positive when multiplying signed numbers. Example: $(+4) \times (+8) = +32$ and $(-4) \times (-8) = +32$. If the signs are opposite, the product is negative. Example: $(+4) \times (-8) = -32$ and $(-4) \times (+8) = -32$. When more than two factors are multiplied together, the sign of the product is determined by how many negative factors are present. If there are an odd number of negative factors then the product is negative, whereas an even number of negative factors indicates a positive product. Example: $(+4) \times (-8) \times (-2) = +64$ and $(-4) \times (-8) \times (-2) = -64$.

### Division

**Division** is the opposite operation to multiplication; one number (the **divisor**) tells us how many parts to divide the other number (the **dividend**) into. The result of division is called the **quotient**. Example: $20 \div 4 = 5$. If 20 is split into 4 equal parts, each part is 5. With division, the order of the numbers does matter, $20 \div 4 \neq 4 \div 20$.

The rules for dividing signed numbers are similar to multiplying signed numbers. If the dividend and divisor have the same sign, the quotient is positive. If the dividend and divisor have opposite signs, the quotient is negative. Example: $(-4) \div (+8) = -0.5$.

**Review Video: Mathematical Operations**
Visit mometrix.com/academy and enter code: 208095

### Parentheses

**Parentheses** are used to designate which operations should be done first when there are multiple operations. Example: $4 - (2 + 1) = 1$; the parentheses tell us that we must add 2 and 1, and then subtract the sum from 4, rather than subtracting 2 from 4 and then adding 1 (this would give us an answer of 3).

**Review Video: Mathematical Parentheses**
Visit mometrix.com/academy and enter code: 978600

### Exponents

An **exponent** is a superscript number placed next to another number at the top right. It indicates how many times the base number is to be multiplied by itself. Exponents provide a shorthand way to write what would be a longer mathematical expression, Example: $2^4 = 2 \times 2 \times 2 \times 2$. A number with an exponent of 2 is said to be "squared," while a number with an exponent of 3 is said to be "cubed." The value of a number raised to an exponent is called its power. So $8^4$ is read as "8 to the 4th power," or "8 raised to the power of 4."

**Review Video: Exponents**
Visit mometrix.com/academy and enter code: 600998

### *Roots*

A **root**, such as a square root, is another way of writing a fractional exponent. Instead of using a superscript, roots use the radical symbol ($\sqrt{\ }$) to indicate the operation. A radical will have a number underneath the bar, and may sometimes have a number in the upper left: $\sqrt[n]{a}$, read as "the $n^{\text{th}}$ root of $a$." The relationship between radical notation and exponent notation can be described by this equation:

$$\sqrt[n]{a} = a^{\frac{1}{n}}$$

The two special cases of $n = 2$ and $n = 3$ are called square roots and cube roots. If there is no number to the upper left, the radical is understood to be a square root ($n = 2$). Nearly all of the roots you encounter will be square roots. A square root is the same as a number raised to the one-half power. When we say that $a$ is the square root of $b$ ($a = \sqrt{b}$), we mean that $a$ multiplied by itself equals $b$: ($a \times a = b$).

A **perfect square** is a number that has an integer for its square root. There are 10 perfect squares from 1 to 100: 1, 4, 9, 16, 25, 36, 49, 64, 81, 100 (the squares of integers 1 through 10).

**Review Video: Roots**
Visit mometrix.com/academy and enter code: 795655

**Review Video: Perfect Squares and Square Roots**
Visit mometrix.com/academy and enter code: 648063

### *Word Problems and Mathematical Symbols*

When working on word problems, you must be able to translate verbal expressions or "math words" into math symbols. This chart contains several "math words" and their appropriate symbols:

| Phrase | Symbol |
|---|---|
| equal, is, was, will be, has, costs, gets to, is the same as, becomes | $=$ |
| times, of, multiplied by, product of, twice, doubles, halves, triples | $\times$ |
| divided by, per, ratio of/to, out of | $\div$ |
| plus, added to, sum, combined, and, more than, totals of | $+$ |
| subtracted from, less than, decreased by, minus, difference between | $-$ |
| what, how much, original value, how many, a number, a variable | $x$, $n$, etc. |

**Review Video: Understanding Word Problems**
Visit mometrix.com/academy and enter code: 499199

### *Examples of Translated Mathematical Phrases*

- The phrase four more than twice a number can be written algebraically as $2x + 4$.
- The phrase half a number decreased by six can be written algebraically as $\frac{1}{2}x - 6$.
- The phrase the sum of a number and the product of five and that number can be written algebraically as $x + 5x$.

- You may see a test question that says, "Olivia is constructing a bookcase from seven boards. Two of them are for vertical supports and five are for shelves. The height of the bookcase is twice the width of the bookcase. If the seven boards total 36 feet in length, what will be the height of Olivia's bookcase?" You would need to make a sketch and then create the equation to determine the width of the shelves. The height can be represented as double the width. (If $x$ represents the width of the shelves in feet, then the height of the bookcase is $2x$. Since the seven boards total 36 feet, $2x + 2x + x + x + x + x + x = 36$ or $9x = 36$; $x = 4$. The height is twice the width, or 8 feet.)

## Subtraction with Regrouping

A great way to make use of some of the features built into the decimal system would be regrouping when attempting longform subtraction operations. When subtracting within a place value, sometimes the minuend is smaller than the subtrahend, **regrouping** enables you to 'borrow' a unit from a place value to the left in order to get a positive difference. For example, consider subtracting 189 from 525 with regrouping.

First, set up the subtraction problem in vertical form:

$$\begin{array}{r} 525 \\ -\ 189 \\ \hline \end{array}$$

Notice that the numbers in the ones and tens columns of 525 are smaller than the numbers in the ones and tens columns of 189. This means you will need to use regrouping to perform subtraction:

$$\begin{array}{rrrr} & 5 & 2 & 5 \\ - & 1 & 8 & 9 \\ \hline \end{array}$$

To subtract 9 from 5 in the ones column you will need to borrow from the 2 in the tens columns:

$$\begin{array}{rrrr} & 5 & 1 & 15 \\ - & 1 & 8 & 9 \\ \hline & & & 6 \end{array}$$

Next, to subtract 8 from 1 in the tens column you will need to borrow from the 5 in the hundreds column:

$$\begin{array}{rrrr} & 4 & 11 & 15 \\ - & 1 & 8 & 9 \\ \hline & & 3 & 6 \end{array}$$

Last, subtract the 1 from the 4 in the hundreds column:

$$\begin{array}{rrrr} & 4 & 11 & 15 \\ - & 1 & 8 & 9 \\ \hline & 3 & 3 & 6 \end{array}$$

**Review Video: Subtracting Large Numbers**
Visit mometrix.com/academy and enter code: 603350

Mathematics

## Order of Operations

The **order of operations** is a set of rules that dictates the order in which we must perform each operation in an expression so that we will evaluate it accurately. If we have an expression that includes multiple different operations, the order of operations tells us which operations to do first. The most common mnemonic for the order of operations is **PEMDAS**, or "Please Excuse My Dear Aunt Sally." PEMDAS stands for parentheses, exponents, multiplication, division, addition, and subtraction. It is important to understand that multiplication and division have equal precedence, as do addition and subtraction, so those pairs of operations are simply worked from left to right in order.

For example, evaluating the expression $5 + 20 \div 4 \times (2 + 3)^2 - 6$ using the correct order of operations would be done like this:

- **P:** Perform the operations inside the parentheses: $(2 + 3) = 5$
- **E:** Simplify the exponents: $(5)^2 = 5 \times 5 = 25$
    - The expression now looks like this: $5 + 20 \div 4 \times 25 - 6$
- **MD:** Perform multiplication and division from left to right: $20 \div 4 = 5$; then $5 \times 25 = 125$
    - The expression now looks like this: $5 + 125 - 6$
- **AS:** Perform addition and subtraction from left to right: $5 + 125 = 130$; then $130 - 6 = 124$

**Review Video: Order of Operations**
Visit mometrix.com/academy and enter code: 259675

## Properties of Operations

### The Commutative Property

The commutative property applies to addition and multiplication and states that these operations can be completed in any order. The **commutative property of addition** states that numbers and terms can be added together in any order to still get the same value. For example, $3 + 4 = 7$ and $4 + 3 = 7$. Also, we can use the commutative property of addition to show that $3x + 4 + 2^2$ is equivalent to $4 + 3x + 2^2$ and $2^2 + 4 + 3x$. When adding terms, you can add in any order and get the same value.

The **commutative property of multiplication** states that numbers and terms can be multiplied in any order to get the same value. For example, $12 \times 3$ is equivalent to $3 \times 12$. Additionally, we can use the commutative property of multiplication to assume that $(5 + 3) \times (36 - 6)$ is equivalent to $(36 - 6) \times (5 + 3)$. You can multiply terms in any order and still get the same value.

### The Associative Property

The **associative property of addition** states that if three or more terms are being added together, the value is the same regardless of the groupings.

For example, given the expression $3 + 4 + 6$, these terms can be grouped and added in any form. $3 + 4 + 6$ is equivalent to $(3 + 4) + 6$ and is also equivalent to $3 + (4 + 6)$. This can be applied to write equivalent expressions in a variety of ways.

For example, suppose we are given the expression $5 + (y + 2) + 4$. We can generate equivalent expressions knowing the associative property. Knowing that when three or more terms are added, the grouping is irrelevant, we can say that this expression is equivalent to $5 + y + (2 + 4)$, and it is equivalent to $(5 + y) + (2 + 4)$. It is even equivalent to $5 + y + 2 + 4$.

The **associative property of multiplication** states that if three or more terms are being multiplied together, the value is the same regardless of the grouping. We can use this property to identify and generate equivalent expressions.

For example, given the expression $2 \times 7 \times 3$, these terms can be grouped in any way and still get the same value. $2 \times 7 \times 3$ is equivalent to $(2 \times 7) \times 3$ or $2 \times (7 \times 3)$.

## THE IDENTITY PROPERTY

The **identity property of multiplication** states that when a number is multiplied by 1, you get the same number. That is, anything multiplied by 1 is itself. For example, $2 \times 1 = 2$, or $1 \times -36 = -36$. Using the identity property of multiplication, we can identify and generate equivalent expressions. Let's say that we are given the expression $15 - (3 \times 4)$. We can generate equivalent expressions using the identity property. One equivalent expression example would be $(15 \times 1) - (3 \times 4)$. Another example would be $15 - (1 \times 3 \times 4)$. We can say these expressions are equivalent because the identity property of multiplication states that we can multiply any portion of an expression by 1 to get the same value.

The **identity property of addition** states that when 0 is added to a number, you get the same number. For example, $2 + 0 = 2$, or $0 + -3 = -3$. We can also use this property to identify and generate equivalent expressions. For example, if we are given the expression $2 \times (1 + 2)$, we could write the equivalent expressions $2 \times (0 + 1 + 2)$ or $(2 + 0) \times (1 + 2)$.

## THE INVERSE PROPERTY

The **inverse property of addition** states that the sum of a number and its opposite is always equal to 0. Remember, the opposite of a number is a number that is opposite on the number line from zero, or the same number with the opposite sign. For example, −4 is opposite to 4, and 1,726.9 is opposite to −1,726.9. So, the inverse property of addition states that if you add opposite numbers, their sum is zero. For example, $5 + (-5) = 0$ and $-5 + 5 = 0$.

The **inverse property of multiplication** states that a number multiplied by its reciprocal is always equal to 1. The **reciprocal** of a number is its "flipped" fraction. For example, the reciprocal of 5 is $\frac{1}{5}$, or the reciprocal of $\frac{2}{3}$ is $\frac{3}{2}$. The inverse property of multiplication can be applied for these values, $5 \times \frac{1}{5} = 1$ and $\frac{2}{3} \times \frac{3}{2} = 1$. This is because when you multiply across, you get a fraction that is equal to 1.

$$\frac{2}{3} \times \frac{3}{2} = \frac{6}{6} = 1$$

## THE DISTRIBUTIVE PROPERTY

The **distributive property** explains how multiplication and addition interact. It says that when multiplying one number by the sum of two other numbers, the same result can also be obtained by multiplying the one number by each of the numbers individually and then adding the products. For example, to multiply 2 by the sum of 7 and 3, the direct approach says, "the sum of 7 and 3 is 10, and 2 times 10 is 20." This would be expressed as $2 \times (7 + 3) = 2 \times 10 = 20$. On the other hand, the distributive property states that the same answer can be achieved by multiplying each number inside the parentheses and adding the products. That is, "the product of 2 and 7 is 14, the product of

Mathematics

2 and 3 is 6, and the sum of 14 and 6 is 20." This would be expressed as $2 \times (7 + 3) = 2 \times 7 + 2 \times 3 = 14 + 6 = 20$, and it is demonstrated below.

$$2 \times (7 + 3) = 2 \times 7 + 2 \times 3$$

This same concept can be used when multiplying a number by the difference of two numbers. For example, $5 \times (10 - 4) = 5 \times 10 - 5 \times 4$. Since $5 \times 10 = 50$ and $5 \times 4 = 20$, the result is $50 - 20 = 30$. This answer can be checked by subtracting inside the parentheses first and then multiplying: $5 \times (10 - 4) = 5 \times 6 = 30$.

**Review Video: Commutative, Associative, and Distributive Properties**
Visit mometrix.com/academy and enter code: 483176

## Properties of Exponents

The properties of exponents are as follows:

| Property | Description |
|---|---|
| $a^1 = a$ | Any number to the power of 1 is equal to itself |
| $1^n = 1$ | The number 1 raised to any power is equal to 1 |
| $a^0 = 1$ | Any number raised to the power of 0 is equal to 1 |
| $a^n \times a^m = a^{n+m}$ | Add exponents to multiply powers of the same base number |
| $a^n \div a^m = a^{n-m}$ | Subtract exponents to divide powers of the same base number |
| $(a^n)^m = a^{n \times m}$ | When a power is raised to a power, the exponents are multiplied |
| $(a \times b)^n = a^n \times b^n$<br>$(a \div b)^n = a^n \div b^n$ | Multiplication and division operations inside parentheses can be raised to a power. This is the same as each term being raised to that power. |
| $a^{-n} = \frac{1}{a^n}$ | A negative exponent is the same as the reciprocal of a positive exponent |

Note that exponents do not have to be integers. Fractional or decimal exponents follow all the rules above as well. Example: $5^{\frac{1}{4}} \times 5^{\frac{3}{4}} = 5^{\frac{1}{4}+\frac{3}{4}} = 5^1 = 5$.

**Review Video: Properties of Exponents**
Visit mometrix.com/academy and enter code: 532558

## Factors and Multiples

### Factors and Greatest Common Factor

A whole number $a$ is a **factor** (or **divisor**) of a whole number $b$ if $a$ divides $b$ evenly. In other words, $a$ is a factor of $b$ if the quotient $b \div a$ is a whole number with a remainder of 0. For instance, 3 is a factor of 12 because $12 \div 3 = 4$ with no remainder. Another way to say this is that $a$ is a factor of $b$ if we can multiply $a$ by another whole number to get $b$. So, we can also show that 3 is a factor of 12 by noting that $3 \times 4 = 12$.

Every positive whole number has 1 and itself as factors. If a whole number greater than one has *only* 1 and itself as factors, we call it a **prime number**. For instance, 5 is a prime number because its only factors are 1 and 5. The first several prime numbers are 2, 3, 5, 7, 11, and 13.

If a whole number greater than 1 is not prime—that is, if it has factors besides 1 and itself—then it is a **composite number.** For instance, 10 is a composite number because it has factors 2 and 5 in addition to 1 and 10. The first several composite numbers are 4, 6, 8, 9, 10, 12, 14, and 15.

A **prime factor** of a whole number is a factor that is also a prime number. For example, the prime factors of 12 are 2 and 3. The prime factors of 15 are 3 and 5.

A **common factor** of two (or more) whole numbers is a number that is a factor of both (or all) of them. For example, the factors of 12 are 1, 2, 3, 4, 6, and 12, while the factors of 15 are 1, 3, 5, and 15. The common factors (underlined) of 12 and 15 are 1 and 3.

The **greatest common factor** (**GCF**) of two (or more) whole numbers is the largest number that is a factor of both (or all) of them. For example, the factors of 15 are 1, 3, 5, and 15; the factors of 35 are 1, 5, 7, and 35. Therefore, the greatest common factor of 15 and 35 is 5.

**Review Video: Factors**
Visit mometrix.com/academy and enter code: 920086

**Review Video: Prime Numbers and Factorization**
Visit mometrix.com/academy and enter code: 760669

### Multiples and Least Common Multiple

A whole number $b$ is a **multiple** of a whole number $a$ when $a$ is a factor of $b$. This means that $b$ is the product of $a$ and another whole number. For example, the multiples of 7 are $0 \times 7 = 0, 1 \times 7 = 7, 2 \times 7 = 14, 3 \times 7 = 21, 4 \times 7 = 28, 5 \times 7 = 35, \ldots$. Dividing 0, 7, 14, 21, 28, and 35 by 7 results in the whole numbers 0, 1, 2, 3, 4, and 5, respectively, showing that 7 is a factor of these numbers.

The least common multiple (**LCM**) of two (or more) whole numbers is the smallest number that is a multiple of both (or all) of them. For example, the multiples of 3 are 3, 6, 9, 12, 15, ...; the multiples of 5 are 5, 10, 15, 20, .... The smallest number that appears in both lists is 15, so the least common multiple of 3 and 5 is 15.

**Review Video: Multiples**
Visit mometrix.com/academy and enter code: 626738

**Review Video: Greatest Common Factor and Least Common Multiple**
Visit mometrix.com/academy and enter code: 838699

## Fractions

A **fraction** is a number that is expressed as one integer written above another integer, with a dividing line between them $\left(\frac{x}{y}\right)$. It represents the **quotient** of the two numbers "$x$ divided by $y$." It can also be thought of as $x$ out of $y$ equal parts.

The top number of a fraction is called the **numerator**, and it represents the number of parts under consideration. The 1 in $\frac{1}{4}$ means that 1 part out of the whole is being considered in the calculation.

The bottom number of a fraction is called the **denominator**, and it represents the total number of equal parts. The 4 in $\frac{1}{4}$ means that the whole consists of 4 equal parts. A fraction cannot have a denominator of zero; this is referred to as "*undefined.*"

Fractions can be manipulated, without changing the value of the fraction, by multiplying or dividing (but not adding or subtracting) both the numerator and denominator by the same number. If you divide both numbers by a common factor, you are **reducing** or simplifying the fraction. Two fractions that have the same value but are expressed differently are known as **equivalent fractions**. For example, $\frac{2}{10}, \frac{3}{15}, \frac{4}{20}$, and $\frac{5}{25}$ are all equivalent fractions. They can also all be reduced or simplified to $\frac{1}{5}$.

When two fractions are manipulated so that they have the same denominator, this is known as finding a **common denominator**. The number chosen to be that common denominator should be the least common multiple of the two original denominators. Example: $\frac{3}{4}$ and $\frac{5}{6}$; the least common multiple of 4 and 6 is 12. Manipulating to achieve the common denominator: $\frac{3}{4} = \frac{9}{12}; \frac{5}{6} = \frac{10}{12}$.

**Review Video: Overview of Fractions**
Visit mometrix.com/academy and enter code: 262335

### *Proper Fractions and Mixed Numbers*

A fraction whose denominator is greater than its numerator is known as a **proper fraction**, while a fraction whose numerator is greater than its denominator is known as an **improper fraction**. Proper fractions have values *less than one* and improper fractions have values *greater than one*.

A **mixed number** is a number that contains both an integer and a fraction. Any improper fraction can be rewritten as a mixed number. Example: $\frac{8}{3} = \frac{6}{3} + \frac{2}{3} = 2 + \frac{2}{3} = 2\frac{2}{3}$. Similarly, any mixed number can be rewritten as an improper fraction. Example: $1\frac{3}{5} = 1 + \frac{3}{5} = \frac{5}{5} + \frac{3}{5} = \frac{8}{5}$.

**Review Video: Proper and Improper Fractions and Mixed Numbers**
Visit mometrix.com/academy and enter code: 211077

### *Adding and Subtracting Fractions*

If two fractions have a common denominator, they can be added or subtracted simply by adding or subtracting the two numerators and retaining the same denominator. If the two fractions do not already have the same denominator, one or both of them must be manipulated to achieve a common denominator before they can be added or subtracted. Example: $\frac{1}{2} + \frac{1}{4} = \frac{2}{4} + \frac{1}{4} = \frac{3}{4}$.

**Review Video: Adding and Subtracting Fractions**
Visit mometrix.com/academy and enter code: 378080

### Multiplying Fractions

Two fractions can be multiplied by multiplying the two numerators to find the new numerator and the two denominators to find the new denominator. Example: $\frac{1}{3} \times \frac{2}{3} = \frac{1\times2}{3\times3} = \frac{2}{9}$.

### Dividing Fractions

Two fractions can be divided by flipping the numerator and denominator of the second fraction and then proceeding as though it were a multiplication problem. Example: $\frac{2}{3} \div \frac{3}{4} = \frac{2}{3} \times \frac{4}{3} = \frac{8}{9}$.

**Review Video: Multiplying and Dividing Fractions**
Visit mometrix.com/academy and enter code: 473632

### Multiplying a Mixed Number by a Whole Number or a Decimal

When multiplying a mixed number by something, it is usually best to convert it to an improper fraction first. Additionally, if the multiplicand is a decimal, it is most often simplest to convert it to a fraction. For instance, to multiply $4\frac{3}{8}$ by 3.5, begin by rewriting each quantity as a whole number plus a proper fraction. Remember, a mixed number is a fraction added to a whole number and a decimal is a representation of the sum of fractions, specifically tenths, hundredths, thousandths, and so on:

$$4\frac{3}{8} \times 3.5 = \left(4 + \frac{3}{8}\right) \times \left(3 + \frac{1}{2}\right)$$

Next, the quantities being added need to be expressed with the same denominator. This is achieved by multiplying and dividing the whole number by the denominator of the fraction. Recall that a whole number is equivalent to that number divided by 1:

$$= \left(\frac{4}{1} \times \frac{8}{8} + \frac{3}{8}\right) \times \left(\frac{3}{1} \times \frac{2}{2} + \frac{1}{2}\right)$$

When multiplying fractions, remember to multiply the numerators and denominators separately:

$$= \left(\frac{4 \times 8}{1 \times 8} + \frac{3}{8}\right) \times \left(\frac{3 \times 2}{1 \times 2} + \frac{1}{2}\right)$$
$$= \left(\frac{32}{8} + \frac{3}{8}\right) \times \left(\frac{6}{2} + \frac{1}{2}\right)$$

Now that the fractions have the same denominators, they can be added:

$$= \frac{35}{8} \times \frac{7}{2}$$

Finally, perform the last multiplication and then simplify:

$$= \frac{35 \times 7}{8 \times 2} = \frac{245}{16} = \frac{240}{16} + \frac{5}{16} = 15\frac{5}{16}$$

### Comparing Fractions

It is important to master the ability to compare and order fractions. This skill is relevant to many real-world scenarios. For example, carpenters often compare fractional construction nail lengths when preparing for a project, and bakers often compare fractional measurements to have the correct ratio of ingredients. There are three commonly used strategies when comparing fractions. These strategies are referred to as the common denominator approach, the decimal approach, and the cross-multiplication approach.

## Using a Common Denominator to Compare Fractions

The fractions $\frac{2}{3}$ and $\frac{4}{7}$ have different denominators. $\frac{2}{3}$ has a denominator of 3, and $\frac{4}{7}$ has a denominator of 7. In order to precisely compare these two fractions, it is necessary to use a common denominator. A common denominator is a common multiple that is shared by both denominators. In this case, the denominators 3 and 7 share a multiple of 21. In general, it is most efficient to select the least common multiple for the two denominators.

Rewrite each fraction with the common denominator of 21. Then, calculate the new numerators as illustrated below.

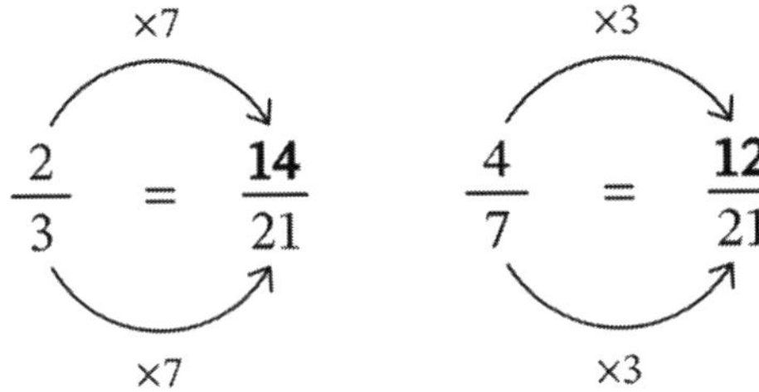


For $\frac{2}{3}$, multiply the numerator and denominator by 7. The result is $\frac{14}{21}$.

For $\frac{4}{7}$, multiply the numerator and denominator by 3. The result is $\frac{12}{21}$.

Now that both fractions have a denominator of 21, the fractions can accurately be compared by comparing the numerators. Since 14 is greater than 12, the fraction $\frac{14}{21}$ is greater than $\frac{12}{21}$. This means that $\frac{2}{3}$ is greater than $\frac{4}{7}$.

## Using Decimals to Compare Fractions

Sometimes decimal values are easier to compare than fraction values. For example, $\frac{5}{8}$ is equivalent to 0.625 and $\frac{3}{5}$ is equivalent to 0.6. This means that the comparison of $\frac{5}{8}$ and $\frac{3}{5}$ can be determined by comparing the decimals 0.625 and 0.6. When both decimal values are extended to the thousandths place, they become 0.625 and 0.600, respectively. It becomes clear that 0.625 is greater than 0.600 because 625 thousandths is greater than 600 thousandths. In other words, $\frac{5}{8}$ is greater than $\frac{3}{5}$ because 0.625 is greater than 0.6.

## Using Cross-Multiplication to Compare Fractions

Cross-multiplication is an efficient strategy for comparing fractions. This is a shortcut for the common denominator strategy. Start by writing each fraction next to one another. Multiply the numerator of the fraction on the left by the denominator of the fraction on the right. Write down the result next to the fraction on the left. Now multiply the numerator of the fraction on the right by the denominator of the fraction on the left. Write down the result next to the fraction on the right. Compare both products. The fraction with the larger result is the larger fraction.

Consider the fractions $\frac{4}{7}$ and $\frac{5}{9}$.

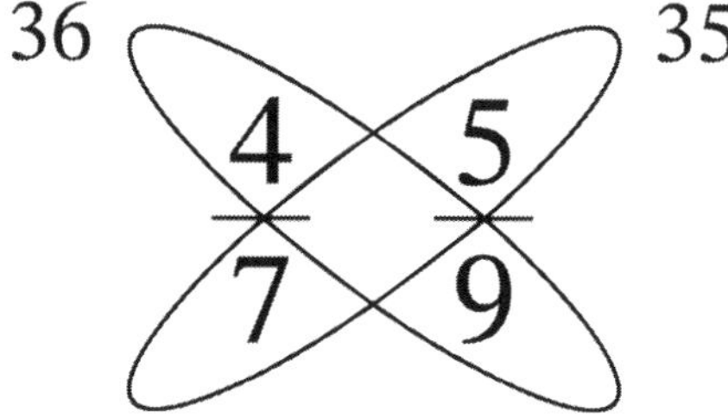


36 is greater than 35. Therefore, $\frac{4}{7}$ is greater than $\frac{5}{9}$.

## Decimals

Decimals are one way to represent parts of a whole. Using the place value system, each digit to the right of a decimal point denotes the number of units of a corresponding *negative* power of ten. For example, consider the decimal 0.24. We can use a model to represent the decimal. Since a dime is worth one-tenth of a dollar and a penny is worth one-hundredth of a dollar, one possible model to represent this fraction is to have 2 dimes representing the 2 in the tenths place and 4 pennies representing the 4 in the hundredths place:

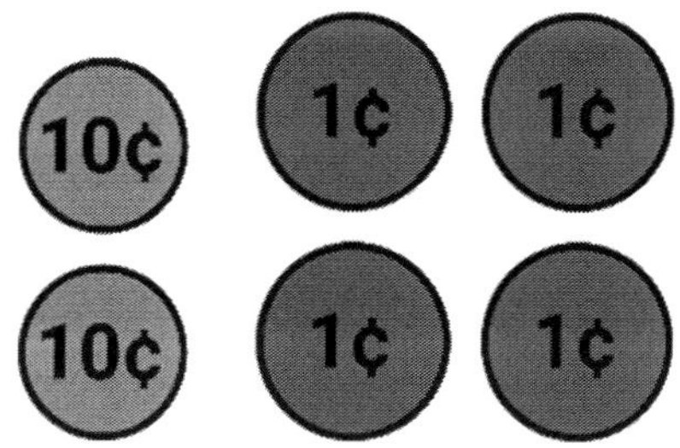


To write the decimal as a fraction, put the decimal in the numerator with 1 in the denominator. Multiply the numerator and denominator by tens until there are no more decimal places. Then simplify the fraction to lowest terms. For example, converting 0.24 to a fraction:

$$0.24 = \frac{0.24}{1} = \frac{0.24 \times 100}{1 \times 100} = \frac{24}{100} = \frac{6}{25}$$

**Review Video: Decimals**
Visit mometrix.com/academy and enter code: 837268

### *Operations with Decimals*

#### Adding and Subtracting Decimals

When adding and subtracting decimals, the decimal points must always be aligned. Adding decimals is just like adding regular whole numbers. Example: $4.5 + 2.0 = 6.5$.

If the problem-solver does not properly align the decimal points, an incorrect answer of 4.7 may result. An easy way to add decimals is to align all of the decimal points in a vertical column visually. This will allow you to see exactly where the decimal should be placed in the final answer. Begin

Mathematics

adding from right to left. Add each column in turn, making sure to carry the number to the left if a column adds up to more than 9. The same rules apply to the subtraction of decimals.

**Review Video: Adding and Subtracting Decimals**
Visit mometrix.com/academy and enter code: 381101

### Multiplying Decimals

A simple multiplication problem has two components: a **multiplicand** and a **multiplier**. When multiplying decimals, work as though the numbers were whole rather than decimals. Once the final product is calculated, count the number of places to the right of the decimal in both the multiplicand and the multiplier. Then, count that number of places from the right of the product and place the decimal in that position.

For example, $12.3 \times 2.56$ has a total of three places to the right of the respective decimals. Multiply $123 \times 256$ to get 31,488. Now, beginning on the right, count three places to the left and insert the decimal. The final product will be 31.488.

**Review Video: How to Multiply Decimals**
Visit mometrix.com/academy and enter code: 731574

### Dividing Decimals

Every division problem has a **divisor** and a **dividend**. The dividend is the number that is being divided. In the problem $14 \div 7$, 14 is the dividend and 7 is the divisor. In a division problem with decimals, the divisor must be converted into a whole number. Begin by moving the decimal in the divisor to the right until a whole number is created. Next, move the decimal in the dividend the same number of spaces to the right. For example, 4.9 into 24.5 would become 49 into 245. The decimal was moved one space to the right to create a whole number in the divisor, and then the same was done for the dividend. Once the whole numbers are created, the problem is carried out normally: $245 \div 49 = 5$.

**Review Video: Dividing Decimals**
Visit mometrix.com/academy and enter code: 560690

**Review Video: Dividing Decimals by Whole Numbers**
Visit mometrix.com/academy and enter code: 535669

## Percentages

**Percentages** can be thought of as fractions that are based on a whole of 100; that is, one whole is equal to 100%. The word **percent** means "per hundred." Percentage problems are often presented in three main ways:

- Find what percentage of some number another number is.
  - Example: What percentage of 40 is 8?
- Find what number is some percentage of a given number.
  - Example: What number is 20% of 40?
- Find what number another number is a given percentage of.
  - Example: What number is 8 20% of?

There are three components in each of these cases: a **whole** ($W$), a **part** ($P$), and a **percentage** (%). These are related by the equation: $P = W \times \%$. This can easily be rearranged into other forms that may suit different questions better: $\% = \frac{P}{W}$ and $W = \frac{P}{\%}$. Percentage problems are often also word problems. As such, a large part of solving them is figuring out which quantities are what. For example, consider the following word problem:

*In a school cafeteria, 7 students choose pizza, 9 choose hamburgers, and 4 choose tacos. What percentage of student choose tacos?*

To find the whole, you must first add all of the parts: $7 + 9 + 4 = 20$. The percentage can then be found by dividing the part by the whole $\left(\% = \frac{P}{W}\right)$: $\frac{4}{20} = \frac{20}{100} = 20\%$.

**Review Video: Computation with Percentages**
Visit mometrix.com/academy and enter code: 693099

### Calculating Percent Change

Suppose a quantity has a particular value (the *old value*) and then we add something (the *change*) to it to get another value (the *new value*). We can describe this process by the simple equation $(\text{old value}) + \text{change} = (\text{new value})$. If we know the old and new values, we can rearrange this equation to find the change, getting $\text{change} = (\text{new value}) - (\text{old value})$. For instance, if a store's price for a box of computer paper goes from \$20 last week to \$25 this week, this is a change of $(\text{new value}) - (\text{old value}) = \$25 - \$20 = \$5$. Or, if the size of the freshman class at a college goes from 500 students one year to 440 students the next year, this is a change of $(\text{new value}) - (\text{old value}) = 440 - 500 = -60$ students. So, we see that change can be positive or negative.

Instead of the word *change*, we sometimes use the words *increase* or *decrease* to specify whether the value goes up or down, respectively. In the examples above, the price of computer paper increases by \$5 and the freshman class decreases by 60 students. Note that the decrease is 60 students and not -60 because the word *decrease* already means that the value goes down. So, *increase* is the same as positive change and *decrease* is the opposite or negative change.

If the changing quantity represents an amount (how much of something there is), we can also calculate the **percent change**. This is the change expressed as a percentage of the old amount. To calculate this, we divide the change by the old amount and express the quotient as a percent. That is, we use the formula $\text{percent change} = \frac{\text{change}}{\text{old value}}$, converting the resulting decimal answer to a percent. In the examples above, the price of a box of computer paper has a percent change of $\frac{\text{change in price}}{\text{old price}} = \frac{\$5}{\$20} = 0.25 = 25\%$, and the size of the freshman class at the college has a percent change of $\frac{\text{change in enrollment}}{\text{old enrollment}} = \frac{-60}{500} = -0.12 = -12\%$. We can also use the terms *percent increase* and *percent decrease*, saying that the price of computer paper increases by 25% and the size of the freshman class decreases by 12%. Note that the denominator is always the old amount, never the new amount.

Mathematics

Example: Your landlord raises your rent from $1,500 to $1,700 per month. To find the percent change in your rent (rounded to the nearest tenth of a percent), you calculate as follows.

$$\text{percent change in rent} = \frac{\text{change in rent}}{\text{old rent}} = \frac{(\text{new rent}) - (\text{old rent})}{\text{old rent}}$$
$$= \frac{\$1{,}700 - \$1{,}500}{\$1{,}500} = \frac{\$200}{\$1{,}500} = 0.1333\ldots \approx 13.3\%$$

Therefore, the percent change in your rent is approximately 13.3%.

**Review Video: Percent Change**
Visit mometrix.com/academy and enter code: 907890

## Converting Between Percentages, Fractions, and Decimals

Converting decimals to percentages and percentages to decimals is as simple as moving the decimal point. To *convert from a decimal to a percentage*, move the decimal point **two places to the right**. To *convert from a percentage to a decimal*, move it **two places to the left**. It may be helpful to remember that the percentage number will always be larger than the equivalent decimal number. Example:

$$0.23 = 23\% \qquad 5.34 = 534\% \qquad 0.007 = 0.7\%$$
$$700\% = 7.00 \qquad 86\% = 0.86 \qquad 0.15\% = 0.0015$$

To convert a fraction to a decimal, simply divide the numerator by the denominator in the fraction. To convert a decimal to a fraction, put the decimal in the numerator with 1 in the denominator. Multiply the numerator and denominator by tens until there are no more decimal places. Then simplify the fraction to lowest terms. For example, converting 0.24 to a fraction:

$$0.24 = \frac{0.24}{1} = \frac{0.24 \times 100}{1 \times 100} = \frac{24}{100} = \frac{6}{25}$$

Fractions can be converted to a percentage by finding equivalent fractions with a denominator of 100. Example:

$$\frac{7}{10} = \frac{70}{100} = 70\% \quad \frac{1}{4} = \frac{25}{100} = 25\%$$

To convert a percentage to a fraction, divide the percentage number by 100 and reduce the fraction to its simplest possible terms. Example:

$$60\% = \frac{60}{100} = \frac{3}{5} \quad 96\% = \frac{96}{100} = \frac{24}{25}$$

**Review Video: Converting Fractions to Percentages and Decimals**
Visit mometrix.com/academy and enter code: 306233

**Review Video: Converting Percentages to Decimals and Fractions**
Visit mometrix.com/academy and enter code: 287297

**Review Video: Converting Decimals to Fractions and Percentages**
Visit mometrix.com/academy and enter code: 986765

**Review Video: Converting Decimals, Improper Fractions, and Mixed Numbers**
Visit mometrix.com/academy and enter code: 696924

## Rational and Irrational Numbers

The term **rational** means that the number can be expressed as a ratio or fraction. That is, a number, $r$, is rational if and only if it can be represented by a fraction $\frac{a}{b}$ where $a$ and $b$ are integers and $b$ does not equal 0. The set of rational numbers includes integers and decimals. If there is no finite way to represent a value with a fraction of integers, then the number is **irrational**. Common irrational numbers are $\pi$ and the square roots of whole numbers that are not perfect squares (e.g., $\sqrt{5}$ or $\sqrt{21}$). The sum or product of an integer and an irrational number is always irrational (e.g., $3\pi$ or $7 + \sqrt{6}$).

**Review Video: Rational and Irrational Numbers**
Visit mometrix.com/academy and enter code: 280645

**Review Video: Ordering Rational Numbers**
Visit mometrix.com/academy and enter code: 419578

**Review Video: Irrational Numbers on a Number Line**
Visit mometrix.com/academy and enter code: 433866

## Proportions and Ratios

### Proportions

There is a **proportion** between two variable quantities if there is a constant relationship between their products or quotients, a relationship that does not change as the quantities themselves change.

Given variable quantities $x$ and $y$, we say that they are **directly proportional** (or that $y$ **varies directly with** $x$) if their quotient or *ratio* is constant—that is, if there is a constant $k$ such that $\frac{y}{x} = k$ is always true. Another way of saying this is that $y$ is a constant multiple of $x$, so that $y = kx$ is always true. We call the number $k$ the **constant of proportionality**. For example, if you drive at a constant 50 miles per hour, then the distance, $y$, that you travel in miles is 50 times the number of hours, $x$, that you drive. In symbols, $y = 50x$ miles (or $\frac{y}{x} = 50$ mph). So, the distance you travel, $y$, is directly proportional to (or varies directly with) the time you travel, $x$, with constant of proportionality $k = 50$ mph.

The quantities $x$ and $y$ are **inversely proportional** (or $y$ varies inversely with $x$) if their product is constant—that is, if there is a constant $k$ such that $xy = k$ is always true. Another way of saying this is to say that $y$ is a constant multiple of the reciprocal of $x$ so that $y = \frac{k}{x}$ is always true. For instance, suppose you drive at speed (rate) $y$ mph for $x$ hours, going a total of 120 miles. Since rate × time = distance, we get $xy = 120$ miles (or $y = \frac{120}{x}$ miles per hour). Thus, your driving speed, $y$, is inversely proportional to (or varies inversely with) your drive time, $x$, with constant of proportionality $k = 120$ miles.

**Review Video: Proportions**
Visit mometrix.com/academy and enter code: 505355

## Ratios

A **ratio** expresses the sizes of two quantities relative to each other. For instance, suppose we have 3 copies of sheet music to share among 6 singers. We can divide the singers into groups of 2 and give each group 1 copy of the music. Thus, there is 1 copy of the music for every 2 singers, and we say that the **ratio** of sheet music to singers is 1 to 2, which we write either as a fraction $\frac{1}{2}$ or using a colon $1 : 2$. Of course, it is also true there are 3 copies for every 6 singers so that the ratio of sheet music to singers is also 3 to 6, which we write as $\frac{3}{6}$ or $3 : 6$. So, the ratios $\frac{1}{2}$ and $\frac{3}{6}$ express the same relative quantities of music and singers. We say that these ratios are equal or **equivalent**, and we note that ratios are equal precisely when their fractions are equal (so, in this case, $\frac{1}{2} = \frac{3}{6}$ as fractions). We can also express the quantities in the other order and say that the ratio of singers to music is $\frac{2}{1}$ or $2 : 1$ (or $\frac{6}{3}$ or $6 : 3$).

**Review Video: Ratios**
Visit mometrix.com/academy and enter code: 996914

## Constant of Proportionality

If variable quantities $x$ and $y$ are proportional and we know a pair of corresponding values for them, then we can find their constant of proportionality. If they are directly proportional, we use the formula $\frac{y}{x} = k$. If they are inversely proportional, we use the formula $xy = k$

Example: The cost in dollars, $y$, of buying fence posts is directly proportional to the number, $x$, that you buy. If it costs \$51 to buy 17 fence posts, what is the constant of proportionality? Because of direct proportionality, we know that $\frac{y}{x} = k$. Since this works for every pair of corresponding $x$- and $y$-values, it also works for $x = 17$ and $y = 51$. This gives us $\frac{51}{17} = k$, which simplifies to $k = 3$. Note also that this is the unit price, namely \$3 per fence post.

### Work/Unit Rate

**Unit rate** expresses a quantity of one thing in terms of one unit of another. For example, if you travel 30 miles every two hours, a unit rate expresses this comparison in terms of one hour: in one hour you travel 15 miles, so your unit rate is 15 miles per hour. Other examples are how much one ounce of food costs (price per ounce) or figuring out how much one egg costs out of the dozen (price per 1 egg, instead of price per 12 eggs). The denominator of a unit rate is always 1. Unit rates are used to compare different situations to solve problems. For example, to make sure you get the best deal when deciding which kind of soda to buy, you can find the unit rate of each. If soda #1 costs $1.50 for a 1-liter bottle, and soda #2 costs $2.75 for a 2-liter bottle, it would be a better deal to buy soda #2, because its unit rate is only $1.375 per 1-liter, which is cheaper than soda #1. Unit rates can also help determine the length of time a given event will take. For example, if you can paint 2 rooms in 4.5 hours, you can determine how long it will take you to paint 5 rooms by solving for the unit rate per room and then multiplying that by 5.

**Review Video: Rates and Unit Rates**
Visit mometrix.com/academy and enter code: 185363

## Cross Multiplication

### Finding an Unknown in Equivalent Expressions

It is often necessary to apply information given about a rate or proportion to a new scenario. For example, if you know that Jedha can run a marathon (26.2 miles) in 3 hours, how long would it take her to run 10 miles at the same pace? Start by setting up equivalent expressions:

$$\frac{26.2\text{ mi}}{3\text{ hr}} = \frac{10\text{ mi}}{x\text{ hr}}$$

Now, cross multiply and solve for $x$:

$$\begin{aligned} 26.2x &= 30 \\ x &= \frac{30}{26.2} = \frac{15}{13.1} \\ x &\approx 1.15\text{ hrs } or \text{ } 1\text{ hr } 9\text{ min} \end{aligned}$$

So, at this pace, Jedha could run 10 miles in about 1.15 hours or about 1 hour and 9 minutes.

**Review Video: Cross Multiplying Fractions**
Visit mometrix.com/academy and enter code: 893904

## Linear Expressions

### Terms and Coefficients

**Mathematical expressions** consist of a combination of one or more values arranged in terms that are added together. As such, an expression could be just a single number, including zero. A **variable term** is the product of a real number, also called a **coefficient**, and one or more variables, each of which may be raised to an exponent. Expressions may also include numbers without a variable, called **constants** or **constant terms**. The expression $6s^2$, for example, is a single term where the coefficient is the real number 6 and the variable term is $s^2$. Note that if a term is written as simply a variable to some exponent, like $t^2$, then the coefficient is 1, because $t^2 = 1t^2$.

Mathematics

### LINEAR EXPRESSIONS

A **single variable linear expression** is the sum of a single variable term, where the variable has no exponent, and a constant, which may be zero. For instance, the expression $2w + 7$ has $2w$ as the variable term and 7 as the constant term. It is important to realize that terms are separated by addition or subtraction. Since an expression is a sum of terms, expressions such as $5x - 3$ can be written as $5x + (-3)$ to emphasize that the constant term is negative. A real-world example of a single variable linear expression is the perimeter of a square, four times the side length, often expressed: $4s$.

In general, a **linear expression** is the sum of any number of variable terms so long as none of the variables have an exponent and none of the terms have two variables multiplied together. For example, $3m + 8n - \frac{1}{4}p + 5.5q - 1$ is a linear expression, but $3y^3$ and $5xy$ are not. In the same way, the expression for the perimeter of a general triangle $(a + b + c)$ is linear, but the expression for the area of a square $(s^2)$ is not.

## Slope

### FINDING SLOPE GIVEN GRAPH OR TABLE

On a graph with two points, $(x_1, y_1)$ and $(x_2, y_2)$, the **slope** is found with the formula $m = \frac{y_2 - y_1}{x_2 - x_1}$; where $x_1 \neq x_2$ and $m$ stands for slope. If the value of the slope is **positive**, the line has an *upward direction* from left to right. If the value of the slope is **negative**, the line has a *downward direction* from left to right. Consider the following example:

A new book goes on sale in bookstores and online stores. In the first month, 5,000 copies of the book are sold. Over time, the book continues to grow in popularity. The data for the number of copies sold is in the table below.

| **# of Months on Sale** | 1 | 2 | 3 | 4 | 5 |
|---|---|---|---|---|---|
| **# of Copies Sold (In Thousands)** | 5 | 10 | 15 | 20 | 25 |

So, the number of copies that are sold and the time that the book is on sale is a proportional relationship. In this example, an equation can be used to show the data: $y = 5x$, where $x$ is the number of months that the book is on sale. Also, $y$ is the number of copies sold. So, the slope of the corresponding line is $\frac{\text{rise}}{\text{run}} = \frac{5}{1} = 5$.

### FINDING SLOPE GIVEN AN EQUATION

When given an equation of a line, it is necessary to solve for $y$ to determine the slope of the line. Given the equation $6x + 2y = 8$, find the slope. First, subtract $6x$ from both sides of the equation, resulting in $2y = -6x + 8$. Then divide both sides of the equation by 2, resulting in $y = -3x + 4$. This then allows us to conclude that the slope of the line is $m = -3$, the coefficient of $x$. Once an equation is in the form $y = mx + b$, the slope and y-intercept can easily be determined. For this reason, we refer to the equation $y = mx + b$ as "slope-intercept form" of the equation of a line.

**Review Video: Finding the Slope of a Line**
Visit mometrix.com/academy and enter code: 766664

# Linear Equations

Equations like $5x = 100$ and $8x - 120 = 200$ and $6x + 4y = 240$ are **linear equations**. Linear equations are named based off the number of distinct variables they include. For example, the equation $3x + 30 = 8x$ is a **one-variable linear equation** because it involves only the single variable $x$. It does not matter that $x$ appears more than once. Any equations that can be written as $ax + b = 0$, where $a \neq 0$, falls into this category. Furthermore, the equation $3x - 5y = 14 + 9y$ is a **two-variable linear equation** because it involves the two variables $x$ and $y$. The equation $7x + 8y - 12z + 14w = 56$ is a linear equation in four variables.

## Satisfying the Equation

When given a one-variable linear equation, the goal is typically to solve it. This means that we want to find the number that makes the equation true if we substitute it for the variable. That number is the **solution,** or root, of the equation. For instance, the equation $5x = 10$ has the solution $x = 2$. This is true because when 2 is substituted for x, the result is $5 \cdot 2 = 10$, which is true. On the other hand, $x = 6$ can not be a solution because $5 \cdot 6 \neq 10$, so it is false. Two equations with the same solution are **equivalent equations**. For example, the equations $5x = 10$ and $5x + 3 = 13$ are equivalent because both have the same solution of $x = 2$.

## Determining a Solution Set

The **solution set** is the set of all solutions of an equation. In the previous example, the solution set would be 2. Solutions to a linear equation in two variables consist of pairs of numbers. For instance, the equation $6x + 4y = 240$ has the solution $x = 20$ and $y = 30$ since $6 \cdot 20 + 4 \cdot 30 = 240$ is true. We can write this solution as the ordered pair (20,30) and plot it as a point on the coordinate plane. Such equations usually have infinitely many solutions; and if we plot the points for all these solutions we get a line, which is a picture of all the solutions. We call this **graphing the equation**. When an equation has no true solutions, it is referred to as an **empty set**.

## Linear Equation Forms

Linear equations can be written many ways. Below is a list of some forms linear equations can take:

- **Standard Form**: $Ax + By = C$; the slope is $\frac{-A}{B}$ and the $y$-intercept is $\frac{C}{B}$
- **Slope Intercept Form**: $y = mx + b$, where $m$ is the slope and $b$ is the $y$-intercept
- **Point-Slope Form**: $y - y_1 = m(x - x_1)$, where $m$ is the slope and $(x_1, y_1)$ is a point on the line
- **Two-Point Form**: $\frac{y-y_1}{x-x_1} = \frac{y_2-y_1}{x_2-x_1}$, where $(x_1, y_1)$ and $(x_2, y_2)$ are two points on the given line
- **Intercept Form**: $\frac{x}{x_1} + \frac{y}{y_1} = 1$, where $(x_1, 0)$ is the point at which a line intersects the $x$-axis, and $(0, y_1)$ is the point at which the same line intersects the $y$-axis

**Review Video: Slope-Intercept and Point-Slope Forms**
Visit mometrix.com/academy and enter code: 113216

**Review Video: Converting Between Standard and Slope-Intercept Forms**
Visit mometrix.com/academy and enter code: 982828

**Review Video: Linear Equations Basics**
Visit mometrix.com/academy and enter code: 793005

# Solving Equations

## Manipulating Equations

### Like Terms

Like terms are terms in an equation that have the same variable, regardless of whether they also have the same coefficient. This includes terms that *lack* a variable; all constants (i.e., numbers without variables) are considered like terms. If the equation involves terms with a variable raised to different powers, the like terms are those that have the variable raised to the same power.

For example, consider the equation $x^2 + 3x + 2 = 2x^2 + x - 7 + 2x$. In this equation, 2 and –7 are like terms; they are both constants. The terms $3x$, $x$, and $2x$ are like terms, they all include the variable $x$ raised to the first power. The terms $x^2$ and $2x^2$ are like terms, they both include the variable $x$, raised to the second power. The terms $2x$ and $2x^2$ are not like terms; although they both involve the variable $x$, the variable is not raised to the same power in both terms. The fact that they have the same coefficient, 2, is not relevant.

**Review Video: Rules for Manipulating Equations**
Visit mometrix.com/academy and enter code: 838871

### Carrying Out the Same Operation on Both Sides of an Equation

When solving an equation, the general procedure is to carry out a series of operations on both sides of an equation, choosing operations that simplify the equation when doing so. The reason why the same operation must be carried out on both sides of the equation is because that leaves the meaning of the equation unchanged, and yields a result that is equivalent to the original equation. This would not be the case if we carried out an operation on one side of an equation and not the other. Consider what an equation means: it is a statement that two values or expressions are equal. If we carry out the same operation on both sides of the equation—add 3 to both sides, for example—then the two sides of the equation are changed in the same way, and so remain equal. If we do that to only one side of the equation—add 3 to one side but not the other—then that wouldn't be true; if we change one side of the equation but not the other then the two sides are no longer equal.

### Combining Like Terms

Combining like terms refers to adding or subtracting like terms—terms with the same variable—and therefore reducing sets of like terms to a single term. The main advantage of doing this is that it simplifies the equation. Often, combining like terms can be done as the first step in solving an equation, though it can also be done later, such as after distributing terms in a product.

For example, consider the equation $2(x + 3) + 3(2 + x + 3) = -4$. The 2 and the 3 in the second set of parentheses are like terms, and we can combine them, yielding $2(x + 3) + 3(x + 5) = -4$. Now we can carry out the multiplications implied by the parentheses, distributing the outer 2 and 3 accordingly: $2x + 6 + 3x + 15 = -4$. The $2x$ and the $3x$ are like terms, and we can add them together: $5x + 6 + 15 = -4$. Now, the constants 6, 15, and –4 are also like terms, and we can combine them as well: subtracting 6 and 15 from both sides of the equation, we get $5x = -4 - 6 - 15$, or $5x = -25$, which simplifies further to $x = -5$.

**Review Video: Solving Equations by Combining Like Terms**
Visit mometrix.com/academy and enter code: 668506

### *Canceling Terms on Opposite Sides of an Equation*

Two terms on opposite sides of an equation can be canceled if and only if they *exactly* match each other. They must have the same variable raised to the same power and the same coefficient. For example, in the equation $3x + 2x^2 + 6 = 2x^2 - 6$, $2x^2$ appears on both sides of the equation and can be canceled, leaving $3x + 6 = -6$. The 6 on each side of the equation *cannot* be canceled, because it is added on one side of the equation and subtracted on the other. While they cannot be canceled, however, the 6 and -6 are like terms and can be combined, yielding $3x = -12$, which simplifies further to $x = -4$.

It's also important to note that the terms to be canceled must be independent terms and cannot be part of a larger term. For example, consider the equation $2(x + 6) = 3(x + 4) + 1$. We cannot cancel the $x$'s, because even though they match each other they are part of the larger terms $2(x + 6)$ and $3(x + 4)$. We must first distribute the 2 and 3, yielding $2x + 12 = 3x + 12 + 1$. Now we see that the terms with the $x$'s do not match, but the 12s do, and can be canceled, leaving $2x = 3x + 1$, which simplifies to $x = -1$.

### *Isolating Variables*

To isolate a variable means to manipulate the equation so that the variable appears by itself on one side of the equation, and does not appear at all on the other side. Generally, an equation or inequality is considered to be solved once the variable is isolated and the other side of the equation or inequality is simplified as much as possible. In the case of a two-variable equation or inequality, only one variable needs to be isolated; it will not usually be possible to simultaneously isolate both variables.

For a linear equation—an equation in which the variable only appears raised to the first power—isolating a variable can be done by first moving all the terms with the variable to one side of the equation and all other terms to the other side. (*Moving* a term really means adding the inverse of the term to both sides; when a term is *moved* to the other side of the equation its sign is flipped.) Then combine like terms on each side. Finally, divide both sides by the coefficient of the variable, if applicable. The steps need not necessarily be done in this order, but this order will always work.

**Review Video: Solving Equations for Specific Variables**
Visit mometrix.com/academy and enter code: 130695

**Review Video: Solving Equations Involving Algebraic Fractions**
Visit mometrix.com/academy and enter code: 237770

**Review Video: Solving One-Step Equations**
Visit mometrix.com/academy and enter code: 777004

## Solving One-Variable Linear Equations

### *Equations with One Solution (the Usual Case)*

To solve a one-variable linear equation, we use the techniques above to isolate the variable.

1. If any coefficients or constants are fractions, it is often helpful first to multiply both sides of the equation by the least common denominator (of all fractions) to clear the fractions.
2. Simplify both sides of the equation by combining any like terms.
3. Put all terms with the variable on one side of the equation and all constant terms on the other side, by adding or subtracting the same terms on both sides of the equation.

Mathematics

4. Divide both sides by the coefficient of the variable (or multiply both sides by its reciprocal).
5. When we have a value for the variable, we can check it by substituting the value into the original equation to make sure it produces a true result.

Consider the following example for solving the equation $\frac{2}{3}x + 8 = 14$:

| | |
|---|---|
| $3 \cdot \left(\frac{2}{3}x + 8\right) = 3 \cdot 14$ | Clear fractions by multiplying both sides by 3. |
| $2x + 24 = 42$ | Simplify, remembering to apply the distributive property. |
| $2x + 24 - 24 = 42 - 24$ | Subtract 24 from both sides to isolate $2x$. |
| $2x = 18$ | Simplify by combining like terms. |
| $\frac{2x}{2} = \frac{18}{2}$ | Divide both sides by 2 to isolate $x$. |
| $x = 9$ | Simplify |

Finally, we check this answer by substituting $x = 9$ into the original equation to make sure we get a true result.

$$\frac{2}{3}x + 8 = \frac{2}{3}(9) + 8 = 6 + 8 = 14$$

This is correct, so the value of $x$ is 9.

**Review Video: Solving Equations Using the Distributive Property**
Visit mometrix.com/academy and enter code: 765499

### *Equations with More Than One Solution*

Some types of non-linear equations, such as equations involving squares of variables, may have more than one solution. For example, the equation $x^2 = 4$ has two solutions: 2 and –2. Equations with absolute values can also have multiple solutions: $|x| = 1$ has the solutions $x = 1$ and $x = -1$.

It is possible for a linear equation to have more than one solution but only if the equation is true regardless of the value of the variable. We call such an equation an **identity**. In this case, the equation has infinitely many solutions, because every possible value of the variable is a solution. We discover that a linear equation is an identity when our attempts to isolate the variable cause the variable to disappear, leaving a *true* equation involving only constants. For example, consider the equation $2(3x + 5) = x + 5(x + 2)$. Distributing, we get $6x + 10 = x + 5x + 10$; combining like terms gives $6x + 10 = 6x + 10$, and the $6x$-terms cancel to leave $10 = 10$. This is clearly true, so the original equation is an identity. We could also cancel the 10's leaving $0 = 0$, which is also is clearly true—in general if both sides of the equation can be reduced to match one another exactly, the original equation is an identity.

### *Equations with No Solution*

Some types of non-linear equations, such as equations involving squares of variables, may have no solution. For example, the equation $x^2 = -2$ has no solutions in the real numbers because the square of a real number must be positive. Similarly, $|x| = -1$ has no solution because the absolute value of a number is always positive.

It is also possible for a linear equation to have no solution. We call such an equation a **contradiction.** We discover that a linear equation is a contradiction when our attempts to isolate the variable cause the variable to disappear, leaving a *false* equation involving only constants. For example, the equation $2(x+3)+x=3x$ has no solution. We can see this by trying to solve it: first we distribute, leaving $2x+6+x=3x$. Combining like terms gives us $3x+6=3x$, and cancelling the term $3x$ on both sides leaves us with $6=0$. This is clearly false, so the original equation is a contradiction, having no solutions.

## FEATURES OF EQUATIONS THAT REQUIRE SPECIAL TREATMENT

A linear equation is an equation in which variables only appear by themselves: not multiplied together, not with exponents other than one, and not inside absolute value signs or any other functions. For example, the equation $x+1-3x=5-x$ is a linear equation; while $x$ appears multiple times, it never appears with an exponent other than one, or inside any function. The two-variable equation $2x-3y=5+2x$ is also a linear equation. In contrast, the equation $x^2-5=3x$ is *not* a linear equation, because it involves the term $x^2$. The equation $\sqrt{x}=5$ is not linear, because it involves a square root. The equation $(x-1)^2=4$ is not linear because even though there's no exponent on the $x$ directly, it appears as part of an expression that is squared. The two-variable equation $x+xy-y=5$ is not linear because it includes the term $xy$, where two variables are multiplied together.

As we see above, linear equations can always be solved (or shown to have no solution) by combining like terms and performing simple operations on both sides of the equation. Some non-linear equations can be solved by similar methods, but others may require more advanced methods of solution, if they can be solved analytically at all.

### *SOLVING EQUATIONS INVOLVING ROOTS*

In an equation involving roots, the first step is to isolate the term with the root, if possible, and then raise both sides of the equation to the appropriate power to eliminate it. Consider an example equation, $2\sqrt{x+1}-1=3$. In this case, begin by adding 1 to both sides, yielding $2\sqrt{x+1}=4$, and then dividing both sides by 2, yielding $\sqrt{x+1}=2$. Now square both sides, yielding $x+1=4$. Finally, subtracting 1 from both sides yields $x=3$.

Squaring both sides of an equation (or raising both sides to any *even* power) may, however, yield a spurious solution—a solution to the squared equation that is *not* a solution of the original equation. It's therefore necessary to plug the solution back into the original equation to make sure it works. In this case, it does: $2\sqrt{3+1}-1=2\sqrt{4}-1=2(2)-1=4-1=3$.

The same procedure applies for other roots as well. For example, given the equation $3+\sqrt[3]{2x}=5$, we can first subtract 3 from both sides, yielding $\sqrt[3]{2x}=2$ and isolating the root. Raising both sides to the third power yields $2x=2^3$; i.e., $2x=8$. We can now divide both sides by 2 to get $x=4$.

**Review Video: Solving Equations Involving Roots**
Visit mometrix.com/academy and enter code: 297670

### *SOLVING EQUATIONS WITH EXPONENTS*

In solving an equation with powers of a variable, sometimes it is possible to eliminate all but one term involving the variable. In that case, we can isolate the power of the variable and then take the appropriate root of both sides to eliminate the exponent. For instance, for the equation $2x^3+17=5x^3-7$, we can subtract $5x^3$ from both sides to get $-3x^3+17=-7$, and then subtract 17 from

Mathematics

both sides to get $-3x^3 = -24$. Finally, we can divide both sides by -3 to get $x^3 = 8$. Since this isolates the cube of the variable, we can take the cube root of both sides to get $x = \sqrt[3]{8} = 2$.

One important but often overlooked point is that equations with an exponent greater than 1 may have more than one answer. The solution to $x^2 = 9$ isn't simply $x = 3$; it's $x = \pm 3$ (that is, $x = 3$ or $x = -3$). For a slightly more complicated example, consider the equation $(x-1)^2 - 1 = 3$. Adding 1 to both sides yields $(x-1)^2 = 4$; taking the square root of both sides yields $x - 1 = 2$. We can then add 1 to both sides to get $x = 3$. However, there's a second solution. We also have the possibility that $x - 1 = -2$, in which case $x = -1$. Both $x = 3$ and $x = -1$ are valid solutions, as can be verified by substituting them both into the original equation.

**Review Video: Solving Equations with Exponents**
Visit mometrix.com/academy and enter code: 514557

**Review Video: Adding and Subtracting with Exponents**
Visit mometrix.com/academy and enter code: 875756

### *Solving Equations with Absolute Values*

When solving an equation with an absolute value, the first step is to isolate the absolute value term. We then consider two possibilities: when the expression inside the absolute value is positive or when it is negative. In the former case, the expression in the absolute value equals the expression on the other side of the equation; in the latter, it equals the additive inverse of that expression—the expression times negative one. We consider each case separately and finally check for spurious solutions.

For instance, consider solving $|2x - 1| + x = 5$ for $x$. We can first isolate the absolute value by moving the $x$ to the other side: $|2x - 1| = -x + 5$. Now, we have two possibilities. First, that $2x - 1$ is positive, and hence $2x - 1 = -x + 5$. Rearranging and combining like terms yields $3x = 6$, and hence $x = 2$. The other possibility is that $2x - 1$ is negative, and hence $2x - 1 = -(-x + 5) = x - 5$. In this case, rearranging and combining like terms yields $x = -4$. Substituting $x = 2$ and $x = -4$ back into the original equation, we see that they are both valid solutions.

Note that the absolute value of a sum or difference applies to the sum or difference as a whole, not to the individual terms; in general, $|2x - 1|$ is not equal to $|2x + 1|$ or to $|2x| - 1$.

**Review Video: Solving Absolute Value Equations**
Visit mometrix.com/academy and enter code: 501208

### *Extraneous Solutions*

An **extraneous solution** may arise when we square both sides of an equation (or raise both sides to an even power) as a step in solving it or under certain other operations on the equation. It is a solution to the squared or otherwise modified equation that is *not* a solution of the original equation. To identify an extraneous solution, it's useful when you solve an equation involving roots or absolute values to plug the solution back into the original equation to make sure it's valid.

### *Two-Variable Equations*

Similar to methods for a one-variable equation, solving a two-variable equation involves isolating a variable: manipulating the equation so that a variable appears by itself on one side of the equation, and not at all on the other side. However, in a two-variable equation, you will usually only be able to isolate one of the variables; the other variable may appear on the other side along with constant terms, or with exponents or other functions. If an equation has multiple variables, the problem should tell you which variable to isolate.

**Review Video: Solving Equations with Variables on Both Sides**
Visit mometrix.com/academy and enter code: 402497

## Rounding and Estimation

**Rounding** is reducing the digits in a number while still trying to keep the value similar. The result will be less accurate but in a simpler form and easier to use. Whole numbers can be rounded to the nearest ten, hundred, or thousand, for instance.

To round a number, we make it a little smaller (rounding down) or a little larger (rounding up) to get a number that ends in zeros. We specify the number of zeros by naming the last place that we will not "zero out." For example, to round 8,327 to the nearest hundred, we round down to 8,300, zeroing out every digit to the right of the hundreds place. To round 4,728 to the nearest thousand, we round up to 5,000, increasing the thousands digit by one (to make the number larger) and zeroing out every digit to the right of the thousands place.

We decide whether to round down or up by looking at the first digit we are going to zero out. If it is less than 5 (namely, 0, 1, 2, 3, or 4) we round down. If it is greater than or equal to 5 (namely, 5, 6, 7, 8, or 9) we round up by adding 1 to the place we are rounding to. So, rounding 8,327 to the nearest hundred, we round down to 8,300 because the tens digit, 2, is less than 5. And rounding 4,728 to the nearest thousand, we round up to 5,000, increasing the thousands digit by 1, because the hundreds digit, 7, is greater than or equal to 5.

This even works with decimals. For example, rounding 39.7426 to the nearest tenth, we round down to 39.7000 (or simply 39.7) because the hundredths digit, 4, is less than 5. And rounding 0.019823 to the nearest thousandth, we round up to 0.020000 (or simply 0.02) by increasing the thousandths digit by 1, because the ten-thousandths digit, 8, is greater than or equal to 5.

When you are asked to estimate the solution to a problem, you will need to provide only an approximate figure or **estimation** for your answer. In this situation, you will need to round each number in the calculation to the level indicated (nearest hundred, nearest thousand, etc.) or to a level that makes sense for the numbers involved. When estimating a sum **all numbers must be rounded to the same level**. You cannot round one number to the nearest thousand while rounding another to the nearest hundred.

For instance, suppose you are considering buying four pieces of equipment for your home office. Their prices are $485, $1,217, $750, and $643. To estimate their total cost, you might round each price to the nearest hundred and add the rounded figures, getting an estimate of $\$500 + \$1,200 + \$800 + \$600 = \$3,100$. By estimating instead of making an exact calculation, you give up a little accuracy to get a simpler calculation.

**Review Video: Rounding and Estimation**
Visit mometrix.com/academy and enter code: 126243

## Scientific Notation

Scientific notation is a way of writing large numbers in a shorter form. The form $a \times 10^n$ is used in scientific notation, where $a$ is greater than or equal to 1 but less than 10, and $n$ is the number of

Mathematics

places the decimal must move to get from the original number to $a$. Example: The number 230,400,000 is cumbersome to write. To write the value in scientific notation, place a decimal point between the first and second numbers, and include all digits through the last non-zero digit ($a = 2.304$). To find the appropriate power of 10, count the number of places the decimal point had to move ($n = 8$). The number is positive if the decimal moved to the left, and negative if it moved to the right. We can then write 230,400,000 as $2.304 \times 10^8$. If we look instead at the number 0.00002304, we have the same value for $a$, but this time the decimal moved 5 places to the right ($n = -5$). Thus, 0.00002304 can be written as $2.304 \times 10^{-5}$. Using this notation makes it simple to compare very large or very small numbers. By comparing exponents, it is easy to see that $3.28 \times 10^4$ is smaller than $1.51 \times 10^5$, because 4 is less than 5.

**Review Video: Scientific Notation**
Visit mometrix.com/academy and enter code: 976454

## Metric and Customary Measurements

### Metric Measurement Prefixes

| | | |
|---|---|---|
| Giga- | One billion | 1 *giga*watt is one billion watts |
| Mega- | One million | 1 *mega*hertz is one million hertz |
| Kilo- | One thousand | 1 *kilo*gram is one thousand grams |
| Deci- | One-tenth | 1 *deci*meter is one-tenth of a meter |
| Centi- | One-hundredth | 1 *centi*meter is one-hundredth of a meter |
| Milli- | One-thousandth | 1 *milli*liter is one-thousandth of a liter |
| Micro- | One-millionth | 1 *micro*gram is one-millionth of a gram |

**Review Video: How the Metric System Works**
Visit mometrix.com/academy and enter code: 163709

### Measurement Conversion

When converting between units, the goal is to maintain the same meaning but change the way it is displayed. In order to go from a larger unit to a smaller unit, multiply the number of the known amount by the equivalent amount. When going from a smaller unit to a larger unit, divide the number of the known amount by the equivalent amount.

For complicated conversions, it may be helpful to set up conversion fractions. In these fractions, one fraction is the **conversion factor**. The other fraction has the unknown amount in the numerator. So, the known value is placed in the denominator. Sometimes, the second fraction has the known value from the problem in the numerator and the unknown in the denominator. Multiply the two fractions to get the converted measurement. Note that since the numerator and the denominator of the factor are equivalent, the value of the fraction is 1. That is why we can say that the result in the new units is equal to the result in the old units even though they have different numbers.

It can often be necessary to chain known conversion factors together. As an example, consider converting 512 square inches to square meters. We know that there are 2.54 centimeters in an inch and 100 centimeters in a meter, and we know we will need to square each of these factors to achieve the conversion we are looking for.

$$\frac{512\text{ in}^2}{1}\times\left(\frac{2.54\text{ cm}}{1\text{ in}}\right)^2\times\left(\frac{1\text{ m}}{100\text{ cm}}\right)^2=\frac{512\,\cancel{\text{in}^2}}{1}\times\left(\frac{6.4516\,\cancel{\text{cm}^2}}{1\,\cancel{\text{in}^2}}\right)\times\left(\frac{1\text{ m}^2}{10{,}000\,\cancel{\text{cm}^2}}\right)=0.330\text{ m}^2$$

**Review Video: Measurement Conversions**
Visit mometrix.com/academy and enter code: 316703

**Review Video: Converting Kilograms to Pounds**
Visit mometrix.com/academy and enter code: 241463

## Common Units and Equivalents

### Metric Equivalents

| | |
|---|---|
| 1000 μg (microgram) | 1 mg |
| 1000 mg (milligram) | 1 g |
| 1000 g (gram) | 1 kg |
| 1000 kg (kilogram) | 1 metric ton |
| 1000 mL (milliliter) | 1 L |
| 1000 μm (micrometer) | 1 mm |
| 1000 mm (millimeter) | 1 m |
| 100 cm (centimeter) | 1 m |
| 1000 m (meter) | 1 km |

### Distance and Area Measurement

| Unit | Abbreviation | US equivalent | Metric equivalent |
|---|---|---|---|
| **Inch** | in | 1 inch | 2.54 centimeters |
| **Foot** | ft | 12 inches | 0.305 meters |
| **Yard** | yd | 3 feet | 0.914 meters |
| **Mile** | mi | 5280 feet | 1.609 kilometers |
| **Acre** | ac | 4840 square yards | 0.405 hectares |
| **Square Mile** | sq. mi. or mi.$^2$ | 640 acres | 2.590 square kilometers |

### Capacity Measurements

| Unit | Abbreviation | US equivalent | Metric equivalent |
|---|---|---|---|
| **Fluid Ounce** | fl oz | 8 fluid drams | 29.573 milliliters |
| **Cup** | c | 8 fluid ounces | 0.237 liter |
| **Pint** | pt. | 16 fluid ounces | 0.473 liter |
| **Quart** | qt. | 2 pints | 0.946 liter |
| **Gallon** | gal. | 4 quarts | 3.785 liters |
| **Teaspoon** | t or tsp. | 1 fluid dram | 5 milliliters |
| **Tablespoon** | T or tbsp. | 4 fluid drams | 15 or 16 milliliters |
| **Cubic Centimeter** | cc or cm$^3$ | 0.271 drams | 1 milliliter |

### Weight Measurements

| Unit | Abbreviation | US equivalent | Metric equivalent |
|---|---|---|---|
| **Ounce** | oz | 16 drams | 28.35 grams |
| **Pound** | lb | 16 ounces | 453.6 grams |
| **Ton** | tn. | 2,000 pounds | 907.2 kilograms |

### Volume and Weight Measurement Clarifications

Always be careful when using ounces and fluid ounces. They are not equivalent.

| | |
|---|---|
| 1 pint = 16 fluid ounces | 1 fluid ounce ≠ 1 ounce |
| 1 pound = 16 ounces | 1 pint ≠ 1 pound |

Having one pint of something does not mean you have one pound of it. In the same way, just because something weighs one pound does not mean that its volume is one pint.

In the United States, the word "ton" by itself refers to a short ton or a net ton. Do not confuse this with a long ton (also called a gross ton) or a metric ton (also spelled *tonne*), which have different measurement equivalents.

1 US ton = 2000 pounds ≠ 1 metric ton = 1000 kilograms

## Precision, Accuracy, and Error

Measurements of physical quantities (e.g., length, area, volume, weight, mass, and time) in the real world are never perfect. Measurements miss the true value, and repeated measurements produce different values. For this reason, fields that depend on good measurement have technical terms, precision and accuracy, that describe how particular ways of measuring a quantity produce good or bad results. Note that these terms apply not to single measurements but to repeated measurements of the same quantity using the same procedure.

**Precision** describes the consistency of measurements. Measurements that cluster closely together, with little variation from one measurement to the next, have high precision. Measurements that vary a great deal from one measurement to the next have low precision.

**Accuracy** describes the closeness of measurements to the true value of the quantity being measured or, more technically, the tendency of measurements to cluster around the true value (though we do not usually know the true value; otherwise, we would not bother to measure it).

An analogy from archery may help. An outstanding archer aiming at the center of the target (the true value) produces a tight cluster of arrows around the center (high accuracy, high precision). Under the same circumstances a modestly good archer produces a loose cluster around the center (high accuracy, low precision). If, however, there is a strong crosswind and the archers do nothing to compensate for it, the outstanding archer's shots will cluster tightly around a point away from the center (low accuracy, high precision); and the modestly good archer's shots will cluster loosely around a point away from the center (low accuracy, low precision).

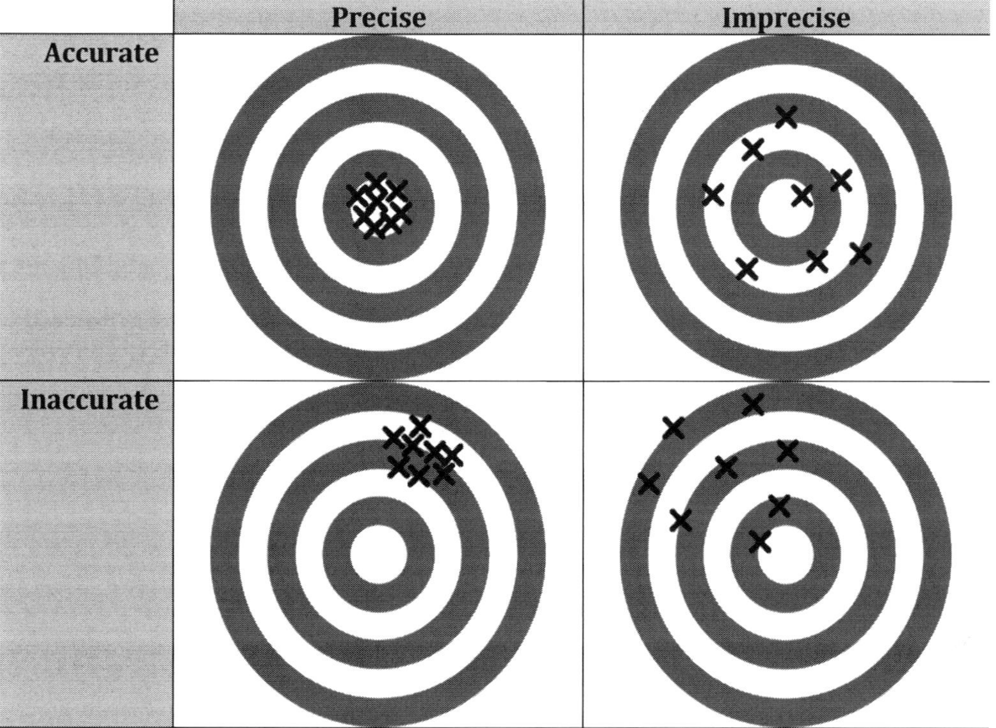


**Error** in measurement is not a mistake but simply the difference between the true value and the measured value. Since we seldom know the true value, we seldom know the exact error; but sometimes we know a limit on how big the error can be (an error bound), in which case we can use the plus-or-minus sign, $\pm$, to indicate how far the true value might lie from the measured value. For instance, if we measure the length of a metal bar as 25.6 cm and we know the error in our measurement is no more than 0.03 cm (some sources call this **approximate error**), then we might report the length of the bar as $25.6 \pm 0.03$ cm, which means it lies between 25.57 cm and 25.63 cm.

A particularly important application of this comes from the necessity of rounding whenever we make a measurement. For instance, if we measure the length of a pencil using a ruler marked off in whole inches (no fractions), then we must round our measurement to the nearest inch. Thus, if we report the length as 8 inches, it means that the actual value lies somewhere between 7.5 inches and 8.5 inches, which is to say $8 \pm 0.5$ inches. This built-in error bound due to rounding is called the **maximum possible error**, and it is always half the magnitude of the smallest unit used in the measurement. Determining the smallest unit can be somewhat subtle, involving the rules for significant figures commonly used in physics, chemistry, and other fields.

**Review Video: Precision, Accuracy, and Error**
Visit mometrix.com/academy and enter code: 520377

## Chapter Quiz

Ready to see how well you retained what you just read? Scan the QR code to go directly to the chapter quiz interface for this study guide. If you're using a computer, simply visit the online resources page at **mometrix.com/resources719/nystceatas-29098** and click the Chapter Quizzes link.

# Instructional Support

Transform passive reading into active learning! After immersing yourself in this chapter, put your comprehension to the test by taking a quiz. The insights you gained will stay with you longer this way. Scan the QR code to go directly to the chapter quiz interface for this study guide. If you're using a computer, simply visit the online resources page at **mometrix.com/resources719/nystceatas-29098** and click the Chapter Quizzes link.

## General Pedagogy

### Developmentally Appropriate Practices

#### *Developmentally Appropriate Practice*

Developmentally appropriate practice **(DAP)** is an approach to teaching grounded in theories of child development. It is derived from the belief that children are naturally curious learners who feel encouraged to take initiative in their own learning when provided a stimulating environment. This approach allows for a great deal of choice in learning experiences. The teacher's role is to facilitate active learning by creating developmentally appropriate activities based on the awareness of similarities between children in various developmental stages and the knowledge that each child develops at a different rate. With this knowledge, the teacher can then adjust the curriculum, activities, and assessments to fit the needs of individual students based on an awareness of age, cultural, social, and individual expectations.

#### *Creating Instruction Tailored to Cognitive Development*

A developmentally responsive teacher understands that the needs of students change as they mature through the stages of cognitive development. Furthermore, an effective teacher uses this knowledge to plan instruction that coincides with each developmental level. The early childhood teacher understands the needs and abilities of preoperational children and designs instruction that focuses on interacting with the world around them through hands-on activities and pretend play. Such activities foster exploration of the environment, roles, and connections. Developmentally responsive elementary school teachers are aware of the logical thinking patterns that occur during the concrete operational stage. Thus, they create instruction that allows children to interact with tangible materials to help them draw logical conclusions about their environment and understand abstract ideas. As children reach adolescence, a developmentally responsive teacher understands the increased ability to think abstractly, hypothetically, and reflectively in the formal operational stage. They use this knowledge to create instruction that encourages discussion, debate, creative problem solving, and opportunities to develop opinions, beliefs, and values.

#### *Cognitive Development*

##### Importance in Design of Appropriate Learning Experiences That Facilitate Growth

Teachers must understand their students' cognitive developmental abilities relative to their grade levels in order to create effective, engaging learning experiences that facilitate growth. This understanding allows teachers to develop age-appropriate instruction, activities, and assessments that challenge students based on their skills and abilities while remaining attainable. In knowing how students in a given grade level think and learn, the teacher can develop instruction that effectively facilitates learning and growth, such as creating opportunities for purposeful play with young children, opportunities for middle-school aged students to engage in logical problem solving, or activities that promote the development of abstract thinking and reasoning with adolescents. In addition, understanding students' cognitive abilities of each developmental level allow the teacher to better understand the nuances that exist within them, as students ultimately develop at their own pace and have individual learning needs.

#### IMPACT ON TEACHING AND LEARNING

Students' thinking and learning develops as they mature and their thought processes and worldviews change. Consequently, teaching and learning must adapt to accommodate these changes and facilitate growth. In the early years of cognitive development, children learn through interacting with the surrounding environment using their physical senses and engage in independent play. To facilitate this, young children need learning experiences that stimulate their development through exploration. As children reach early elementary school, they begin to think symbolically and play with others. Purposeful play and interaction with learning materials becomes an important part of learning at this stage. Teachers should act as facilitators and provide multiple opportunities for children to engage in purposeful, self-directed play with interactive materials as they learn to categorize the world around them. By later childhood, children think concretely and logically, thus needing hands-on learning experiences that provide opportunities for classification, experimentation, and problem-solving skills to facilitate their level of cognition and promote development. As children reach adolescence, they are increasingly able to think abstractly and consider hypothetical situations beyond what is concretely present. To enhance learning, teachers must provide opportunities for exploring different perspectives, values, and synthesizing information to engage in creative problem solving.

### *APPROPRIATE INSTRUCTIONAL ACTIVITIES*

The following are some examples of appropriate instructional activities for early childhood, middle-level, and high school students:

- **Early childhood:** Activities that allow for exploration, play, and movement while teaching young children to function and cooperate in a group setting are most valuable in early childhood classrooms. **Movement activities** such as dancing, jumping rope, using outdoor play equipment, and structured and unstructured play are beneficial in developing gross motor skills and teaching young children to properly interact with others. **Whole-group** activities such as circle time, class songs, and read-aloud sessions are also valuable in teaching young children appropriate communication skills within a group. **Thematic learning stations**, such as a science center, dramatic play area, library corner, block area, art center, and technology center, allow young children to explore their own interests on a variety of topics while developing creative and imaginative skills. **Sensory play** stations that include items like a sand box or water table are beneficial in further developing motor skills and allowing young children to explore and experiment with a variety of textures. Young children also require opportunities for quiet activities, such as nap time, self-selected reading, or meditation throughout the day in order to process information, reflect, and rest after active movement.

- **Middle-level**: Students at this age are best supported by the implementation of **hands-on** learning activities that develop **logical reasoning** and **collaboration** skills. Collaborative activities used for this purpose include science experiments, mathematical word problems, the use of manipulatives, and projects that allow opportunities for building, creating, disassembling, and exploring. Social and emotional learning activities are also important in developing middle school students' skills in these domains. Incorporating class meetings, community building activities, and self-reflection activities is valuable for teaching social and emotional skills. In addition, cooperative learning opportunities should be implemented frequently across subject areas to further develop students' abilities to work productively with others. Examples include literacy circles, creating teams for class review games, or group presentations.
- **High school:** Instructional activities for high school students should be designed to foster the development of **abstract** and **hypothetical** thinking abilities while preparing them to become productive members of society as they enter adulthood. Activities such as debates, class discussions, and mock trials are beneficial in providing high school students the opportunity to employ abstract reasoning, consider solutions to hypothetical situations, and develop empathy for opposing viewpoints. Assignments that require students to engage in the research process are valuable opportunities for developing higher-order thinking skills, as they encourage students to analyze, compare, and interpret information as well as seek evidence to support their claims. In addition, incorporating activities that benefit the community, such as fundraisers or food and clothing drives, are beneficial in teaching high school students the importance of positively contributing to society.

### *Developmentally Appropriate Learning Experiences and Assessments*

Effective developmentally appropriate instruction requires careful consideration when planning to ensure that students' individual needs across domains are supported to facilitate growth and a positive learning experience. The teacher must consider the developmental stage of their students based upon their age group as well as students' individual differences. With this knowledge in mind, teachers must ensure that they provide an inclusive learning environment that fosters growth and development by creating challenging yet attainable activities based on students' needs. Likewise, teachers must evaluate whether learning experiences and assessments are appropriate for the age, development, culture, and learning differences of the students. Learning experiences must provide opportunities for hands-on, cooperative, and self-directed learning, exploration, and participation to allow students to interact with their environment and build experiences. Additionally, lessons and activities should be flexible in nature to allow for inquiry and build upon students' prior experiences. Effective and developmentally appropriate assessments are aimed at monitoring student progress and allow for flexibility based on students' learning differences. They should be intended to provide feedback to the teacher on how to better adapt instruction to meet students' individual needs and foster developmental growth.

### *Development of Life Skills and Attitudes in Middle School-Age Children*

Middle school-age children are at a pivotal development point in which they experience rapid and profound change. In this transition, they often demonstrate characteristics of younger and older children. They are at a critical stage for developing the beliefs, attitudes, and habits that will be the foundation for their futures. Teachers must understand the implications of these changes and design instruction that addresses students' learning needs and facilitates the development of important life skills such as working and getting along with others, appreciating diversity, and committing to continued schooling. Cooperative learning and team building strategies instill the importance of working together positively to solve problems, building on one another's strengths, and valuing the perspectives of others. These strategies also teach students to appreciate diversity through encouraging them to work with peers with different backgrounds and experiences. Additionally, teachers can teach students to embrace diversity through creating a culturally responsive classroom environment that models acceptance and incorporates elements of students' differences into instruction to demonstrate the value of diverse perspectives. Teachers promote positive attitudes toward academics that encourage a commitment to continued schooling by teaching organization, time management, and goal-setting skills that instill a growth mindset and provide a foundation for success.

### *Impact of Student Characteristics on Teaching and Learning*

#### Young Children

The developmental level of young children is characterized by defining attributes that impact teaching and learning and for which several considerations must be made to design and implement effective instruction. As the attention span of young children is limited, the teacher must think about how to effectively act as a facilitator for learning more often than directly instructing students. **Direct instruction** must be delivered in small, manageable chunks to accommodate students' attention spans and ensure they retain and understand new concepts. Thus, the teacher must evaluate which elements of the curriculum require structured learning while allowing for flexibility within instruction to accommodate student inquiry. Young children also need frequent **movement**, **physical activity**, and **social interaction**, as they learn and build experiences concretely through moving, playing, interacting with, and exploring their environment. To create a learning environment that accommodates these characteristics, the teacher must consider the physical arrangement of the classroom and whether it adequately allows for movement. Additionally, teachers must incorporate **structured** and **unstructured activities** that foster and promote exploration, inquiry, play, cooperative learning, and hands-on interactions with the learning environment. With these considerations in mind, the teacher enhances students' learning experiences by tailoring instruction to their developmental characteristics.

#### Middle School-Age Children

As middle school-age children transition from childhood to adolescence, they experience vast changes across all developmental domains. Consequently, they exhibit characteristics that affect teaching and learning that require careful consideration when adapting instruction to their unique learning needs. While these students require increasing independence as they mature, they still need a structured, predictable environment to ease the transition into high school. The teacher must create a balance between fostering independence and growth while providing a schedule and routine. Opportunities for self-directed learning and student choice as well as strategies for self-assessment and reflection foster autonomy and self-responsibility over learning while the teacher facilitates and monitors progress. Strategies to teach effective organizational and time management skills further promote independence and prepare students for success upon entering high school. As middle school-age students develop, the importance of peers becomes increasingly prevalent because they begin to search for their identities and shape their own values and beliefs. Teachers must ensure to provide opportunities for cooperative and small group learning to facilitate students' social development while considering the importance of promoting positive peer relationships at this impressionable developmental level.

#### Adolescent Children

The developmental changes that occur in adolescence result in distinct characteristics as students in this age group transition into young adulthood. During this stage, students are discovering their identities, values, and beliefs and begin to explore long-term career and life choices. As they navigate their development and shape the people they will become, social relationships come to be increasingly important. Teachers must consider the impact of these characteristics when developing instruction to effectively address the unique needs of this age group and establish foundational attitudes, habits, and skills necessary for success in life. Effective instruction encourages adolescents to consider different perspectives, morals, and values to broaden their worldviews and foster the development of their own beliefs. Lessons and activities should allow for exploration of personal interests, skills, and abilities as students shape their personalities and begin to consider long-term life goals. Moreover, teachers should incorporate strategies that assist adolescents in setting goals to successfully foster a growth mindset and provide a foundation for success. Additionally, as socialization is highly influential at this stage, teachers must consider the importance of incorporating cooperative learning strategies and opportunities for socialization within instruction to encourage healthy peer relationships and foster positive identity development.

### *Interconnection of Developmental Domains*

Developmental domains are deeply interconnected. If one area of a child's development is negatively impacted, it is likely to pose negative consequences on other developmental areas. Proper physical development, for example, is key to developing cognitively, socially, and emotionally because physical development allows children to acquire the necessary gross and fine motor skills to explore and experiment with the world around them and interact with others. Physical development includes development of the brain. Factors such as poor nutrition, sleep, or prenatal exposure to drugs potentially hinder brain development. Consequentially, this may result in cognitive delays and, ultimately, lead to social or emotional developmental delays through negatively impacting the child's ability to interact with others, build relationships, emotionally regulate, or communicate effectively.

**Review Video: Early Childhood Developmental Domains**
Visit mometrix.com/academy and enter code: 100380

### *Factors to Consider When Selecting Materials for Learning and Play*

To plan meaningful, integrated, and active learning and play experiences, the teacher must have a deep understanding of both the developmental stage of the students and an understanding of students' individual needs. With this knowledge in mind, there are several factors that the teacher must consider when choosing materials that support active learning, play experiences, and the development of the whole child. Materials should be adaptable in use to facilitate development in multiple areas. Versatility is also important in fostering imagination and creativity. Teachers must consider how the chosen materials will support the understanding of concepts covered in instruction as well as how they will support conceptual, perceptual, and language development. Furthermore, teachers must ensure that materials are age-appropriate and stimulating and that they encourage active participation both independently and cooperatively.

### *Characteristics of a Developmentally Responsive Classroom*

A developmentally responsive classroom is one in which the teacher understands the cognitive, physical, social, and emotional developmental stages of students while recognizing nuances and individual developmental differences within these stages. Teachers must understand that developmental domains are interconnected, Teachers must effectively respond to unique developmental differences by designing a learner-centered curriculum and classroom environment that caters to each student's abilities, needs, and developmental levels to develop the whole child. The developmentally responsive classroom is engaging, supportive, and provides challenging learning opportunities based on individual learner abilities. There are several factors teachers must consider in the developmentally responsive classroom when planning an appropriate, engaging, and challenging learning experience. Teachers must have a deep understanding of which teaching strategies will most effectively appeal to students of varying developmental levels and be prepared to teach content in multiple ways. Furthermore, teachers must consider how to plan and organize activities, lessons, breaks, and the overall classroom environment. This includes considering how to arrange the classroom, which activity areas to include, spacing, and classroom equipment. The developmentally responsive classroom should promote positivity and productivity through creating a supportive yet challenging learning atmosphere that welcomes and respects differences, thus encouraging students' curiosity and excitement for learning.

## Diverse Student Populations

### *Understanding Students' Diverse Backgrounds and Needs*

#### Self-Education

Educating oneself on students' diverse backgrounds and needs enhances one's overall understanding of their students and creates a culturally sensitive, accepting classroom environment tailored to students' individual needs. There are several avenues through which teachers should educate themselves in an effort to build an accepting and respectful classroom climate. Communication is key for learning about diversities; thus, it is important for teachers to foster and maintain positive communications with students' families to deepen understanding of cultures, beliefs, lifestyles, and needs that exist within their classrooms. This could include learning some language of students with different cultural backgrounds, attending family nights at school, or participating in social events within their students' communities to integrate themselves into the culture. Furthermore, teachers can learn more about their students' backgrounds and needs through gaining an understanding of student differences, incorporating these diversities into the curriculum, and encouraging students to participate in learning by sharing aspects of their lives with the class.

#### Teaching, Learning, and Classroom Climate Benefits

A deep understanding of students' diverse backgrounds and needs provides multiple benefits for teaching, learning, and overall classroom climate. Knowledge of students' diversities allows teachers to understand the individual needs and abilities of their students and tailor instruction accordingly to maximize student development and achievement. Additionally, it allows teachers to know which authentic materials to incorporate in lessons and instructions to best create an engaging, relevant, and respectful learning experience that fosters student interest in learning and promotes success. Furthermore, by enhancing understanding of students' diverse backgrounds and needs, teachers consequently begin to model an attitude of inclusivity, acceptance, and respect for differences, which is then reflected by students and achieves a positive, welcoming classroom climate that promotes diversity.

### *Implications for Teaching, Learning, and Assessment in Diverse Classrooms*

In any classroom, a teacher will encounter a wide range of variances among individual students that inevitably will influence teaching, learning, and assessment. Diversities in ethnicity, gender, language background, and learning exceptionality will likely exist simultaneously in a single classroom. Educators must be prepared to teach to these diversities while concurrently teaching students the value and importance of diversity. The curriculum and classroom environment must be adjusted to meet individual student needs and create an **inclusive**, **respectful**, and **equitable** environment that welcomes differences and allows for success in learning. This begins with the teacher developing an understanding of the unique diversities that exist within their students and using this knowledge to **differentiate** curriculum, materials, activities, and assessments in such a way that students of all needs, interests, backgrounds, and abilities feel encouraged and included. Furthermore, the teacher must understand how to instill appropriate supports to accommodate the diverse needs of students and how to modify the classroom environment in such a way that is reflective of the diversity of the students.

### *Considerations for Teaching in Diverse Classrooms*

#### Ethnically Diverse Classrooms

As society becomes increasingly diverse, teachers will certainly encounter classrooms with students of multiple ethnicities. Thus, to create an accepting and respectful classroom environment that allows for success in learning for all students, there are several factors to consider. Teachers must educate themselves on the various ethnicities within their classroom. This includes being mindful of the **social norms, values, beliefs, traditions,** and **lifestyles** of different ethnic groups and learning to communicate with students and families in a respectful, culturally sensitive manner. Additionally, teachers must make a conscious effort to incorporate aspects of each ethnicity into the curriculum, activities, and classroom environment to create an inclusive atmosphere that teaches the acceptance, respect for, and celebration of differences. Teachers must be **culturally competent** and ensure that all materials are accurate, relevant, authentic, and portray the different ethnicities within the classroom in a respectful, unbiased manner. Furthermore, teachers must consider how their own ethnicity impacts their teaching style and interactions with students, how they may be perceived by other ethnic groups, and how to respond in a manner that fosters respect and inclusivity.

#### Gender-Diverse Classrooms

When approaching a gender-diverse classroom, teachers need to consider their perceptions and expectations of different genders as well as their interactions with different genders. Teachers should also consider how the classroom environment and materials portray gender differences. Teachers must work to eliminate possible stereotypical beliefs so that all students feel respected, accepted, and encouraged to participate. Furthermore, teachers must consider how their behavior acts as a model for how students perceive gender roles and should act in a way that eliminates gender divisiveness. Teachers should use gender-neutral language when addressing students and ensure that all students receive equal attention. Teachers must maintain equal academic and behavioral expectations between genders and be sure to equally praise and discipline students so that neither gender feels superior or inferior to another. Regarding curriculum and classroom materials, teachers must ensure that the classroom environment encourages equal participation in, access to, and choice of all activities and procedures. Activities and materials should provide equal opportunities and foster collaboration between genders. Furthermore, teachers must ensure that curriculum materials avoid gender stereotypes and highlight each gender equally in order to create an accepting and respectful learning environment that provides equal opportunities for students of all genders to develop their individual identities and abilities.

#### Linguistically Diverse Classrooms

In a **linguistically diverse** classroom, teachers must consider how to effectively demonstrate value for students' native languages while simultaneously supporting the development of necessary language skills to thrive in the school setting. By accepting and encouraging students to use their native languages, teachers can establish an inclusive learning environment that celebrates linguistic differences and encourages students to want to build upon their language skills. Through this, teachers create an equitable learning environment that allows for academic success. To develop English language skills, teachers must first consider each student's language ability, level of exposure to English prior to entering the classroom, and the level of language learning support each student has at home. Teachers can then implement effective instructional strategies and supports to modify curriculum in a way that addresses students' language needs. Teachers must also consider the implications of the classroom environment on language acquisition. By creating an atmosphere that encourages language acquisition through **literacy-rich resources** and **cooperative learning**, teachers promote the use of language skills and ultimately provide opportunities for success for all students.

### Linguistic Supports and Instructional Strategies for English Language Proficiency

Incorporating a variety of linguistic aids and instructional strategies is beneficial in supporting ELL students of varying levels of English language proficiency. **Visual representations** to accompany instruction, such as posters, charts, pictures, slide shows, videos, tables, or anchor charts, are valuable in providing clarification and reference while promoting vocabulary acquisition. When delivering instruction, **body language** such as hand gestures, eye contact, and movement to mimic verbal directions and explanations can provide clarification to enhance understanding. These students may also require **translation devices** for clarification, an interpreter to help with understanding instructions and new concepts, alternate assignments with simplified language, or **individualized instruction** from an ESL teacher. Frequently checking for understanding and providing clarification as necessary throughout instruction are necessary to ensuring ELL students understand learning materials, instructions, and assessments. In addition, creating a print- and literacy-rich environment is valuable in promoting English language acquisition. This can be done by including word walls for new vocabulary, reading materials that vary in complexity, labels, and opportunities for speaking, reading, and writing within instruction.

### Learning Disabilities and Other Exceptionalities

In a classroom where learning disabilities and exceptionalities are present, teachers must consider accommodations for students of various learning needs while fostering an atmosphere of respect and acceptance. Teachers must understand the individual learning needs of each student and differentiate instruction accordingly to create an equitable and inclusive learning atmosphere. For **learning disabled** students, teachers must consider accommodations that allow for inclusion in all areas of curriculum and instruction. Such considerations may include extended work time, individualized instruction, and cooperative learning activities to ensure that learning disabled students are provided the necessary supports to achieve academic success. For students with other exceptionalities, such as **gifted and talented** students, teachers need to consider ways to provide challenging and stimulating opportunities for expansion and enrichment of curriculum. Furthermore, teachers must be aware of their own interactions with students in order to demonstrate and encourage respect and acceptance among students. By providing supports for individual student success, teachers can effectively highlight students' strengths and teach students to accept and celebrate differences in learning abilities.

## Educating Students about Diversity

### *Goals of Teaching Diversity in the Classroom*

Teaching diversity in the classroom aims to establish a welcoming and inclusive classroom environment that encourages academic achievement and whole-child development. Diversity education works to develop students' understanding, acceptance, and respect for others' perspectives while instilling the concept that people are ultimately more alike than different and that diversity should be celebrated. Teaching the importance of differences creates a positive, inclusive classroom atmosphere in which all students feel respected, safe, and valued by their teacher and peers. Such an environment promotes academic achievement among students in that it encourages participation in learning and builds the self-esteem necessary for positive growth and development. Furthermore, teaching diversity has a significant role in **whole-child development** in that it instills the ability to understand and respect multiple frames of reference, thus increasing the child's ability to problem solve, cooperate with others, and develop a broader global perspective. Additionally, it allows for the development of cultural competency and ultimately creates accepting and respectful contributors to society.

**Review Video: Multiculturalism/Celebrating All Cultures**
Visit mometrix.com/academy and enter code: 708545

### *Recognizing and Eliminating Personal Biases*

Personal biases are often subtle and unconscious, yet it is essential that teachers work to recognize and eliminate them to create an accepting and respectful classroom environment. Personal biases may negatively impact teaching style, interactions with students, student learning, and self-esteem. In eliminating personal bias, teachers ensure that they establish an inclusive classroom environment where each student is treated fairly. Furthermore, students' beliefs toward diversity are influenced by the attitudes and behaviors modeled by their teacher; therefore, eradicating personal bias is vital in positively influencing students to accept and respect differences. To eliminate personal bias, teachers must **reflect** on their own culture's attitudes toward diversity as well as how these attitudes influence their interactions toward other groups, and work to make positive changes. Teachers must **educate** themselves on the diversities among their students and work to deepen their understanding of different groups through **communicating** with families, **integrating** themselves into students' communities, and participating in **professional development** that focuses on **cultural competency** and the importance of teaching diversity. Through making positive changes against personal biases, teachers foster a classroom environment that promotes diversity and empowers all students to be successful.

### *Impact of Diverse Cultural Climate in the Classroom*

Creating a diverse cultural climate in the classroom results in an empowering and engaging learning environment that facilitates academic success. An atmosphere that respects and accepts differences fosters a sense of inclusivity and welcoming among teachers and students, which allows students to feel comfortable with differences, safe in their own identities, and comfortable to engage in learning. This fosters a positive attitude toward learning that promotes academic achievement. Additionally, when students accept one another's differences in a diverse cultural climate, they are better able to work together and adopt creative problem-solving solutions through others' perspectives, which results in success in learning. Furthermore, a successfully diverse cultural climate reflects the diversity of the students within it, which ultimately creates a more engaging and relevant academic environment that sparks motivation and curiosity toward learning. Learning environments that reflect students' diversity create a sense of unity and belonging in the classroom and positively contribute to success in learning through building students' self-esteem and self-concept to empower them in believing they can achieve academic success.

### Authentic Classroom Materials

**Authentic classroom materials** are artifacts from various cultures, events, or periods of time. These items enhance the relevancy of instruction by promoting students' real-world connection to learning and may also be used to incorporate students' backgrounds and experiences into the classroom to increase engagement. Such materials include magazines, newspapers, advertisements, restaurant menus, and recipes. In addition, resources such as video clips, films, television shows, documentaries, news segments, and music serve as authentic media sources to incorporate into instruction. Original works or documents, including art pieces, literature, poetry, maps, or historical records, are also valuable authentic resources for providing students with a real-world learning experience.

#### Locating and Implementing

**Authentic classroom materials** and resources are integral in creating a classroom environment that fosters engaging, relevant, and positive learning experiences. Teachers must work to develop an understanding of the diversities among their students and use this knowledge to locate and implement authentic classroom materials into daily instruction. In doing so, teachers create a positive learning environment that accepts and respects differences through incorporating **relevant** and **familiar** materials that make students from all backgrounds feel valued and included in instruction. When students can see aspects of their culture reflected in authentic learning materials, they can make **personal connections** between what they are learning and their own lives. This makes learning become more valuable, engaging, and relevant, thereby promoting success in learning.

### Incorporating Diversity Education into the Classroom

Incorporating diversity into the classroom maximizes student opportunities for academic success through creating a welcoming, empowering, and inclusive atmosphere. Teachers can implement multiple strategies to incorporate **diversity education** into the curriculum both as its own unit and woven into content instruction once they develop an understanding of the diversities among their own students. Through **building relationships** with students, teachers can use their knowledge of students' lives to incorporate aspects of their backgrounds into the curriculum by creating specific **cultural lessons** on food, music, language, art, and history. Additionally, **cultural comparison** studies are an effective method of teaching students the value of diversity and highlighting the fact that people from different backgrounds often have more similarities than differences. Teachers can further implement diversity education by encouraging students to participate in learning through having them share elements of their culture and background with the class through activities such as show and tell or hosting family nights. Furthermore, integrating **cooperative learning** activities into instruction allows and encourages students from different backgrounds to work together and gain an understanding of the perspectives and backgrounds of others.

### Incorporating Diversity in the Curriculum

Incorporating diversity into the curriculum is vital for teaching the value and importance of differences and for contributing to a respectful and accepting environment. Additionally, it is imperative that diversity education extend from the curriculum to the entire classroom environment to maximize student growth and opportunity to reach potential. When students learn in an atmosphere that celebrates diversity and identifies strengths in differences, they feel a sense of belonging and confidence that encourages them to engage in learning, thus maximizing the potential for academic success. Teachers can effectively integrate diversity into the classroom environment through making authentic cultural materials such as texts, music, and art readily accessible for students. Additionally, providing several opportunities for students to collaborate and socialize in a natural setting allows them to gain an understanding and respect for their peers' backgrounds. By encouraging students to share aspects of their own lives and backgrounds with the class through cultural activities, teachers facilitate a diverse climate that celebrates differences.

### *Culturally Responsive Teaching*

**Culturally responsive teaching** is an instructional approach in which the teacher practices awareness, inclusivity, and sensitivity regarding the social and cultural diversities that are present within the classroom. With this awareness in mind, the culturally responsive teacher designs curriculum, instruction, activities, and assessments that are inclusive and reflective of students' social and cultural backgrounds and experiences. When planning instruction and learning experiences, teachers can demonstrate awareness of social and cultural norms through consciously educating themselves on the beliefs, values, and norms of their students. This is achieved through connecting with students and building positive relationships to learn about their individual backgrounds and locate authentic learning materials that are reflective of their experiences. Through communicating with students' parents, family members, and members of the community, teachers can practice and build awareness of the diverse social and cultural norms of their students to gain an understanding of how to design culturally responsive instruction. By educating themselves on the social and cultural norms of their students, teachers can effectively ensure that students' diversities are reflected in all areas of instruction in a culturally sensitive manner to create an empowering learning environment that engages all students.

| Practices for Culturally Responsive Teaching | |
|---|---|
| 1 | Create an inclusive classroom environment. |
| 2 | Recognize personal biases and work to eliminate them. |
| 3 | Self-educate on the community and students' social and cultural backgrounds. |
| 4 | Use curriculum that reflects students' diversities using authentic materials. |
| 5 | Frequently communicate with students' families. |
| 6 | Build positive interpersonal relationships with students. |
| 7 | Be involved in the community. |

## Instructional Techniques

### *Implementing Multiple Instructional Techniques to Maximize Student Learning*

Incorporating multiple instructional techniques into the classroom maximizes student learning by enhancing intellectual involvement and overall engagement. When instructional material is presented through a variety of means, it facilitates an **active learning** environment in which students' interest is captured and they are motivated to participate in learning. Varying teaching strategies stimulates engagement and fosters achievement by encouraging students to actively participate in their own learning and implement critical thinking skills to consider information more deeply. Students' understanding is strengthened when content is presented in different ways through various instructional techniques by providing them with multiple frames of reference for making connections and internalizing new concepts. In addition, utilizing multiple instructional techniques allows the teacher to effectively **differentiate instruction** to access multiple learning styles and address individual student needs to ensure understanding and enhance the overall learning process.

### *Instructional Strategies to Differentiate Instruction*

Implementing a variety of strategies for differentiation helps to ensure that instruction appeals to students' varying learning styles and needs. By incorporating **multiple modalities** into direct instruction, such as visual representations, written directions, video or audio clips, songs, graphs, or mnemonic devices, teachers can differentiate the presentation of new concepts and information. Using strategies to differentiate instructional activities is also beneficial in diversifying the learning experience. By providing opportunities for **independent, collaborative**, and **hands-on** learning, teachers can ensure that learning is accessible and engaging to all students. In addition, learning activities should allow for a degree of flexibility in order to appeal to students' varying needs and preferences. Activities such as task cards, educational technology resources, and learning stations provide this **flexibility** and allow for a student-directed experience in which students can choose to learn in the way that best suits their needs. Similarly, assigning open-ended projects as summative assessments allows for a degree of **student-choice**, thus differentiating the method in which students demonstrate their understanding.

### *Varying the Teacher and Student Roles in the Instructional Process*

Varying the roles of the teacher and students as an instructional technique is beneficial in creating an engaging, dynamic classroom environment that maximizes learning. When different roles are implemented, instruction is diversified, thus stimulating student interest and engagement. In addition, certain teacher and student roles are most applicable and effective in specific learning situations. When teachers acknowledge this and understand when to adopt and assign particular roles, they can effectively deliver instruction in a way that deepens student understanding and fosters success in learning. In presenting new content, directions, or modeling new skills, for example, the roles of **lecturer** and student **observer** are effective. In hands-on learning situations, students can take on the role of **active participant** while the teacher acts as a **facilitator** to create a student-centered and engaging learning environment in which students are given ownership over their own learning. Such variation enhances intellectual involvement by promoting critical thinking and problem-solving skills through self-directed learning. Skillfully assigning different roles throughout the learning process also allows the teacher to effectively address students' individual learning needs and preferences to promote engagement and enhance the learning experience.

### *Fostering Intellectual Involvement and Engagement*

Effective instruction includes a variety of strategies for fostering intellectual involvement and engagement to promote academic success. Presenting instruction using various approaches provides multiple avenues for learning new content, thus ensuring and strengthening student understanding to facilitate achievement. In addition, diversifying instructional strategies creates variety in the classroom that effectively stimulates students' interest and motivation to engage in learning. Strategies such as **cooperative learning**, **discussion**, and **self-directed opportunities** encourage active student participation that enhances intellectual involvement by allowing students to build on background knowledge, deepen understanding by exploring others' perspectives, and take ownership over their own learning. This ultimately increases student engagement and motivation for success in learning. Similarly, incorporating **inquiry**, **problem-solving**, and **project-based** strategies promotes curiosity in learning, creativity, and the development of critical thinking skills that stimulate intellectual participation and engagement to create a productive learning environment. Implementing **digital resources** and media throughout instruction is integral in enhancing academic success by making learning relevant, interesting, and differentiated to accommodate various learning needs. At the end of a lesson or activity, allowing students the opportunity to reflect is a valuable strategy in increasing intellectual involvement, retainment, and academic success by facilitating personal connections with learning to build understanding.

### *Actively Engaging Students by Incorporating Discussion into Instruction*

Classroom discussion is a valuable instructional technique in engaging students throughout the learning process. When teachers skillfully pose higher-level questions in discussions, they establish an active learning environment in which students are encouraged and motivated to participate, thus enhancing overall engagement. Effective discussions prompt students to become **intellectually invested** in instruction by promoting the use of **critical** and **higher-order thinking** skills to consider information more deeply and devise creative solutions to problems. In addition, discussions stimulate engagement by providing students the opportunity to express their own thoughts and reasoning regarding a given topic to establish a sense of ownership over their learning. Furthermore, discussions foster a collaborative learning environment that actively engages students by prompting them to understand others' perspectives, consider alternative approaches, and build on one another's experiences to make deeper connections to learning.

### *Promoting Student Inquiry*

The promotion of inquiry is a valuable instructional technique in enhancing student engagement and intellectual involvement. In an **inquiry-based** learning environment, students are encouraged to explore instructional material and devise their own conclusions or solutions to problems. This increases the effectiveness of the learning process by providing students with a sense of agency over their own learning. In addition, implementing this strategy fosters curiosity, self-motivation, and active participation, as it allows for hands-on, **student-led** learning that increases overall engagement. Incorporating inquiry into the classroom stimulates critical and higher-order thinking skills as students construct their own understanding by interacting with learning materials, analyzing their findings, and synthesizing their learning to create new conclusions, results, and responses. To effectively incorporate inquiry into the learning process, the teacher must provide several opportunities for self-directed learning, project-based learning, and student choice to stimulate curiosity. Questions must be open-ended, and students must be encouraged to hypothesize, predict, and experiment in their learning. The teacher must be flexible in instruction to allow space and opportunity for exploration and allow time for reflection and extended learning opportunities to facilitate further inquiry.

### *Incorporating Problem-Solving into Instruction*

Providing opportunities for creative problem solving within instruction effectively creates an engaging and successful learning experience. Students become more **intellectually involved** when encouraged to actively participate in learning and utilize **critical thinking skills** to test hypotheses, analyze results, and devise creative solutions to problems. This hands-on, **student-directed** approach promotes success in learning by allowing students to interact with learning materials as they seek answers to complex ideas and problems in an engaging environment. Problem-solving enables students to make deeper connections to their learning to enhance understanding, as this strategy prompts them to employ and develop background knowledge. In addition, problem-solving activities allow for collaborative learning in which students can actively engage with peers to build on one another's knowledge and experience, thus enhancing successful learning.

### *Intellectual Involvement, Active Student Engagement, and Success in Learning*

A productive learning environment is composed intellectually involved students that are actively engaged in successful learning. A strong correlation exists between **intellectual involvement**, **active student engagement**, and **success in learning**, and each component is necessary for effective instruction. Effective instruction consists of challenging students based on their abilities and teaching them to think deeply about new ideas and concepts. This ultimately encourages students' intellectual involvement, as it prompts them to utilize their critical thinking skills to build on their background knowledge, consider alternative perspectives, and synthesize their learning to devise creative solutions. When students are intellectually involved in instruction, they become more personally invested and engaged, as learning becomes relevant, interesting, and challenging. Engaged students are active participants in their learning, thus enhancing their overall productivity and academic success.

### *Effectively Structuring Lessons*

When developing instruction, it is imperative that the teacher is knowledgeable on how to effectively structure lessons to maximize student engagement and success. Each lesson must include a clear **objective** and explicitly state the process for achieving it. To initiate engagement, effective lessons begin with an **opening**, or "warm-up," activity to introduce a new topic, diagnose student understanding, and activate prior knowledge. Instruction of new material must be delivered through a variety of teaching strategies that are consciously tailored to students' individual learning needs to enhance participation and ensure comprehension. Direct instruction should be followed by **active learning** activities with clear directions and procedures to allow students to practice new concepts and skills. Throughout a successful lesson, the teacher checks frequently for understanding and comprehension by conducting a variety of **formative assessments** and adjusts instruction as necessary. Including **closure** activities is essential to successful learning, as it gives students the opportunity to reflect, process information, make connections, and demonstrate comprehension. In structuring lessons effectively according to students' learning needs, the teacher establishes a focused and engaging learning environment that promotes academic success.

**Example of a Daily Lesson Plan Structure**

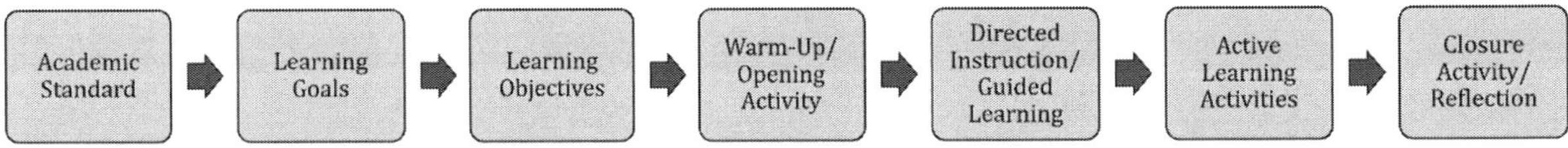


### *Flexible Instructional Groupings*

**Flexible instructional groupings** provide the teacher and students with a versatile, engaging environment for successful learning. Skillfully grouping students allows for productive, cooperative learning opportunities in which individual strengths are enhanced and necessary support is provided, thus enhancing motivation and engagement. When working in groups, students' understanding of instruction is strengthened, as they are able to learn and build upon one another's background knowledge, perspectives, and abilities. Instructional groups can include students of the **same** or **varied abilities** depending on the learning objective and task to increase productivity and provide scaffolding as necessary for support. This strategy is effective in enabling the teacher to **differentiate** instruction and adjust groups as needed to accommodate varying learning styles, abilities, and interests to maximize engagement and success in learning.

### *Effective Pacing of Lessons and Importance of Flexibility to Students' Needs*

Effective pacing is imperative to focused and engaging instruction. Teachers must be conscientious of the pace of their instruction and ensure that it is reflective of their students' learning needs and sustains their attention. Instruction that is delivered too quickly results in confusion and discouragement, whereas if instruction is too slow, students will lose interest and become disengaged. A well-paced lesson states clear learning goals and objectives while clearly outlining the means to achieve them to elicit student motivation. The teacher must consider the most **efficient** and **engaging** instructional strategies for presenting new material to establish a steady pace and maintain it by incorporating smooth **transitions** from one activity to the next. It is important that teachers are conscious of the rate of instruction throughout all stages of learning while maintaining **flexibility** in pacing in order to be responsive to their students. As individual students have different learning needs and processing times, they may require a faster or slower rate of instruction to understand new concepts and remain engaged in learning. Frequent checks for understanding and reflection activities are essential strategies in determining if the pace of instruction must be adjusted to accommodate students' needs.

### *Connecting Content to Students' Prior Knowledge and Experiences*

Implementing effective instructional strategies for connecting content to students' prior knowledge and experiences enhances the relevancy of learning and fosters deeper connections that strengthen understanding. To achieve this, teachers must educate themselves on students' backgrounds, experiences, communities, and interests to determine what is important and interesting to them. With this knowledge in mind, teachers can successfully locate and implement **authentic materials** into instruction to enhance relevancy. Additionally, encouraging students to bring materials to class that reflect their backgrounds and including these materials in instruction makes learning relevant by allowing students to make **personal connections** to content. Instructional strategies such as brainstorming, KWL charts, prereading, and anticipation guides allow the teacher to determine what students know prior to learning a new concept, thus enabling them to connect content to students' background knowledge in a relevant way. Incorporating digital resources further enhances relevancy in learning. Teachers can locate videos or audio clips that relate to instruction and reflect students' background experiences and interests. Using digital resources to introduce a new concept is a valuable strategy in developing students' **schema** on a topic to build prior knowledge and make learning meaningful by fostering connections.

#### Making Learning Relevant and Meaningful

For learning to be relevant and meaningful, it is essential that teachers present content in a way that connects with students' **prior knowledge** and experiences. When students are able to apply new ideas and information to what they already know through effective instructional techniques, it facilitates strong **personal connections** that make learning relevant and meaningful. In addition, personal connections and **relevancy** are strengthened when teachers consciously incorporate materials to reflect students' individual backgrounds and experiences in instruction. Linking content to students' background experiences enables them to relate instruction to real-world situations, thus establishing a sense of purpose for learning by making it applicable to their lives. Intentionally connecting content with students' prior knowledge and experiences enhances the effectiveness of the instructional process and fosters positive attitudes toward learning.

#### Enhancing Student Engagement and Success in Learning

Engaging instruction employs a variety of instructional strategies and materials to create a relevant, meaningful, and successful learning experience. Effective content establishes a clear and applicable purpose for instruction that increases student participation in the learning process. Presenting relevant and meaningful content enhances understanding and engagement by enabling students to create real-world, **personal connections** to learning based upon their own backgrounds and experiences. In addition, when instruction is tailored to reflect students' unique interests and preferences, content becomes more appealing and students' willingness to learn is enhanced. When students can perceive content through their own frames of reference with instructional materials that reflect their unique differences, they are able to effectively internalize and relate information to their lives, thus increasing engagement. Engaged learning ultimately facilitates academic success in that when students are motivated to learn, they demonstrate positive attitudes toward learning and are more likely to actively participate.

## Adapting Instruction to Individual Needs

### *Evaluating Activities and Materials to Meet Learning Needs*

The careful selection of instructional activities and materials is integral to accommodating students' varying characteristics and needs. When evaluating the appropriateness of activities and materials, several considerations must be made. Teachers must consider whether activities and materials align with state and district **academic standards**. Teachers must also evaluate the quality and effectiveness of the activities and materials in supporting students' unique differences as they achieve learning goals and objectives. All materials and activities must be **developmentally appropriate** across domains yet adaptable to individual students' learning needs. In addition, they must be challenging yet feasible for student achievement relative to students' grade levels and abilities to promote engagement and the development of critical and **higher-order thinking** skills. Teachers must evaluate activities and materials for versatility to allow for student choice and differentiation in order to address varying characteristics and needs. Teachers must also ensure that activities and materials are accurate, **culturally sensitive**, and reflective of students' diversities to foster an inclusive learning environment that promotes engagement.

#### Instructional Resources and Technologies

The implementation of varied instructional resources and technologies is highly valuable in supporting student engagement and achievement. Effective use of resources and technologies requires teachers to evaluate their appropriateness in addressing students' individual characteristics and learning needs for academic success. Teachers must be attuned to students' unique differences in order to seek high quality technologies and resources that address their students' needs and support the achievement of learning goals and objectives. Technologies and resources must be **accurate**, **comprehensible**, easily **accessible** to students, and **relevant** to the curriculum and the development of particular skills. Teachers must also consider the grade-level and **developmental appropriateness** of technologies and resources as well as their adaptability to allow for differentiation. Effective technologies and resources are interactive, engaging, and multifaceted to allow for varying levels of complexity based on students' abilities. This allows teachers to provide appropriate challenges while diversifying instruction to appeal to varied characteristics and learning needs, thus fostering an engaging environment that supports success in learning for all students.

### *Adapting Activities and Materials to Meet Individual Characteristics and Needs*

In effective instruction, activities and materials are adapted to accommodate students' individual characteristics and needs. Teachers must be attuned to students' unique differences and understand how to adjust activities and materials accordingly to facilitate academic success and growth. To achieve this, teachers must incorporate a **variety** of activities and materials that appeal to all styles of learners. Activities and materials should provide **student choice** for engagement in learning and demonstration of understanding. By differentiating instruction, teachers can effectively scaffold activities and materials to provide supports as necessary as well as include extensions or alternate activities for enrichment. **Chunking** instruction, allowing extra time as necessary, and accompanying activities and materials with aids such as graphic organizers, visual representations, and anticipation guides further differentiates learning to accommodate students' learning characteristics and needs. Conducting **formative assessments** provides teachers with valuable feedback regarding student understanding and engagement, thus allowing them to modify and adjust the complexity of activities and materials as necessary to adapt to varied characteristics and learning differences.

#### Instructional Resources and Technologies

When teachers understand students' individual characteristics and needs, they can adapt instructional resources and technologies accordingly to maximize learning. To do so effectively, the teacher must incorporate a diverse array of **multifaceted** resources and technologies that support and enhance learning through a variety of methods. This ensures that varying learning needs are met, as students of all learning styles are provided with several avenues for building and strengthening understanding. Additionally, the teacher can adapt resources and technologies to accommodate individual students by **varying the complexity** to provide challenges, support, and opportunities for enrichment based on ability level. Supplementing technologies and resources with **scaffolds**, such as extra time, visual representations, or opportunities for collaborative learning, further enables the teacher to adapt to individual learning needs. When effectively implemented and adapted to students' characteristics and needs, instructional technologies and resources serve as valuable tools for differentiating curriculum to enhance the learning experience.

## Flexible and Responsive Instructional Practices

### *Evaluation of Instruction*

Evaluating the appropriateness of instructional materials, activities, resources, and technologies is integral to establishing a successful learning environment. Doing so provides students with high-quality and inclusive instruction by ensuring **clarity**, **accuracy**, **relevancy**, and **reflection** of student diversities. By determining whether these components of instruction meet varying characteristics and learning needs, the teacher can deliver **student-centered** instruction that is challenging based on individual ability and promote development and academic success. This process also allows the teacher to effectively **differentiate** instruction to provide necessary personalized support for success in achieving learning targets as well as create engaging learning opportunities tailored to students' unique differences and interests. Effectively determining the appropriateness of activities, materials, resources, and technologies in meeting students' learning needs ultimately maximizes academic achievement and fosters positive attitudes toward learning that establish a foundation for future success.

### *Continuous Monitoring of Instructional Effectiveness*

Successful instruction must be flexible and adaptable to meet students' dynamic learning needs. To achieve this, teachers must continuously monitor the effectiveness of their instruction to determine if their teaching strategies, activities, and communication are effective. Frequent evaluation of instructional effectiveness is necessary to ensure that students understand **foundational concepts** before moving on to more advanced concepts. **Adaptations** to instruction, communication, or assessment may be necessary to ensure students are able to comprehend and retain concepts before moving on to more advanced topics. **Remediation** of missed concepts is often much more challenging and less successful than checking for comprehension within context and providing more detailed instruction. This ultimately fosters long-term achievement, as the teacher can identify and address student needs as they arise and prevent compounding issues. Continuous monitoring enables the teacher to ensure that learning opportunities are engaging, relevant, and challenging based on students' ability levels, as it provides immediate feedback on the effectiveness of instruction, which allows the teacher to make necessary changes. This ultimately enhances instruction by establishing a student-centered learning environment that is tailored to individual needs, interests, and abilities.

#### Pre-Instructional, Peri-Instructional, and Post-Instructional Strategies

Instructional effectiveness must be monitored on a whole-class and individual level throughout all stages of teaching. Prior to instruction, administering **pre-tests** provides teachers with insight regarding whole-class and individual understanding. This enables teachers to select effective and appropriate instructional strategies that can be differentiated to meet individual needs. Pre-tests allow teachers to identify and clarify misunderstandings before instruction to ensure effectiveness. During instruction, **observation** of students' participation in instruction during independent and group activities enables the teacher to evaluate overall and individual understanding and engagement. Frequent checks for understanding and **formative assessments** throughout instruction provide feedback on whole-group and individual learning, as the teacher can assess understanding and participation to adapt teaching strategies or individualize instruction. Leading student discussions allows the teacher to identify areas of misunderstanding among the class or individuals who may need reteaching through a different approach. Closure and reflection activities after instruction are valuable in monitoring effectiveness, as they indicate both whole-class and individual comprehension and retainment of new concepts. Likewise, incorporating **summative assessments** and analyzing the results provides teachers with information regarding the overall effectiveness of their teaching process as well as students' individual strengths and weaknesses to consider for future instruction.

### Applying Feedback to Make Necessary Changes to Instruction

Continuous monitoring of instruction indicates the instruction's effectiveness on a **whole-class** and **individual** level, as it provides the teacher with immediate insight into student understanding, progress, and areas for improvement. Monitoring instructional effectiveness enables the teacher to evaluate students' **pace** in achieving learning goals and adjust the rate of instruction as necessary. Additionally, it allows the teacher to identify whole-class and individual **misconceptions** that require correction to ensure students do not fall behind schedule in meeting academic benchmarks. If monitoring reveals misunderstanding among the whole class, the teacher must alter the overall instructional approach and teaching strategies to clarify and regain understanding. Individual misconceptions indicate the need to differentiate instruction, adjust groupings, and provide supports and remediation as necessary to ensure the student progresses at the same rate as the rest of the class. By identifying student strengths and weaknesses through consistent monitoring of instructional effectiveness, the teacher can effectively make instructional decisions that are attuned to whole-class and individual student needs to maximize learning.

## *Flexibility in Instruction*

### Situations Requiring Flexibility

The classroom environment is dynamic in nature. Teachers will inevitably encounter situations throughout instruction and assessment in which **flexibility** is integral to successful teaching and learning. As students have varying learning styles, needs, and interests, teachers may find that their instructional approaches are ineffective in maintaining engagement and may need to adjust strategies, activities, or assessments to better meet learning needs. Students may have difficulty grasping new material, which could result in a lack of engagement in instructional activities and, potentially, disruptive behavior. Teachers must consistently be attuned to students' levels of comprehension and allow flexibility in their lesson plans to modify strategies, activities, or pacing as necessary to facilitate engagement and understanding before advancing in instruction. Students may also progress more quickly than others through instructional activities or assessments. **Scaffolding** activities to include opportunities for extension and enrichment allow for flexibility within instruction and ensure that all students are adequately challenged and engaged in learning. Throughout instruction and assessments, teachers may find valuable, unexpected learning opportunities. By remaining open and flexible to these instances, teachers can enhance the learning process and strengthen student understanding by incorporating them into instruction.

## Enhancing the Overall Learning Experience

**Flexibility** is an integral component of effective instruction, as it enables the teacher to adequately address and accommodate students' individual needs and interests for maximized success in learning. When teachers consider their lesson plans as **frameworks** while allowing for flexibility, they demonstrate an awareness of their students' individual differences and the potential for deviation from original instruction. This enables them to more effectively modify instructional and assessment strategies, activities, and approaches to create a **responsive**, **student-centered** environment that enhances the overall learning experience and promotes achievement. When instructional activities and assessments are adaptable to accommodate students' needs and interests, learning becomes more personalized and relevant, thus strengthening understanding and increasing motivation to engage in active learning. A flexible approach to instruction and assessment also provides students with the ability to explore content of interest on a deeper level and potentially encounter unanticipated learning opportunities that foster personal connections and enhance learning. In addition, this approach allows for **versatility** in assessment, as flexibility enables the teacher to modify assessments by providing necessary support to meet students' individual needs and supports students' choice in demonstrating learning.

## Poor Student Comprehension

Throughout instruction and assessments, students may have difficulty **comprehending** new or difficult material despite being engaged in instruction. This may lead to confusion that can cause students to become discouraged and disengaged in learning as well as have continued and compounded difficulty in grasping increasingly complex concepts. Difficulties with comprehension hinders academic success, as students who struggle face challenges in building the foundation of understanding necessary for advancing through curriculum. To ensure student comprehension throughout all stages of learning, the teacher must be aware of students' individual learning styles and needs and be able to respond flexibly to obstacles they may encounter. **Formative assessments** during instruction enable the teacher to evaluate the level of student comprehension and identify areas of need for flexible **adjustment** or additional support. This includes modifying **pacing** and allowing additional time for student processing to ensure understanding. In addition, the original lesson plan may require **chunking** into smaller, more manageable parts to allow students to internalize new concepts before moving on. The teacher may also need to respond flexibly to students' needs during instruction by **differentiating** teaching strategies, activities, groupings, or assessments to ensure that material is accessible and comprehensible to all students for enhanced success.

## Unanticipated Learning Opportunities

**Unanticipated learning opportunities**, when embraced by the teacher, are often highly valuable in establishing a classroom environment that promotes student engagement, motivation, and success. These instances often divert from the original lesson plan, but when utilized effectively, they serve to strengthen student understanding and foster **personal connections** for an enhanced learning experience. Facilitating such opportunities allows students to investigate topics that are interesting and relevant to them on a deeper level, thus increasing active engagement and promoting **self-directed** learning. This ultimately supports students in forming connections and recognizing the real-world applications of their learning, which increases the likelihood that they will internalize and **retain** new information. Responding flexibly to unanticipated learning opportunities includes acknowledging students' questions and comments as well as demonstrating an awareness of their individual differences and learning needs. This enables the teacher to maximize the effectiveness of these opportunities by facilitating student-led instruction that is attuned to their learning styles, interests, and preferences for enhanced engagement and achievement.

### Conducting Ongoing Assessments and Making Adjustments

Conducting **ongoing assessments** throughout instruction provides teachers with continuous feedback regarding student comprehension, engagement, and performance. When practiced consistently, teachers are more attuned and responsive to students' individual learning needs. This enables them to effectively modify instructional strategies, activities, and assessments accordingly for a **student-centered** learning environment that provides the support necessary for enhanced engagement, comprehension, and achievement. It allows teachers to identify and address areas of **misconception** and student need to ensure understanding prior to progressing through the curriculum. Feedback from ongoing evaluation of student performance indicates areas of instruction in which adjustment is necessary to effectively support students in achieving learning goals. Teachers may need to adjust their pacing to ensure comprehension and engagement as well as differentiate instruction based on feedback regarding individual progress to ensure all students are adequately challenged and supported based on their ability levels. Student groupings may need to be adjusted to scaffold instruction and facilitate increased comprehension. When teachers effectively apply feedback from ongoing assessments of student engagement and performance, they can tailor instruction to accommodate their individual needs and interests to enhance success in learning.

### Progressing Ahead of Schedule

Throughout instruction, teachers will encounter instances in which individual students or the whole class progresses **faster than anticipated**. When this arises, the teacher must be prepared to respond flexibly to ensure that all students are engaged, on task, and challenged based on their ability levels. Lesson plans should be **scaffolded** to include opportunities for enrichment and extended learning for students who finish before others. This includes incorporating materials such as increasingly complex texts, practice activities, and project opportunities. Teachers can also establish a designated area in the classroom in which individuals or small groups that finish early can participate in **extended learning** or **review** activities that reinforce learning objectives. Such activities allow students to explore instructional topics on a deeper level for strengthened understanding and ensure they are engaging productively in meaningful activities that are relevant to instruction. When the whole class progresses faster than expected, the teacher can respond flexibly by incorporating **total participation** activities to reinforce instructional material. Activities such as review games, class discussions, and digital resources for extra practice ensure that the class remains engaged in instruction when they finish a lesson early.

## Schedules, Routines, and Activities for Young Children

### *Ideal Schedule for Young Children*

An ideal schedule for young children reflects their developmental characteristics and capabilities to maximize their learning. A **predictable** routine is necessary for young children to feel secure in their learning environment, so each day should follow a similar schedule while allowing room for **flexibility** if an activity takes longer than expected. Each day should begin with a clear routine, such as unpacking, a warm-up activity, and a class meeting to allow students to share thoughts, ask questions, and allow the teacher to discuss what will occur that day. This establishes a positive tone for the day while focusing the attention on learning. Similarly, the end of the day should have a specific routine, such as cleaning up materials and packing up for dismissal. Young children learn best by physically interacting with and exploring their environments. As such, each day should include large blocks of time for **active movement** throughout the day in the form of play, projects, and learning centers. Periods of **rest** must follow such activities, as this enables young children to process and internalize what they learned. **Direct instruction** should occur before active movement periods and last approximately 15-20 minutes to sustain engagement and attention toward learning.

| Example Daily Schedule for the Early Childhood Education Classroom | |
|---|---|
| 8:00-8:30 | Welcome, unpack, morning work |
| 8:30-8:45 | Circle time, review class calendar |
| 8:45-9:30 | Literacy/language arts |
| 9:30-10:15 | Learning stations |
| 10:15-11:00 | Math |
| 11:00-11:30 | Music/dance/movement |
| 11:30-12:15 | Lunch |
| 12:15-1:00 | Recess/unstructured play |
| 1:00-1:20 | Rest/quiet time |
| 1:20-2:00 | Science |
| 2:00-2:45 | Creative arts |
| 2:45-3:15 | Daily reflection, pack up, dismissal |

Some examples of restful and active movement activities for young children are discussed below:

- **Restful:** Incorporating restful activities into the early childhood classroom are beneficial in helping young children process and retain new concepts and providing them the opportunity to unwind after active movement activities. Examples of such activities include nap time, class meditation, self-reflection activities, independent art projects, or self-selected reading time. Teachers can also read aloud to students or play an audiobook during these periods.
- **Active:** Providing young children with multiple opportunities for active movement throughout the day is beneficial in promoting the development of gross motor skills, connections to learning, and the ability to function in a group setting. Active movement opportunities should include whole-class, small group, and independent activities. Examples include class dances, songs, games, nature walks, or total participation activities such as gallery walks or four corners. Physical education activities, such as jump rope, tag, sports, or using playground equipment are also beneficial. Young children should also be provided with ample time for both structured and unstructured play throughout the day.

### *Balancing Restful and Active Movement Activities*

A schedule that balances **rest** and **active movement** is necessary for positive cognitive, physical, emotional, and social development in young children. Connecting learning to active movement strengthens students' understanding of new concepts, as it allows them to physically explore and interact with their environment, experiment with new ideas, and gain new experiences for healthy **cognitive development**. In addition, incorporating active movement encourages the use of **gross motor skills** and provides students with the space to physically express themselves in an appropriate setting, thus promoting physical and emotional development. Active movement also encourages the development of positive **interpersonal skills** as young children interact and explore with one another. Restful periods are equally as important to the development of young children. Incorporating rest after a period of active movement further strengthens young children's connection to learning by providing them the opportunity to reflect, process, and internalize new information.

### *Providing Large Blocks of Time for Play, Projects, and Learning Centers*

Providing young children with ample time for play, projects, and learning centers throughout the school day is integral to fostering their development across domains. Young children learn most effectively through active movement as they physically interact with their environment, and incorporating large blocks of time for such activities allows them to do so. Significant time dedicated to active play, projects, and learning centers on a variety of topics allows young children to explore and experiment with the world around them, test new ideas, draw conclusions, and acquire new knowledge. This supports healthy **physical** and **cognitive development**, as it provides young children the opportunity to engage in learning across subject areas while connecting it to active movement for strengthened understanding. In addition, allowing large blocks of time for these activities is necessary for **social** and **emotional development**, as it provides young children the space to interact with one another and develop important skills such as cooperation, sharing, conflict resolution, and emotional self-regulation. Dedicating large blocks of time to play, projects, and learning centers establishes a student-led, hands-on learning environment that is reflective of the developmental characteristics and needs of young children.

### *Characteristics of Young Children in Relation to Interactions with Others*

Designing group activities that align with the ability of young children to collaborate while supporting social development requires a realistic understanding of their capacity to do so. This entails understanding the **developmental characteristics** of young children at varying stages, including how the nature of their interactions with others evolves. Young children learn by exploring and interacting with their environments, so they need ample opportunities for play and active movement to do so; however, the teacher must recognize that the way young children play and collaborate develops over time. Young children typically exhibit little interest in actively playing with others until approximately age four. Until then, they progress through stages of solitary play, observing their peers, playing independently alongside others, and, eventually, loosely interacting (sometimes with the same toys) while still primarily engaging in independent play. During these stages, it is important that teachers foster **collaboration** by providing multiple opportunities for play as well as learning materials that encourage **cooperation** and **sharing**. The teacher must, however, maintain the understanding that these children have yet to develop the capacity to intentionally work with others. Once this ability is developed, the teacher can integrate coordinated group activities that encourage collaboration toward a common goal.

### *Considerations When Designing Group Activities for Young Children*

For young children, thoughtfully designed group activities are integral in promoting development across domains. These opportunities facilitate social and emotional development by encouraging collaboration and positive communication. They also facilitate physical and cognitive growth by allowing children to play, explore, and interact with others in the learning environment. It is important that teachers carefully consider the particulars of group activities when planning to ensure maximized learning and development. Teachers must consider the **developmental characteristics** of their students' age groups, including their capacity to collaborate with others. This enables the teacher to plan group activities that align with students' abilities while promoting collaboration and development. All **learning materials** must be carefully selected to encourage collaboration, sharing, and the development of positive social skills at a developmentally appropriate level. The teacher must also consider **desired learning outcomes** and the nature of the learning taking place to determine whether group activities should be structured or unstructured. Unstructured play is valuable in allowing students to develop their social and emotional skills in a natural setting, whereas structured, teacher-led group activities allow for more focused learning. Desired outcomes also determine the size of groups for the activity to best promote collaboration and learning.

### *Activities that Reflect and Develop Young Children's Ability to Collaborate*

Young children benefit from a variety of **whole-class** and **small-group** activities designed to reflect and develop their collaborative skills. When the teacher incorporates group activities to encourage cooperation, sharing, and positive interactions, young children gain important social and emotional skills necessary for development across domains. Whole-group activities such as **circle time** provide young children with the opportunity to interact with others, express ideas, and ask questions in a developmentally appropriate setting. This activity develops important collaborative skills, such as taking turns, active listening, and respectful communication. Other **whole-group activities**, such as reading aloud, group songs, dances, games, or class nature walks, are effective in teaching young children how to productively contribute to and function in a group setting. **Small-group activities** can be incorporated throughout all aspects of structured and unstructured learning to develop young children's collaborative skills. Learning centers, such as a science area, pretend play area, or building block center, provide materials that encourage collaboration while allowing students to interact with others according to their abilities in a student-led setting. Problem-solving activities, such as puzzles, games, age-appropriate science experiments, or scavenger hunts, are effective in teaching young children how to work together toward a common goal.

### *Managing Group Activities to Promote Collaborative Skills and Accountability*

Well-planned group activities are beneficial in developing students' collaborative skills and sense of individual accountability. Such group activities are well-organized, effectively managed, and intentionally structured with a **clear goal** or problem that must be solved while allowing room for creativity to enhance the collaborative process. When designing these activities, the teacher must incorporate enough **significant components** to ensure all students within the group can productively contribute. If the assignment is too simple, students can easily complete it on their own, whereas a multifaceted activity instills a sense of interdependence within the group that fosters the development of collaborative skills. To promote individual accountability, **meaningful roles** and responsibilities should be assigned to each group member because when students feel others are relying on their contributions to complete a task, they develop a sense of ownership that motivates active participation. To further develop collaborative skills and individual accountability, students should be graded both as a **whole group** and **individually**. This encourages group cooperation while ensuring that students' individual contributions are recognized. Including **self-assessments** at the end of group activities is beneficial in allowing students to reflect on the quality of their contributions to the group and ways they could improve their collaborative skills.

Thoughtful consideration of how to best organize and manage collaborative activities helps establish an environment that supports students in learning to work together productively and assume responsible roles within a group. When planning group activities, the teacher must consider the **desired learning outcomes** and the **nature of the task** to determine whether there are enough significant components that would benefit from collaboration. **Group size** must also be considered to most effectively foster collaboration and individual accountability when assuming responsible roles. Groups with too few students may be inadequate for addressing all the components of a complex task, whereas grouping too many students together limits productive collaboration and makes it difficult for each member to assume a significant, responsible role. The teacher must be selective regarding which students are grouped together to best facilitate productive collaboration. This includes determining which students will work well together as well as grouping students that may need support with those who can provide scaffolding. It is also important to consider how **responsibilities** will be divided to ensure each member is given a significant role that allows him or her to contribute productively to the group. How students' contributions will be monitored and **assessed** should also be considered.

## Assessment Methodology

### *Assessment Methods*

Effective teaching requires multiple methods of assessment to evaluate student comprehension and instructional effectiveness. Assessments are typically categorized as diagnostic, formative, summative, and benchmark and are applicable at varying stages of instruction. **Diagnostic** assessments are administered before instruction and indicate students' prior knowledge and areas of misunderstanding to determine the path of instruction. **Formative** assessments occur continuously to measure student engagement, comprehension, and instructional effectiveness. These assessments indicate instructional strategies that require adjustment to meet students' needs in facilitating successful learning and include strategies like checking for understanding, observations, total participation activities, and exit tickets. **Summative** assessments are given at the end of a lesson or unit to evaluate student progress in reaching learning targets and identify areas of misconception for reteaching. Such assessments can be given in the form of exams and quizzes or be project-based activities in which students demonstrate their learning through hands-on, personalized methods. Additionally, portfolios serve as valuable summative assessments in allowing students to demonstrate their progress over time and provide insight regarding individual achievement. **Benchmark** assessments occur less frequently and encompass large portions of curriculum. These assessments are intended to evaluate the progress of groups of students in achieving state and district academic standards.

#### Assessment Types

- **Diagnostic:** These assessments can either be formal or informal and are intended to provide teachers with information regarding students' level of understanding prior to beginning a unit of instruction. Examples include pretests, KWL charts, anticipation guides, and brainstorming activities. Digital resources, such as online polls, surveys, and quizzes are also valuable resources for gathering diagnostic feedback.
- **Formative:** These assessments occur throughout instruction to provide the teacher with feedback regarding student understanding. Examples include warm-up and closure activities, checking frequently for understanding, student reflection activities, and providing students with color-coded cards to indicate their level of understanding. Short quizzes and total participation activities, such as four corners, are also valuable formative assessments. Numerous digital resources, including polls, surveys, and review games, are also beneficial in providing teachers with formative feedback to indicate instructional effectiveness.
- **Summative:** Summative assessments are intended to indicate students' levels of mastery and progress toward reaching academic learning standards. These assessments may take the form of written or digital exams and include multiple choice, short answer, or long answer questions. Examples also include projects, final essays, presentations, or portfolios to demonstrate student progress over time.
- **Benchmark:** Benchmark assessments measure students' progress in achieving academic standards. These assessments are typically standardized to ensure uniformity, objectivity, and accuracy. Benchmark assessments are typically given as a written multiple choice or short answer exam, or as a digital exam in which students answer questions on the computer.

**Review Video: Formative and Summative Assessments**
Visit mometrix.com/academy and enter code: 804991

### Determining Appropriate Assessment Strategies

As varying assessment methods provide different information regarding student performance and achievement, the teacher must consider the most applicable and effective assessment strategy in each stage of instruction. This includes determining the **desired outcomes** of assessment as well as the information the teacher intends to ascertain and how they will apply the results to further instruction. **Age-** and **grade-level-**appropriateness must be considered when selecting which assessment strategies will enable students to successfully demonstrate their learning. Additionally, the teacher must be cognizant of students' individual differences and learning needs to determine which assessment model is most **accommodating** and reflective of their progress. It is also important that teachers consider the practicality of assessment strategies and methods they will use to implement the assessment for maximized feedback regarding individual and whole-class progress in achieving learning goals.

### Assessments That Reflect Real-World Applications

Assessments that reflect **real-world applications** enhance relevancy and students' ability to establish personal connections to learning that deepen understanding. Implementing such assessments provides authenticity and enhances engagement by defining a clear and practical purpose for learning. These assessments often allow for hands-on opportunities for demonstrating learning and can be adjusted to accommodate students' varying learning styles and needs while measuring individual progress; however, assessments that focus on real-world applications can be subjective, thus making it difficult to extract concrete data and quantify student progress to guide future instructional decisions. In addition, teachers may have difficulty analyzing assessment results on a large scale and comparing student performance with other schools and districts, as individual assessments may vary.

### Diagnostic Tests

**Diagnostic tests** are integral to planning and delivering effective instruction. These tests are typically administered prior to beginning a unit or lesson and provide valuable feedback for guiding and planning instruction. Diagnostic tests provide **preliminary information** regarding students' levels of understanding and prior knowledge. This serves as a baseline for instructional planning that connects and builds upon students' background knowledge and experiences to enhance success in learning. Diagnostic tests allow the teacher to identify and clarify areas of student misconception prior to engaging in instruction to ensure continued comprehension and avoid the need for remediation. They indicate areas of student strength and need as well as individual instructional aids that may need to be incorporated into lessons to support student achievement. In addition, these tests enable the teacher to determine which instructional strategies, activities, groupings, and materials will be most valuable in maximizing engagement and learning. Diagnostic tests can be **formal** or **informal** and include pre-tests, pre-reading activities, surveys, vocabulary inventories, and graphic organizers (such as KWL charts). These tests are used to assess student understanding prior to engaging in learning. Diagnostic tests are generally not graded, as there is little expectation that all students in a class possess the same baseline of proficiency at the start of a unit.

### Formative Assessments

Formative assessments are any assessments that take place in the **middle of a unit of instruction**. The goals of formative assessments are to help teachers understand where a student is in his or her progress toward **mastering** the current unit's content and to provide the students with **ongoing feedback** throughout the unit. The advantage of relying heavily on formative assessments in instruction is that it allows the teacher to continuously **check for comprehension** and adjust instruction as needed to ensure that the whole class is adequately prepared to proceed at the end of the unit. To understand formative assessments well, teachers need to understand that any interaction that can provide information about the student's comprehension is a type of formative assessment which can be used to inform future instruction.

Formative assessments are often a mixture of formal and informal assessments. **Formal formative assessments** often include classwork, homework, and quizzes. Examples of **informal formative assessments** include simple comprehension checks during instruction, class-wide discussions of the current topic, and exit slips, which are written questions posed by teachers at the end of class, which helps the teacher quickly review which students are struggling with the concepts.

### *Summative Assessments*

**Summative assessment** refers to an evaluation at the end of a discrete unit of instruction, such as the end of a course, unit, or semester. Classic examples of summative assessments include end-of-course assessments, final exams, or even qualifying standardized tests such as the SAT or ACT. Most summative assessments are created to measure student mastery of particular **academic standards**. Whereas formative assessment generally informs current instruction, summative assessments are used to objectively demonstrate that each individual has achieved adequate mastery of the standards in question. If a student has not met the benchmark, he or she may need extra instruction or may need to repeat the course.

These assessments usually take the form of **tests** or formal portfolios with rubrics and clearly defined goals. Summative assessments are usually high-stakes, heavily-weighted, and they should always be formally graded. These types of assessments often feature a narrower range of question types, such as multiple choice, short answer, and essay questions to help with systematic grading.

**Project-based** assessments are beneficial in evaluating achievement, as they incorporate several elements of instruction and highlight real-world applications of learning. This allows students to demonstrate understanding through a hands-on, individualized approach that reinforces connections to learning and increases retainment. **Portfolios** of student work over time serve as a valuable method for assessing individual progress toward reaching learning targets. Summative assessments provide insight regarding overall instructional effectiveness and are necessary for guiding future instruction in subsequent years but are not usually used to modify current instruction.

> **Review Video: Assessment Reliability and Validity**
> Visit mometrix.com/academy and enter code: 424680

### *Benchmark Assessments*

**Benchmark assessments** are intended to quantify, evaluate, and compare individual and groups of students' achievement of school-wide, district, and state **academic standards.** They are typically administered in specific intervals throughout the school year and encompass entire or large units of curriculum to determine student mastery and readiness for academic advancement. Benchmark assessments provide data that enable the teacher to determine students' progress toward reaching academic goals to guide current and continued instruction. This data can be utilized by the school and individual teachers to create learning goals and objectives aligned with academic standards. It can also be used to plan instructional strategies, activities, and assessments to support students in achieving these academic standards. In addition, benchmark assessments provide feedback regarding understanding and the potential need for remediation to allow the teacher to instill necessary supports in future instruction that prepare students for success in achieving learning targets.

### Alignment of Assessments with Instructional Goals and Objectives

To effectively monitor student progress, assessments must align with **instructional goals** and **objectives**. This allows the teacher to determine whether students are advancing at an appropriate pace to achieve state and district academic standards. When assessments are aligned with specific learning targets, the teacher ensures that students are learning relevant material to establish a foundation of knowledge necessary for growth and academic achievement. To achieve this, teachers must determine which instructional goals and objectives their students must achieve and derive instruction, content, and activities from these specifications. Instruction must reflect and reinforce learning targets, and the teacher must select the most effective strategies for addressing students' needs as they work to achieve them. Assessments must be reflective of content instruction to ensure they are aligned with learning goals and objectives, as well as to enable the teacher to evaluate student progress in mastering them. The teacher must clearly communicate learning goals and objectives throughout all stages of instruction to provide students with clarity on expectations. This establishes a clear purpose and focus for learning that enhances relevancy and strengthens connections to support student achievement.

### Clearly Communicating Assessment Criteria and Standards

Students must be clear on the purpose of learning throughout all stages of instruction to enhance understanding and facilitate success. When assessment **criteria** and **standards** are clearly communicated, the purpose of learning is established, and students are able to effectively connect instructional activities to learning goals and criteria for assessment. Communicating assessment criteria and standards provides students with clarity on tasks and learning goals they are expected to accomplish as they prepare themselves for assessment. This allows for more **focused instruction** and engagement in learning, as it enhances relevancy and student motivation. Utilizing appropriate forms of **rubrics** is an effective strategy in specifying assessment criteria and standards, as it informs students about learning goals they are working toward, the quality of work they are expected to achieve, and skills they must master to succeed on the assessment. Rubrics indicate to students exactly how they will be evaluated, thus supporting their understanding and focus as they engage in learning to promote academic success.

#### Rubrics for Communicating Standards

The following are varying styles of rubrics that can be used to communicate criteria and standards:

- **Analytic:** Analytic rubrics break down criteria for an assignment into several categories and provide an explanation of the varying levels of performance in each one. This style of rubric is beneficial for detailing the characteristics of quality work as well as providing students with feedback regarding specific components of their performance. Analytic rubrics are most effective when used for summative assessments, such as long-term projects or essays.
- **Holistic:** Holistic rubrics evaluate the quality of the student's assignment as a whole rather than scoring individual components. Students' scores are determined based upon their performance across multiple performance indicators. This style of rubric is beneficial for providing a comprehensive evaluation but limits the amount of feedback that students receive regarding their performance in specific areas.
- **Single-point:** Single-point rubrics outline criteria for assignments into several categories. Rather than providing a numeric score to each category, however, the teacher provides written feedback regarding the students' strengths and ways in which they can improve their performance. This style of rubric is beneficial in providing student-centered feedback that focuses on their overall progress.

- **Checklist:** Checklists typically outline a set of criteria that is scored using a binary approach based upon completion of each component. This style increases the efficiency of grading assignments and is often easy for students to comprehend but does not provide detailed feedback. This method of grading should generally be reserved for shorter assignments.

#### COMMUNICATING HIGH ACADEMIC EXPECTATIONS IN ASSESSMENTS

The attitudes and behaviors exhibited by the teacher are highly influential on students' attitudes toward learning. Teachers demonstrate belief in students' abilities to be successful in learning when they communicate **high academic expectations**. This promotes students' **self-concept** and establishes a **growth mindset** to create confident, empowered learners that are motivated to achieve. High expectations for assessments and reaching academic standards communicates to students the quality of work that is expected of them and encourages them to overcome obstacles as they engage in learning. When communicating expectations for student achievement, it is important that the teacher is aware of students' individual learning needs to provide the necessary support that establishes equitable opportunities for success in meeting assessment criteria and standards. Setting high expectations through assessment criteria and standards while supporting students in their learning enhances overall achievement and establishes a foundation for continuous academic success.

#### EFFECTIVE COMMUNICATION AND IMPACT ON STUDENT LEARNING

Communicating high academic expectations enhances students' self-concept and increases personal motivation for success in learning. To maximize student achievement, it is important that the teacher set high academic expectations that are **clearly** communicated through **age-appropriate** terms and consistently reinforced. Expectations must be reflected through learning goals and objectives and must be **visible** at all times to ensure student awareness. Teachers must be **specific** in communicating what they want students to accomplish and clearly detail necessary steps for achievement while assuming the role of facilitator to guide learning and provide support. Providing constructive **feedback** throughout instruction is integral in reminding students of academic expectations and ensuring they are making adequate progress toward reaching learning goals. When high academic expectations are communicated and reinforced, students are empowered with a sense of confidence and self-responsibility for their own learning that promotes their desire to learn. This ultimately enhances achievement and equips them with the tools necessary for future academic success.

### *ANALYZING AND INTERPRETING ASSESSMENT DATA*

Teachers can utilize multiple techniques to effectively analyze and interpret assessment data. This typically involves creating charts and graphs outlining different data subsets. They can list each learning standard that was assessed, determine how many students overall demonstrated proficiency on the standard, and identify individual students who did not demonstrate proficiency on each standard. This information can be used to differentiate instruction. Additionally, they can track individual student performance and progress on each standard over time.

Teachers can take note of overall patterns and trends in assessment data. For example, they can determine if any subgroups of students did not meet expectations. They can consider whether the data confirms or challenges any existing beliefs, implications this may have on instructional planning and what, if any, conclusions can be drawn from this data.

Analyzing and interpreting assessment data may raise new questions for educators, so they can also determine if additional data collection is needed.

### USING ASSESSMENT DATA TO DIFFERENTIATE INSTRUCTION FOR INDIVIDUAL LEARNERS

By analyzing and interpreting assessment data, teachers can determine if there are any specific learning standards that need to be retaught to their entire classes. This may be necessary if the data shows that all students struggled in these specific areas. Teachers may consider reteaching these standards using different methods if the initial methods were unsuccessful.

Teachers can also form groups of students who did not demonstrate proficiency on the same learning standards. Targeted instruction can be planned for these groups to help them make progress in these areas. Interventions can also be planned for individual students who did not show proficiency in certain areas. If interventions have already been in place and have not led to increased learning outcomes, the interventions may be redesigned. If interventions have been in place and assessment data now shows proficiency, the interventions may be discontinued.

If assessment data shows that certain students have met or exceeded expectations in certain areas, enrichment activities can be planned to challenge these students and meet their learning needs.

### *ALIGNING ASSESSMENTS WITH INSTRUCTIONAL GOALS AND OBJECTIVES*

Assessments that are congruent to instructional goals and objectives provide a **clear purpose** for learning that enhances student understanding and motivation. When learning targets are reflected in assessments, instructional activities and materials become more **relevant**, as they are derived from these specifications. Such clarity in purpose allows for more focus and productivity as students engage in instruction and fosters connections that strengthen overall understanding for maximized success in learning. Aligning assessments with instructional goals and objectives ensures that students are learning material that is relevant to the curriculum and academic standards to ensure **preparedness** as they advance in their academic careers. In addition, it enables the teacher to evaluate and monitor student progress to determine whether they are progressing at an ideal pace for achieving academic standards. With this information, the teacher can effectively modify instruction as necessary to support students' needs in reaching desired learning outcomes.

### *NORM-REFERENCED TESTS*

On **norm-referenced tests**, students' performances are compared to the performances of sample groups of similar students. Norm-referenced tests identify students who score above and below the average. To ensure reliability, the tests must be given in a standardized manner to all students.

Norm-referenced tests usually cover a broad range of skills, such as the entire grade-level curriculum for a subject. They typically contain a few questions per skill. Whereas scores in component areas of the tests may be calculated, usually overall test scores are reported. Scores are often reported using percentile ranks, which indicate what percentage of test takers scored lower than the student being assessed. For example, a student's score in the 75th percentile means the student scored better than 75% of other test takers. Other times, scores may be reported using grade-level equivalency.

One advantage of norm-referenced tests is their objectivity. They also allow educators to compare large groups of students at once. This may be helpful for making decisions regarding class placements and groupings. A disadvantage of norm-referenced tests is that they only indicate how well students perform in comparison to one another. They do not indicate whether or not students have mastered certain skills.

### *Criterion-Referenced Tests*

**Criterion-referenced tests** measure how well students perform on certain skills or standards. The goal of these tests is to indicate whether or not students have mastered certain skills and which skills require additional instruction. Scores are typically reported using the percentage of questions answered correctly or students' performance levels. Performance levels are outlined using terms such as *below expectations*, *met expectations*, and *exceeded expectations*.

One advantage of criterion-referenced tests is that they provide teachers with useful information to guide instruction. They can identify which specific skills students have mastered and which skills need additional practice. Teachers can use this information to plan whole-class, small-group, and individualized instruction. Analyzing results of criterion-referenced tests over time can also help teachers track student progress on certain skills. A disadvantage of criterion-referenced tests is that they do not allow educators to compare students' performances to samples of their peers.

### *Ways That Standardized Test Results Are Reported*

- **Raw scores** are sometimes reported and indicate how many questions students answered correctly on a test. By themselves, they do not provide much useful information. They do not indicate how students performed in comparison to other students or to grade-level expectations.
- **Grade-level equivalents** are also sometimes reported. A grade-level equivalent score of 3.4 indicates that a student performed as well as an average third grader in the fourth month of school. It can indicate whether a student is performing above or below grade-level expectations, but it does not indicate that the student should be moved to a different grade level.
- **Standard scores** are used to compare students' performances on tests to standardized samples of their peers. Standard deviation refers to the amount that a set of scores differs from the mean score on a test.
- **Percentile ranks** are used on criterion-referenced tests to indicate what percentage of test takers scored lower than the student whose score is being reported.
- **Cutoff scores** refer to predetermined scores students must obtain in order to be considered proficient in certain areas. Scores below the cutoff level indicate improvement is needed and may result in interventions or instructional changes.

### *Formal and Informal Assessments*

Assessments are any method a teacher uses to gather information about student comprehension of curriculum, including improvised questions for the class and highly-structured tests. **Formal assessments** are assessments that have **clearly defined standards and methodology** and which are applied consistently to all students. Formal tests should be objective and scrutinized for validity and reliability since they tend to carry higher weight for the student. Summative assessments, such as end-of-unit tests, lend themselves to being formal tests because it is necessary that a teacher test the comprehension of all students in a consistent and thorough way.

Although formal assessments can provide useful data about student performance and progress, they can be costly and time-consuming to implement. Administering formal assessments often interrupts classroom instruction and may cause testing anxiety.

**Informal assessments** are assessments that do not adhere to formal objectives, and they do not have to be administered consistently to all students. As a result, they do not have to be scored or recorded as a grade and generally act as a **subjective measure** of class comprehension. Informal assessments can be as simple as asking the students to raise their hands if they are ready to proceed to the next step or asking a particular question of an individual student.

Informal assessments do not provide objective data for analysis, but they can be implemented quickly and inexpensively. Informal assessments can also be incorporated into regular classroom instruction and activities, making them more authentic and less stressful for students.

### USING VARIOUS ASSESSMENTS

The goal of **assessment** in education is to gather data that, when evaluated, can be used to further student learning and achievement. **Standardized tests** are helpful for placement purposes and to reflect student progress toward goals set by a school district or state. If a textbook is chosen to align with district learning standards, the textbook assessments can provide teachers with convenient, small-scale, regular checks of student knowledge against the target standard.

In order be effective, teachers must know where their students are in the learning process. Teachers use a multitude of **formal and informal assessment methods** to do this. Posing differentiated discussion questions is an example of an informal assessment method that allows teachers to gauge individual student progress rather than their standing in relation to a universal benchmark.

Effective teachers employ a variety of assessments, as different formats assess different skills, promote different learning experiences, and appeal to different learners. A portfolio is an example of an assessment that gauges student progress in multiple skills and through multiple media. Teachers can use authentic or performance-based assessments to stimulate student interest and provide visible connections between language-learning and the real world.

### ASSESSMENT RELIABILITY

**Assessment reliability** refers to how well an assessment is constructed and is made up of a variety of measures. An assessment is generally considered **reliable** if it yields similar results across multiple administrations of the assessment. A test should perform similarly with different test administrators, graders, test-takers, and over multiple iterations. Factors that affect reliability include the day-to-day wellbeing of the student (students can sometimes underperform), the physical environment of the test, the way it is administered, and the subjectivity of the scorer (with written-response assessments).

Perhaps the most important threat to assessment reliability is the nature of the **exam questions** themselves. An assessment question is designed to test knowledge of a certain construct. A question is reliable in this sense if students who understand the content answer the question correctly. Statisticians look for patterns in student marks, both within the single test and over multiple tests, as a way of measuring reliability. Teachers should watch out for circumstances in which a student or students answer correctly a series of questions about a given concept (demonstrating their understanding) but then answer a related question incorrectly. The latter question may be an unreliable indicator of concept knowledge.

#### MEASURES OF ASSESSMENT RELIABILITY

- **Test-retest reliability** refers to an assessment's consistency of results with the same test-taker over multiple retests. If one student shows inconsistent results over time, the test is not considered to have test-retest reliability.
- **Intertester reliability** refers to an assessment's consistency of results between multiple test-takers at the same level. Students at similar levels of proficiency should show similar results.

- **Inter-rater reliability** refers to an assessment's consistency of results between different administrators of the test. This plays an especially critical role in tests with interactive or subjective responses, such as Likert-scales, cloze tests, and short answer tests. Different raters of the same test need to have a consistent means of evaluating the test-takers' performance. Clear rubrics can help keep two or more raters consistent in scoring.
- **Intra-rater reliability** refers to an assessment's consistency of results with one rater over time. One test rater should be able to score different students objectively to rate subjective test formats fairly.
- **Parallel-forms reliability** refers to an assessment's consistency between multiple different forms. For instance, end-of-course assessments may have many distinctive test forms, with different questions or question orders. If the different forms of a test do not provide the same results, the test is said to be lacking in parallel-forms reliability.
- **Internal consistency reliability** refers to the consistency of results of similar questions on a particular assessment. If there are two or more questions targeted at the same standard and at the same level, they should show the same results across each question.

### *Assessment Validity*

**Assessment validity** is a measure of the relevancy that an assessment has to the skill or ability being evaluated and the degree to which students' performance is representative of their mastery of the topic of assessment. In other words, a teacher should ask how well an assessment's results correlate to what it is looking to assess. Assessments should be evaluated for validity on both the **individual question** level and as a **test overall**. This can be especially helpful in refining tests for future classes. The overall validity of an assessment is determined by several types of validity measures.

An assessment is considered **valid** if it measures what it is intended to measure. One common error that can reduce the validity of a test (or a question on a test) occurs if the instructions are written at a reading level the students can't understand. In this case, it is not valid to take the student's failed answer as a true indication of his or her knowledge of the subject. Factors internal to the student might also affect exam validity: anxiety and a lack of self-esteem often lower assessments results, reducing their validity as a measure of student knowledge.

An assessment has content validity if it includes all the **relevant aspects** of the subject being tested—if it is comprehensive, in other words. An assessment has **predictive validity** if a score on the test is an accurate predictor of future success in the same domain. For example, SAT exams purport to have validity in predicting student success in a college. An assessment has construct validity if it accurately measures student knowledge of the subject being tested.

#### Measures of Assessment Validity

- **Face validity** refers to the initial impression of whether an assessment seems to be fit for the task. As this method is subjective to interpretation and unquantifiable, it should not be used singularly as a measurement of validity.
- **Construct validity** asks if an assessment actually assesses what it is intended to assess. Some topics are more straightforward, such as assessing if a student can perform two-digit multiplication. This can be directly tested, which gives the assessment a strong content validity. Other measures, such as a person's overall happiness, must be measured indirectly. If an assessment asserted that a person is generally happy if he or she smiles frequently, it would be fair to question the construct validity of that assessment because smiling is unlikely to be a consistent measure of all peoples' general happiness.

- **Content validity** indicates whether the assessment is comprehensive of all aspects of the content being assessed. If a test leaves out an important topic, then the teacher will not have a full picture as a result of the assessment.
- **Criterion validity** refers to whether the results of an assessment can be used to **predict** a related value, known as **criterion**. An example of this is the hypothesis that IQ tests would predict a person's success later in life, but many critics believe that IQ tests are not valid predictors of success because intelligence is not the only predictor of success in life. IQ tests have shown validity toward predicting academic success, however. The measure of an assessment's criterion validity depends on how closely related the criterion is.
- **Discriminant validity** refers to how well an assessment tests only that which it is intended to test and successfully discriminates one piece of information from another. For instance, a student who is exceptional in mathematics should not be able to put that information into use on a science test and gain an unfair advantage. If the student is able to score well due to his or her mathematics knowledge, the science test did not adequately discriminate science knowledge from mathematics knowledge.
- **Convergent validity** is related to discriminant validity, but takes into account that two measures may be distinct but correlated. For instance, a personality test should distinguish self-esteem from extraversion so that they can be measured independently, but if an assessment has convergent validity, it should show a correlation between related measures.

### *Practicality*

An assessment is **practical** if it uses an appropriate amount of human and budgetary resources. A practical exam doesn't take very long to design or score, nor does it take students very long to complete in relation to other learning objectives and priorities. Teachers often need to balance a desire to construct comprehensive or content-valid tests with a need for practicality: lengthy exams consume large amounts of instruction time and may return unreliable results if students become tired and lose focus.

### *Assessment Bias*

An assessment is considered biased if it disadvantages a certain group of students, such as students of a certain gender, race, cultural background, or socioeconomic class. A **content bias** exists when the subject matter of a question or assessment is familiar to one group and not another. For example, a reading comprehension passage that discusses an event in American history would be biased against students new to the country. An **attitudinal bias** exists when a teacher has a pre-conceived idea about the likely success of an assessment of a particular individual or group. A **method bias** arises when the format of an assessment is unfamiliar to a given group of students. **Language bias** occurs when an assessment utilizes idioms, collocations, or cultural references unfamiliar to a group of students. Finally, **translation bias** may arise when educators attempt to translate content-area assessments into a student's native language—rough or hurried translations often result in a loss of nuance important for accurate assessment.

### *Authentic Assessments*

An authentic assessment is an assessment designed to closely resemble something that a student does, or will do, in the real world. For example, students will never encounter a multiple-choice test requiring them to choose the right tense of a verb, but they will encounter contexts in which they have to write a narration of an event that has antecedents and consequents spread out in time—like narrating their version of what caused a traffic accident. The latter is an example of a potential **authentic assessment**.

Well-designed authentic assessments require a student to exercise **advanced cognitive skills** (e.g., solving problems, integrating information, performing deductions), integrate **background knowledge**, and confront **ambiguity**. Research has demonstrated that mere language proficiency is not predictive of future language success—learning how to utilize knowledge in a complex context is an essential additional skill.

The terms "authentic" and "performance-based" are often used interchangeably when describing assessments; however, a performance-based assessment doesn't necessarily have to be grounded in a possible authentic experience.

### *Performance-Based Assessments*

A performance-based assessment is one in which students demonstrate their learning by performing a **task** rather than by answering questions in a traditional test format. Proponents of **performance-based assessments** argue that they lead students to use **high-level cognitive skills** since they focus on how to put their knowledge to use and plan a sequence of stages in an activity or presentation. They also allow students more opportunities to individualize their presentations or responses based on preferred learning styles. Research suggests that students welcome the chance to put their knowledge to use in real-world scenarios.

Advocates of performance-based assessments suggest that they avoid many of the problems of language or cultural bias present in traditional assessments, allowing more accurate assessment of how well students learned the underlying concepts. In discussions regarding English as a second language, they argue that performance assessments come closer to replicating what should be the true goal of language learning—the effective use of language in real contexts—than do more traditional exams. Critics point out that performance assessments are difficult and time-consuming for teachers to construct and for students to perform. Finally, performative assessments are difficult to grade in the absence of a well-constructed and detailed rubric.

### *Technology-Based Assessments*

**Technology-based assessments** provide teachers with multiple resources for evaluating student progress to guide instruction. They are applicable in most formal and informal instructional settings and can be utilized as formative and summative assessments. Technology-based assessments simplify and enhance the efficiency of determining comprehension and instructional effectiveness, as they quickly present the teacher with information regarding student progress. This data enables the teacher to make necessary adjustments to facilitate student learning and growth. Implementing this assessment format simplifies the process of aligning them to school and district academic standards. This establishes objectivity and uniformity for comparing results and progress among students. It also helps ensure that all students are held to the same academic expectations. While technology-based assessments are beneficial, there are some shortcomings to consider. This format may not be entirely effective for all learning styles in demonstrating understanding, as individualization in technology-based assessment can be limited. These assessments may not illustrate individual students' growth over time but rather their mastery of an academic standard, thus hindering the ability to evaluate overall achievement. As technology-based evaluation limits hands-on opportunities, the real-world application and relevancy of the assessment may be unapparent to students.

#### Advantages and Disadvantages of Technology-Based Assessments

Technology-based assessments can have many advantages. They can be given to large numbers of students at once, limited only by the amounts of technological equipment schools possess. Many types of technology-based assessments are instantly scored, and feedback is provided quickly.

Students are sometimes able to view their results and feedback at the conclusion of their testing sessions. Data can be quickly compiled and reported in easy-to-understand formats. Technology-based assessments can also often track student progress over time.

Technology-based assessments can have some disadvantages as well. Glitches and system errors can interfere with the assessment process or score reporting. Students must also have the necessary prerequisite technological skills to take the assessments, or the results may not measure the content they are designed to measure. For example, if students take timed, computer-based writing tests, they should have proficient typing skills. Otherwise, they may perform poorly on the tests despite strong writing abilities. Other prerequisite skills include knowing how to use a keyboard and mouse and understanding how to locate necessary information on the screen.

### *Portfolio Assessments*

A **portfolio** is a collection of student work in multiple forms and media gathered over time. Teachers may assess the portfolio both for evidence of progress over time or in its end state as a demonstration of the achievement of certain proficiency levels.

One advantage of **portfolio assessments** is their breadth. Unlike traditional assessments, which focus on one or two language skills, portfolios may contain work in multiple forms, such as writing samples, pictures, and graphs designed for content courses, video and audio clips, student reflections, teacher observations, and student exams. A second advantage is that they allow a student to develop work in authentic contexts, including in other classrooms and at home.

In order for portfolios to function as an objective assessment tool, teachers should negotiate with students in advance of what genres of work will be included and outline a grading rubric that makes clear what will be assessed, such as linguistic proficiency, use of English in academic contexts, and demonstrated use of target cognitive skills.

### *Curriculum-Based Assessments*

Curriculum-based assessments, also known as **curriculum-based measurements (CBM)**, are short, frequent assessments designed to measure student progress toward meeting curriculum **benchmarks**.

Teachers implement CBMs by designing **probes**, or short assessments that target specific skills. For example, a teacher might design a spelling probe, administered weekly, that requires students to spell 10 unfamiliar but level-appropriate words. The data from these assessments can be tracked over time to measure student progress toward defined grade-level goals.

CBM has several clear advantages. If structured well, the probes have high reliability and validity. Furthermore, they provide clear and objective evidence of student progress—a welcome outcome for students and parents who often grapple with less-clear and subjective evidence. Used correctly, CBMs also motivate students and provide them with evidence of their own progress; however, while CBMs are helpful in identifying areas of student weaknesses, they do not identify the causes of those weaknesses or provide teachers with strategies for improving instruction.

### *Textbook Assessments*

Textbook assessments are the assessments provided at the end of a chapter or unit in an approved textbook. **Textbook assessments** present several advantages for a teacher: they are already made; they are likely to be accurate representations of the chapter or unit materials; and, if the textbook has been prescribed or recommended by the state, it is likely to correspond closely to Common Core or other tested standards.

Textbook assessments can be limiting for students who lag in the comprehension of academic English or whose preferred learning style is not verbal. While textbooks may come with DVDs or recommended audio links, ESOL teachers will likely need to supplement these assessment materials with some of their own findings. Finally, textbook assessments are unlikely to represent the range of assessment types used in the modern classroom, such as a portfolio or performance-based assessments.

#### *PEER ASSESSMENT*

A peer assessment is when students grade one another's work based on a teacher-provided framework. **Peer assessments** are promoted as a means of saving teacher time and building student metacognitive skills. They are typically used as **formative** rather than summative assessments, given concerns about the reliability of student scoring and the tensions that can result if student scores contribute to overall grades. Peer assessments are used most often to grade essay-type written work or presentations. Proponents point out that peer assessments require students to apply metacognition, build cooperative work and interpersonal skills, and broaden the sense that the student is accountable to peers and not just the teacher. Even advocates of the practice agree that students need detailed rubrics in order to succeed. Critics often argue that low-performing students have little to offer high-performing students in terms of valuable feedback—and this disparity may be more pronounced in ESOL classrooms or special education environments than in mainstream ones. One way to overcome this weakness is for the teacher to lead the evaluation exercise, guiding the students through a point-by-point framework of evaluation.

## CLASSROOM ROUTINES AND PROCEDURES

### INFLUENCE ON CLASSROOM CLIMATE, PRODUCTIVITY, STUDENT BEHAVIOR, AND LEARNING

A well-managed classroom focused on productivity, positive behavior, and success in learning relies on the effectiveness and consistency of **routines** and **procedures** instilled for daily activities. By implementing these at the beginning of the school year and continuously reinforcing them throughout, the teacher establishes an orderly, efficient classroom that facilitates students' ability to productively engage in learning. Classroom management, student behavior, and productivity are enhanced by structured routines and procedures, as students who understand expectations are more inclined to follow them. Such structure provides students with a sense of predictability and security in their environment that contributes to their willingness to participate in learning. Routines and procedures simplify daily tasks and allow for smooth transitions between activities. This minimizes opportunities for student distraction or disruption, thus promoting positive behavior, increasing instructional time, and enhancing students' ability to focus on learning in an orderly, productive classroom climate.

**Review Video: Classroom Management - Rhythms of Teaching**
Visit mometrix.com/academy and enter code: 809399

### CONSIDERATIONS REGARDING AGE-APPROPRIATENESS TO ENSURE EFFECTIVENESS

Classroom procedures and routines must reflect the characteristics and capabilities of the **age group** of the students. It is important that teachers understand and apply their knowledge of students' **developmental levels** across domains when considering which routines and procedures to establish in their classrooms. In doing so, teachers ensure that expectations are age-appropriate, realistic, and effective in creating an orderly, productive environment. Procedures and routines must always be clear, succinct, and limited in number to avoid overwhelming students; however, in communicating them, the teacher must use comprehensible language relative to students' age-groups. The nature of learning must be considered when determining age-appropriate routines and procedures. For young children, procedures for cleaning up toys after playtime is appropriate, whereas procedures for turning in homework and taking assessments applies to older students. The degree to which students are expected to perform routines and procedures independently must also be considered and reflective of their capabilities. Young children may need a great deal of assistance, whereas older students can perform certain tasks independently. Consequences for not following expectations must be appropriate to students' age groups. Losing free play time may be appropriate for young children, whereas parent communication may be effective for older students.

### EXAMPLES OF AGE-APPROPRIATE ROUTINES AND PROCEDURES

**Young children:** Young children can reasonably be expected to perform **basic daily routines** independently, although they likely will need frequent reminders. Daily procedures may include having young children hang up their coats, put away lunchboxes, and unpack their backpacks at the beginning of the day as they prepare to begin morning work. Similarly, young children can be expected to independently follow end-of-day procedures and routines, such as packing up their backpacks, cleaning up learning materials, and lining up at the door for dismissal. Young children should be able to follow simple behavioral procedures as well, such as keeping hands to themselves, responding to attention signals from the teacher, and cleaning up learning materials before transitioning between activities. Young children also benefit from being assigned classroom "jobs," such as line leader, paper collector, or teacher assistant, as these routines instill a sense of accountability and self-responsibility.

**Middle-level:** Middle-level students can be expected to follow a variety of routines and procedures with **increasing levels of independence**. These students can reasonably be expected to enter the classroom on time and prepare necessary learning materials. In addition, middle-level students can be held responsible for independently turning in homework according to the procedures for doing so and beginning their morning work. Middle-level students should be able to follow procedures for accessing learning materials, transitioning to cooperative learning activities, cleaning up their own materials before moving to a new activity, and non-instructional tasks, such as sharpening pencils, using the restroom, or throwing away trash with minimal reminders from the teacher.

**High school:** Routines and procedures in the high school classroom should **reflect** students' levels of **maturity and increasing capabilities for independence** as they approach adulthood. These students can reasonably be expected to independently come to class on time, prepared, and follow procedures for turning in homework and beginning morning work. In addition, high school students can be expected to follow procedures for direct instruction, cooperative learning activities, and independently transitioning between activities. High school students can be held to a greater degree of accountability regarding grading procedures, tardiness and attendance, and procedures for turning in late assignments.

### FACILITATING AN ORGANIZED, PRODUCTIVE ENVIRONMENT THAT MAXIMIZES STUDENT LEARNING

Clear routines and procedures for daily classroom activities are necessary to create an organized, productive environment that maximizes student learning. In order to be effective, routines and procedures must be reflective of the teacher's **instructional** and **classroom management** style, explicitly stated, and consistently reinforced. This ensures expectations are relevant, realistic, and that students are continuously aware of them as they engage in learning. Procedures for entering and exiting the classroom as well as how students will begin and end their day, establish a structured, **predictable** routine that enhances focus on instruction. Smooth **transition procedures** maintain order and enhance efficiency when moving between activities, as they eliminate idle time, minimize student distraction, and allow for increased time dedicated to productive teaching and learning. Such transition procedures include how and when to access and clean up materials, move from independent to collaborative group work, or move between learning stations. The teacher must also consider procedures for performing non-instructional activities, such as sharpening pencils or going to the restroom, as these further avoid disruptions to instructional time. Procedures and routines establish organization and efficiency in the classroom by simplifying tasks to allow for increased productive instructional time and enhanced student learning.

While the specifics of routines may vary depending upon the teacher's classroom management style and students' learning needs, many common procedures and routines share similar guidelines.

- **Entering the classroom/morning routine:** A procedure for the beginning of class ensures that students enter the room in an orderly manner with a clear understanding of what is expected of them. This routine should include entering the room quietly, unpacking necessary items for class, turning in homework, and working on an opening activity while the teacher takes attendance.
- **Leaving the classroom/packing up routine:** A procedure for packing up and leaving the classroom at the end of class or the school day ensures that students have all of their necessary materials, leave the room clean and organized, and exit in an orderly manner. Such a routine may include cleaning up learning materials, putting away assignments or papers, straightening desks, throwing away trash, packing up backpacks, and lining up by the door prior to dismissal. Students may be assigned specific jobs for cleaning up and organizing the room.
- **Turning in work:** Procedures for turning in classwork and homework allow for smoother transitions between activities and limit interruptions to instruction. This should occur at a specific time during the class period and can include designating a "turn in" box in the classroom for students to hand in assignments, or having students pass their papers to the front in a specific order. A student may be designated to collect papers at the end of an activity as well.
- **Using the restroom:** Restroom procedures limit student distraction and interruptions to instruction. Restroom breaks should generally not occur during direct instruction, and students should be permitted to go one at a time to avoid misbehavior. Students should be given a restroom pass, sign out before leaving the room, and sign back in upon returning to ensure that the teacher is always aware of students' whereabouts. Specific hand signals in which students can silently request permission to use the restroom are beneficial in further minimizing disruptions.
- **Transitions between activities:** Procedures for transitions allow for an orderly learning environment in that they indicate to students when and how to move between activities in the classroom. These procedures should include an attention signal and a clear explanation of the steps for transitioning, such as cleaning up materials from the previous activity, and a signal to indicate when students are permitted to move. Students should be expected to transition between activities quickly, quietly, and without disruption.
- **Non-instructional tasks:** Procedures for non-instructional tasks limit interruptions to instructional time for more focused learning. Activities such as getting a tissue, sharpening pencils, and throwing away trash should occur during specific times when the teacher is not directly instructing and should be done quietly and without disruption.
- **Managing student behavior:** Clear procedures for misbehavior establish a predictable, orderly learning environment. These procedures should be explicit, consistent, and follow a logical sequence. They may include a verbal warning, seating change, loss of privileges, or communication with home.

- **Accessing and using materials, supplies, and technology:** Procedures for these activities are beneficial in limiting disruption, maintaining organization, and avoiding interruptions to instruction. Such procedures indicate when and how to access and use materials, supplies, and technology in a respectful and orderly manner. The teacher should clearly communicate expectations for access and use as well as utilize a specific signal to indicate when students are permitted to move. These procedures should also include methods for proper cleanup at the end of the activity.
- **Finishing work early:** A procedure for finishing work early minimizes idle time and limits student disruption. Students who finish early may be permitted to work on other assignments or read quietly, or the teacher can dedicate an area of the room for extra practice and review activities for students to work on if they finish early. The teacher may also permit early finishers to assist other students in applicable learning situations.
- **Emergency drills:** Procedures for emergency drills ensure that students know how to complete them in a safe, orderly manner. When the drill begins, students should immediately stop what they are doing, leave all materials on their desks, and line up by the door in an organized fashion. Students should exit the room with the teacher and move quickly and quietly through the hallways to the designated drill location. For emergency drills that occur inside the classroom, students should move quickly and quietly to a previously designated location within the room and remain there until the drill is over.
- **Attention signal:** A dedicated signal to capture students' attention indicates that they need to stop what they are doing, focus, and listen quietly to the teacher for further information or instructions. This signal could be in the form of a hand signal, call and response, phrase, or sound and should be used consistently.
- **Direct instruction:** A procedure for direct instruction is beneficial in maintaining students' focus on learning. This should include steps for active listening, including sitting up straight, facing the teacher, maintaining eye contact, and refraining from distracting neighboring classmates. Students should have clear steps regarding how to ask questions, such as raising their hands or utilizing color-coded cards to indicate levels of understanding, and how to take notes, when applicable.
- **Independent work:** An independent work procedure limits distractions and promotes students' ability to focus. This should include communicating expectations for quiet time during this period, including refraining from talking to neighboring peers, working at and remaining in assigned seats, and engaging in the proper procedure if a student finishes early. A student can indicate a need for assistance by raising a hand or utilizing a dedicated signal to request help, such as color-coded cards.
- **Collaborative work:** A procedure for collaborative work indicates to students how to move from independent to group activities. This includes moving to a group setting without disruption, maintaining a normal volume, communicating respectfully, and cleaning up materials when finished before moving back to assigned seats in an orderly manner.

### *Non-Instructional Duties and Instructional Activities Maximizing Efficiency*

Many non-instructional duties, such as taking attendance, grading papers, and facilitating communication, can be coordinated with instructional activities when effective **routines** and **procedures** are instilled to accomplish them. This enhances overall efficiency in the classroom, as time is not lost on completing administrative tasks, allowing more time dedicated to instruction. Taking attendance, for example, can be incorporated into students' morning work routines, as they can mark their own presence as part of the procedure for entering the classroom and beginning the day. Grading and communication with colleagues or families can take place during independent work, assessments, or recreational time. The teacher can also observe, monitor, and assess students' progress as they engage in learning. Student **self-correction** in lieu of formal grading can be beneficial in allowing students to reflect on their performance, seek areas for improvement, and strengthen their understanding while integrating grading as an instructional activity. In addition, a variety of **digital resources** are available that allow for immediate student feedback and communication with families throughout instruction. In utilizing such resources, the teacher can efficiently coordinate administrative duties with instructional activities to maximize time for student learning.

### *Effective Time Management*

Practicing effective time management is beneficial in establishing an efficient, orderly classroom environment focused on productivity and maximizing student learning. By instilling specific **procedures** for managing daily routines such as transitioning, accessing materials and supplies, and using technology, the teacher can ensure that these tasks are completed in a timely manner while minimizing time lost on non-instructional activities and student distraction. This allows more time to be focused on instruction and student learning. To achieve this, procedures for such tasks must be **explicit** and consistently reinforced. Prior to transitioning between activities, accessing materials, or using technology, the teacher must provide a clear, detailed explanation of each step of the procedure as well as expectations for how students will complete it. Modeling the procedure is beneficial in providing a visual example to ensure student understanding. In order to be effective, each procedure must include a specific **signal** to indicate when students can begin, and the teacher must consistently monitor to ensure students are completing the task correctly. When students have a clear understanding on how to accomplish daily activities, they can do so quickly, effectively, and without disruption. This increases overall efficiency in the classroom and maximizes time dedicated to student learning.

### *Using Technology to Perform Administrative Tasks*

Technology resources are widely available to assist teachers in accomplishing a variety of administrative tasks and are highly beneficial in establishing a **well-managed**, **organized**, and **productive** learning environment. Tasks such as taking attendance, maintaining gradebooks, or facilitating communication can be completed more efficiently through the use of technology. This allows for more time dedicated to productive teaching and learning as well as smoother transitions between activities, as time is not lost on completing such duties. Increased efficiency in completing administrative duties is beneficial in sustaining students' attention, engagement, and productivity in learning, as it minimizes idle time that could lead to distraction or disruption. In addition, utilizing technology to perform administrative duties enhances overall organization, as all tasks performed digitally can be stored in a single area on the device used for easy access and recall of information. Through email, digital apps, or class websites, the teacher can efficiently communicate with colleagues and students' families to update them regarding important events, assignments, and individual progress. This creates a sense of connectedness between the teacher and community that contributes to a positive, productive classroom climate.

### *Volunteers and Paraprofessionals*

#### Enhancing and Enriching Instruction

**Paraprofessionals** and **volunteers** are highly valuable in enhancing and enriching the overall learning experience, as their efforts contribute to an organized, positive, and productive classroom environment. These aides collaborate with the teacher throughout planning and instruction to implement best practices in meeting students' learning needs. Paraprofessionals and volunteers can lead small groups of students as they engage in instruction for a more focused, **student-centered** learning experience. They can also provide additional support to struggling students while the teacher engages in whole-class instruction. Specifically, paraprofessionals are typically licensed in the educational field and are qualified to provide **individual accommodations** to students with individual learning needs to create an inclusive learning environment. In addition, working with paraprofessionals and volunteers is beneficial in creating an efficient, organized classroom that enhances student learning, as they can assist with **non-instructional duties** that allow for smooth transitions during instruction, such as preparing learning materials, handing back papers, or grading assignments. **Classroom management** is also enhanced when paraprofessionals and volunteers are present, as they can assist in reinforcing expectations and monitoring behavior to ensure all students are positively and productively engaging in learning.

#### Monitoring Their Performance in the Classroom

Paraprofessionals and volunteers are invaluable resources for creating a positive, productive classroom environment; however, to ensure the contributions of these aides are consistently beneficial in meeting students' needs and maximizing learning, it is important to continuously monitor their performance in the classroom. Paraprofessionals and volunteers are typically interviewed by administration prior to entering the classroom to determine whether their qualifications are aligned with meeting students' needs to enhance instruction. The administration is also often responsible for monitoring their performance throughout the school year. Specifically, paraprofessionals are licensed in the field of education and are often formally evaluated against specific **performance measurement tools**. **Observations** by administration can either be scheduled or conducted as an informal "walk-through" to assess how the paraprofessional or volunteer interacts with the teacher and students and his or her effectiveness in contributing to a productive learning environment. Teachers can also monitor the performance of volunteers and paraprofessionals in their classrooms. By analyzing **students' progress** when working with these aides and eliciting **feedback** from students, teachers can determine their effectiveness in enhancing the learning experience. Frequently communicating with paraprofessionals and volunteers provides valuable insight regarding whether they contribute to a positive classroom climate focused on student learning.

## Behavior Management Theory

### *Managing and Monitoring Student Behavior*

#### Behaviorism and Conditioning

The theoretical school of **behaviorism** was established by John B. Watson and further developed by Ivan Pavlov and B.F. Skinner. Behaviorism emphasizes the role of environmental and experiential learning in the behavior of animals and humans. Simply put, if a person experiences a desirable result from a particular behavior, that person is more likely to perform the behavior in pursuit of the result. Likewise, undesirable results cause a person to avoid performing an associated behavior. This process of **reinforcing** or rewarding good behaviors and **punishing** unwanted behaviors is known as conditioning. Behaviorists use the terms *positive* and *negative* to refer to the mode of conditioning. The term ***positive*** refers to an added stimulus, such as giving a child a treat as positive reinforcement or giving added homework as positive punishment. ***Negative*** refers to removing a stimulus, such as taking recess away as a negative punishment or taking away extra classwork as negative reinforcement for students performing their homework independently. In the classroom, the teacher has the opportunity to help students learn to meet specific behavioral expectations. The tools of behaviorism may be carefully employed in the classrooms through positive and negative punishments and rewards. Classroom rules and expectations should be made clear as soon as possible and reinforced through verbal praise, prizes, or special privileges. Likewise, negative behaviors should be discouraged through verbal warnings, loss of privileges, and communication with the family or administrators when necessary.

### Choice Theory

Choice theory, developed by **William Glasser**, states that behavior is chosen, either consciously or unconsciously, to meet the **five basic needs** of survival, love and belonging, power, freedom, and fun. Rather than implement positive and negative reinforcements to drive behavior, the teacher must aim to teach students self-responsibility for their actions. This includes encouraging students to reflect and consider the reasons for their actions and attempt to rectify any misbehavior. This method relies on the notion that if students understand how their desire to meet certain needs impacts their actions, they are more likely to engage in positive behavior. In the classroom, the teacher focuses on meeting students' **five basic needs** to encourage positive behavior by creating a classroom climate that emphasizes **communication, relationship building**, and **self-reflection**. This includes establishing positive relationships with students, holding class discussions, and teaching conflict resolution skills to create a safe, welcoming learning environment. Instructional activities are tailored to individual needs, and students have a great deal of choice in their own learning with the intention of promoting positive behavior by meeting their needs for power and freedom.

### Assertive Discipline Theory

The **Assertive Discipline theory** was developed by **Lee** and **Marlene Canter**. This theory states that the teacher is in charge of **instruction**, **the classroom**, and **students' behavior**. The expectation is that the teacher establishes clear behavioral standards that protect their right to teach and students' right to learn without distraction or disruption. Negative consequences for unwanted behavior are instilled to deter students from deviating from behavioral expectations. This theory argues that if teachers are viewed as firm and consistent, students will have a greater respect for them and ultimately engage in positive behavior. In the classroom, the teacher is in control of **establishing** and **consistently reinforcing** standards for student behavior. This establishes a sense of predictability, as students are clear on what is expected of them as they engage in learning. Students are expected to comply with the teacher's expectations, and a system of **negative consequences** are in place to discourage unwanted behavior. Positive behavior is rewarded to further reinforce desired behavior. The teacher in this classroom believes that creating such an environment enhances students' ability to focus on learning without disruption.

### Student-Directed Learning Theory

The **student-directed learning theory**, or the idea of the **democratic classroom**, was founded by **Alfie Kohn** and emphasizes the importance of **student choice** and **classroom community** in influencing behavior. This includes having students contribute to the development of behavioral expectations, as this helps students understand their purpose while instilling a sense of ownership and accountability. Instructional activities are tailored to accommodate students' individual interests and natural curiosity while emphasizing cooperation to foster an engaging learning environment that promotes positive behavior. This theory focuses on eliciting students' intrinsic motivation to engage in positive behavior rather than relying on positive and negative reinforcements. In the classroom, students primarily direct their own learning based upon their **natural curiosity** while the teacher acts as a **facilitator**. Students contribute to the development of behavioral expectations that are instilled to promote respect and focus on learning. **Active engagement**, **cooperation**, and **collaborative learning** are emphasized over direct instruction. Students may be engaging in differing activities simultaneously as the teacher moves around the classroom to monitor progress and assist as necessary.

### Social Learning Theory and Behavior Management

The **social learning theory**, developed by **Albert Bandura**, asserts that one's **environment** and the **people** within it heavily influence behavior. As humans are social creatures, they learn a great deal by **observing** and **imitating** one another. This theory is also rooted in the importance of **self-efficacy** in achieving desired behavior, as students must be motivated and confident that they can effectively imitate what they observe. In the classroom, the teacher establishes behavioral expectations and focuses on **modeling** positive behaviors, attitudes, and interactions with the intention of encouraging students to do the same. The teacher recognizes and praises positive behavior from students to elicit the same behavior from others. The teacher also emphasizes a growth mindset in the classroom to promote students' sense of self-efficacy.

### *Behavior Standards and Expectations for Students at Developmental Levels*

Behavioral standards that emphasize respect for oneself, others, and property are necessary in creating a safe, positive, and productive learning environment for students of all ages; however, as students at varying developmental levels differ in their capabilities across domains, behavioral expectations must be **realistic**, **applicable**, and reflect an **awareness** of these **differences** while encouraging growth. Young children, for example, are learning to interact with others and function in a group setting. Behavioral expectations must be attuned to this understanding while promoting the development of positive interpersonal skills. Young children also require ample opportunities for active movement and cannot reasonably be expected to sit still for long periods of time. Middle-level students are at a unique transitional period in their development and often exhibit characteristics of both young children and adolescents. Behavioral standards for these students must recognize the significant social, emotional, cognitive, and physical changes occurring at this stage by emphasizing self-control, emotional regulation, and positive interactions. As older students prepare for adulthood, they can generally be expected to conduct themselves with a degree of maturity and responsibility in a variety of settings. Appropriate behavioral standards for these students emphasize self-responsibility, respectful interactions, and independently completing necessary tasks.

### *Effective Management of Student Behavior*

#### Management and Significance in Positive, Productive, and Organized Environments

Promoting **appropriate behavior** and **ethical work habits** while taking specific measures to **manage student behavior** creates a safe, organized, and productive classroom. Such an environment is beneficial for students' motivation, engagement, and ability to focus on learning. This is achieved by communicating and consistently reinforcing **high** yet **realistic behavioral expectations** for all students. This, when combined with **relationship building** strategies, establishes a positive rapport between the teacher and students that encourages appropriate behavior and ethical work habits. Students are more inclined to adhere to expectations for behavior and work habits when their relationship with the teacher is founded on mutual understanding and respect. In addition, students who feel they are a part of developing academic and behavioral expectations feel a greater sense of **ownership** and responsibility to follow them, and, therefore, it is beneficial to include students in this process. Encouraging students to **self-monitor** their behavior and utilize conflict resolution strategies furthers this sense of accountability, as it prompts students to positively manage their own actions and work habits. Misbehavior must be addressed appropriately and in a timely manner, and consequences must follow a logical sequence, such as a verbal warning, followed by loss of privileges or communication with family.

**Review Video: Student Behavior Management Approaches**
Visit mometrix.com/academy and enter code: 843846

**Review Video: Promoting Appropriate Behavior**
Visit mometrix.com/academy and enter code: 321015

#### Strategies

Proactively implementing effective behavior management strategies is beneficial to establishing and maintaining a positive, productive learning environment. The **physical environment** should be arranged in such a way that facilitates ease of movement while limiting the amount of free space that could encourage student disruption. Planning for **smooth transitions** from one activity to the next further discourages behavioral disruptions. Desks should be arranged so that students can easily view the teacher, projector, chalkboard, or other information pertinent to learning. Expectations for behavior, procedures, and routines, including consequences, should be predictable, consistent, succinct, and visible at all times. Allowing students to participate in the development of classroom procedures and routines is valuable in providing students with a sense of personal accountability that increases the likelihood that they will follow them. Students also often respond well to incentives for modeling appropriate behavior, such as a **PBIS reward system**, verbal praise, or a positive phone call home. Nonverbal strategies are valuable in subtly managing student behavior throughout instruction, such as hand gestures, proximity, or eye contact. Misbehavior should be addressed discreetly and privately so as to avoid embarrassing the student or encouraging further disruption.

#### Importance of Consistency

Standards for behavior must be enforced consistently in order to establish a well-managed classroom in which students can focus on learning. This includes communicating **clear expectations**, holding all students equally accountable with specific **positive and negative consequences**, and **following through** on implementing them. In doing so, the teacher ensures that students are always aware of the behavior expected from them and what will happen if they do not adhere to the standards. When students are clear regarding behavioral expectations and assured that they will be enforced, they are more inclined to demonstrate appropriate conduct. This creates a predictable, secure environment that promotes student motivation, engagement, and focused productivity in learning. Consistently enforcing behavior standards gives the teacher a sense of credibility among students, and, therefore, students are more likely to respect and adhere to these expectations. In addition, holding all students to the same high behavioral standards contributes to a positive classroom climate in which all students feel they are treated fairly.

## Materials and Resources

### *Materials and Resources That Enhance Student Learning and Engagement*

#### Instructional Materials and Resources

The careful selection of instructional materials and resources for lesson plans is an integral component of enhancing student engagement and the overall learning experience. Lesson materials should be relevant to students' interests so as to facilitate personal connections to learning and ultimately, deepen understanding. In building positive relationships with students by educating themselves on students' backgrounds and interests, teachers can effectively locate and implement varied instructional materials and resources that are relevant to students and foster motivation for learning. Additionally, interactive materials, such as manipulatives or other hands-on learning resources, enhance learning and engagement through encouraging participation. Similarly, cooperative learning materials encourage student participation and engagement through fostering collaboration. Teachers can also enhance learning experiences through incorporating authentic materials that are relevant to instruction such as maps, brochures, historical documents, or similar materials that enhance student engagement and learning.

#### Technological Resources

Technology is integrated in nearly every aspect of life as a tool to enhance and assist in daily activities. This notion also applies in the classroom, as technological resources are an excellent method of increasing student engagement and interest, supporting students in their individual learning needs, and enhancing learning. The use of computers, tablets, smartphones, and other technological resources serve to improve understanding of classroom instruction, foster relevancy and personal connections, and scaffold instruction to address diverse learning styles and needs. Additionally, teachers have myriad digital resources available in the form of interactive websites, videos clips, and apps that can be implemented to enrich lessons and increase development across all subject areas. Often, these resources accommodate students' individual learning needs through providing increasingly challenging activities based on individual skill level, and the teacher can utilize these resources to tailor instruction to address individual student needs. Technological resources can also add authenticity to learning experiences, making them more engaging and enhancing student learning. Virtual field trips or science experiments can provide real-world connections to instruction by recreating authentic learning experiences without students having to leave the classroom.

### COMMUNITY RESOURCES

Community resources are beneficial in enriching instruction to foster engagement and enhance student learning. They provide students the opportunity to connect and apply what they learn in the classroom with the real world. This ultimately makes learning more authentic, as students are able to see the relevancy of what they are learning. This enhances learning by making it more engaging. Through field trips, teachers can incorporate community resources such as museums, art exhibits, science centers, and even local areas such as parks or historical sites into curriculum to accompany material learned in class. Additionally, if access to field trips is limited, teachers can take advantage of community outreach programs that bring learning experiences to classrooms. Reaching out to members of the community that are relevant to topics being covered in class, such as scientists or local historians, can be beneficial in allowing students to understand how what they are learning is applicable outside of the classroom. Locating and implementing community resources enhances student learning and engagement through making learning authentic, relevant, and applicable in the real world.

### DEVELOPMENTALLY APPROPRIATE MATERIALS AND RESOURCES

To create engaging and effective learning experiences, instructional materials and resources must be developmentally appropriate. Teachers must have a solid understanding of the general cognitive, physical, social, and emotional developmental levels of their students as well as individual differences in skills and abilities to properly select developmentally appropriate materials. The age and developmental level appropriateness of instructional resources can be determined by considering the material's size, height, and level of difficulty for students. Whether materials accommodate individual differences in skill level, ability, or interest can be determined by their versatility. If a resource can be used in multiple ways, it will appeal to a variety of learning needs and interests and support development across domains. Developmentally appropriate materials are reflective and considerate of students' diversities. Teachers can determine this by using their knowledge of students' backgrounds to select materials that incorporate and are sensitive to their students' cultural differences to support development by fostering personal connections to learning.

## Equity in Education

### *Equality vs. Equity*

**Equality** refers to providing everyone with the same resources when working toward a goal, regardless of the unique needs or situation of the individual. **Equity** means considering an individual's needs and circumstances to provide the proper supports that allow the individual a fair opportunity to achieve a common goal. In the classroom, creating an equitable environment requires the consideration of students' individual learning styles, needs, and personal situations and using this knowledge to instill necessary supports to help each student achieve the same objectives relative to their peers. Equity in the classroom is especially important for closing the achievement gap, particularly in low socioeconomic areas, because many of these students come from disadvantaged situations and need additional help to gain a fair opportunity for academic success.

**Review Video: Equality vs Equity**
Visit mometrix.com/academy and enter code: 685648

### *Supports Utilized to Provide an Equitable Learning Environment*

The nature of academic, physical, and behavioral supports depends largely on the needs of the individual student; however, some common supports are effective in addressing an array of needs to facilitate an equitable learning environment. Students with **learning disabilities** may benefit from academic supports such as preferential seating near the front of the room and minimized distractions to enhance focus. Modified test questions or alternate assignments, graphic organizers, scaffolded texts, extra copies of class notes, and individualized instruction are also valuable in enhancing focus, preventing students from becoming overwhelmed, and ensuring learning activities are aligned with students' capabilities. Students with **physical disabilities** may require wheelchair access, a sign language interpreter or scribe, braille text, enlarged fonts, or the use of technology devices to aid in reading and writing. Common **behavioral supports** in the classroom include opportunities for frequent breaks or movement as needed, a daily check-in with a caseworker or other dedicated staff member, or a behavior chart to allow students to self-monitor.

### *Establishing High Academic Expectations*

In any classroom, establishing high academic standards is imperative for motivating and empowering students to succeed. By communicating high expectations clearly and frequently, the teacher demonstrates belief that each student can overcome obstacles and excel academically, thus inspiring student engagement, curiosity for learning, and an overall positive and productive learning environment. To create an environment of high academic standards, the teachers' expectations must be apparent in instruction. The teacher must provide lessons and activities that are rigorous but not so challenging that students are unable to complete them without assistance, as this would disempower and disengage students from learning. The teacher must set achievable learning goals based on knowledge of student abilities and encourage self-reflection. Additionally, the teacher must utilize knowledge of students' individual needs to instill necessary supports to help students in achieving tasks and create an equitable environment for learning. This will ultimately empower students to overcome obstacles and motivate them for academic success.

## LEGAL AND ETHICAL OBLIGATIONS SURROUNDING STUDENT RIGHTS

### *LEGAL REQUIREMENTS FOR EDUCATORS*

#### SPECIAL EDUCATION SERVICES

Establishing an inclusive, equitable learning environment for students with disabilities requires educators to adhere to strict legal guidelines regarding special education services. According to **IDEA (Individuals with Disabilities Education Act)**, educators must provide students with disabilities a **free and appropriate public education (FAPE)** in the **least restrictive environment (LRE)**. To do this effectively, educators are required to fully comply with students' **IEPs (Individual Education Plans)** at all times. This includes providing students requiring special education services with the necessary supports, accommodations, and modifications according to their IEPs throughout all stages of instruction. Educators must also document the academic and behavioral progress of these students in relation to the goals outlined in their IEPs to report to the designated case manager. In addition, the specifics of students' special education services must be kept confidential in order to protect their privacy. Adhering to these legal requirements promotes equity in the classroom by ensuring that the unique needs of students with disabilities are met, thus allowing them to effectively participate and engage in learning.

> **Review Video: Legal and Ethical Issues**
> Visit mometrix.com/academy and enter code: 934372
>
> **Review Video: IEPs**
> Visit mometrix.com/academy and enter code: 153484
>
> **Review Video: Development of the Individuals with Disabilities Education Act**
> Visit mometrix.com/academy and enter code: 100350

#### FERPA

Understanding and observing the legal requirements related to students' and families' rights is integral to maintaining their confidentiality and establishing a safe, secure learning environment. Educators are required to follow the guidelines of **FERPA (Family Educational Rights and Privacy Act)** regarding students' education records and personally identifiable information. According to FERPA, educators may not release students' education records or personally identifiable information except in authorized situations, such as when the student enrolls in another school or the information is requested by a financial aid institution to which the student has applied. In all other instances, the educator must have written permission to disclose this information. FERPA also provides students' parents or legal guardians the right to access their child's education records and request that the education records be amended. While educators may not disclose personally identifiable information, they are permitted to release directory information regarding the student, including their name, phone number, or student identification number; however, educators must provide an appropriate amount of time to allow for the refusal of such disclosure. It is also important to note that the rights guaranteed under FERPA become applicable only to students once they have turned 18 or begun postsecondary education.

#### DISCIPLINE PROCEDURES AND STUDENT CODE OF CONDUCT

Adhering to legal requirements regarding student discipline procedures is necessary to ensure a safe, orderly, and unbiased learning environment. School districts are responsible for developing a **student code of conduct** to distribute among teachers, staff, students, and families. This document outlines expectations for student behavior as well as specific consequences for varying degrees of infractions that may occur on school grounds. Educators must strictly adhere to the guidelines stated in the student code of conduct when enacting disciplinary measures. This includes ensuring that consequences for student misbehavior align with the nature of the action and do not interfere with the student's right to a free public education. Disciplinary actions must be free of bias and must not endanger the student's physical, mental, or emotional health. In addition, the educator must document instances of student discipline and keep these records confidential to protect the student's right to privacy. Extended suspensions and expulsions must be reserved for instances in which all other disciplinary measures have been exhausted. In such cases, the student is entitled to a hearing at the board of education, and teachers must provide adequate instructional materials for the time that the student is out of the classroom.

Guidelines for acceptable student behavior on school property are outlined in a student code of conduct. Providing students with this reference helps to ensure that the school functions in a safe, orderly, and productive manner so as to create and maintain an environment focused on learning. This document typically addresses a number of topics related to **daily school procedures**, including student dress code standards, acceptable use policies for the internet and digital devices, attendance, grading policies, and academic integrity. Student codes of conduct also address **potential behavioral issues**, such as acceptable conduct while riding school buses, the use of illegal substances on school property, and harmful or disruptive behavior, including bullying, harassment, or fighting. The expectations iterated in student codes of conduct are typically accompanied by an ascending matrix of classroom, administrative, and district-level **consequences** that coincide with the severity and frequency of student infractions.

### Establishing an Equitable Learning Environment for All Students

An **equitable environment** is one in which students receive the individual support necessary to facilitate their success in learning. Establishing such an environment requires educators to adhere to several legal guidelines to ensure all students are provided with fair access to learning opportunities. Educators must be sure that all students are included in the educational program, and may not discriminate based upon students' races, religions, genders, backgrounds, disabilities, or any other differentiating characteristics. All students must be provided with equal access to learning materials, resources, technologies, and supports. In addition, educators must fully comply with all accommodations outlined in students' **IEPs**, **504 plans**, and **Behavior Intervention Plans (BIP)**, and implement all required supports to provide them with equitable access to learning.

**Review Video: 504 Plans and IEPs**
Visit mometrix.com/academy and enter code: 881103

### Child Abuse

One of the primary responsibilities of an educator is to ensure the safety of all students. In order to do so, it is important that educators understand and follow all legal requirements related to child abuse. Within the classroom, educators are responsible for establishing a safe, secure learning environment. All interactions with students must be appropriate and refrain from harming students' **physical**, **mental**, or **emotional health**. Educators must also recognize the signs of potential **child abuse** or **neglect** among their students. If any abuse or neglect is suspected, educators are legally required to report it immediately to the proper agency according to their state and local laws regardless of whether there is concrete evidence, as waiting to report it may place the student in continued danger. Reports of potential child abuse or neglect must be **confidential** so as to protect the students' privacy. Depending on the protocols established by individual school districts, educators may be required to notify their school's administration and resource officer of the report.

#### Significance of Understanding and Adhering to Legal Requirements

Understanding the legal requirements for educators ensures that teachers know what is expected of them to maintain professionalism and establish a safe, secure learning environment. This avoids misconception regarding the teacher's **roles** and **responsibilities** within the educational program so that teachers understand how to adhere to legal guidelines properly. When teachers are aware of the legal requirements they must follow, they are more effectively able to implement the appropriate protocols for addressing specific education-related situations. This includes instances related to establishing an equitable learning environment, providing special education services, interacting appropriately with students, colleagues, and families as well as protecting students' privacy. In addition, understanding the legal requirements for educators ensures that they are aware of their own professional rights and how to protect themselves in various education-related situations.

### *Ethical Guidelines*

#### Confidentiality

Adhering to ethical guidelines in relation to confidentiality is an important part of demonstrating professionalism as well as protecting the privacy of students, their families, and others in the school building. Teachers are required to follow all standards outlined by **FERPA** regarding student and family privacy. This includes preserving the confidentiality of all **personally identifiable information** about students, such as grades, medical history, discipline records, or special education services, except in authorized situations. By following these guidelines, teachers ensure that they do not release any information that may compromise the safety of students or their families. In addition, when students and families feel their personal information is kept confidential, they are more likely to seek necessary supports from the educational program without the fear of being stigmatized. Similarly, teachers must follow ethical guidelines to protect the privacy of their colleagues. Any knowledge about a colleague's personal information must be kept confidential so as to establish positive, professional relationships founded on mutual trust. Doing so facilitates productive collaboration among colleagues to benefit student success in learning.

#### Interactions with Students and Others in the School Community

The daily interactions among students, teachers, staff, and administration largely determine the quality of the school environment. A positive, safe, and professional school community is one in which educators adhere to ethical guidelines regarding interactions with one another and students. Communication with colleagues must be respectful of one another's privacy and confidentiality. This includes avoiding gossip and ensuring that all discussions about colleagues are factual, neutral, and professional in nature. In addition, interactions with members of the school community must **avoid discrimination** of any sort. Similarly, all interactions with students must be inclusive, accepting, and respectful of differences. In addition, educators must maintain proper **boundaries** when communicating with students. This includes avoiding communication outside of the school setting except in authorized situations and ensuring that all interactions maintain professionalism. Any interactions with students must avoid compromising their **physical or mental health**, **safety**, or **ability to learn**. By adhering to these ethical guidelines, educators can ensure that all communication with students and members of the school community contribute to establishing and maintaining a safe, appropriate, and professional learning environment.

## Roles and Responsibilities within the Local Education System

### *Department Chairpersons*

**Department chairpersons** are appointed to act as **leaders** within their subject areas. These individuals are responsible for a variety of instructional and administrative duties to ensure the **efficacy** of their academic department in supporting the goals and mission of the school. This includes contributing to curriculum development, communicating instructional expectations from administration to their colleagues, and ensuring that daily instruction within the department aligns with campus and district academic standards. Department chairpersons also serve as **resources** for their teams, including collaborating with them to design instructional activities and assessments, offering support, and facilitating positive communication with administration. When working with administration, department chairpersons discuss the progress of their departments in meeting academic goals, collaborate to develop strategies for assisting faculty in supporting student learning, and ensure their colleagues have the support, materials, and resources necessary for effective instruction. In addition, department chairpersons are often responsible for coordinating department activities and programs that promote student achievement and contribute to creating a positive school community.

### *School Principal*

The primary role of the **principal** is establishing and maintaining a **school culture** that supports students, teachers, staff, and families in the educational program. This role comprises a multifaceted array of responsibilities that extend to nearly every aspect of the school. The principal is responsible for supervising the **daily operations** of the school to ensure a safe, orderly environment in which teachers, staff, and students are working in alignment with the school's mission. To achieve this, the principal must communicate expectations for a positive, productive school community, ensure academic and behavioral policies are followed by staff and students, and assign staff members specific duties to facilitate an organized, efficient learning environment. In addition, it is important that the principal support staff, students, and families by engaging in frequent, open communication, addressing concerns, and providing resources necessary to promote growth and achievement. The principal is also responsible for ensuring that the school's educational program is effective in supporting teachers, staff, and students in the achievement of academic standards. This includes overseeing curriculum, monitoring instructional practices, measuring the school's performance in relation to district academic standards, as well as communicating the progress and needs of the school to the board of education.

### *Board of Trustees*

Each school within a district is overseen by a **board of trustees** responsible for making decisions to ensure that the educational program supports students' learning needs for academic achievement. The board of trustees is composed of a group of **elected individuals** who are typically members of the community in which they serve. As such, they have an understanding of the educational needs of the students within the community and can apply this knowledge to make effective decisions regarding the learning program. Members within a board of trustees are responsible for creating an educational program in alignment with students' needs as well as setting goals and developing strategies that support students in achieving them. This includes determining a **budget plan, allocating resources**, and making **administrative decisions** that benefit the school. In addition, board members are responsible for analyzing assessment data to make informed decisions regarding strategies to best support individual schools within the district and ensuring that measures are being implemented to effectively meet students' learning needs.

### *Curriculum Coordinators*

**Curriculum coordinators** are responsible for the **development** and **implementation** of curriculum that is aligned with campus and district academic goals. These individuals work closely with teachers and administrators to analyze student progress in relation to the educational program, primarily through **assessment scores**, to determine the overall effectiveness of the curriculum in supporting students' achievement. Analyzing student progress enables curriculum coordinators to identify strengths and areas for improvement within the curriculum to make adjustments that best meet students' learning needs as they work to achieve learning targets. Ensuring that curriculum aligns with academic standards and students' learning needs facilitates more effective teaching and learning. Doing so provides teachers with a clear understanding of how to adequately prepare students for success, thus allowing them to design focused instruction and implement necessary supports to promote the achievement of campus and district academic standards.

### *School Technology Coordinators*

Incorporating technology into the classroom is highly valuable in diversifying instructional strategies to promote student learning and engagement. School **technology coordinators** facilitate this integration to enhance teaching and learning, as they are responsible for the **organization, maintenance**, and **allocation** of available technology resources within the school building. This includes ensuring that all technology is functional, updated, properly stored, and accessible to teachers. These individuals are also responsible for **staying current** on developing digital resources that could be implemented to improve the learning experience as well as communicating with the board of education regarding **acquiring** technology resources for their schools. Doing so ensures that teachers have the materials necessary to best support students' learning. In addition, technology coordinators **educate** teachers and staff on the uses of technology resources as well as strategies to implement them in the classroom for more effective instruction.

### *Special Education Professionals*

Special education professionals work with students of various disabilities, their teachers, and families to provide an equitable, inclusive environment that supports learning and development. These individuals are responsible for creating an educational plan that is tailored to support the unique needs of disabled students and ensuring that this plan is followed in all areas of the school. Special educators develop **individualized education programs** (IEPs) according to students' areas of need, develop academic and behavioral goals, as well as provide supports and modifications to accommodate students in achieving them. Special education professionals work with teachers to educate them on the proper implementation of individualized accommodations to ensure all students have the support necessary to successfully engage in learning. This includes collaborating with teachers to adapt and modify curriculum, instructional activities, and assessments to meet the individual needs of students with disabilities. In addition, special educators may work alongside classroom teachers in a team-teaching setting or provide individualized instruction as necessary. Students' academic and behavioral progress is monitored over time, and special educators communicate this information to families in order to collaborate in developing future goals and strategies to support achievement.

### *Roles and Responsibilities of Professionals Within the Education Program*

The roles and responsibilities of various professionals within the educational program are described as follows:

- **Principal**—The principal is responsible for ensuring that the daily operations of the school function in a safe, orderly manner that aligns with the goals of the educational program. This includes delegating tasks to staff, enforcing academic and behavioral policies, ensuring instructional practices support student achievement, and communicating with students, staff, and families to establish a positive learning environment.
- **Vice principal**—The vice principal's role is to assist the principal in supervising the daily operations of the school to create a safe, orderly, and productive learning environment. The vice principal is responsible for working with teachers, staff, students, and families to support them in the educational program. This includes enforcing academic and behavioral policies, addressing concerns, facilitating communication, and ensuring instructional practices support student achievement of campus and district academic goals.
- **Board of trustees**—The board of trustees is responsible for developing an educational program that reflects the learning needs of students within the community. This includes developing educational goals, strategies to support students in achieving them, and ensuring that schools within the district are in alignment with the educational program. The board of trustees is also responsible for administrative decisions such as developing a budget plan and allocating resources to schools within the district according to students' needs.
- **Curriculum coordinator**—Curriculum coordinators are responsible for developing a curriculum that aligns with campus and district academic goals and ensuring it is implemented properly to support student achievement. This includes working with teachers and administrators to measure student progress within the curriculum and adjusting instructional strategies as necessary to support student success.
- **Assessment coordinator**—Assessment coordinators schedule, disperse, and collect standardized assessments and testing materials within the school building. They are responsible for educating teachers on proper assessment protocols to ensure that all practices align with district policies, collaborating with them to develop strategies that support student achievement, and ensuring all students are provided with necessary accommodations according to individual need.
- **Technology coordinator**—Technology coordinators facilitate the integration of digital resources into the curriculum. They are responsible for acquiring, organizing, maintaining, and allocating technology within the school. These individuals also work with teachers and staff to educate them on ways to utilize technology resources to enhance instruction.
- **Department chair**—Department chairpersons act as leaders among the teachers within their content areas. Their responsibilities include contributing to curriculum development, facilitating communication between administration and their colleagues, and ensuring instructional practices align with the educational program. They also collaborate with members of their team to develop instructional practices that best support student achievement of campus and district academic goals.
- **Teacher assistant**—The teacher assistant's role is to support the classroom teacher in both instructional and non-instructional duties. This includes assisting with the preparation, organization, and cleanup of lesson materials, working with small groups of students, managing student behavior, and ensuring the classroom functions in a safe, orderly manner.

- **Paraprofessional**—Paraprofessionals are licensed within the field of education and are responsible for assisting the teacher with daily classroom operations. This includes working with individual or small groups of students to provide instructional support, assisting with the preparation of lesson plans and materials, managing student behavior, and completing administrative duties.
- **Speech-language pathologist**—Speech-language pathologists are special education professionals who work with students who have varying degrees of language and communication difficulties. They are responsible for evaluating and diagnosing disabilities related to speech and language as well as developing individualized treatment programs. Speech-language pathologists then work with these students to remedy language and communication disabilities as well as collaborate with teachers, staff, and families regarding ways to support their progress.
- **ESL specialist**—ESL (English as a second language) specialists work with students for whom English is not their native language. They are responsible for evaluating students' levels of English language proficiency across the domains of reading, writing, speaking, and listening, determining necessary linguistic supports, and working with teachers to develop strategies that support English language acquisition. ESL specialists also work with individual or small groups of students to monitor progress and develop English language proficiency skills.
- **Guidance counselor**—The role of guidance counselors is to support students' social, emotional, academic, and behavioral needs. This includes providing counseling services, mediation, and, for upper grade level students, advice regarding course selection and career choices. These individuals communicate with teachers, staff, and families to develop and implement plans to support students' personal growth and academic achievement.
- **School nurse**—The school nurse is responsible for providing a range of healthcare to students and staff in the school building. This includes evaluating the physical, mental, and emotional health of students and staff as well as delivering general first-aid treatments. School nurses are also responsible for organizing and dispersing prescribed medications to students in accordance with their healthcare plan and educating teachers and staff regarding best practices for ensuring students' health and safety. School nurses may work with special education professionals to assess students' needs in the development of an individualized education program.
- **Building service worker**—Building service workers are responsible for the general maintenance of the school building and outside campus. This includes ensuring that all areas, equipment, and furniture are clean, functional, and safe for student and staff use. These individuals are also responsible for transporting heavy equipment and furniture throughout the school building.
- **Secretary**—The school secretary is responsible for assisting the principal, vice principal, and other office personnel in daily administrative duties. This individual assumes a variety of responsibilities to ensure the efficient function of daily operations within the school. Their responsibilities include communicating with students, families, and other office visitors, directing phone calls to the appropriate location, handling financial matters, and coordinating the school calendar.

- **Library/media specialist**—Library and media specialists coordinate the organization, maintenance, and allocation of all library and media resources within the school building. They are responsible for educating students regarding the proper use of library and media resources to locate information, including how to navigate the internet safely and appropriately for educational purposes. Library and media specialists also direct students toward reading material aligned with their literacy skills and provide teachers with learning materials to incorporate into instruction.
- **Instructional leadership team (ILT)**—An instructional leadership team is composed of individuals responsible for educating teachers regarding current and relevant instructional philosophies and practices to enhance student learning. These individuals collaborate with teachers to educate them regarding how to implement instructional strategies, activities, and assessments to effectively meet students' learning needs and support their achievement of campus and district academic goals.
- **School resource officer**—The role of the school resource officer is to maintain a safe, orderly environment for teachers, staff, and students. They are responsible for ensuring the physical security of the school, handling legal infractions within the school, and addressing conflicts among students. The school resource officer also works with administration and staff to develop emergency drill procedures.
- **Pupil personnel worker (PPW)**—Pupil personnel workers are responsible for addressing issues that hinder the academic achievement of at-risk students. These individuals communicate with teachers, administration, staff, and families to ensure these students are supported both within and outside of the school building. This includes addressing issues related to behavior, crisis intervention, attendance, and home lives. Pupil personnel workers direct families toward school and community support resources and collaborate with teachers to implement supports that facilitate success in learning.

## Team Teaching and Professional Collaboration

### *Team Teaching*

**Team teaching** refers to the collaboration of two or more teachers, paraprofessionals, instructional aides, or special education workers in planning and delivering instruction and assessments. There are **several structures** to this approach to accommodate varying teaching styles and student needs. One teacher may provide direct instruction while another engages in lesson activities or monitors student progress. Similarly, one teacher may instruct while another observes and collects information to improve future planning. Students may be grouped with teachers according to their needs to provide differentiation, or teachers may participate simultaneously and equally in all aspects of the learning process. The intention of this approach is to create a **student-centered environment** focused on enhancing and deepening the learning experience. Team teaching is beneficial in allowing increased **individualized instruction** that more effectively meets students' learning needs. Additionally, when multiple teachers are present, students have access to varying **ideas** and **perspectives** that strengthen their understanding. Team teaching also benefits teachers, as it enables them to utilize one another's strengths for improved instruction. There are, however, limitations to this approach. Differences in **classroom management** styles, **teaching practices**, and **personalities**, when not addressed properly through respectful communication and flexibility, hinder the effectiveness of team teaching.

### *Vertical Teaming*

Communication and collaboration among teachers of varying grade levels is integral to effective instruction that supports students' learning and development. Through **vertical teaming**, content specific teachers **across grade levels** have the opportunity to work together in discussing and planning curriculum, instruction, assessments, and strategies that prepare students for achievement. Teachers of lower grade levels are often unsure of what students in upper grade levels are learning. As a result, these teachers may be uncertain of the skills and abilities their students need to be adequately prepared for success as they transition through grade levels. Likewise, teachers of upper grade levels are often unsure of what students have learned in previous grades, thus hindering their ability to adequately plan instruction and implement necessary learning supports. Vertical teaming facilitates the communication necessary for teachers across grade levels to collaborate in **establishing expectations for preparedness** at each grade level and developing a common curriculum path. This enhances teaching and learning, in that teachers are more effectively able to plan instruction that is aligned with learning targets and prepare students with the necessary knowledge, tools, and supports for continued academic success.

### *Horizontal Teaming*

**Horizontal teaming** refers to the collaboration of **same grade level** teachers and staff that work with a common group of students. These teams may comprise teachers within a **single subject area** or **across disciplines** and may also include special education workers, grade-level administrators, paraprofessionals, and guidance counselors. Horizontal teaming is beneficial in facilitating the **coordinated planning** of curriculum, instruction, assessments, and discussion regarding students' progress in the educational program. In addition, this method of teaming provides teachers and staff the opportunity to work together in developing educational goals, addressing areas of need, and implementing strategies to support students' success in learning. Horizontal teaming is also beneficial in encouraging teachers and staff to cooperate with one another in alignment with the goals and mission of the school to create a positive learning community focused on promoting student achievement.

### *Benefits of Mentors in Enhancing Professional Knowledge and Skills*

**Mentors** within the school community are typically experienced teachers who are available to offer support, guidance, and expertise to new teachers. As these individuals typically have a great deal of experience as educators, they are highly valuable resources in increasing professional knowledge and improving teaching skills. Mentors can provide **strategies, tools**, and **advice** for planning and delivering instruction, classroom management, and meeting students' learning needs to promote achievement. This includes suggesting ideas and resources for lesson activities and assessments as well as techniques for differentiating instruction, enhancing student engagement, and promoting positive behavior. In addition, mentors can offer insight on how to effectively **navigate the school community**, including how to interact appropriately with colleagues and superiors, complete administrative duties, and communicate effectively with students' families. Regularly working with mentors in the school building ensures that new teachers are supported in developing the knowledge and skills necessary to become effective educators.

### *Interaction with Professionals in the School Community*

In order for an educational community to function effectively, professionals in the building must work together cohesively on a daily basis to support the school's mission and student learning. The nature of these interactions significantly determines the climate and culture of the school environment. Appropriate, professional interactions are important in facilitating the productive collaboration necessary to create a positive school community that promotes student success in learning. All interactions must therefore be **respectful**, **constructive**, and **sensitive** to the varying backgrounds, cultures, and beliefs among professionals in the school community. This includes using **appropriate language**, practicing **active listening**, and ensuring that discussions regarding colleagues, superiors, students, and other individuals in the building remain positive. When interacting in a team setting, it is important to maintain open dialogue and support one another's contributions to the educational program. All professionals in the school building must understand one another's roles and appreciate how these roles function together to support the educational program. Doing so ensures that collaboration is productive, purposeful, and aligned with enhancing students' learning experience.

### *Supportive and Cooperative Relationships with Professional Colleagues*

#### Supports Learning and Achievement of Campus and District Goals

Effective collaboration among school staff and faculty members is reliant on establishing and maintaining supportive, cooperative professional relationships. Doing so facilitates a sense of **mutual respect** and **open communication** that allows colleagues to work together constructively in developing educational goals, plans to support students in achieving them, and strategies to address areas of need within the educational program. Mutual support and cooperation are also beneficial in fostering the **coordinated planning** of curriculum, learning activities, assessments, and accommodations to meet students' individual needs for academic achievement. Such professional relationships allow for more effective teaching and learning, as students are supported by a school community that works together cohesively to promote learning and the achievement of campus and district academic goals.

#### Strategies for Establishing and Maintaining Relationships

Building and maintaining professional relationships founded on mutual support and cooperation is integral in creating a positive, productive school community focused on student achievement. **Frequent communication** with colleagues in a variety of settings is an important factor in establishing and sustaining such professional relationships. Maintaining continuous and open communication allows professional colleagues in the school building to develop the respect for and understanding of one another necessary to establish a strong rapport. By participating together in **school activities**, **events**, and **programs**, teachers and staff members can build connections while contributing to enhancing the school community and climate. **Community building** strategies, such as participating in activities or games that require teamwork, are also valuable opportunities for developing supportive and cooperative professional relationships among colleagues. In addition, **collaborating** with one another in regard to curriculum, lesson planning, and promoting student achievement contributes significantly to developing positive professional relationships. There are multiple avenues for such collaboration, including participating in professional learning communities (PLC's), department meetings, vertical or horizontal teaming, or engaging in team teaching. Doing so provides teachers and staff the opportunity to communicate and develop mutual goals that support the educational program and student learning.

**Review Video: Collaborating with Other Professionals**
Visit mometrix.com/academy and enter code: 100351

# PARTICIPATING IN THE LOCAL EDUCATIONAL COMMUNITY

## IMPACT OF VOLUNTEERING ON POSITIVE EDUCATIONAL COMMUNITY

Participating in school activities, events, and projects positively impacts the nature of the school community and culture. When teachers and staff members volunteer their time to contribute in such a way, it strengthens **connections** to the school community that foster positive attitudes toward it. By actively engaging in activities, events, and projects, teachers and staff have the opportunity to collaborate in making **positive contributions** to the school community. This facilitates the development of relationships among colleagues that enhance their ability to work cooperatively in creating a positive learning atmosphere that benefits students and the educational program. Students are more supported in such an environment and develop positive attitudes toward learning and strong relationships with their teachers that enhance the overall school **climate**. In addition, as students are influenced by the behaviors, actions, and attitudes modeled by adults in the building, contributing positively to the school community encourages them to do the same.

## PARTICIPATION OPPORTUNITIES

Participating in school activities, events, and projects is valuable in integrating oneself into the school community while making positive contributions. Such participation can occur through a variety of avenues, both within and outside of the school campus. Teachers can assist in school fundraisers, food and clothing drives, or field trips. They can also serve as tutors and lead school clubs or other extracurricular activities. By attending school sporting events, recitals, concerts, and plays, teachers can participate in the school community while supporting students. Events such as open-house nights, parent-teacher nights, and public forum meetings are also valuable opportunities to participate in the school community in a way that positively contributes to students' learning.

## ENHANCING THE EDUCATIONAL COMMUNITY

As teachers work closely with students, colleagues, and administration, their contributions to the school and district are integral in enhancing the school community. Teachers provide valuable insight regarding the needs of the educational program and ways to improve the school environment. As such, their participation in the school and district is beneficial in helping to ensure the needs of staff and students are adequately met to create a positive educational community. In addition, active participation in the school and district facilitates the collaboration necessary for establishing relationships among colleagues that contribute to a positive school culture and climate. Teachers can contribute to building such an educational community in a variety of ways. By participating in **school activities**, **events**, and **projects**, teachers can work cooperatively to create a positive learning atmosphere. Teachers can also attend **school meetings** and serve on focused **committees** to solve problems and influence decisions that improve the nature of the school environment. At the district level, teachers can communicate with members of the board of education and participate in **public forums** to express ideas, discuss concerns, and offer input regarding ways to enhance the educational community.

# Instruction Related to Reading and Writing

## Developmental Literacy

### *Literacy*

Literacy is commonly understood as the **ability to read and write**. UNESCO, the United Nations Educational, Scientific, and Cultural Organization, has further defined literacy as the "ability to identify, understand, interpret, create, communicate, compute, and use printed and written materials associated with varying contexts." Under the UNESCO definition, understanding cultural, political, and historical contexts of communities falls under the definition of literacy. While **reading literacy** may be gauged simply by the ability to read a newspaper, **writing literacy** includes spelling, grammar, and sentence structure. To be literate in a foreign language, one would also need to be able to understand a language by listening and be able to speak the language. Some argue that visual representation and numeracy should be included in the requirements one must meet to be considered literate. **Computer literacy** refers to one's ability to utilize the basic functions of computers and other technologies. Subsets of reading literacy include phonological awareness, decoding, comprehension, and vocabulary.

### *Phonological Awareness*

A subskill of literacy, phonological awareness is the ability to perceive sound structures in a spoken word, such as syllables and the individual phonemes within syllables. **Phonemes** are the sounds represented by the letters in the alphabet. The ability to separate, blend, and manipulate sounds is critical to developing reading and spelling skills. Phonological awareness is concerned with not only syllables, but also **onset sounds** (the initial sound in a word, such as /k/ in 'cat') and **rime** (the sounds that follow the onset in a word, such as /at/ in 'cat'). Phonological awareness is an auditory skill that does not necessarily involve print. It should be developed before the student has learned letter to sound correspondences. A student's phonological awareness is an indicator of future reading success.

**Review Video: Phonological and Phonemic Awareness, and Phonics**
Visit mometrix.com/academy and enter code: 197017

**Review Video: Components of Oral Language Development**
Visit mometrix.com/academy and enter code: 480589

### *Communication Development Within a Child's First Five Years of Life*

Language and communication development depend strongly on the language a child develops within the first five years of life. During this time, three developmental periods are observed. At birth, the first period begins. This period is characterized by infant crying and gazing. Babies communicate their sensations and emotions through these behaviors, so they are expressive; however, they are not yet intentional. They indirectly indicate their needs through expressing how they feel, and when these needs are met, these communicative behaviors are reinforced. These expressions and reinforcement are the foundations for the later development of intentional communication. This becomes possible in the second developmental period, between 6 and 18 months. At this time, infants become able to coordinate their attention visually with other people relative to things and events, enabling purposeful communication with adults. During the third developmental period, from 18 months on, children come to use language as their main way of communicating and learning. Preschoolers can carry on conversations, exercise self-control through language use, and conduct verbal negotiations.

### Milestones of Normal Language Development by the 2 Years Old

By the time most children reach the age of 2 years, they have acquired a vocabulary of about 150 to 300 words. They can name various familiar objects found in their environments. They are able to use at least two prepositions in their speech (e.g., *in*, *on*, and/or *under*). Two-year-olds typically combine the words they know into short sentences. These sentences tend to be mostly noun-verb or verb-noun combinations (e.g., "Daddy work," "Watch this"). They may also include verb-preposition combinations (e.g., "Go out," "Come in"). By the age of 2 years, children use pronouns, such as *I*, *me*, and *you*. They typically can use at least two such pronouns correctly. A normally developing 2-year-old will respond to some commands, directions, or questions, such as "Show me your eyes" or "Where are your ears?"

### Aspects of Human Language Abilities from Before Birth to 5 Years of Age

Language and communication abilities are integral parts of human life that are central to learning, successful school performance, successful social interactions, and successful living. Human language ability begins before birth: the developing fetus can hear not only internal maternal sounds, but also the mother's voice, others' voices, and other sounds outside the womb. Humans have a natural sensitivity to human sounds and languages from before they are born until they are about 4½ years old. These years are critical for developing language and communication. Babies and young children are predisposed to greater sensitivity to human sounds than other sounds, orienting them toward the language spoken around them. Children absorb their environmental language completely, including vocal tones, syntax, usage, and emphasis. This linguistic absorption occurs very rapidly. Children's first 2½ years particularly involve amazing abilities to learn language, including grammatical expression.

#### 6 Months, 12 Months, and 18 Months

Individual differences dictate a broad range of language development that is still normal. However, parents observing noticeably delayed language development in their children should consult professionals. Typically, babies respond to hearing their names by 6 months of age, turn their heads and eyes toward the sources of human voices they hear, and respond accordingly to friendly and angry tones of voice. By the age of 12 months, toddlers can usually understand and follow simple directions, especially when these are accompanied by physical and/or vocal cues. They can intentionally use one or more words with the correct meaning. By the age of 18 months, a normally developing child usually has acquired a vocabulary of roughly 5 to 20 words. Eighteen-month-old children use nouns in their speech most of the time. They are very likely to repeat certain words and/or phrases over and over. At this age, children typically are able to follow simple verbal commands without needing as many visual or auditory cues as at 12 months.

#### Three Years

By the time they are 3 years old, most normally developing children have acquired vocabularies of between 900 and 1,000 words. Typically, they correctly use the pronouns *I*, *me*, and *you*. They use more verbs more frequently. They apply past tenses to some verbs and plurals to some nouns. 3-year-olds usually can use at least three prepositions; the most common are *in*, *on*, and *under*. The normally developing 3-year-old knows the major body parts and can name them. 3-year-olds typically use 3-word sentences with ease. Normally, parents should find approximately 75 to 100 percent of what a 3-year-old says to be intelligible, while strangers should find between 50 and 75 percent of a 3-year-old's speech intelligible. Children this age comprehend most simple questions about their activities and environments and can answer questions about what they should do when they are thirsty, hungry, sleepy, hot, or cold. They can tell about their experiences in ways that adults can generally follow. By the age of 3 years, children should also be able to tell others their name, age, and sex.

### Four Years

When normally developing children are 4 years old, most know the names of animals familiar to them. They can use at least four prepositions in their speech (e.g., *in*, *on*, *under*, *to*, *from*, etc.). They can name familiar objects in pictures, and they know and can identify one color or more. Usually, they are able to repeat four-syllable words they hear. They verbalize as they engage in their activities, which Vygotsky dubbed "private speech." Private speech helps young children think through what they are doing, solve problems, make decisions, and reinforce the correct sequences in multistep activities. When presented with contrasting items, 4-year-olds can understand comparative concepts like bigger and smaller. At this age, they are able to comply with simple commands without the target stimuli being in their sight (e.g., "Put those clothes in the hamper" [upstairs]). Four-year-old children will also frequently repeat speech sounds, syllables, words, and phrases, similar to 18-month-olds' repetitions but at higher linguistic and developmental levels.

### Five Years

Once most children have reached the age of 5 years, their speech has expanded from the emphasis of younger children on nouns, verbs, and a few prepositions, and is now characterized by many more descriptive words, including adjectives and adverbs. Five-year-olds understand common antonyms, such as big/little, heavy/light, long/short, and hot/cold. They can now repeat longer sentences they hear, up to about 9 words. When given three consecutive, uninterrupted commands, the typical 5-year-old can follow these without forgetting one or two. At age 5, most children have learned simple concepts of time like today, yesterday, and tomorrow; day, morning, afternoon, and night; and before, after, and later. Five-year-olds typically speak in relatively long sentences and normally should be incorporating some compound sentences (with more than one independent clause) and complex sentences (with one or more independent and dependent clauses). Five-year-old children's speech is also grammatically correct most of the time.

## *Activities That Teach Phonological Awareness*

Classroom activities that teach phonological awareness include language play and exposure to a variety of sounds and the contexts of sounds. Activities that teach phonological awareness include:

- Clapping to the sounds of individual words, names, or all words in a sentence
- Practicing saying blended phonemes
- Singing songs that involve phoneme replacement (e.g., The Name Game)
- Reading poems, songs, and nursery rhymes out loud
- Reading patterned and predictable texts out loud
- Listening to environmental sounds or following verbal directions
- Playing games with rhyming chants or fingerplays
- Reading alliterative texts out loud
- Grouping objects by beginning sounds
- Reordering words in a well-known sentence or making silly phrases by deleting words from a well-known sentence (perhaps from a favorite storybook)

## *Teaching of Reading Through Phonics*

**Phonics** is the process of learning to read by learning how spoken language is represented by letters. Students learn to read phonetically by sounding out the **phonemes** in words and then blending them together to produce the correct sounds in words. In other words, the student connects speech sounds with letters or groups of letters and blends the sounds together to determine the pronunciation of an unknown word. Phonics is a method commonly used to teach **decoding and reading**, but it has been challenged by other methods, such as the whole language approach. Despite the complexity of pronunciation and combined sounds in the English language, phonics is a highly effective way to teach reading. Being able to read or pronounce a word does not mean the student comprehends the meaning of the word, but context aids comprehension. When phonics is used as a foundation for decoding, children eventually learn to recognize words automatically and advance to decoding multisyllable words with practice.

### *Alphabetic Principle and Alphabet Writing Systems*

The **alphabetic principle** refers to the use of letters and combinations of letters to represent speech sounds. The way letters are combined and pronounced is guided by a system of rules that establishes relationships between written and spoken words and their letter symbols. Alphabet writing systems are common around the world. Some are **phonological** in that each letter stands for an individual sound and words are spelled just as they sound. However, keep in mind that there are other writing systems as well, such as the Chinese **logographic** system and the Japanese **syllabic** system.

**Review Video: Print Awareness and Alphabet Knowledge**
Visit mometrix.com/academy and enter code: 541069

### *Facts Children Should Know About Letters*

To be appropriately prepared to learn to read and write, a child should learn:

- That each letter is **distinct** in appearance
- What **direction and shape** must be used to write each letter
- That each letter has a **name**, which can be associated with the shape of a letter
- That there are **26** letters in the English alphabet, and letters are grouped in a certain order
- That letters represent **sounds of speech**
- That **words** are composed of letters and have meaning
- That one must be able to **correspond** letters and sounds to read

### *Development of Language Skills*

Children learn language through interacting with others, by experiencing language in daily and relevant context, and through understanding that speaking and listening are necessary for effective communication. Teachers can promote **language development** by intensifying the opportunities a child has to experience and understand language.

Teachers can assist language development by:

- Modeling enriched vocabulary and teaching new words
- Using questions and examples to extend a child's descriptive language skills
- Providing ample response time to encourage children to practice speech
- Asking for clarification to provide students with the opportunity to develop communication skills
- Promoting conversations among children
- Providing feedback to let children know they have been heard and understood, and providing further explanation when needed

### *Relationship Between Oral and Written Language Development*

Oral and written language development occur simultaneously. The acquisition of skills in one area supports the acquisition of skills in the other. However, oral language is not a prerequisite to written language. An immature form of oral language development is babbling, and an immature form of written language development is scribbling. **Oral language development** does not occur naturally, but does occur in a social context. This means it is best to include children in conversations rather than simply talk at them. **Written language development** can occur without direct instruction. In fact, reading and writing do not necessarily need to be taught through formal lessons if the child is exposed to a print-rich environment. A teacher can assist a child's language development by building on what the child already knows, discussing relevant and meaningful events and experiences, teaching vocabulary and literacy skills, and providing opportunities to acquire more complex language.

### PRINT-RICH ENVIRONMENT

A teacher can provide a **print-rich environment** in the classroom in a number of ways. These include:

- **Displaying** the following in the classroom:
  - Children's names in print or cursive
  - Children's written work
  - Newspapers and magazines
  - Instructional charts
  - Written schedules
  - Signs and labels
  - Printed songs, poems, and rhymes
- Using **graphic organizers** such as KWL charts or story road maps to:
  - Remind students about what was read and discussed
  - Expand on the lesson topic or theme
  - Show the relationships among books, ideas, and words
- Using **big books** to:
  - Point out features of print, such as specific letters and punctuation
  - Track print from left to right
  - Emphasize the concept of words and the fact that they are used to communicate

### BENEFITS OF PRINT AND BOOK AWARENESS

**Print and book awareness** helps a child understand:

- That there is a **connection** between print and messages contained on signs, labels, and other print forms in the child's environment
- That reading and writing are ways to obtain information and communicate ideas
- That **print** written in English runs from left to right and from top to bottom
- That a book has **parts**, such as a title, a cover, a title page, and a table of contents
- That a book has an **author** and contains a **story**
- That **illustrations** can carry meaning
- That **letters and words** are different
- That **words and sentences** are separated by spaces and punctuation
- That different **text forms** are used for different functions
- That print represents **spoken language**
- How to **hold** a book

### DECODING

Decoding is the method or strategy used to make sense of printed words and figure out how to correctly pronounce them. In order to **decode**, a student needs to know the relationships between letters and sounds, including letter patterns; that words are constructed from phonemes and phoneme blends; and that a printed word represents a word that can be spoken. This knowledge will help the student recognize familiar words and make informed guesses about the pronunciation of unfamiliar words. Decoding is not the same as comprehension. It does not require an understanding of the meaning of a word, only a knowledge of how to recognize and pronounce it. Decoding can also refer to the skills a student uses to determine the meaning of a **sentence**. These skills include applying knowledge of vocabulary, sentence structure, and context.

**Review Video: Phonics (Encoding and Decoding)**
Visit mometrix.com/academy and enter code: 821361

### *Role of Fluency in Literacy Development*

**Fluency** is the goal of literacy development. It is the ability to read accurately and quickly. Evidence of fluency includes the ability to recognize words automatically and group words for comprehension. At this point, the student no longer needs to decode words except for complex, unfamiliar ones. He or she is able to move to the next level and understand the **meaning** of a text. The student should be able to self-check for comprehension and should feel comfortable expressing ideas in writing. Teachers can help students build fluency by continuing to provide:

- Reading experiences and discussions about text that gradually increase in level of difficulty
- Reading practice, both silently and out loud
- Word analysis practice
- Instruction on reading comprehension strategies
- Opportunities to express responses to readings through writing

**Review Video: Fluency**
Visit mometrix.com/academy and enter code: 531179

### *Role of Vocabulary in Literacy Development*

When students do not know the meaning of words in a text, their comprehension is limited. As a result, the text becomes boring or confusing. The larger a student's **vocabulary** is, the better their reading comprehension will be. A larger vocabulary is also associated with an enhanced ability to **communicate** in speech and writing. It is the teacher's role to help students develop a good working vocabulary. Students learn most of the words they use and understand by listening to the world around them (adults, other students, media, etc.) They also learn from their reading experiences, which include being read to and reading independently. Carefully designed activities can also stimulate vocabulary growth, and should emphasize useful words that students see frequently, important words necessary for understanding text, and difficult words and phrases, such as idioms or words with more than one meaning.

### *Teaching Techniques Promoting Vocabulary Development*

A student's **vocabulary** can be developed by:

- Calling upon a student's **prior knowledge** and making comparisons to that knowledge
- **Defining** a word and providing multiple examples of the use of the word in context
- Showing a student how to use **context clues** to discover the meaning of a word
- Providing instruction on **prefixes**, **roots**, and **suffixes** to help students break a word into its parts and decipher its meaning
- Showing students how to use a **dictionary and a thesaurus**
- Asking students to **practice** new vocabulary by using the words in their own writing

- Providing a **print-rich environment** with a word wall
- Studying a group of words related to a **single subject**, such as farm words, transportation words, etc. so that concept development is enhanced

### *Affixes, Prefixes, and Root Words*

**Affixes** are syllables attached to the beginning or end of a word to make a derivative or inflectional form of a word. Both prefixes and suffixes are affixes. A **prefix** is a syllable that appears at the beginning of a word that creates a specific meaning in combination with the root or base word. For example, the prefix *mis* means wrong. When combined with the root word *spelling*, the word *misspelling* is created, which means wrong spelling. A **root word** is the base of a word to which affixes can be added. For example, the prefix *in-* or *pre-* can be added to the latin root word *vent* to create *invent* or *prevent*, respectively. The suffix *-er* can be added to the root word *manage* to create *manager*, which means one who manages. The suffix *-able*, meaning capable of, can be added to *manage* to create *managable*, which means capable of being managed.

### *Suffixes*

A **suffix** is a syllable that appears at the end of a word that creates a specific meaning in combination with the root or base word. There are three types of suffixes:

- **Noun suffixes**—Noun suffixes can change a verb or adjective to a noun. They can denote the act of, state of, quality of, or result of something. For example, *-ment* added to *argue* becomes *argument*, which can be understood as the result of arguing or the reasons given to prove an idea. Noun suffixes can also denote the doer, or one who acts. For example, *-eer* added to *auction* becomes *auctioneer*, meaning one who auctions. Other examples include *-hood*, *-ness*, *-tion*, *-ship*, and *-ism*.
- **Verb suffixes**—These change other words to verbs and denote to make or to perform the act of. For example, *-en* added to *soft* makes *soften*, which means to make soft. Other verb suffixes are *-ate* (perpetuate), *-fy* (dignify), and *-ize* (sterilize).
- **Adjectival suffixes**—These suffixes change other words to adjectives and include suffixes such as *-ful*, which means full of. When added to *care*, the word *careful* is formed, which means full of care. Other examples are *-ish* and *-less*.

### *Strategies to Improve Reading Comprehension*

Teachers can model the strategies students can use on their own to better comprehend a text through a read-aloud. First, the teacher should do a walk-through of the story **illustrations** and ask, "What's happening here?" The teacher should then ask students to **predict** what the story will be about based on what they have seen. As the book is read, the teacher should ask open-ended questions such as, "Why do you think the character did this?" and "How do you think the character feels?" The teacher should also ask students if they can **relate** to the story or have background knowledge of something similar. After the reading, the teacher should ask the students to **retell** the story in their own words to check for comprehension. Possible methods of retelling include performing a puppet show or summarizing the story to a partner.

**Review Video: Grammar Skills and Reading Comprehension**
Visit mometrix.com/academy and enter code: 411287

### *Role of Prior Knowledge in Determining Appropriate Literacy Education*

Even preschool children have some literacy skills, and the extent and type of these skills have implications for instructional approaches. **Comprehension** results from relating two or more pieces of information. One piece comes from the text, and another piece might come from **prior**

**knowledge** (something from a student's long-term memory). For a child, that prior knowledge comes from being read to at home; taking part in other literacy experiences, such as playing computer or word games; being exposed to a print-rich environment at home; and observing parents' reading habits. Children who have had **extensive literacy experience** are better prepared to further develop their literacy skills in school than children who have not been read to, have few books or magazines in their homes, are seldom exposed to high-level oral or written language activities, and seldom witness adults engaged in reading and writing. Children with a scant literacy background are at a disadvantage. The teacher must not make any assumptions about their prior knowledge, and should use intense, targeted instruction. Otherwise, the student may have trouble improving their reading comprehension.

**Review Video: Importance of Promoting Literacy in the Home**
Visit mometrix.com/academy and enter code: 862347

## Teaching Reading

### *Recommendations for Teaching Reading*

- Students often benefit from the explicit instruction of new vocabulary. Vocabulary knowledge can be reinforced implicitly by integrating the new words into activities and future texts.
- Reading comprehension can also be improved by explicitly preparing students for reading activities. An example of explicit instruction prior to a reading assignment is to explicitly describe a particular type of plot device that is used in a passage before the students encounter the device in the reading. Guided readings and summaries help prepare a student to comprehend an assigned passage.
- Peer discussions are also known to help improve reading comprehension, as students can help each other develop decoding skills through discussions about the meaning and interpretation of texts.
- Reading comprehension is often affected by students' motivation to read the passage. Teachers should employ motivational strategies, such as frequent assessments or rewards, to keep students engaged when reading.

### *Guiding the Literacy Instruction of Students*

- Throughout the school day, educators should give students explicit instruction and supportive practice in using strategies that have been proven to effectively improve reading comprehension.
- Educators should use a higher quantity and quality of continued, open discussions about the content that students are reading.
- Educators should sustain high standards for students. Students should be expected to be able to answer questions about the text that they read, the vocabulary that they learn, and any applications of the text.
- Educators should work to enhance the degree to which students are motivated to read and are engaged with reading.
- Educators should teach students content knowledge that is essential to their mastery of concepts that are critical to their understanding and success.

### *Literacy Instruction Strategies to Use Before and During Reading*

Instructional activities initiated before students read have a number of purposes:

- To activate the prior knowledge of the students
- To generate questions they may want to ask about the subject and reading before they read
- To discuss the vocabulary words they will encounter in the text when they read it
- To encourage students to make predictions about what they will be reading
- To help students to identify a purpose for their reading

Activities initiated during reading include the following purposes:

- To engage students with the text
- To help students to self-monitor their own reading comprehension
- To teach students how to summarize the text
- To help them integrate new information from the text with their existing knowledge
- To help them make and verify predictions about the text
- To enable them to create graphic organizers to aid comprehension
- To facilitate their use of mental imagery related to the text

### *Instructional Activities Used After Students Have Read Assigned Text*

After students read some text, teachers will initiate various instructional activities to support and evaluate their reading comprehension. Some of the purposes of instructional activities conducted after reading text include the following:

- To have students reflect on the content of the lesson
- To identify where they found this content in the text they read
- To have students consider and study questions the teacher provided to guide their reading and have them give answers to those questions based on what they read and their own prior knowledge
- To have students evaluate the accuracy of predictions they previously made about the text during instructional activities conducted before and during reading
- To have students engage in discussion of the text to express, share, and compare their responses to the text
- To have students summarize or retell the narrative, events, or information they read in the text using their own words, demonstrating comprehension and application.

### *Instructing Students to Apply Cognitive Strategies*

Teachers can follow several steps to teach students how to apply the same cognitive strategies that excellent readers routinely employ to comprehend the text that they read. First, the teacher should give the students **direct instruction** in each cognitive strategy—e.g., inferring, questioning, summarizing, etc.

This direct instruction should include the following:

- The teacher should give the students a definition of the strategy, and explain it.
- The teacher should explain what purpose is served by the strategy during the act of reading.
- The teacher should also identify the most important characteristics of the strategy.
- Then the teacher should give the students concrete examples of the strategy and non-examples (i.e., examples of actions that do not use the strategy).

- Following direct instruction, the teacher should use think-alouds to model the use of the cognitive strategy for students.
- Then the teacher should give the students guided practice in applying the strategy.

### "Mindless Reading" Versus Highly Effective Reading

Many students who struggle with reading mistakenly are simply "zoning out" while moving their eyes across the page. This is known as "Mindless Reading." In contrast, effective readers apply cognitive strategies to keep engaged and process the text they read. One strategy that can be employed to help prevent mindless reading is group reading, either aloud or silently. The key to enforcing engagement is to use frequent recaps or comprehension checks. Teachers should encourage discussion between small groups of students reading a passage and should ask challenging and rigorous questions that require paying close attention to the story. Asking students to apply themes or questions about the text to their own life is a good way to keep students engaged, as well.

### Readability

Before assigning texts, teachers should evaluate the text's level of readability so they can best set their students up for success. **Readability** refers to a how easily an individual can read a passage. There are several different methods and formulas for evaluating a text's readability. These can be aligned to students' reading levels and inform teachers, parents, and students of which books and materials are the best fit for a student's reading skills. Readability can be determined using factors such as the number of words, syllables per word, and difficult or uncommon words in a passage. Below are a few common algorithms used to determine readability.

#### Flesch Reading Ease and Gunning Fog Scale Level

The Flesch Reading Ease and Gunning Fog Scale Level methods primarily use syllable count and the length of the sentences in a passage to determine readability. The **Flesch Reading Ease** method is measured on a 100-point scale, with different ranges of scores corresponding to a certain level of education. The Flesch-Kincade Grade Level method converts this score to a grade level, suggesting that a typical student of that grade level can read the passage. The **Gunning Fog Scale Level** method gives a text a score that corresponds to a category of difficulty. Texts that receive a score in the zero to five range are considered readable, scores that range from five to 10 are hard, scores that range from 10 and 15 are difficult, and scores that range from 15 to 20 are very difficult.

#### Dale-Chall Score

The **Dale-Chall Score** evaluates text based on whether or not the words within it are common or not. This method starts with a set list of words that are considered easy. Scores are given based on the number of words in passage that are not on that list. These scores range from zero to 9.9. Scores equal to or below 4.9 suggest that the passage can be easily read by a typical fourth-grader, while scores exceeding 9.0 suggest that a reader would need to be at a college level to easily read the passage.

#### Fry Readability Grade Level

The **Fry Readability Grade Level** analyzes a passage based on the number of syllables and sentences per 100 words. These values are documented on a graph, using the two factors as axes. The readability and appropriate grade level of a text are determined by which portions of the graph the text falls under based on its 100-word sample. This method is often completed using multiple 100-word samples for higher accuracy.

### *Reading Comprehension Strategies for Informational Texts*

#### Paired Reading Strategy to Identify Main Ideas and Details

Students can support one another's comprehension of informational text by working in pairs. Each student silently reads a portion of text. One summarizes the text's main point, and then the other must agree or disagree and explain why until they reach an agreement. Then each person takes a turn at identifying details in the text portion that support the main idea that they have identified. Finally, they repeat each step with their roles reversed. Each pair of students can keep track of the central ideas and supporting details by taking notes in two columns: one for main ideas and the other for the details that support those main ideas.

#### Text Coding

Text coding or text monitoring is recommended as an active reading strategy to support student comprehension of informational texts. As they read, students make text code notations on Post-it Notes or in the margins of the text. Teachers should model text coding for students one or two codes at a time until they have demonstrated all eight codes: A check mark means "I know this." An "X" means "This is not what I expected." An asterisk (*) means "This is important." A question mark means "I have a question about this." Two question marks mean "I am really confused about this." An exclamation point means "I am surprised at this." An "L" means "I have learned something new from this." And RR means "I need to reread this part."

#### Connections and Distinctions Among Elements in Text

Students should be able to analyze how an informational text makes connections and distinctions among ideas, events, or individuals, such as by comparing or contrasting them, making analogies between them, or dividing them into categories to show similarities and differences. For example, teachers can help eighth-graders analyze how to divide animals into categories of carnivores, which eat only meat; herbivores, which eat only plants; and omnivores, which eat both meat and plants. Teachers and students can identify the author's comparisons and contrasts of groups. Teachers can help students analyze these processes by supplying sentence frames. For example, "A _____ is a _____, so _____" and "A _____ is a _____ which means _____." The students fill these empty spaces in, creating sentences such as, "A frog is a carnivore, so it eats only meat," and "A rabbit is an herbivore, which means it eats only plants."

### *Denotative and Connotative Meaning*

Similar to literal and figurative language, **denotation** is the literal meaning, or dictionary definition, of a word whereas **connotation** is the feelings or thoughts associated with a word that are not included in its literal definition. For example, "politician" and "statesman" have the same denotation, but in context, "politician" may have a negative connotation while "statesman" may have a positive connotation. Teachers can help students understand positive or negative connotations of words depending on their sentence contexts. For example, the word "challenge" has a positive connotation in this sentence: "Although I finished last, I still accomplished the challenge of running the race." Teachers can give students a multiple-choice game wherein they choose whether "challenge" here means (A) easy, (B) hard, (C) fun, or (D) taking work to overcome. The word "difficult" has a negative connotation in this sentence: "I finished last in the race because it was difficult." Students choose whether "difficult" here means (A) easy, (B) hard, (C) fun, or (D) lengthy. Positive and negative connotations for the same word can also be taught. Consider the following sentence: "When the teacher asked Johnny why he was in the restroom so long, he gave a *smart* answer." In this context, "smart" means disrespectful and carries a negative connotation. But in the sentence, "Johnny was *smart* to return to class from the restroom right away," the same word means wise and carries a positive connotation.

### PROMOTING STUDENT INTEREST IN READING

When instructing students in the study of literature, it is important to encourage students' interest in literature. This can help students engage in the literature more deeply and better appreciate what they learn about it. Educators can promote students' interest in literature by allowing students to choose what they read. Letting students individually choose or vote on reading materials gives them an opportunity to make choices and gain a sense of responsibility over their education. Students may also gain interest in literature from participating in peer discussions. Giving students the opportunity to share their observations and ideas with each other, and potentially build upon each other's thoughts, also contributes to a sense of responsibility over their learning and education. Students should also be encouraged to appreciate the value of the literature they are reading. If students can relate literature to themselves, the world, history, or other topics and concepts that interest them, they may be better enabled to see the value of what they are reading and its ability to have an impact. Emphasizing text-to-self, text-to-world, and text-to-text relationships equips students to make their own connections with literature, which promotes their interest in literature.

#### ASSIGNMENTS TO PROMOTE STUDENT INTEREST

Observing relationships between literature and reality can also allow students to see similarities between their observations, their peer's experiences, and various pieces of literature. Many of these similarities are relevant to common human experiences, including emotions, psychology, various relationships, and the stages and progression of life. Once students learn to observe these similarities and themes within literature, they are better equipped to analyze and interpret the function of these elements in a particular work. One way to foster a student's analysis and interest in the work's purpose is to create assignments relevant to the message, plot, or moral of the literature they are studying. These may include analysis essays, student-taught lessons, or interpretive illustrations of concepts or messages. This analysis may be aided by identifying rhetorical and figurative devices in the same work and connecting the use of these devices to the present themes. The application of literary theories and criticism can also reveal the function or relevance of these themes and show a text's treatment of the human experience.

#### TEXT CONNECTIONS AND STUDENT INTEREST

Text-to-self and text-to-world connections also encourage students to understand the personal and societal relevance of a particular work. Students can be encouraged to make text-to-self connections when they can relate the text to their personal lives. This can be facilitated by teaching texts that feature protagonists that are close in age to the students in the class or texts that take place in a familiar region. By teaching or assigning texts that align to current events, teachers can promote students' interest in literature's timeless applicability to world, national, and local events and developments. Alternatively, when teaching texts that do not have characters or events that bear strong resemblance to the students or current events, teachers can still ask students to identify smaller similarities between their lives and the text.

#### LITERATURE AND STUDENT INTEREST

While students may not choose to read classic British or American literature for leisure, their opinions on assigned readings can inform what they do choose to read on their own. Commonly assigned novels and short stories fall into genres that are still popular today. Students can determine which works they enjoy, consider what genre that work may belong to, and choose their leisurely reading accordingly. For example, *1984* by George Orwell takes place in a dystopian society. This is a common theme in young-adult fiction, so students who enjoyed *1984* may look for novels with similar settings. *Frankenstein* by Mary Shelley is an example of early science fiction, so students who like *Frankenstein* can be encouraged to read other science-fiction novels. These similarities may also be used to pique students' interest in assigned readings by highlighting the similarities between classic literature and contemporary fiction.

### Technology and Reading

Students today have considerable access and exposure to technology. Students often use technology for entertainment and social interaction, but technology can also be used and enjoyed in education. Technology can be used to increase students' engagement and interest in literature and to promote their comprehension of the material. Different types of technology can appeal to different students and their learning styles. Games and activities related to literature and lessons make the material interactive and give students an opportunity to see the material applied and presented in an alternative way. Projects and assignments that require students to use technology give students an opportunity to create a unique product and reflect what they valued most about the literature. Technology also allows students to interact with each other and the material outside of class, encouraging their engagement by enabling them to collaborate and make their own connections.

Technology can also promote students' comprehension by presenting literature in various mediums. Many e-books and digital texts integrate tools that allow users to look up definitions, pronunciations, and other information while they are reading without distracting from the text. This promotes comprehension by providing helpful resources that support the reader's comprehension of the text. Audiobooks can also aid in reading comprehension. Some students are more receptive of information they hear, rather than information they read. Students who read a text and listen to a narration of that text simultaneously may be able to focus on the text more deeply and comprehend the information better.

### Incorporating Young Adult Literature in the Classroom

Young-adult literature includes a variety of genres and themes. One prominent trend in young-adult literature is plots that take place in dystopian societies in the future. These novels compare to commonly taught novels, such as *1984* by George Orwell, and offer a commentary on the time at which they were written. Many young-adult novels also compare to books like Charles Dickens's *Great Expectations*, which features a young boy growing into adulthood and navigating society and his relationship with others. This is also a common element in several young-adult novels. Many modern young-adult novels also include topics that are valuable for consideration, but are not thoroughly discussed in older works, or are presented in a way that is no longer accurate or accepted. However, young-adult literature is prone to change frequently, as it includes works from a variety of genres and is subject to the trends in the society from which it emerges. The complete body of young-adult literature is very diverse. Some popular examples of young-adult novels include Lois Lowry's *The Giver* (1993), Suzanne Collins's *The Hunger* Games (2008), and Brandon Sanderson's *The Rithmatist* (2013). While these books are often written for teenage readers, the subjects they cover and their popularity give them the potential to be effective educational resources.

### Personal Response to the Text

As students read texts, the teacher can promote their connection with the text by guiding their responses. This can include encouraging connections such as text-to-text, text-to-world, or text-to-self. Students can make these connections verbally, in activities like group discussions or oral reports, or in their writing. These activities can be used with any type of text, and may help students connect readings to other subjects or areas of the curriculum. Though they may not do it consciously, students are already making connections as they read. Consciously thinking about these connections and communicating them to others may help students comprehend their reading and increase their interest in the material. Text-to-self connections are particularly effective for helping students form meaning from the text. Each student has unique experiences that may help them relate to different parts of the text or even alter the meaning they derive from the text.

### *Promoting Respect for Other Cultures through Assigned Reading*

Teachers can also promote respect for other cultures and their differences through assigned readings. Literature has been shaped by literary movements from cultures all over the world, providing a diverse volume of world literature. Even within American literature, there is a variety of authors whose works can meet other educational criteria and introduce students to different cultures and ways of thinking within their own country. Having students read these works will inform them of different perspectives on historical periods and events, allowing them to see the experiences and talents of people unlike themselves. Assigning students readings from a variety of world literature, including British literature, will help them understand and respect international diversity. To help students understand and respect national diversity, it is helpful to assign works from literary periods that are sometimes overlooked, such as Native American literature, the Harlem Renaissance, the Dark Romantics, and the Lost Generation. Authors who have given overlooked groups a voice through their writings include Maya Angelou, Mark Twain, Martin Luther King Jr., William Carlos Williams, John Steinbeck, and Amy Tan. Incorporating diverse contemporary literature can also help students respect their peers and community members.

## Teaching Writing

### *Research-Based Strategies to Teach Effective Writing*

Effective instruction for teaching writing skills includes

- Explicitly teaching students stages of the writing process and techniques to plan, draft, revise, and edit their writing.
- Modeling of effective writing practices and independent student practice of the elements of the writing process. Students can often benefit from summarizing text as practice for writing clearly, concisely, and accurately.
- Collaborative writing helps students plan, write, edit, and revise writing cooperatively. Classmates can take turns reviewing each other's writing, giving both positive feedback for reinforcement and constructive feedback for improvement.
- Setting specific goals for writing assignments to target particular writing skills.
- Teaching students to combine sentences to improve the grammatical complexity of their work.
- The process writing approach is a strategy in which teachers give students opportunities for extended practice with planning, writing, and review.
- Teaching students to consider their audience or be provided with an authentic audience, such as their classmates.
- Inquiry strategies include setting clear goals for writing and examining concrete data, such as observing others and documenting their own responses. Inquiry strategies may also include application of learning to compositions.
- Prewriting strategies help students generate and organize ideas, access background knowledge, research topics, and visualize their ideas on a graphic organizer or other visual aid.
- Using mnemonic devices, checklists, graphic organizers, outlines, and other procedural strategies can help students plan and revise their writing.

- Teaching students to ask themselves questions and make self-statements to help formulate ideas in prewriting and editing.
- Teaching self-regulation to help students monitor their own writing output.

### *Informative/Explanatory Writing*

#### Instructional Methods to Guide Student Writing

Teachers can use **mentor texts**, which they can find from multiple everyday sources, and align them with the writing standards for their students' grade levels. Teachers can compose informative or explanatory texts in front of their classes to **model composition** for them. They can use the "thinking out loud" technique for additional modeling. This demonstrates the process of defining and expressing ideas clearly in writing and supporting those ideas with details like explanations, descriptions, definitions, examples, anecdotes, and processes. Teachers should employ **scaffolding** with students in which they begin with explicit instruction, proceed to modeling, and then provide activities for practice. These activities can include guided writing exercises, shared writing experiences, cooperative practice (collaborating with classmates), feedback that refers to the learning objectives that the teachers have established, or peer conferences.

#### Necessary Skills for Informative Writing

For students to write in an informative context, they must be able to locate and select pertinent information from primary and secondary sources. They must also combine their own experiences and existing knowledge with this new information they find. They must not only select facts, details, and examples relevant to their topics but also learn to incorporate this information into their writing. At the same time, students need to develop their skills in various writing techniques, such as comparing and contrasting, making transitions between topics or points, and citing scenarios and anecdotes related to their topics. In teaching informative writing, teachers must "read like writers" to use mentor texts to consider author craft and technique. They can find mentor texts in blogs, websites, newspapers, novels, plays, picture books, and many more. Teachers should know the grade-level writing standards for informative writing to select classroom-specific, appropriate mentor texts.

#### Guidelines for Grades K-5

Teachers can pose questions related to the content area subjects they are teaching for students to answer, and they can invite and make use of interesting elementary-grade student questions like, "Why did immigrants come to America?" "Why does my face turn red in cold weather?" or "Why does my dog drool?" In lower elementary grades, students may choose or be assigned topics, give some definitions and facts about the topics, and write concluding statements. Students in upper elementary grades should be able to introduce topics, focus them, group information logically, develop topics with enough details, connect ideas, use specific academic vocabulary, and write conclusions. To develop these skills, students must have many opportunities for researching information and writing informative or explanatory text. Up to one-third of elementary student writing should be informative or explanatory text. Children must read informational texts with depth and breadth, and use writing as a learning tool, to fulfill the objective of building knowledge through reading and writing.

#### Expectations and Recommendations for Grades 6-12

Standards for high school students include using informative or explanatory text to communicate and investigate complex concepts, information, and ideas. They should be able to effectively choose, analyze, and organize content and write accurately and clearly. Informative or explanatory text is recommended to comprise approximately 40 percent of high school students' writing across curriculum content subjects. Teachers can present brief mentor texts that use informative writing in creative, engaging ways to students as demonstrations. Using mentor texts as templates, teachers can model composing similar texts about other topics. Teachers then have students apply this format to write about topics the students select, giving them support or scaffolding. Thereafter, teachers can have students write short texts on various topics that necessitate using prior knowledge and doing research. "Thinking aloud" to model the cognitive writing process is also important. Teachers should assign frequent short research instead of traditional longer library-research term papers. Authentic writing tasks include conducting and reporting survey/interview research, producing newspaper front pages, and composing web pages.

### Questions to Determine Content and Format

When student writers have chosen a viewpoint or idea about which to write, teachers can help them select what content to include and identify which writing format is most appropriate for their subject. They should have students ask themselves what their readers need to know to enable them to agree with the viewpoint in the writing, or to believe what the writer is saying. Students can imagine another person hearing them say what they will write about, and responding, "Oh, yeah? Prove that!" Teachers should have students ask themselves what kinds of evidence they need to prove their positions and ideas to skeptical readers. They should have students consider what points might cause the reader to disagree. Students should consider what knowledge their reading audience shares in common with them. They should also consider what information they need to share with their readers. Teachers can have students adapt various writing formats, organizing techniques, and writing styles to different purposes and audiences to practice choosing writing modes and language.

### Considerations to Teach Students About Occasions, Purposes, and Audiences

Teachers can explain to students that organizing their ideas, providing evidence to support the points they make in their writing, and correcting their grammar and mechanics are not simply for following writing rules or correctness for its own sake, but rather for ensuring that specific reader audiences understand what they intend to communicate. For example, upper-elementary-grade students writing for lower-elementary-grade students should write in print rather than script, use simpler vocabulary, and avoid writing in long, complex, compound, or complex-compound sentences. The purpose for writing guides word choice, such as encouraging readers to question opposing viewpoints or stimulate empathy or sympathy. It also influences narrative, descriptive, expository, or persuasive or argumentative format. For instance, business letters require different form and language than parent thank-you notes. When writing to affect the reader's opinion, words that evoke certain emotions, descriptions that appeal to beliefs, and supporting information can all help to persuade.

### Style and Voice Instruction

When instructing students to develop their writing skills, it is important to help them develop style and their own voice. Style and voice make writing unique to the author and allow writers be creative. Style and voice can be carefully incorporated when writing academically or formally, but should not compromise the authority, accuracy, or formality of the composition. Voice and style can include elements such as tone, mood, or even literary devices and figurative language. To help students develop their voice, it is helpful to have them refer to what they know. Students can look to writings they enjoy and consider the author's style and voice. Students who can recognize style and voice in others' work are more equipped to detect their own style or voice.

Students can also identify what makes their speaking voice or patterns unique and determine whether these elements are transferrable to their writing. Having groups or pairs of students look at samples of each other's writing to look for style and voice can be effective, also. This collaborative approach helps students practice detecting style and voice while learning what style and voice others see in their writing. Students should remember to keep grammar and context in mind as they develop their voice, as these elements are still important for clear and appropriate writing. Voice and style can also grow from each student's personal experiences and perspective, as they impact the way individuals understand and communicate information.

### STANDARDS FOR CITING TEXTUAL EVIDENCE

Reading standards for informational texts expect sixth-graders to cite textual evidence to support their inferences and analyses. Seventh-graders are expected additionally to identify several specific pieces of textual evidence to defend each of their conclusions. Eighth-graders are expected to differentiate strong from weak textual evidence. Ninth- and Tenth-graders are expected to be able to cite thorough evidence as well as strong evidence from text. Eleventh- and Twelfth-graders are expected, in combination with the previous grade-level standards, to determine which things are left unclear in a text. Students must be able to connect text to their background knowledge and make inferences to understand text, judge it critically, draw conclusions about it, and make their own interpretations of it. Therefore, they must be able to organize and differentiate between main ideas and details in a text to make inferences about them. They must also be able to locate evidence in the text.

### PLAGIARISM AND LIABILITY

When using resources created by others or creating original media for instruction, it is important to abide by ethical and legal standards. These standards include copyright laws and standards for fair use and liability. While many of these laws and standards are enforced nationwide, states and local governments may have unique expectations and requirements for media usage. Complying with these regulations demonstrates respect for the law and the creators of the media. Fostering this respect in students and teaching them to avoid plagiarism and violation of these regulations is also valuable.

### BENEFITS OF ENCOURAGING STUDENT WRITING

Teaching students to write effectively and study the writings of others can inspire them to use their writing skills in other areas of life. Students can use writing for a variety of purposes, such as personal growth, reflection, learning, problem solving, and expression. Writing leisurely may entail practices such as keeping a journal or writing creatively. This allows students to reflect on their daily lives and express their thoughts and feelings freely. Writing for leisure also allows students to practice metacognition, or thinking about their own thought processes. This helps students recognize patterns in their own thoughts and clarify thoughts that they may not have fully considered or developed. Journaling can also help students keep a record of their thoughts so they can compare their past entries to the present and evaluate their own growth.

#### WRITING FOR REFLECTION

Writing for personal use and reflection also helps students learn about themselves by leading them to understand and consider their thoughts more intentionally. This can also promote problem solving by allowing students to write their thoughts in one place and see connections or patterns that reveal solutions to problems, or more clearly reveal their problems. Writing in a journal also helps students explore their thoughts more willingly because the writing is private and done on the student's own time.

# Instruction Related to Mathematics

## Instruction and Assessment

### *Instruction*

#### Mathematical Jargon

Mathematical language is hard for beginners. Words such as "or" and "only" have more precise meanings than in everyday speech. Also confusing to beginners are words such as "open" and "field" that have been given specific mathematical meanings. **Mathematical jargon** includes technical terms such as homeomorphism and integrable. But there is a reason for special notation and technical jargon. Mathematics requires more precision than everyday speech. Mathematicians refer to this precision of language and logic as rigor.

#### Rigor

Rigor is fundamentally a matter of mathematical proof. Mathematicians want their theorems to follow from axioms by means of systematic reasoning. This is to avoid mistaken "theorems", based upon fallible intuitions, of which many instances have occurred in the history of the subject. The level of rigor expected in mathematics has varied over time; the Greeks expected detailed arguments, but at the time of Isaac Newton the methods employed were less rigorous. Problems inherent in the definitions used by Newton would lead to a resurgence of careful analysis and formal proof in the 19th century. Today, mathematicians continue to argue amongst themselves about computer-assisted proofs. Because large computations are hard to verify, such proofs may not be sufficiently rigorous. Axioms in traditional thought were "self-evident truths," but that conception is problematic. At a formal level, an axiom is just a string of symbols which has an intrinsic meaning only in the context of all derivable formulas of an axiomatic system. It was the goal of Hilbert's program to put all of mathematics on a firm axiomatic basis, but according to Gödel's incompleteness theorem every (sufficiently powerful) axiomatic system has undecidable formulas; and thus, a final axiomatization of mathematics is impossible. Nonetheless mathematics is often imagined to be (as far as its formal content) nothing but set theory in some axiomatization, in the sense that every mathematical statement or proof could be cast into formulas within set theory.

#### Numerals and Naming Systems

Some of the systems for representing numbers in previous and present cultures are well known. Roman numerals use a few letters of the alphabet to represent numbers up to the thousands, but are not intended for arbitrarily large numbers and can only represent positive integers. Arabic numerals are a family of systems originating in India, passing to medieval Islamic civilization and then to Europe, and now are the standard in global culture. They have undergone many curious changes with time and geography, but can represent arbitrarily large numbers and have been adapted to negative numbers, fractions, and other real numbers.

Less-well-known systems include some that are written and can be read today, such as the Hebrew and Greek method of using the letters of the alphabet, in order, for digits 1–9, tens 10–90, and hundreds 100–900.

A completely different system is that of the quipu, which the Inca used to record numbers on knotted strings.

#### Finger Counting

Many systems of finger counting have been, and still are, used in various parts of the world. Most are not as obvious as holding up a number of fingers. The position of fingers may be most important. One continuing use for finger counting is for people who speak different languages to communicate prices in the marketplace.

### Cognitive Theorists and Constructivists

**Constructivists** believe that students may construct knowledge by themselves. In other words, students are actively engaged in the construction of their own knowledge. Students will assimilate and accommodate in order to build new knowledge, based on previous knowledge. Thus, in planning instruction based on constructivism, a teacher would focus on grouping designs, environment, problem-solving tasks, and inclusion of multiple representations. The goal in such a classroom would be for students to construct knowledge on their own. There are different levels of constructivism, including weak constructivism and radical constructivism.

**Cognitivists** differ from constructivists in that they believe that active exploration is important in helping students make sense of observations and experiences. However, the students are not expected to invent or construct knowledge by themselves. They are only expected to make sense of the mathematics. In planning instruction based on cognitivism, a teacher would employ similar methods to those discussed above, with the focus on active exploration. Students would do a lot of comparisons of mathematical methods in making sense of ideas.

### Constructivism

Three types of constructivism are weak constructivism, social constructivism, and radical constructivism. **Weak constructivists** believe that students construct their own knowledge, but also accept certain preconceived notions or facts. **Social constructivists** believe that students construct knowledge by interacting with one another and holding discussions and conversations. **Radical constructivists** believe that all interpretations of knowledge are subjective, based on the individual learner. In other words, there is no real truth; it is all subjective. Classroom instructional planning based on a weak constructivist viewpoint might involve incorporation of some accepted theorems and definitions, while continuing to plan active explorations and discussions. Planning based on a social constructivist viewpoint might involve group activities, debates, discussion forums, etc. Planning based on a radical constructivist viewpoint would involve activities that are open-ended, where there is more than one correct answer. The problems would invite more than one correct answer.

### Project-Based Learning

**Project-based learning** is learning that centers on the solving of a problem. Students learn many different ideas by solving one "big" problem. For example, for a unit on sine and cosine functions, a teacher may design a problem whereby the students are asked to model a real-world phenomenon using both types of functions. Students must investigate the effects of changes in amplitude, period, shifts, etc., on the graphs of the functions. Students will also be able to make connections between the types of functions when modeling the same phenomenon. Such a problem will induce high-level thinking.

Project-based learning is derived from constructivist theory, which contends that students learn by doing and constructing their own knowledge.

### Cooperative Learning

**Cooperative learning** simply means that students will learn by cooperating with one another. Students will be placed into groups of a size determined by the teacher. With such an approach, students work together to succeed in learning. Students may work together to learn a topic, complete an assignment, or compete with other groups.

Examples of cooperative learning include Think-Pair-Share and Jigsaw. **Think-Pair-Share** is a cooperative learning strategy that involves thinking about some given topic, sharing ideas, thoughts, or questions with a partner, and then sharing the partner discussion with the whole group. For example, in the mathematics classroom, a teacher may ask the class to think about the meaning of a proportional relationship. Each student would think for a set period of time, share ideas with a partner, and then each partner group would share their ideas regarding the meaning of proportionality. **Jigsaw** is another cooperative learning strategy that involves dividing among each group member reading material or ideas to be learned. Each student will then read his or her information, summarize it, and share the findings or ideas with the group. In mathematics, students might be given information on modeling with cosine and sine functions. Students could then share what they learned about real-world phenomena modeled by each. Different students may also be assigned to read in-depth material on amplitude, period, shifts, etc.

### Control Strategies

"**Control strategies**" is another name for "metacognitive learning strategies," which indicate any strategy that promotes a learner's awareness of his or her level of learning. With such strategies, the student will work to determine what he or she knows and does not know regarding a subject. Possible control strategies are thinking, self-regulation, and discussing ideas with peers.

Example:

> A student may discover his or her level of "knowing" about functions by keeping a journal of any questions he or she might have regarding the topic. The student may list everything that he or she understands, as well as aspects not understood. As the student progresses through the course, he or she may go back and reconfirm any correct knowledge and monitor progress on any previous misconceptions.

### Memorization and Elaboration Strategies

**Memorization** is simply a technique whereby rote repetition is used to learn information. **Elaboration** strategies involve the connection of new information to some previously learned information. In mathematics, for example, students may use elaboration strategies when learning how to calculate the volume of a cone, based on their understood approach for calculating the volume of a cylinder. The student would be making connections in his or her mind between this new skill and other previously acquired skills. A memorization technique would simply involve memorization of the volume of a cone formula, as well as ways to evaluate the formula.

### Prior Knowledge

Three ways of activating students' prior knowledge are concept mapping, visual imagery, and comparing and contrasting. With **concept mapping**, a student would detail and connect all known aspects of a mathematics topic. Ideas would be grouped into subgroups. Such an approach would allow a student to see what he or she does not know, prompting the activation of any prior knowledge on the subject. **Visual imagery** is simply the use of any pictures or diagrams to promote activation of prior knowledge. For example, giving a picture of Pascal's triangle would likely activate students' prior knowledge regarding the binomial theorem. **Comparing and contrasting** means that the student will compare and contrast ideas or approaches. For example, a student might be given a mapping of an inverse function. He or she could then compare and contrast this mapping to a known mapping of a function, in order to decide how they are the same and different. This would activate a student's prior understanding of functions and the definition thereof.

Three methods for ascertaining, or assessing, students' prior knowledge are portfolios, pre-tests, and self-inventories. **Portfolios** are simply a compilation of prior student activity related to mathematics topics. For example, a portfolio might show a student's work with transforming functions. **Pre-tests** are designed to measure a student's understanding of mathematics topics that will be taught in the course during the year. **Self-inventories** are just what the name implies: inventories that ask the students to name, list, describe, and explain information understood about various mathematics topics.

Once a teacher has assessed students' level of prior knowledge regarding some mathematics topic, he or she may use that information to scaffold the instruction. In other words, the teacher may decide to further break down the mathematics material into more integral parts. Exact processes or steps may be shown, including justification for using certain properties or theorems. More examples may be shown, while including examples of many different variations of problems, in order to ensure that students are not simply memorizing one approach that will be incorrectly applied to any problem of that sort. The teacher may also decide that more group work, peer cooperation, and discussion are needed.

For example, suppose a teacher determines that students have very little understanding of logic and valid arguments. The teacher may decide to re-teach the creation of truth tables, including truth values for intersections and "if $p$, then $q$" statements. The teacher may also decide to re-teach how a truth table may be used to show if an argument is valid. Students may be placed into groups and asked to determine the validity of several simple arguments. Once students understand the concept, they may move on to more rigorous arguments, including equivalence relations.

## Concept Whereby Usage of Manipulatives Would Increase Conceptual Understanding

Understanding of how to solve one-variable equations would certainly be enhanced by using rods and counters. With this manipulative, the rod would represent the variable, or $x$, while the counters would represent the constants on each side of the equation. A sample diagram of the equation, $x + 4 = 8$, is shown below. Note that the vertical line represents the equals sign.

In order to solve the equation (and isolate $x$), four counters may be removed from each side of the mat. This process is shown below:

Now, the final illustration is:

Thus, the solution is $x = 4$. The manipulative helps students understand the meaning of the subtraction property of equality in action, without simply memorizing its meaning.

## Piaget's Cognitive Development Theory

**Piaget's cognitive development theory** is aligned with **constructivism**. In fact, constructivism is built on his ideas. Piaget's cognitive development theory indicates that students actively participate in the construction of their own knowledge via assimilation and accommodation. Current cognitive theorists do not believe that students have to construct their own knowledge, but instead that they only have to make sense of what they are observing.

The four stages of learning, as developed by Piaget, are sensorimotor, preoperational, concrete operational, and formal operational. The defined stages show the progression from concrete thinking to abstract thinking. In other words, a child would need an object to understand properties, in the first stage. By the fourth stage, the child would be able to think abstractly, without some concrete form. In mathematics, this idea might be illustrated by first working with diagrams and manipulatives of numbers and then later writing symbolic forms of the numbers, including the numerals. This would illustrate the progression from 0 to 7 years. In the years of 11 to adulthood, much deeper abstraction is utilized. For example, people would be able to discuss functions and general properties, without looking at any concrete graphs or representations.

**Review Video: Piaget's Cognitive Development Theory**
Visit mometrix.com/academy and enter code: 100376

## Progression That a Student Undergoes as He or She Learns Mathematics

When learning mathematics, students begin with concrete representations and ideas. Later, students are able to abstract meaning and make generalizations. Students will also be asked to apply abstract ideas from one topic to another mathematics topic. In other words, students would move from concrete representations, ideas, and facts to symbolic representations and generalizations. Piaget outlined such a progression in his general four stages of cognitive learning. For example, a student may first learn about solving equations by using a balance scale. After the student understands the process, he or she can solve alone, using the symbolic equations. He or she would also be able to describe the process for solving any equation.

## Direct Instruction Versus Student-Centered Instruction

**Direct instruction** is instruction whereby the teacher delivers all content knowledge to be learned, and students, more or less, passively listen. The teacher employs a step-by-step instruction method for learning content. Student-centered instruction is learning whereby the teacher serves as a facilitator of learning and students actively participate in their own learning. Research has shown that students show a higher level of procedural and conceptual understanding when learning in a student-centered approach. Direct instruction might be more appropriate when teaching basic or fundamental theorems. Student-centered learning might be more appropriate when helping students make connections or develop higher-level thinking regarding a topic.

## Cooperative Learning Task Versus Traditional Task

**Think-Pair-Share** is an activity whereby a topic is first given for consideration on an individual basis. Next, the students are arranged in pairs and asked to discuss the topic (e.g., any questions, comments, generalizations, etc.). Finally, each pair will contribute to a whole-class discussion on the topic.

In mathematics, students would likely develop a higher level of understanding by using such an activity as Think-Pair-Share when learning about trigonometric functions. For example, students might be asked to consider different real-world situations that may be modeled with sine and cosine functions. Students could individually make a list and then share with a partner. Each partner group could then contribute to a whole class list. This list could be used as a reference sheet.

### Implementing Technology in Classroom Instruction

Technology may be implemented in the mathematics classroom in many ways. For example, Excel may be used to perform regressions, calculate lines of best fit, calculate correlation coefficients, plot residuals, show convergence or divergence of a sequence, etc. Calculators may be used to evaluate and graph functions, find area under the normal curve, calculate combinations and permutations, perform statistical tests, etc. Graphing software, such as GeoGebra, may be used to graph and explore many shapes and functions. Students may also use it to graph reflections, rotations, translations, and dilations.

### Modifying Instruction to Accommodate English-Language Learners

In mathematics specifically, instruction may be modified to include illustrations of ideas, in addition to given words. Audio may also be included for problem tasks. English-language learners may also be grouped with other fluent English-speaking students in order to assist with learning of the mathematics topic. Students will be able to hear the conversation, in addition to seeing the topic in print. In addition, problems may be broken down into smaller pieces, which can help the student focus on one step at a time. Further, additional one-on-one time with the teacher may be needed, whereby the teacher reads aloud and illustrates examples to be learned.

### Effective Learning Environment for ELL Students

Characteristics of an effective learning environment for ELL students include creation of a low threshold for anxiety, use of pictures to teach vocabulary and mathematics ideas, implementation of graphic organizers, explicit teaching of vocabulary words, and use of active learning strategies. The latter two are extremely important, since ELL students need to learn exact terms and exact definitions while also engaging with fellow students, as opposed to sitting alone at a desk. Research completed by professors at the University of Houston and University of California list collaborative learning, use of multiple representations, and technology integration as important facets of an effective learning environment for ELL students (Waxman & Tellez, 2002).

### Closed-Ended Mathematics Question and Then Rewritten in an Open-Ended Manner

Closed-Ended:

- Look at the graph of $y = x^2 + 2$. Decide if the graph represents a function.

Open-Ended:

- Provide an example of an equation that represents a function. Provide an example of an equation that does not represent a function. Explain how the graphs of the two equations compare to one another.

The first question will elicit a simple, straightforward response, or "Yes, it is a function."

The second question prompts the student to come up with two equations and then describe how the graphs of the two equations would compare. There is more than one possible answer, and the student has to make a comparison as well.

### Good Questioning Response Techniques

A few good questioning response techniques are:

- Make sure the wait time is sufficient;
- Do not include leading prompts within questions;
- Ask more questions based on student answers;
- Confirm or restate correct student comments.

The key to good questioning response techniques is to show the student that his or her comments are important and to connect those comments to other student comments. The student should feel that he or she has made a contribution to the community of learners. A teacher should always ask a meaningful, thought-provoking question and provide sufficient time for the student to provide a meaningful and well-thought-out response. Student answers should lead to more questions and ideas and not serve as an endpoint.

### NCTM Categories of Questions That Teachers Should Ask

The professional standards describe five categories of questions that teachers should ask. These categories are: 1) working together to make sense of problems; 2) individually making sense of problems; 3) reasoning about mathematics; 4) providing conjectures about mathematics; and 5) making connections within and outside of mathematics. Sample questions include "What does this mean?," "How can you prove that?," and "What does this relate to?". Categories 4 and 5 are high level and include questions that prompt students to invent ideas and make meaningful connections.

### Accountants and Mathematical Modeling

Accountants use mathematical modeling in a variety of ways. For example, an accountant models the future value of a certificate of deposit (CD) using the compound interest formula. An accountant also may fit a regression line to a client's overall savings over $x$ years. An accountant may model tax payments with residual plots. Accountants may use past income tax returns to predict future tax expenses. Accountants may compare rates of return when investing in different mutual funds, by fitting and comparing regression lines.

### Scientists and Functions

Scientists use functions to model real-world phenomena. For example, scientists use quadratic functions to model the height of an object tossed into the air or dropped from a certain height. Scientists use sine and cosine functions to model real-world occurrences such as the depth of water at various times of the day, the movement of a pendulum, etc. Scientists use exponential functions to analyze and predict the number of bacteria present after $x$ amount of time. Scientists also use functions when analyzing the time it takes a rocket to reach a destination.

### Making Mathematics Relevant to Students' Lives

Teachers can make mathematics relevant to students, using a variety of strategies. Teachers may include items relevant and pertinent to students within question stems, such as including "iPad," "apps," and video game names. Teachers should pose questions that are similar to what students may have asked themselves, such as, "If I invest this much money in an account and save for $x$ years, after how many years will I have $y$ dollars?" Teachers should include real-world problems to solve, and not simply include rote solving of equations. Students should know what sorts of scenarios may be modeled with rational expressions. Many researchers believe that curricula should be centered on the "real world," with all facets of mathematics learning spawning from that center. In other words, students often know how to convert a decimal to a percentage, but when reading *The Wall Street Journal*, they may not be able to interpret a percentage yield.

## ASSESSMENT

### ASSESSMENT TOOL

A **mathematics assessment tool** is used to assess a student's prior knowledge, current knowledge, skill set, procedural knowledge, conceptual understanding, depth of understanding, and ability to make abstractions and generalizations. Perhaps the most important purpose of such a tool is to help the student develop and modify instruction. A teacher may determine that students are ready to surpass the current lesson or need it to be much more scaffolded. A teacher may also use the assessment to track students' progress. For example, a portfolio might show students' initial understanding of functions and end with their work with function modeling.

When a teacher needs to decide on an appropriate assessment tool, he or she needs to consider the purpose of the assessment. For example, if the purpose of an assessment is to direct the instruction, a pre-test may be a good assessment to use. If the purpose of the assessment is to determine the level of student understanding, then a whole-class discussion may be desired. If the purpose of an assessment is to assess student understanding of a unit of material, then an exam would be appropriate. If a teacher wishes to analyze student understanding and ability to abstract knowledge, then a performance assessment may be used. If a teacher wishes to check off skills mastered by students, then a checklist would be appropriate.

### VALID TEST

A test is valid if it tests what it is supposed to test. In other words, a test is valid if it appropriately covers the material it is supposed to cover. For example, a topic not taught in class should not be included on a valid test. In order to construct a valid test, a teacher should make a list of all standards covered during that time period. The teacher should also closely mirror the design of problems examined in class, for homework, and in group discussions. Finally, the teacher should make sure that there is an even balance of questions to cover all of the material.

### VALID EXAM

In order to select a **valid exam**, a teacher should make sure that the test aligns with the objectives and standards covered in the unit. The teacher should also make sure that the test problems are similar to those covered during class time. The teacher should make sure the percentages of questions devoted to each objective are balanced. In order for a test to be valid, it must be reliable, meaning that it produces similar results with different groups. A teacher may wish to check the validity and reliability results of an exam.

In general, an exam is considered **invalid** if it does not measure what it is supposed to measure. The exam may include questions from another unit. It may include questions with different wording techniques, making it much more difficult. The exam may include representations different from those covered in class. An invalid exam would not be reliable, meaning the results would not be consistent with different administrations of the exam. Biased questions and wording may also make an exam invalid.

### ASSESSING STUDENTS' UNDERSTANDING OF WHAT HAS BEEN TAUGHT

In order to assess thought processes, **open-ended questions** are needed. The teacher may wish to have students write an essay, write entries in a mathematics journal, undergo a performance task, or participate in a debate or discussion. The teacher may also design a pre-test that includes all constructed response questions. In particular, a performance task requires students to justify solutions, which provide the teacher with insight into students' understanding and reasoning. In general, the assessment should include questions that ask students to make abstractions and justify their thinking.

### Testing Issue

Example: A student claims that an exam is more difficult and includes more content than what was presented in class. How might a teacher determine if the student's claim is true?

The teacher would need to make a list of all objectives and standards covered during the time period. The teacher would also need to compile all problems and examples covered in class and as homework. Finally, the teacher would need to do a careful analysis of the wording of the problems covered in class and as homework. If any of these items are not aligned to the exam, the teacher would need to go back and re-teach the material, using the created test as a guide for instruction.

### Performance Task

A **performance task** allows the teacher to assess process as well as product, meaning that a teacher can assess students' thought processes as well as their final answer. The level of student learning will be much clearer when reviewing a performance task. A performance task goes beyond a multiple-choice format, allowing for oral and tactile-kinesthetic performances. Furthermore, a performance task may combine several mathematics concepts into one assessment instrument. This type of assessment often includes real-world problems, which helps the student connect mathematics to the outside world.

### Formative and Summative Assessments

**Formative assessments** are those given during the learning process. Formative assessments provide the teacher with information related to a student's progress at various stages throughout a time period. Formative assessments are used to modify instruction as needed. In other words, formative assessments inform instruction. Summative assessments are those given at the end of a learning period. Summative assessments serve to measure the cumulative knowledge gained. Examples of formative assessments include quizzes, checklists, observations, and discussion. Examples of summative assessments include exams, portfolios, performance tasks, and standardized tests.

Four formative assessments include quizzes, checklists, observations, and discussion. **Quizzes** are often short assessments that may include multiple-choice items, short response items, or essay items. Quizzes are often administered following presentation of a portion of a mathematics unit. **Checklists** include a list of skills or concepts that should be mastered or understood. A teacher will check off all items mastered by a student. **Observations** are informal means of assessing students' understanding of a topic. A teacher may observe students' questions, engagement, and performance on projects. **Discussion** is another informal formative assessment. Discussions, both in groups and whole-class formats, allow the teacher to analyze students' thinking.

Four summative assessments include exams, portfolios, performance tasks, and standardized tests. **Exams** may include closed-ended or open-ended questions. Exams may be administered after each unit, semester, or at the end of the year. **Portfolios** include tasks created by a student and may include writing pieces and other large projects. Although the portfolio contains formative work, the tool itself may be used as a summative assessment piece. **Performance tasks** are large-scale problems that include many different components that relate to some big idea. For example, a student may be asked to formulate a plan for modeling a real-world phenomenon with a sine function. The student may be asked to explain how the function would change, given changes to the amplitude, period, shifts, etc. The student may then explain how these components would need to change to fit a new function. **Standardized tests** are tests that compare a student's performance to that of other students. They are often given at the end of the school year.

**Review Video: Formative and Summative Assessments**
Visit mometrix.com/academy and enter code: 804991

**Review Video: Assessment Reliability and Validity**
Visit mometrix.com/academy and enter code: 424680

### Scoring Rubric

A **strong rubric** will include unique performance criteria for each bullet. In other words, a portion of one criteria statement should not be included in a portion of another criteria statement. Each criteria statement should be clearly delineated, describing exactly what the student must be able to do. Furthermore, a strong rubric will often have scoring options, ranging from 0 to 4. When designing the rubric, it is helpful to create a model student response that will warrant each rubric score. It is also helpful to provide a space to provide feedback to students.

### Enhancing Student Understanding

In order for an assessment to enhance student understanding, it should provide an opportunity for the student to learn something. The assessment should be a learning opportunity for the student. It should prompt the student to think deeper about a mathematics topic. In other words, the student should think, "Okay. I understand this. I wonder how the process/solution would change if I did this." The assessment might prompt the student to ask deeper questions in the next class session or complete research on a certain topic. In order to create such an assessment, open-ended and challenging questions should be included on the exam. The exam should not consist of simple, lower-level, one-answer questions.

### Testing Mathematical Misconceptions

In order to design such an assessment, the teacher should include mathematical error-type problems, whereby the student must look at a solution process or conjecture and determine if he or she agrees, of if and where an error occurred. The student would need to identify the error, correct it, and explain why it was erroneous. The assessment should include a variety of mathematical misconceptions. One solution process may include more than one error. A teacher may also simply ask students to participate in a collaborative learning activity, whereby the students must share ideas and thoughts regarding a new mathematical topic.

### Assessing Prior Knowledge

Such a pre-test must not include any leading prompts. It should include open-ended and constructed-response items as well. A pre-test with solely multiple-choice items will not be sufficient, since a student has the option of guessing. The test should include higher-level questions that require connections within the field of mathematics. In other words, the questions should not all be mutually exclusive. They should build on one another. Finally, the test might include student error problems as well.

### Assessing Both Procedural Knowledge and Conceptual Understanding

The assessment should include rote, algorithmic-type problems, as well as those that ask the student to utilize higher-level thinking, abstractions, and generalizations. The test should include open-ended, constructed-response-type problems. A performance task is an excellent assessment for assessing a student's ability to solve a problem, while also examining the student's thought processes, rationales, etc. In order to assess both types of understanding, the assessment will need to ask students to justify and explain solutions. In other words, the assessments should include questions at both ends of Bloom's Taxonomy.

### PRE-TEST AND POST-TEST

A **post-test** should be exactly the same as an administered pre-test. If the teacher is to compare the results of a post-test to a pre-test, then the test and testing conditions should be identical. The **pre-test** assesses students' prior knowledge, while a post-test assesses students post knowledge. Comparing the results, side by side, allows the teacher to track student progress. The teacher may wish to add additional questions to the post-test, but the original questions should remain.

### ASSESSMENT THAT WILL SHOW WHAT STUDENTS DO AND DO NOT KNOW

The teacher should include questions that are straightforward, involve errors, require justification, and require shown work. A student self-assessment is one such tool that would show misconceptions, understood material, and advanced knowledge. The assessment should include more than multiple-choice questions. Designing a performance assessment with scaffolded questions, whereby only one solution may be found based on a previous answer, will also show students' exact level of understanding. A debate format is one type of assessment whereby the teacher will be able to see a student's level of understanding, as he or she seeks to respond with a rebuttal.

### ASSESSMENT TO HONE IN ON ANY ERROR PATTERNS EVIDENT IN STUDENTS' WORK

A **portfolio** would be an excellent assessment for monitoring any student error patterns. The teacher would be able to track student errors as the course progressed. The teacher would be given insight into how, and if, errors improved, or if some knowledge was acquired but other knowledge was still incorrect. The portfolio might include a series of similar questions related to a certain topic. For example, a portfolio may include function transformation questions. A student's ability to transform functions may be tracked, starting with simple linear functions and ending with complex sine functions.

### COMPONENTS THAT MUST BE PRESENT IN AN ASSESSMENT THAT SUPPORTS STUDENT LEARNING

The assessment must require students to **think deeper** than what they have covered in class. It should prompt them to make connections between topics. It should invite different ways of thinking about problem solving. In other words, the student may think, "Okay. I have seen a similar version in class. This problem is slightly different, in that the parabola is shifted left. This is the opposite of shifting right, so I will add the constant to the $x$-term." The assessment will thus solidify the student's understanding of how to shift any function.

### USING ASSESSMENT RESULTS FROM ELL LEARNERS IN ORDER TO MODIFY INSTRUCTION

The teacher would be able to see if language itself is a barrier in learning. In other words, if the group of ELL students, as a whole, show difficulty with a mathematics topic, the teacher may deduce that the content was not clear due to minimal supporting pictures, diagrams, and auditory support. The teacher may decide to reteach the lesson, using more visual cues, verbal pronunciations, explicit vocabulary usage, and peer-group placement. Collaborative learning may be employed.

### A TEACHER'S QUESTIONS REGARDING THE RESULTS OF AN ADMINISTERED EXAM

The teacher may ask the following:

- Did I cover the content in an explicit manner?
- Did I show plenty of examples?
- Did I use multiple representations when teaching the concepts?

- Did I design instruction such as to accommodate all modes of learning?
- Was the test valid?
- Did students have an adequate amount of time to complete the test?
- Why did some groups of students score lower or higher?
- Did any biased questions affect the results?

### Effects of Focus on Career and College Readiness

The focus on college and career-readiness standards prompts publishers and teachers to utilize more real-world problems in instruction and assessments. The focus in mathematics classrooms is shifting to more real-world, cumulative problems that require understanding of many different mathematics concepts in order to solve. Problems are related to science, finance, medicine, etc. The focus includes the ability to apply the algorithms to many different career situations. In summary, the recent focus shifts the instructional design to an application-based status.

### Role of Assessment in a Classroom Focused on Cognitive Instruction

A cognitively guided classroom would be similar to a constructivist classroom, in that **active participation** would be present. However, in a cognitive classroom (as advocated by current cognitive theorists), students are not required to invent their own knowledge. Instead, they must simply make sense of what they are observing and experiencing. They may be assisted by the teacher. Thus, the role of an assessment in such a classroom is to ascertain student thought processes. Such an assessment would ask students to describe thinking and perhaps make connections to other mathematics topics. The assessment must ascertain students' reasoning abilities.

### Instructional Cycle Described by a Learning Theorist

The **5E Learning Model** is based on the thinking of Jean Piaget. It is a constructivist learning model. Piaget believed that students construct their own knowledge via active participation and experiences. Problem solving is integral to student learning. The cycle is listed as engagement, exploration, explanation, elaboration, and evaluation. Thus, with active engagement and exploration, the student is able to develop his or her own explanation, use assimilation and accommodation to make sense of the information, and then evaluate the material and make conjectures, etc.

## Chapter Quiz

Ready to see how well you retained what you just read? Scan the QR code to go directly to the chapter quiz interface for this study guide. If you're using a computer, simply visit the online resources page at **mometrix.com/resources719/nystceatas-29098** and click the Chapter Quizzes link.

# NYSTCE Practice Test #1

Want to take this practice test in an online interactive format?
Check out the online resources page, which includes interactive practice questions and much more: **mometrix.com/resources719/nystceatas-29098**

## Reading

*Refer to the following for questions 1–13:*

A child's educational atmosphere has a profound effect on his or her future. One of the greatest advantages—or disadvantages—a student may face is undoubtedly the size of his or her class. Ideally, class sizes should allow for a teacher to adequately meet the learning needs of each student, with time for answering questions and making sure everyone is on the same page. But in today's education crisis, more and more students are being squeezed into classrooms, stretching teachers to educate a large number of children with a wide variety of learning abilities, aptitudes, and educational needs, not to mention a variety of backgrounds that affect their learning.

A study done on early elementary students found that those in smaller classes scored significantly better on reading than those in larger classes. When these students graduated from high school, they were also more likely to complete college entrance exams. Significantly, minorities and lower income students in the smaller classes were particularly more likely to take steps toward a college education. Clearly, class size had an impact.

While adding new technology or upgrading to state-of-the-art facilities can benefit students, very few of these improvements have the same long-term effect as giving students more teacher time and attention. Lowering the student-to-teacher ratio is crucial to improving education.

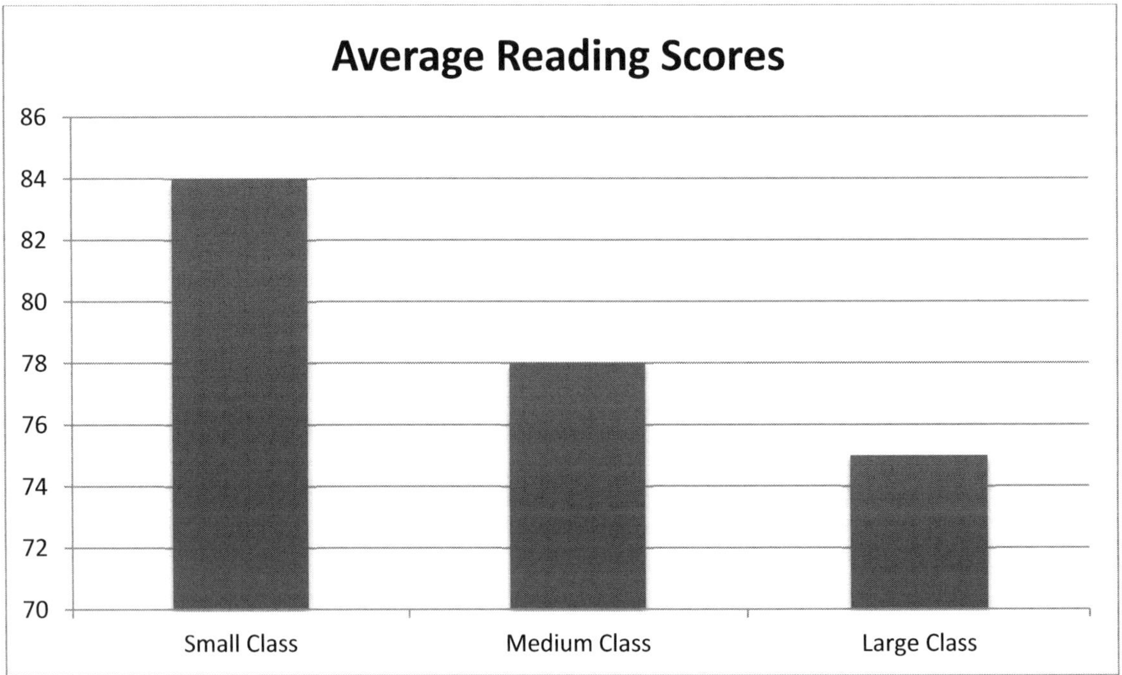


**1. What is the meaning of the word "profound" in the first sentence?**

a. Wise
b. Immense
c. Challenging
d. Confusing

**2. Which of the following best represents the main idea of this passage?**

a. "A child's educational atmosphere has a profound effect on his or her future."
b. "One of the greatest advantages...is undoubtedly the size of his or her class."
c. "A study done on early elementary students found that those in smaller classes scored significantly better..."
d. "While adding...long-term effect as giving students more teacher time and attention."

**3. Where in this passage is the topic sentence?**

a. The first sentence of the passage
b. The second sentence in the passage
c. The third sentence of the passage
d. The fifth sentence of the passage

**4. What is the meaning of the word "aptitudes" in the fourth sentence?**

a. Classes
b. Interests
c. Abilities
d. Needs

**5. From the passage, one can infer that ____________________.**

a. Lowering class sizes is an effective way to improve student learning.
b. Adding new technology to the classroom can significantly improve test scores.
c. Class size has little effect on graduation rates.
d. Students in smaller classes are more likely to obtain STEM degrees.

**6. What is the tone of this passage?**

a. Informative
b. Persuasive
c. Entertaining
d. Warning

**7. Of the following, which best restates the main idea of this passage?**

a. Smaller class sizes promote better learning.
b. Students from small classes are more likely to attend college.
c. Children have differing needs and so they need individualized education.
d. Teachers cannot effectively manage large classes.

**8. Which paragraph of the passage gives examples of how lowering class size affects students?**

a. This information is not included in the passage.
b. This information is stated in the first paragraph.
c. This information is given in the second paragraph.
d. This information is stated in the third paragraph.

**9. Which of the following is not an effect of smaller class sizes, according to the passage?**

a. Higher percentage of students taking college entrance exams
b. Higher percentage of students graduating from high school
c. Higher percentage of minorities seeking college education
d. Higher reading scores

**10. This passage identifies which of the following as beneficial to students?**

a. Low student-to-teacher ratio
b. New technology
c. State-of-the-art facilities
d. All of the above

**11. According to the passage, which of the following test scores were higher in the smaller classes?**

a. All-around academics
b. Mathematics
c. Reading
d. Reading and mathematics

**12. According to the chart, what was the average reading score of students in the medium-sized class?**

a. 75
b. 78
c. 84
d. This information cannot be determined from the chart.

**13. According to the chart, students in the small class outscored students in the large class by how many points, on average?**

a. 6
b. 9
c. 12
d. This information cannot be determined from the chart.

*Refer to the following for questions 14–17:*

> It was the best of times, it was the worst of times, it was the age of wisdom, it was the age of foolishness, it was the epoch of belief, it was the epoch of incredulity, it was the season of Light, it was the season of Darkness, it was the spring of hope, it was the winter of despair, we had everything before us, we had nothing before us, we were all going direct to heaven, we were all going direct the other way – in short, the period was so far like the present period, that some of its noisiest authorities insisted on its being received, for good or for evil, in the superlative degree of comparison only.
>
> Excerpted from *A Tale of Two Cities* by Charles Dickens (1859)

**14. Which of the following ideas did Dickens want to convey in this introduction?**

a. The extreme good and bad described were only imagined by "authorities."
b. Everything could seem to be best or worst depending on the individual.
c. The past era described was indistinguishable from the present one.
d. The readers' present era and this past era both had good and bad.

**15. Of the following statements, which accurately describes textual evidence of Dickens's techniques and their effects?**

a. The rhythm and anaphora reinforce the idea of equal and opposing forces.
b. The presentation of multiple pairs of opposites introduces a paradox motif.
c. The author's use of anastrophe and rhythm emphasizes contrasting opposites.
d. The author uses repetition to slow the pacing of the story.

**16. Among the following, which pair is most figurative in meaning?**

a. Wisdom and foolishness
b. Belief and incredulity
c. Light and darkness
d. Hope and despair

**17. From reading only this introductory paragraph, what can readers infer about the rest of this novel?**

a. The story will likely include equal amounts of good and bad.
b. The story will likely focus more on bad than good.
c. The story will likely explain how good and bad are really the same.
d. The story will likely show how good can come from bad.

*Refer to the following for questions 18–20:*

Vocational counseling at the high school level can be invaluable to students, especially those students who may not know the profession they would eventually like to pursue. Good vocational counseling can be very helpful to steer students to the major or career field that works best with their strengths and interests. Not all high schools have vocational counselors on staff, so in many places a school's guidance counselor will be responsible for this job too.

A skilled vocational counselor will first assist students in assessing those areas where they hold their highest interest and abilities. A number of evaluation instruments can be used to evaluate a student's talents, abilities, and personality traits, and often fields a student may not have considered previously will be discovered during this assessment.

**18. Which of the following would be a good title for the passage?**

a. An Overview of Vocational Counseling
b. Why Students Need Vocational Counseling
c. The Duties of the Vocational Counselor
d. The Value of the Vocational Counselor

**19. According to the passage, the students who benefit most from vocational counseling tend to be:**

a. Those who do not have a chosen profession.
b. Those who are honest about their interests.
c. Those who already know their eventual career choice.
d. Those who have a vocational counselor in their school.

**20. The main purpose of the passage is to:**

a. Argue for vocational counseling as a career choice.
b. Give positive and negative ideas about vocational counseling.
c. Talk about evaluation instruments.
d. Tell what vocational counseling can do for students.

*Refer to the following for questions 21–22:*

Delaying their initial entry to school can cause some children to actually fall behind their peers in learning. Some studies have shown differing early childhood academic achievement results when comparing children from low-income families with those living in middle-income homes. Children from low-income homes tend to begin school with weaker skills than their peers from more advantaged backgrounds. Holding young children back a year before they begin their academic career is sometimes thought to help them mature before beginning school. This practice may actually backfire for some of those children from low-income households. During the additional year at home, these children are thought to miss opportunities to cultivate the basic skills that they could develop while taking part in a learning environment – skills suggested to be absent in some low-income families.

**21. According to the passage, which of the following is true?**

a. Children from low-income homes are always weaker in basic skills than children from higher-income homes.
b. Holding children back a year from starting school is always a mistake.
c. Children from high-income homes often begin school with stronger basic skills than children from lower-income homes.
d. Learning at school is preferable to learning at home.

**22. What is the main purpose of this passage?**

a. To persuade parents to have their kids begin school on time.
b. To explain the problems teachers have with some students.
c. To tell that not all students are starting school with the same basic skills.
d. To explain the disparity in basic skills when kids initially enter school.

*Refer to the following for questions 23–27:*

A teacher has an immense set of responsibilities to juggle, but also has access to a number of resources. Multiple people and organizations are available to aid teachers in their work or to augment the educational experiences of the students. One of these resources is the Library Media Center (LMC), which serves both to provide a broader education for students and to share the teaching tasks of the teacher.

The Library Media Center serves to educate students on multiple topics: research, technology, information literacy, and many others. Students are able to obtain hands-on experience in discovering information and learning how to find what they need. The librarian and other library staff guide the students during their time in the LMC, giving the teacher time to focus on other needs such as planning.

The instruction given in the LMC not only offers an extra learning opportunity for students, but also provides extra help in the classroom for teachers. Teachers can use the resources and instruction that the LMC offers to enrich their lessons, link various subjects together, and engage students more deeply in learning. The school library is more than merely a place to read books; it sparks learning.

**23. Where in this passage is the main idea stated?**

a. The first sentence
b. The second sentence
c. The third sentence
d. The entire first paragraph

**24. Which of these choices is the best example of a topic sentence in this passage?**

a. The first sentence in the first paragraph
b. The second sentence in the first paragraph
c. The first sentence in the second paragraph
d. The second sentence in the second paragraph

**25. Which of the following is a synonym for the word "juggle" in the first sentence?**

a. Succeed
b. Balance
c. Waver
d. Toss

**26. What is the meaning of the word "augment" in the second sentence?**

a. Increase
b. Correct
c. Change
d. Color

**27. Which of the following most accurately restates the main idea of the passage?**

a. Teachers cannot carry the teaching burden alone, so library staff help them.
b. There are many resources available for teachers if they know where to look.
c. Libraries serve to educate students in many ways and to provide assistance to teachers.
d. A library is more than just a place to find books.

## Writing

**28. A number of verb forms are used in headlines. These include simple tenses, infinitive forms, and auxiliary verbs dropped in the passive voice. Which headline below uses a simple tense?**

a. LOST DOG RETURNS
b. GOVERNOR TO VISIT CITY
c. GRADUATE NAMED VALEDICTORIAN
d. HERO GIVEN AWARD

**29. Of the following, which sentence is correctly punctuated?**

a. "I told you that it would be ready next week; it will be ready next week."
b. "I told you, that it would be ready next week it will be ready next week."
c. "I told you that it would be ready next week, it will be ready next week."
d. "I told you that it would be ready next week it will be ready next week."

**30. The statements below exhibit which of the following grammatical errors?**

Many literary scholars also point to the traditions of the Welsh story collection known as the *Mabinogion* for the origins. And even the name of the legendary King Arthur.

a. Incorrectly placed comma
b. Incorrect use of capitalization
c. Incomplete sentence
d. There is no error

**31. The sentence below exhibits which of the following grammatical errors?**

For modern readers, the stories contained within the Arthurian legends are often most familiar because of English poet Alfred, Lord Tennyson, his *Idylls of the King* focuses largely on the romantic triangle of Arthur, Guinevere, and Lancelot.

a. Comma splice
b. Incorrect verb tense
c. Incorrect use of parallelism
d. There is no error

**32. In the sentence below, the expressions "to reflect" and "to enlighten" are examples of which of the following types of verbals?**

While set in the ancient and mythical world of Camelot, Tennyson's *Idylls of the King* often do more to reflect the Victorian issues of his day than to enlighten the reader about the world of King Arthur.

a. adverb
b. gerund
c. participle
d. infinitive

**33. Of the following verbs, which is regular with respect to endings for all tenses?**

a. To be
b. To go
c. To run
d. To walk

**34. Which of these verbs is not correctly conjugated in terms of present, past, and perfect tense endings?**

a. Write, wrote, written
b. Swim, swam, swum
c. Do, did, done
d. Run, ran, ran

**35. In the sentence, "It's only me," what is true about the use of the pronoun "me"?**

a. It may be tolerated in casual speech, but not in formal writing.
b. It is considered acceptable in both spoken and written English.
c. It is technically correct because the pronoun is an object pronoun.
d. It is technically correct because the pronoun is a subject pronoun.

**36. Which of the following versions of this sentence is correct?**

a. Its time for the snake to shed it's skin.
b. It's time for the snake to shed it's skin.
c. It's time for the snake to shed its skin.
d. Its time for the snake to shed its skin.

**37. Fill in the blank in this sentence with the correct choice:**

"Jacqueline, ____ loves picnics, has suggested that we all eat outside."

a. whom
b. which
c. who
d. that

**38. Which of the following is an example of correct demonstrative pronoun use?**

a. This was a great meal last week.
b. That is beautiful weather today.
c. These over there are the nicest.
d. Those are the ones that I want.

**39. Among the following sentences, which one uses the correct modifier?**

a. When Todd and Jimmy race, Todd is the best runner.
b. Out of all the candidates, she was the better choice.
c. In math class, Sue is a better student than Jeffrey is.
d. He scored highest on the first of the two tests given.

**40. Which choice correctly fills in the blank in this sentence?**

The runt of the litter is the ______ of the four puppies.

a. Small
b. Smaller
c. Smallish
d. Smallest

**41. Of these choices, which one is a complete sentence and not a fragment?**

a. "Coming soon to a location near you."
b. "The best and brightest in our nation."
c. "Leave them alone."
d. "Everybody who registers to compete."

**42. Which of the following is an example of a run-on sentence?**

a. I know what you mean I have had the exact same experience.
b. Time flies when we are busy, and we are busy all of the time.
c. They live on a mountaintop; they can see the city from there.
d. Jim watched the football game, but Jerry was not interested.

**43. Among these, which one shows correct sentence division?**

a. While the Japanese bow the Americans shake hands.
b. The children played while the grandparents watched.
c. His car could not be fixed he had to buy another one.
d. We write in English words they write computer code.

**44. Which of these sentences is punctuated correctly?**

a. Run and play now children.
b. Marietta has her hands full: she has ten children.
c. You may not like it, however, that is the way it is.
d. We got along well; and we became good friends.

**45. Of the following sentences, which has correct punctuation?**

a. We are, by the way, quite concerned.
b. She is, for your information an expert.
c. They did on the other hand, plan first.
d. Why, you are the first, to mention this.

**46. Among these choices, which sentence(s) are accurately punctuated?**

a. Many people believe this is true. But, the facts show it is a myth.
b. Many people believe this is true; but, the facts show it is a myth.
c. Many people believe this is true, but the facts show it is a myth.
d. Many people believe this is true but the facts show it is a myth.

**47. The punctuation is correct in which of the following sentence versions?**

a. "Wow! How great to see you! where have you been?"
b. "Wow! how great to see you! where have you been?"
c. "Wow! how great to see you! Where have you been?"
d. "Wow! How great to see you! Where have you been?"

**48. Which of these versions of the sentence capitalizes all words correctly?**

a. She hoped to practice her japanese in Tokyo, though many citizens wanted to practice their english.
b. She hoped to practice her Japanese in Tokyo, though many citizens wanted to practice their English.
c. She hoped to practice her Japanese in tokyo, though many citizens wanted to practice their English.
d. She hoped to practice her japanese in tokyo, though many citizens wanted to practice their english.

**49. In which of the following choices do all words have proper capitalization?**

a. The queen of England is Her Majesty Queen Elizabeth II.
b. The Queen of England is her majesty queen Elizabeth II.
c. The Queen of England is her Majesty Queen Elizabeth II.
d. The queen of england is her majesty queen Elizabeth II.

**50. In the context of each of these sentences, which commonly shared word is correctly spelled?**

a. The police officer was sighted for improper conduct.
b. The police officer was sighted pursuing the suspects.
c. The police officer sighted the motorist for a violation.
d. The police officer sighted several instances for proof.

**51. Which version spells all words correctly in the context of the sentence?**

a. I new you meant slightly used when you said knew.
b. I knew you meant slightly used when saying knew.
c. I new you meant slightly used when you said new.
d. I knew you meant slightly used when you said new.

**52. Of the following, which sentence version spells every word correctly for the context?**

a. If it hurt your feelings, I didn't mean to. I know how you feel to.
b. If it hurt your feelings, I didn't mean too. I know how you feel to.
c. If it hurt your feelings, I didn't mean to. I know how you feel too.
d. If it hurt your feelings, I didn't mean too. I know how you feel too.

**53. Which of these choices applies a capitalization rule correctly?**

a. The Golden Gate Bridge
b. The Golden Gate bridge
c. The Golden gate Bridge
d. The golden gate bridge

**54. What version of this sentence correctly spells every word?**

a. We didn't no there were know lifeguards on duty.
b. We didn't know there were know lifeguards then.
c. We didn't know there were no lifeguards on duty.
d. We didn't no there were no lifeguards there then.

## Mathematics

**55. What is the value of the underlined digit in 8,<u>7</u>06?**

a. 70
b. 700
c. 7
d. 7,000

**56. In which place value is the digit 2 in 9,452.8?**

a. Ones
b. Hundreds
c. Tens
d. Tenths

**57. What is 788 rounded to the nearest ten?**

a. 789
b. 800
c. 790
d. 780

**58. What is 3,895,399 rounded to the nearest thousand?**

a. 3,896,000
b. 5,000
c. 3,895,000
d. 3,895,400

**59. How many meters are equivalent to 7,200 centimeters?**

a. 720,000
b. 720
c. 72
d. 7.2

**60. A homeowner is ordering fencing material to place a fence around her property. The lot is rectangular with a length of 385 feet, and the width is 295 feet. Which of the following is the best estimate of the minimum amount of fencing material she should order?**

a. 1600 feet
b. 700 feet
c. 1,400 feet
d. 1,200 feet

**61. Ms. Robinson has a busy afternoon delivering gifts to family members. First, she drives 5.1 miles to her mother's house. Then, she drives 7.2 miles to her aunt's house, followed by 13.9 miles to her brother's house. Finally, she drives 14.6 miles on the return trip home. What is the best estimate of the total miles Ms. Robinson drives on her trip?**

a. 29 miles
b. 41 miles
c. 39 miles
d. 42 miles

**62. The ticket sales for Monday through Friday of a school fundraiser are 120, 240, 81, 29, and 350. What was the total number of tickets sold?**

a. 720
b. 810
c. 820
d. 819

**63. Chen is planning a trip from San Francisco to Los Angeles that has a distance of 262 miles. If he stops off at his grandparents, it will add an additional 49 miles to his trip. How long is Chen's trip if he visits his grandparents?**

a. 213 miles
b. 311 miles
c. 310 miles
d. 360 miles

**64. Fifty-three pies are donated for the sports fundraiser. If 17 pies are sold the first day, how many pies remain?**

a. 47
b. 37
c. 46
d. 36

**65. What is the difference between 73,752 and 63,721?**

a. 10,031
b. 10,131
c. 10,020
d. 10,021

**66. Felicia's new job requires extensive travel. If she is required to be out of town on business for 157 of 365 days this year, how many days is Felicia in town?**

a. 208
b. 209
c. 218
d. 532

**67. The music club is selling raffle tickets as a fundraiser. Two students each sold 75 tickets on Monday. Three students each sold 45 tickets on Tuesday. And one student sold 95 tickets on Wednesday. How many tickets were sold in all?**

a. 305
b. 335
c. 215
d. 380

**68. What is 1200 × 1200?**

a. 1,440,000
b. 14,400,000
c. 144,000
d. 14,400

**69. A local theater group rents an auditorium with 25 rows of 40 seats each. How many seats does the auditorium contain?**

a. 800 seats
b. 900 seats
c. 1,000 seats
d. 1,200 seats

**70. What is the remainder when 150 is divided by 11?**

a. 1
b. 3
c. 5
d. 7

**71. An employer is dividing a $5000 bonus evenly between 20 employees. What is the amount each employee receives?**

a. $200
b. $500
c. $250
d. $150

**72. Ethan finances a car for $32,460. He is paying for the car in 60 equal monthly payments. How much is his car payment each month?**

a. $431
b. $441
c. $531
d. $541

**73. If Mr. Jackson drives at 55 mph for 3 hours, how far does he drive?**

a. 175 miles
b. 145 miles
c. 155 miles
d. 165 miles

**74. Marshall buys $12\frac{1}{4}$ yards of material for a backdrop for the school play. If he only uses $8\frac{2}{3}$ yards, how much of the material remains?**

a. $3\frac{1}{2}$
b. $3\frac{7}{12}$
c. $4\frac{1}{12}$
d. $3\frac{5}{12}$

**75. What is the sum of $\frac{1}{2}+\frac{1}{3}+\frac{1}{4}$?**

a. $1\frac{1}{12}$
b. 1
c. $1\frac{1}{6}$
d. $1\frac{1}{4}$

**76. Mr. Nelson stocks shelves for a big box store. On Thursday night he stocks 505 jars of tomato sauce that weighed 1.09 pounds each. What is the total weight of tomato sauce that Mr. Nelson stocked?**

a. 550.45 pounds
b. 50.50 pounds
c. 545.95 pounds
d. 540.45 pounds

**77. Mr. Screen drove 412.5 miles in his new car on only 12.5 gallons of gasoline. How many miles per gallon did his new car get?**

a. 31 mpg
b. 33 mpg
c. 35 mpg
d. 37 mpg

**78. Ms. Snead's classroom contains 24 students. If 8 of the students have pets, approximately what percent of the students have pets?**

a. 0.16%
b. 16%
c. 0.33%
d. 33%

**79. Marcie finished 25% of her math problems on the bus. If Marcie finished 8 problems, how many homework problems did she have?**

a. 24
b. 48
c. 16
d. 32

**80. If 60% of Ms. Feece's students prefer apple slices to carrot sticks, what fraction of her students prefer apple slices?**

a. $\frac{2}{3}$
b. $\frac{3}{5}$
c. $\frac{2}{5}$
d. $\frac{5}{8}$

**81. What is 0.0037 written as a percent?**

a. 3.7%
b. 0.037%
c. 37%
d. 0.37%

## Instructional Support

**82. For a student with a haptic learning style, which reading-related activity is most applicable?**

a. Writing a paper about a literary work the student read
b. Sculpting a model of a character or author in literature
c. Listening to a recording of the literary work read aloud
d. Choreographing and performing a dance about a work

**83. Which of these instructional activities is most related to activating student background knowledge?**

a. Assigning students to write about something in their lives similar to what they read
b. Assigning students to look for examples in real life of things they are reading about
c. Assigning students to drill repeatedly as practice to learn reading vocabulary words
d. Assigning students to watch a movie adapted from their required reading material

**84. If a student wants to find comprehensive background information about a reading topic, which instructional resource is most useful?**

a. Glossary
b. Thesaurus
c. Dictionary
d. Encyclopedia

**85. When can students best summarize some text they have been assigned or have chosen to read?**

a. While they skim the text for the first time
b. Before they skim the text for the first time
c. During their first-time reading of that text
d. After they have read that text thoroughly

**86. In the Question-Answer Relationship (QAR) reading comprehension strategy, which type of question is it if the teacher asks students, "How would you feel if what happened in this story happened to you?"**

a. "Right There"
b. "On Your Own"
c. "Author and You"
d. "Think and Search"

**87. When monitoring student reading progress, which teacher activity is most related to lesson planning?**

a. Reteaching specific skills in which students are shown most deficient
b. Allowing more time to teach skills where students are least proficient
c. Eliminating skills all students have fully mastered from the next exam
d. Designing quizzes to reflect instructional proportions in various areas

**88. A teacher collects information on student progress in reading through formative assessment to inform her planning and instruction. Which resulting teacher action most involves instruction?**

a. The teacher writes a new lesson using different strategies.
b. The teacher revises the calendar to address critical needs.
c. The teacher adjusts the pace to fit students' learning rates.
d. The teacher writes shorter quizzes to give more frequently.

**89. When teachers instruct students in writing, which of the following is most appropriate?**

a. Students should draft before editing and proofreading it.
b. Students should draft and edit their writing concurrently.
c. Students should proofread their writing while they edit it.
d. Students should do all three at once, as a holistic process.

**90. Teachers must help students focus their writing to make it effective. Among the following related necessary features, which one is most critical of all to focus in writing?**

a. Topic
b. Purpose
c. Main idea
d. Organization

**91. Among the following factors, which is most related to focused writing?**

a. Perfect grammar and spelling
b. Evocative choices of words
c. Smooth sentence connections
d. A significant unifying perspective

**92. A middle school English teacher has assigned her class to cooperative learning groups for a writing exercise wherein each student edits his/her first draft of a short story. The teacher asks her teaching assistant to supervise one small group. Which feedback that the assistant can give the teacher would be most useful?**

a. The quality of student collaborations
b. The students who seem to write best
c. The things students needed help with
d. The story she found the most creative

**93. A student learning to vary his writing has demonstrated skill in varying sentence length. Now he is trying to vary sentence types, but he is unsure whether he is producing complete sentences or not. Which type of resource would help him with this most?**

a. Dictionaries, online and/or in hardcopies
b. Online and/or hardcopy grammar books
c. Word processor program grammar check
d. Imitating sentences by authors of classics

**94. Within technology that supports student writing, which characteristic related to word processing software programs is often lacking in public schools today?**

a. Portable hardware
b. Bundled software
c. Facilitated revision
d. Typing vs. writing

**95. If a teacher wants to conduct formative assessment of student progress in writing skills to inform lesson planning, upcoming testing, and ongoing instruction, which format would likely give the best information?**

a. Pop quiz
b. Oral test
c. Formal exam
d. Writing sample

**96. Monitoring student writing progress informs the teacher's planning, assessment, and instruction. Of these teacher decisions that student data will inform, which is most related to assessment?**

a. How much time to spend with each writing skill
b. How frequently to gather progress information
c. How to identify strategies for each writing skill
d. How to group students for working on writing

**97. Which of the following statements is most accurate about problem-solving as it relates to K–4 math instruction?**

a. It is a discrete topic and a component of the math program.
b. It is a goal far less important than others in math instruction.
c. It is a process that should pervade the whole math program.
d. It is a set of math concepts and skills that students can learn.

**98. In an elementary school class, the majority of students understand the concept of multiplication after several days of instruction. However, three students are having difficulty. The teacher asks his teaching assistant to help them. Which action by the assistant will most assist these students in grasping the concept?**

a. Have them add several sets of three pennies to a pile one set at a time.
b. Give them calculators and show them how to use them for multiplying.
c. Have them reread the textbook chapter and then ask her any questions.
d. Give them worksheets with a few simple multiplication problems to do.

**99. Mickey, a high school student, just started his first after-school part-time job. His classmate Alonzo started a part-time job last summer and has continued it since school started. Mickey wants to know if he receives the hourly wages promised for all the hours he works. Alonzo wants to know the cumulative results of small raises he has received quarterly over the past nine months. Which resources or procedures can each of them use?**

a. Both students should use graphic organizers to get answers
b. Mickey can add and subtract; Alonzo can multiply and divide
c. Each student should use real money he can count, add, etc.
d. Multiplication and division for Mickey; Alonzo can make a graph

**100. Mr. Kirk, a new teacher at a public high school, has been teaching a trigonometry course when he discovers a number of students know how to look up numbers in a table, plot these values as points, and connect them to make a graph, but they have no idea what a sine or function is. He decides to consult his mentor about how to explain these concepts, and then add some lessons to help students understand them. Student information has informed Mr. Kirk most in which areas?**

a. Planning and instruction
b. Planning, teaching, testing
c. Instruction and assessment
d. Planning and assessment

# Answer Key and Explanations for Test #1

## Reading

**1. B:** *Profound* means "great or intense." While the word can be used to describe wisdom or challenges, it does not actually mean "wise" (A) or "challenging" (C). "Confusing" (D) is a synonym for "confound," not "profound."

**2. B:** This sentence best expresses the main idea; choice A provides additional information supporting it; choice C elaborates on it; and choice D elaborates on the opening sentence of the second paragraph, which can also be considered the topic sentence of the second paragraph.

**3. B:** Topic sentences are often, but not always, the first sentences. In this case, the first sentence (A) introduces the subject but the second sentence is actually the topic sentence. The third sentence (C) supports the topic sentence by adding some information. The fifth sentence (D) is more appropriately the second paragraph's topic sentence rather than the topic sentence of the whole passage.

**4. C:** An *aptitude* is "a natural ability to do something." This is somewhat similar to interests (B) but refers more to a student's actual talent or skill rather than what he or she enjoys. It does not refer to a student's classes (A) or needs (D).

**5. A:** The passage implies that small class sizes may be responsible for improved test scores, and thus improved learning. New technology (B) is mentioned as a potential benefit, but the passage does not specify what kind of benefit. The passage does not mention graduation rates (C), though it refers to students who do graduate. The passage discusses impact on college education, but makes no mention of different types of college degrees (D).

**6. B:** The last sentence of the passage gives an action statement, preceded by arguments to support it. Thus, this is a persuasive passage, trying to convince the reader of something. While it contains information, the tone is not merely informative (A). It is meant to persuade, not entertain (C) or warn (D).

**7. A:** This is the best restatement of the main idea. Choice B makes an assumption that is not fully backed up by the passage, choice C states a supporting piece of information on the topic, and choice D makes another assumption not supported by the passage.

**8. C:** The second paragraph describes the study on class sizes, detailing how they can affect test scores and college entrance.

**9. B:** The passage mentions that students who graduate high school are more likely to pursue college but does not discuss high school graduation rates.

**10. D:** The passage mentions all three as beneficial to students, although the low student-to-teacher ratio is supposed to be most beneficial.

**11. C:** The second paragraph mentions that students in smaller classes scored higher on reading. The passage does not mention all-around academics (A) or mathematics (B, D).

**12. B:** The chart shows that the average reading scores were 84 for the small class (C), 78 for the medium class (B), and 75 for the large class (A).

**13. B:** Students in the small class had an average reading score of 84, while students in the large class averaged 75. This is a difference of 9.

**14. D:** Charles Dickens uses a series of opposites to convey the idea that the period described involves extremes of positive and negative. He also likens the period to the present time in that certain institutions are interested in people believing in these extremes. He does not say that the extremes are only imagined (A), that personal subjectivity dictates whether a given extreme is seen as good or bad (B), or that this past era and the present era are identical (C).

**15. A:** The even rhythm and ample use of anaphora emphasize the concept of equal, opposing forces. Anaphora is the repetition of a phrase to start consecutive clauses, creating a parallel. The presentation of multiple opposites introduces a theme of doubles that highlights conflict rather than contradiction, so choice B is not correct. Choice C is not correct because it mentions anastrophe, which reverses adjective-noun order to noun-adjective, such as in the phrase "ocean blue." Anaphora is relevant here, not anastrophe. Repetition of an entire sentence can be used to slow the pacing in a story, but the repetition here is limited to the beginnings of the clauses. The ending of each clause is different, so there is no slowing effect, making choice D incorrect.

**16. C:** In the sense that Charles Dickens uses them here, *light* and *darkness* do not mean physical illumination or its absence. Their meanings are instead figurative, with *light* referring to good, knowledge, happiness, hope, etc., and *darkness* referring to bad, ignorance, unhappiness, despair, etc. The other three choices all use words whose most literal meaning is applicable, so these pairs are not figurative in meaning.

**17. A:** Because of the balancing of opposites in the introduction, readers can infer that this balance will likely be present throughout the story. There is no reason to expect it will focus more on bad, as choice B states. Though the introduction mentions that the "superlative degree of comparison" is "for good or for evil," it does not suggest that there is really no difference between good and bad, so choice C is incorrect. Choice D is incorrect because, even though the story may show how good can come from bad, there is no reason to view this possibility as particularly likely from reading the passage.

**18. A:** Answer A, "An Overview of Vocational Counseling," most accurately describes the content of the passage, so it is the correct choice. This passage describes the role of the vocational counselor (C) and how vocational counseling benefits students (B). Since the passage covers several aspects of vocational counseling, answers B, C, and D would not be good titles because they are not broad enough to accurately describe the passage.

**19. A:** The passage describes vocational counseling as a useful tool for students who are not sure what career they want to pursue, or do not have a chosen profession (A). Students who receive vocational counseling will likely have a vocational counselor at their school (D). These students should also be honest about their interests to receive the best results (B). However, these factors do not determine whether or not a student needs or would benefit from vocational counseling. Students who already know what career they wish to pursue will not benefit from vocational counseling as much, as the purpose of this counseling is to help them make this decision (C).

**20. D:** This passage gives the reader basic information about vocational counseling and how it helps students (D). Answers A and B suggest that the purpose of the passage is to persuade readers to form an opinion or take action regarding vocational counseling. This is not the purpose of the passage, as it is expository. The purpose of the passage is also not to talk about evaluation instruments (C), as they are a detail mentioned only in the second paragraph.

**21. C:** The passage states that "children from low-income homes tend to begin school with weaker skills than their peers from more advantaged backgrounds," which has the same meaning as answer C. Answers A and B include absolute statements that claim something is true for all students. The passage discusses generalizations, not circumstances that always apply to all students, so these answers are incorrect. The passage does not clearly discuss learning at home, so answer D is also incorrect.

**22. D:** The main purpose of the passage is to inform readers of factors that can cause a disparity in basic skills in students when they begin attending school (D). While this passage discusses the benefits of allowing children to start school on time, it is not a persuasive passage (A). While the passage mentions the visible disparity in students' basic skills (C), this is a detail discussed in the passage, so it is not the main purpose of the passage. Teachers and their potential problems with students (B) are not mentioned in the passage.

**23. C:** The main idea can be found in the third sentence of the first paragraph. The first two sentences bring up the subject of helping teachers and giving students an improved educational experience, but the Library Media Center is not mentioned until the third sentence.

**24. C:** The first sentence of the second paragraph is the best example of a topic sentence as it states the main topic of the paragraph. The first two sentences of the first paragraph (A and B) provide some background for the subject but do not mention the topic. The second sentence in the second paragraph (D) gives details that support that paragraph's topic sentence.

**25. B:** The word *juggle* here refers to the teacher's need to balance many different responsibilities. While the teacher undoubtedly hopes to succeed, that is not the meaning of the word here. A juggler may waver (C) as he or she tosses (D) balls, but the literal meaning of juggling does not apply here.

**26. A:** To *augment* something is to increase it or make it greater. While the library may correct some misinformation (A) or change a student's education (C), these are not the meaning of *augment*. "Color" (D) is *pigment*, not *augment*.

**27. C:** This is the best restatement of the main idea. Choices A and B restate information from the first two sentences, but the main idea is found in the third sentence. Choice D restates a detail from the final paragraph.

## Writing

**28. A:** This headline uses the simple tense. In this case, it's the simple present tense. B uses the infinitive form, while C and D both drop the auxiliary verb in the passive voice.

**29. A:** This version is correctly punctuated because it is a compound-complex sentence, consisting of two independent clauses and a dependent/subordinate (relative) clause. Independent clauses should be separated by a semicolon. In (B) and (D), the two independent clauses have no punctuation separating them, creating a run-on sentence; additionally, (B) has an incorrect comma between the first independent clause and the subordinating conjunction "that," which introduces the relative clause. (If "that" were omitted, it would be correct with or without the comma.) Version (C) incorrectly separates the independent clauses with a comma instead of a semicolon.

**30. C:** The statement "And even the name of the legendary King Arthur" is not a complete sentence and thus cannot stand on its own. The period that is placed before the word *And* should be removed and the two statements combined.

**31. A:** The comma that is located before "his Idylls of the King" represents a comma splice and should be replaced with a period, a semicolon, or a comma and a coordinating conjunction. The two statements before and after the comma represent individual sentences and cannot be joined with a comma alone.

**32. D:** The clue for identifying infinitives is the word *to* before a verb. In this case, *to reflect* and *to enlighten* are excellent examples of infinitives, which are a type of verbal, or a verb form that actually function as a different part of speech. Infinitives (and gerunds) function as nouns.

**33. D:** The verb "to walk" is regular, i.e., it is conjugated with regular endings: walk, walks, walking, walked. "To be" (A) is irregular: am, is, are, were. "To go" (B) is also irregular, with past tense being "went" rather than "goed" (which is not a word). "To run" is irregular, with run in present tense and ran in past, but "have run" and "had run" (not ran) in present perfect and past perfect tenses.

**34. D:** The verb "to run" is "run" in present tense ("I run every day"), "ran" in past tense ("She ran home") and "have/has/had run" in perfect tense ("He had run to the mailbox"). The other choices are all irregular verbs, conjugated correctly here.

**35. A:** Many English grammar experts tolerate the common but incorrect use of "me," "him," "her," "them," and similar object pronouns instead of subject pronouns. A subject pronoun can be the sentence subject (e.g., "I am here"), or rename the subject (e.g., "It is only I"). Object pronouns are objects (e.g., "Dogs like me"). In formal writing, "I" is correct here, not "me." Thus choice (B) is incorrect. Because "me" is an object pronoun but is technically incorrect, choice (C) is wrong. Because "me" is incorrect and is not a subject pronoun, choice (D) is wrong.

**36. C:** The possessive case of the pronoun *it* is correctly spelled *its* without an apostrophe, just as the possessive form of *him* is *his* with no apostrophe. *It's* is a contraction of the pronoun *it* and the verb *is*, used correctly in choices B and C. Choice A uses both incorrectly by omitting the apostrophe from the contraction and adding it to the possessive. Although choice D uses the possessive correctly, it uses the contraction incorrectly by omitting the apostrophe.

**37. C:** The pronoun *who* refers to a person as the sentence or phrase subject (Jacqueline in this case). The pronoun *whom* (A) refers to a person as a sentence or phrase object (e.g., "Whom did you choose?"). The pronouns *which* (B) and *that* (D) refer to a thing rather than to a person.

**38. D:** Demonstrative pronouns can stand alone to replace nouns. (When modifying nouns, they are demonstrative adjectives, e.g., "This meal was great"). "Those" is plural and refers correctly to "the ones." However, "This" (A) should be "That" as it refers to a meal last week; conversely, "That" (B) should be "This" as it refers to weather today. "These" (C) should be "Those" as it refers to things "over there." "These" would refer to things right here.

**39. C:** Comparative modifiers show a difference between two things (or places or people)—Sue and Jeffrey in this case. Superlative modifiers show differences between more than two. Therefore, choice A should use *better*, not *best*, as only two people are compared; choice B should use *best*, not *better*, as she was the choice "Out of all the candidates;" and choice D should use *higher*, not *highest*, as only two test scores are compared.

**40. D:** Grammatically, these adjectives follow a logical progression showing increasing degrees of the attribute: the original is small (A); the comparative, indicating more small, is smaller and is used to compare two things (B); and the superlative, indicating most small, is smallest (D). Smallish (C) is also an adjective based on small, but not comparative or superlative; rather, it indicates approximation, i.e., sort of small or somewhat small.

**41. C:** This is a complete sentence with an implied subject (you), verb, and object. Choice A is a sentence fragment with a verb, adverb, preposition, article, object, and preposition, but no subject. Choice B is a fragment with subjects and a prepositional phrase, but no verb. Choice D is a fragment as it has a subject modified by a dependent clause containing a verb, but the subject has no accompanying verb to create the necessary independent clause.

**42. A:** This is a run-on sentence because it contains two independent clauses but no connection or division. This can be corrected by dividing the clauses into two sentences separated by a period, by dividing the two clauses with a semicolon, or by joining the two clauses with a comma and a coordinating conjunction (e.g., *because*, *since*, or *as*). Choice B correctly divides two independent clauses with a comma and the coordinating conjunction *and*. Choice C correctly divides two independent clauses with a semicolon. Choice D correctly connects two independent clauses with a comma and the coordinating conjunction "but."

**43. B:** This sentence is correct: "while," as a subordinating conjunction, introduces the subordinate (dependent) clause. However, when the subordinate clause comes first (A), a comma should separate it from the following independent clause. The run-on sentence (C) needs a semicolon to divide it; a comma plus a coordinating conjunction like "so" (or a semicolon plus "therefore," "thus," "hence," etc. plus a comma); or a period, making two sentences. Run-on (D) needs either a period, a semicolon, or a comma plus a conjunction like "and" or "but." (Shorter sentences can omit the comma or conjunction.)

**44. B:** Sentence (A) omits a comma before "children" to indicate the first part is addressing them. Without the comma, they become the object of the verb "play." Sentence (B) is punctuated correctly: a semicolon separates independent clauses when the second one explains or completes the first. Sentence (C) incorrectly uses a comma before "however" instead of a semicolon. Conversely, sentence (D) incorrectly uses a semicolon before "and" instead of a comma.

**45. A:** Phrases that interrupt the flow of a sentence ("by the way," in this case) should be set off by commas. Choice B has the first comma but omits the second to set off "for your information." Choice C has the second comma but omits the first to set off "on the other hand." A comma should follow an introductory word like *why*, but there should be no comma after *first* (D).

**46. C:** When joining two independent clauses within one sentence via a coordinating conjunction like "but," a comma should precede the "but." These two clauses can also be correctly divided into two separate sentences. However, there should not be a comma or any other punctuation following "But" when it begins the second sentence (B). Conversely, omitting punctuation before "but" within the same sentence (D) is incorrect.

**47. D:** The first letter of the first word in any sentence must always be capitalized, no matter what that word is. This includes the first word of a new sentence within a quotation, as in this example, which contains two separate sentences following the exclamation "Wow!" Choice (A) capitalizes only the first new sentence, choice (B) capitalizes neither new sentence, and choice (C) capitalizes only the second new sentence.

**48. B:** Proper nouns, e.g., the name of the city Tokyo, always have capitalized initial letters. Not only proper nouns, but also verbs, adjectives, and other parts of speech derived from proper nouns—e.g., "Japanese" and "English"—also always have their first letters capitalized. Option (A) fails to capitalize these language names, option (C) fails to capitalize the city name, and option (D) fails to capitalize all of these.

**49. A:** Formal titles of people, positions, occupations, etc. that come before or after proper names are capitalized. However, nouns naming positions or occupations are not capitalized as their titles are. Therefore, choice A is correct. Choice B incorrectly capitalizes the noun *queen* at the beginning and fails to capitalize the titles *Her Majesty* and *Queen [Elizabeth II]*. Choice C incorrectly capitalizes the noun *queen* and fails to capitalize *Her* in the title. Choice D fails to capitalize the proper noun *England* and the title words *Her Majesty* and *Queen*.

**50. B:** In this sentence, "sighted" means seen and is spelled correctly. In choice A, the word should be spelled "cited" and means officially summoned to appear in court or issued a citation (ticket). In choice C, it should also be "cited," with the same or similar meaning as choice A. In choice D, it should again be spelled "cited," but in this case it means made reference to as examples, support, confirmation, or proof.

**51. D:** The spelling *knew* indicates the past tense of the verb *to know*; the spelling *new* indicates the adjective meaning novel, recent, original, not old, etc. These two meanings cannot be spelled alike or interchangeably. Choice A misspells both words; choice B misspells only *new* as *knew*; and choice C misspells only *knew* as *new*.

**52. C:** The first instance is the preposition "to," meaning in order, and used as the first word of verb infinitives. The second instance is the adverb "too," meaning excessively, or (as in this case) also. Choice A misspells the second instance, choice B misspells both, choice C is correct, and choice D misspells the first instance.

**53. A:** As the name of a landmark structure, this phrase is a proper noun. Not only proper nouns (i.e., names), but also adjectives derived from proper nouns (e.g., *Golden*) should have their initial letters capitalized. *Bridge* is part of the whole name and is included in this capitalization rule (B). The same applies to *Gate* (C). Because all three of the name's words should be capitalized, choice D is incorrect.

**54. C:** The first instance, meaning be aware or cognizant of, is spelled "know"; the second instance, meaning not any, is spelled "no." Choice A reverses these spellings, choice B misspells the second instance, choice C spells both correctly, and choice D misspells the first instance.

## Mathematics

**55. B:** The place value is assigned by the position of the digit. The places to the left of the decimal are ones, tens, hundreds, then thousands, respectively. Since the digit 7 is in the third place to the left of the implied decimal, it's in the hundreds place. The value of this digit is $7 \times 100$, which is 700.

**56. A:** The place value of a digit depends on its location in relation to the decimal point. The places to the left of the decimal are ones, tens, then hundreds, respectively. The places to the right of the decimal are tenths, hundredths, and thousandths, respectively. Since the digit 2 is in the first position to the left of the decimal point, its place value is ones.

**57. C:** The place value of a digit depends on its location in relation to the decimal point. The places to the left of the decimal are ones, tens, then hundreds, respectively. To round a number to a certain place value, look at the digit to the immediate right. If the digit to the right is 5 or more, round up by adding one. If the digit is less than five, round down by keeping the same digit. For this problem, the digit in the tens place is 8. The digit to its immediate right is 8. Since 8 is greater than 5, round up: 788 rounded to the nearest ten is 790.

**58. C:** The place value of a digit depends on its location in relation to the decimal point. The places to the left of the decimal are ones, tens, hundreds, then thousands, respectively. To round a number to a certain place value, look at the digit to the immediate right. If the digit to the right is 5 or more, round up by adding one. If the digit is less than five, round down by keeping the same digit. For this problem, the digit in the thousands place is 5. The digit to its immediate right is 3. Since 3 is less than 5, round down: 3,895,399 rounded to the nearest thousand is 3,895,000.

**59. C:** Since 1 meter equals 100 centimeters, the conversion factor is 100. Since a centimeter is shorter than a meter, we divide by the conversion factor.

$$7{,}200 \text{ cm} \times \frac{1 \text{ m}}{100 \text{ cm}} = 72 \text{ m}$$

Therefore, 7,200 centimeters is equivalent to 72 meters.

**60. C:** The length of the fence is equal to the perimeter of the rectangular property. The perimeter of the property is equal to the sum of twice the length and twice the width. The length is approximately 400 feet, and the width is approximately 300 feet, so the perimeter is $2(400) + 2(300) = 1{,}400$ feet.

**61. B:** A quick estimate of the total miles can be obtained by rounding each leg of the trip to the nearest whole mile and finding the sum: $5 + 7 + 14 + 15 = 41$ miles.

**62. C:** The total number of tickets sold is equal to the sum of the tickets sold each day. The total is equal to $120 + 240 + 81 + 29 + 350$ or 820 tickets.

**63. B:** The length of Chen's trip is equal to the sum of the original distance and the additional miles to see his grandparents. Then the total equals $262 + 49$ or 311 miles.

**64. D:** The amount of pies remaining is equal to the difference between the number of pies donated and the number of pies sold. Then, the amount equals $53 - 17$ or 36 pies.

**65. A:** This is ordinary subtracting with no borrowing: $73{,}752 - 63{,}721 = 10{,}031$.

**66. A:** The number of day's Felicia is in town is equal to the difference between the number of days in a year and the number of days she travels.

$$365 - 157 = 208$$

Therefore, Felicia is in town 208 days this year.

**67. D:** The number of tickets sold is the sum of the tickets sold by each of the students. This sum is $75 + 75 + 45 + 45 + 45 + 95 = 380$ tickets.

**68. A:** To multiply numbers ending in zero, first multiply the numbers (ignoring the zeros) and then add the zeros after the last digit of the product. Then $12 \times 12 = 144$ and adding the four zeros yields 1,440,000.

**69. C:** The number of seats in the auditorium is equal to the product of the number of rows and the number of seats per row. The number of seats equals $25 \times 40$, or 1,000 seats.

**70. D:** Since 11 is not a factor of 150, there is a remainder when 150 is divided by 11. Since $11 \times 13 = 143$, and $150 - 143 = 7$, the remainder is 7.

**71. C:** The amount received by each employee is equal to the total amount of the bonus divided by the number of employees. The amount each employee receives equals $\$5{,}000 \div 20 = \$250$.

**72. D:** The amount of Ethan's car payment is equal to the cost of the car divided by the number of payments. The car payment equals $\$32{,}460 \div 60$ or $541.

**73. D:** The distance travelled is equal to the product of the rate of travel and the time of travel. Since $55 \times 3 = 165$, Mr. Jackson drives 165 miles.

**74. B:** The amount of material remaining is equal to $12\frac{1}{4} - 8\frac{2}{3}$. First, convert both mixed numbers to improper fractions: $\frac{49}{4} - \frac{26}{3}$. Next convert to a common denominator: $\frac{147}{12} - \frac{104}{12}$. Finally, subtract the numerators and convert back to a mixed number: $\frac{147}{12} - \frac{104}{12} = \frac{43}{12} = 3\frac{7}{12}$.

**75. A:** To add these fractions, rewrite each fraction as an equivalent fraction over the least common denominator: $\frac{6}{12} + \frac{4}{12} + \frac{3}{12} = \frac{13}{12}$ or $1\frac{1}{12}$.

**76. A:** The total weight of the tomato sauce Mr. Nelson stocked is equal to the product of the number of jars and the weight of each jar. The total weight equals $505 \times 1.09$ or 550.45 pounds.

**77. B:** The number of miles per gallon is the quotient of the number of miles driven and the number of gallons of gasoline. The number of miles per gallon equals $412.5 \div 12.5$ or 33 mpg.

**78. D:** This question is basically asking, "What percent of 24 is 8?" Let $n$ represent *what percent*, and replace the *of* with a multiplication symbol and the *is* with an equal sign. Then we have $n \times 24 = 8$. To solve this equation, divide both sides by 24. Then $n = 8 \div 24 = 0.3333$. This is in decimal form. To convert a decimal to a percent, move the decimal point two places to the right and add the percent symbol. Then the decimal 0.3333 is 33.33%. Rounded to the nearest percent, this is 33%.

**79. D:** This question is asking, "8 is 25% of what number?" Let $n$ represent *what number*, and replace the *of* with a multiplication sign and the *is* with an equal sign. But first, we need to convert the 25% to a decimal. Remove the percent sign and move the decimal point two places to the left. Then we have $8 = 0.25 \times n$. To solve this equation, divide both sides by 0.25. Then $8 \div 0.25 = n$, so $n = 32$. Marcie had 32 homework problems.

**80. B:** To covert a percent to a fraction, remove the percent symbol and place the number over one hundred. Then 60% is represented by the fraction $\frac{60}{100}$, which reduces to $\frac{3}{5}$.

**81. D:** To convert a decimal to a percent, move the decimal point two places to the right and add the percent symbol. Thus 0.0037 equals 0.37%.

## Instructional Support

**82. B:** A haptic learning style is one in which the student learns best through tactile contact (e.g., touching, feeling, manipulating, and shaping things using the hands). Writing a paper (A) is most applicable for a student with a verbal learning style, learning best through reading and writing. Listening to a recording (C) is most applicable for a student with an auditory learning style, learning better through hearing than through seeing. Dance (D) is most applicable for a student with a kinesthetic learning style, learning best though physical movement.

**83. A:** Activating students' previous experiences and knowledge and connecting new learning to these makes reading material more meaningful to them. One way is having students identify similarities between and relate things in their reading and personal lives. Having them seek examples in real life (B) helps students apply reading more than relate it to prior knowledge. Drilling (C) is better for memorizing, e.g., new vocabulary, irregular spellings/verbs, etc., than for activating prior knowledge. Movies (D) make reading matter multisensory, reducing verbal demand, rather than accessing prior experience.

**84. D:** An encyclopedia offers the most comprehensive information about a variety of academic and other subjects. A glossary (A) is a list that a text includes of vocabulary words or specialized terminology used specifically in that text, with definitions—not a comprehensive information source. A thesaurus (B) provides synonyms and antonyms for words. A dictionary (C) provides spellings, pronunciations, definitions, and usage examples of most words in a language—not limited to text-specific words, and not including other information unrelated to words.

**85. D:** Students can gain some comprehension of the overall topic of text while skimming it for the first time (A), but cannot summarize while skimming. Before skimming (B), they can get a general idea what text is about by previewing the title, heading(s), table of contents, illustrations, etc., but not summarize actual main ideas. They cannot summarize during first reading (C) as they have not finished it yet. Summarizing is an effective comprehension and retention strategy only after students have thoroughly read the text (D).

**86. B:** In the QAR strategy, "Right There" (A) questions ask students to find a single correct answer in text. "Author and You" (C) questions ask students to relate text to their existing knowledge. "Think and Search" (D) questions ask students to recall facts directly from text, usually in multiple locations. "On Your Own" (B) questions ask students to respond from their own experience and knowledge rather than the text.

**87. B:** Using student reading progress information to allow more time for the instruction that students need most is more related to lesson planning than the other choices. Using this information for reteaching (A) is more related to instruction. Using it for eliminating mastered skills from an exam (C) and for designing quizzes in proportion to amounts of instruction (D) are both more related to assessment.

**88. C:** Writing a new lesson using different strategies (A) that might be more effective most involves planning. Revising the calendar to allow more time for instruction to meet critical student needs (B) also involves planning most. Adjusting the instructional pace to fit student learning rates better (C) involves instruction the most among these choices. Writing shorter quizzes to administer more often (D) to divide new learning into smaller and more manageable amounts most involves assessment.

**89. A:** The best way to teach students to write is to instruct them first to compose rough drafts, then to edit their drafts. After editing, once they have achieved a final draft, only then should they proofread their work for mechanical and typing or handwriting errors and correct these. Some students with especial writing gifts or talents may be capable of choices B, C, or D, but they are the minority. Most students (and other writers) must learn and apply the process in sequential steps (A).

**90. B:** Although writers and writing students must focus on a specific topic (A) and/or main idea (C), either or both of these alone are insufficient. They must moreover know why they are writing about these, and what they want their writing to communicate about them—i.e., their purpose for writing (B). Focus interacts reciprocally with organization (D): focus determines structural choices, and good writers make use of suitable organizational choices to reinforce focus. (The same applies to other writing features.)

**91. D:** As experienced writers and teachers advise, if students determine a perspective from which to write, they can establish a clear focus before starting to make writing unified and coherent, and discover what message they want to communicate. In other words, determining perspective helps them find their purpose for writing. Perfect mechanics (A), effective word choice (B), and smoothly connected sentences (C) demonstrate good technical skills in writing, but are useless if the writing is not focused and unified by some central viewpoint or idea, i.e., the student's reason for writing.

**92. C:** The writing exercise focused on students editing their own drafts. Though they were assigned to cooperative learning groups, how well they collaborated (A) is not the most useful information for the teacher. Neither is identifying exemplary student writers (B), nor identifying the most creative writing (D). To help the teacher plan ongoing instruction best, her assistant can inform her of what kinds of help she observed the students needed in editing their own writing.

**93. B:** Dictionaries will help a student with word meanings, spellings, pronunciations, and usage, but not with sentence structure. The grammar check functions in word processing programs (C) are typically unreliable: they frequently detect some errors but not others; try to "correct" already acceptable constructions; and, lacking artificial intelligence, also lack the informed judgment of knowledgeable humans. The greatest authors (e.g., Shakespeare) frequently break grammatical rules with the expertise to do so effectively (D). Grammar books and guides (B) supply rules for writing complete sentences.

**94. A:** Word processing software presents a great boon to most students in public schools. However, many schools today lack accompanying computer hardware that is portable, durable, and cost-effective. Technology companies have produced and continue developing tablet computers and similar devices as solutions, but most public schools do not have these yet. Spell-check, style-check and other related software programs typically bundled (B) with word processing programs offer added advantages to students. Word processing programs facilitate revision (C), another advantage. Many students having fine motor deficits can learn to type more easily than handwrite (D), which is another asset.

**95. D:** A pop quiz (A) or an oral test (B) may yield some information about what students do and do not know about writing, but will not show their actual use of writing skills. Formal examinations (C) are typically not used as formative assessments during instruction, but as summative assessments after instruction. However, writing samples (D) require students to demonstrate and enable teachers to evaluate how students are writing at the time, progress made, skills mastered, and skills or areas needing more instruction.

**96. B:** How often to collect information on student progress is most related to assessment among these choices. How much time to spend on each writing skill (A) is more related to planning. Identifying strategies (both to use and to teach) for each writing skill (C) is more related to instruction. Grouping students (D) is more related to planning.

**97. C:** According to education experts, in K–4 math instruction, problem-solving is not a separate topic or part of a math program (A), but is among the foremost goals of math instruction (B). It is a process that should spread throughout the whole math program (C), and it supplies the context wherein students can learn math concepts and skills, rather than actually being those math concepts and skills (D).

**98. A:** Giving the students a hands-on learning activity using concrete objects that are also familiar will make the abstract math concept simpler for them to understand. Concrete, manipulative objects are important for teaching abstract concepts to younger students who typically do not yet think abstractly. Calculators (B) do not explain the concept. Rereading the textbook and asking questions (C) does not provide concrete objects or hands-on learning. These three students cannot apply the concept by working even simple problems (D) until they first understand it.

**99. D:** Graphic organizers (A) can make differences, similarities, and relationships more visual, but will not necessarily help these students with what they want to know. Mickey can determine whether his hours worked times pay per hour equals his total wages by multiplying and/or dividing; Alonzo can determine how much his raises have added to his earnings by graphing them across the time period. Choice (B) cites the wrong math procedures for what each student wants to determine. Counting real money (C) will not efficiently or practically give them the data they want as simple computations and graphing will.

**100. A:** Informed by student progress data, Mr. Kirk's decision to consult his mentor about how to explain these concepts is most related to instruction, while his decision to add lessons with this instruction is most related to planning. Neither decision is related to assessment.

# NYSTCE Practice Test #2

## Reading

*Refer to the following for questions 1–9:*

**Classroom Management**

While each teacher has a unique method of classroom management and cannot be completely categorized as one certain type, most tend toward one of four main styles. These styles depend on the amount of control and involvement a teacher takes. A teacher with both high involvement and high control is Authoritative. An Authoritarian teacher also exhibits a high level of control, but low involvement. Some teachers exhibit high involvement but low control. These teachers are termed Indulgent. Finally, a Permissive teacher has low involvement and low control. The style a teacher uses determines, to a significant degree, both the environment of the classroom and the success of the teaching.

An Authoritative teacher provides a stable environment with clear expectations. Rules are enforced and the teacher is invested in the students, who learn to be responsible and to take on leadership. Students under Authoritarian teachers, on the other hand, can feel uncared for, as behavior is strictly enforced but the teacher may not take time to explain rules and concepts or truly invest in the individuals. Indulgent teachers take time to talk to students and help them but rules are feebly enforced. Students know their teacher cares for them, but this style can lead to a chaotic environment that hampers learning. Permissive teachers allow excess freedom for students and give little direction, which can result in poor behavior and lack of learning.

While each style can have benefits, the Authoritative style is typically the most effective for student learning because it provides an orderly and caring atmosphere. Students know they must behave but they also know the teacher cares about them and will take time to explain concepts and listen to questions. The strictness is tempered by kindness, and students not only learn better but also grow better emotionally in an Authoritative environment.

**1. Which of the following is the most accurate meaning of *feebly*, as used in the fourth sentence of paragraph 2?**

a. Weakly
b. In a senile fashion
c. Haphazardly
d. Rarely

**2. The word *tempered* in the last sentence is closest in meaning to which related word?**

a. The noun *temper*, meaning the heat of anger
b. The adjective *temperate*, meaning moderate
c. The noun *temper*, meaning one's disposition
d. The adjective *temperamental*, meaning sensitive

**3. Of these choices, where is the main idea of this article best expressed?**

a. In the article's title
b. In the first sentence of the first paragraph
c. In the last sentence of the first paragraph
d. In the last sentence of the last paragraph

**4. What can be stated about the topic sentences in this selection?**

a. The first sentence of each paragraph is that paragraph's topic sentence.
b. None of the three paragraphs has a true topic sentence, only a main idea.
c. The first and third paragraphs begin with a topic sentence, while the second paragraph has no clear topic sentence.
d. Each paragraph concludes with the topic sentence.

**5. Where in the article are the results of the different classroom management styles discussed?**

a. All three paragraphs
b. Paragraph 3
c. Paragraphs 1 and 3
d. Paragraphs 2 and 3

**6. Which two classroom management styles exhibit a low level of involvement?**

a. Authoritative and Indulgent
b. Authoritarian and Indulgent
c. Authoritarian and Permissive
d. Indulgent and Permissive

**7. Which sentence in the first paragraph is the best example of a topic sentence?**

a. The first sentence
b. The second sentence
c. The final sentence
d. None of these

**8. What best describes the sequence of the paragraphs in this article?**

a. Main Idea, Supporting Details, Summary
b. Problem, Solution, Summary
c. Introduction, Cause, Effect
d. Introduction, Supporting Details, Application

**9. What kind of graph would be best to depict the number of teachers using each style of classroom management in a particular school?**

a. A line graph
b. A bar graph
c. A scatter plot
d. A Venn diagram

*Refer to the following for questions 10–18:*

While the pros and cons of using technology in teaching have been argued for decades, it is undoubtedly an integral part of the classroom now. Teachers are expected to utilize technology to further the education of their students, both in the classroom and out. This can provide new ways not only to teach, but also to engage students in their own learning. Yet it can also provide new challenges.

Nearly every school has a wide range of student backgrounds; economic backgrounds, ethnic/cultural backgrounds, and learning styles can vary greatly, along with other details like level of parental involvement. This variety can make it tricky when using technology, especially out of the classroom. For instance, an idea to host an online forum for homework help may seem advantageous, but some students may not have Internet access or a computer. Even students who can access the forum may need other methods, such as video for those who need auditory teaching along with the text.

Despite these challenges, technology brings a host of opportunities to enhance learning and enable students to participate more in their education. Students can connect with teachers and other students outside the classroom, expand their research competence, and be more "hands-on" rather than simply listening to a lecture. Despite technology's drawbacks of cost and challenge to implement, the potential for educational enhancement is immense.

**10. Which of the following is the best meaning for *host*, as seen in the first sentence of the third paragraph?**

a. Supporting role
b. Dearth
c. Multitude
d. Exclusive selection

**11. A suitable synonym for the word *competence* in the second sentence of the third paragraph would be which of these choices?**

a. Victory
b. Knowledge
c. Aggression
d. Ability

**12. Which sentence serves as the most direct introductory statement?**

a. The opening sentence of the first paragraph
b. The second sentence of the first paragraph
c. The first sentence of the second paragraph
d. The entire second paragraph

**13. What is the best restatement of the main idea of the text?**

a. There are both positive and negative aspects of technology.
b. Different student backgrounds make it a challenge to use technology in education.
c. The benefits of using technology in education outweigh the challenges.
d. Students can have many new experiences with technology that would be impossible without it.

**14. Regarding summary statements, which choice is most accurate about this text?**

a. The entire first paragraph is a summary statement.
b. There is no summary statement in this selection.
c. The entire last paragraph is a summary statement.
d. The final sentence is a summary statement.

**15. Which paragraph(s) of this text name the drawbacks of using technology in schools?**

a. The first and second paragraphs
b. The second and third paragraphs
c. The second paragraph only
d. All three paragraphs

**16. What is the tone of this selection?**

a. Persuasive
b. Confrontational
c. Informative
d. Concerned

**17. Is the final sentence of the selection a fact or an opinion, and does it show bias?**

a. Fact, bias
b. Opinion, bias
c. Fact, no bias
d. Opinion, no bias

**18. How can the three paragraphs of the text be described?**

a. Introduction, Argument and Counterargument, Summary
b. Introduction, Counterargument, Argument and Summary
c. Argument, Counterargument, Summary
d. Introduction, Argument, Counterargument

*Refer to the following for questions 19–21:*

Jo's face was a study next day, for the secret rather weighed upon her, and she found it hard not to look mysterious and important. Meg observed it, but did not trouble herself to make inquiries, for she had learned that the best way to manage Jo was by the law of contraries, so she felt sure of being told everything if she did not ask. She was rather surprised, therefore, when the silence remained unbroken, and Jo assumed a patronizing air, which decidedly aggravated Meg, who in turn assumed an air of dignified reserve and devoted herself to her mother. This left Jo to her own devices, for Mrs. March had taken her place as nurse, and bade her rest, exercise, and amuse herself after her long confinement. Amy being gone, Laurie was her only refuge, and much as she enjoyed his society, she rather dreaded him just then, for he was an incorrigible tease, and she feared he would coax the secret from her.

(*Little Women* by Louisa May Alcott)

**19. What can you infer about Laurie?**

a. He was stoic.
b. He was taciturn.
c. He was unruly.
d. He was uncanny.

**20. From what point of view is this passage written?**

a. First person
b. Second person
c. Third person
d. Fourth person

**21. The phrase *was a study* implies that:**

a. Jo looked jubilant.
b. Jo looked secretive.
c. Jo looked disheveled.
d. Jo looked angry.

*Refer to the following for questions 22–24:*

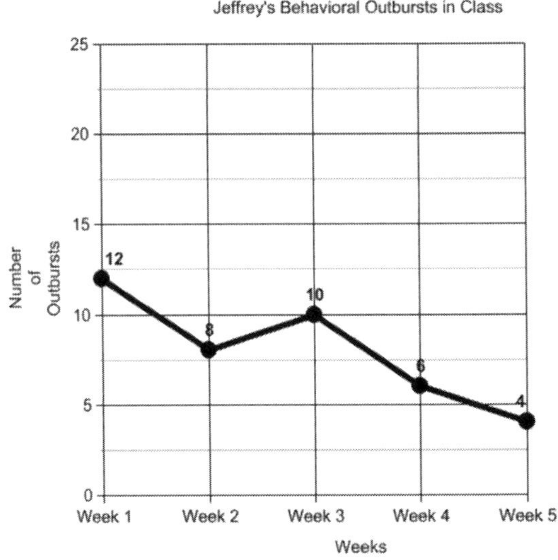


**22. This student received an intervention to reduce behavioral outbursts in class. What effect has this had by the fifth week, according to the graph's data?**

a. His outbursts have decreased by one-third of what they were.
b. His outbursts have decreased to one-third of what they were.
c. His outbursts have decreased by one-half of what they were.
d. His outbursts have decreased to one-half of what they were.

**23. What is the overall pattern of the target behavior over the five weeks shown?**

a. Decreasing overall, with one increase from Week 2 to Week 3
b. Increasing overall, with one decrease from Week 3 to Week 4
c. Decreasing overall, with instability shown by interim changes
d. Increasing overall, with two decreases between Weeks 1 to 5

**24. Using the graphed values, what is the average number of outbursts Jeffrey had over the weeks shown?**

a. 40
b. 12
c. 8
d. 4

*Refer to the following for question 25:*

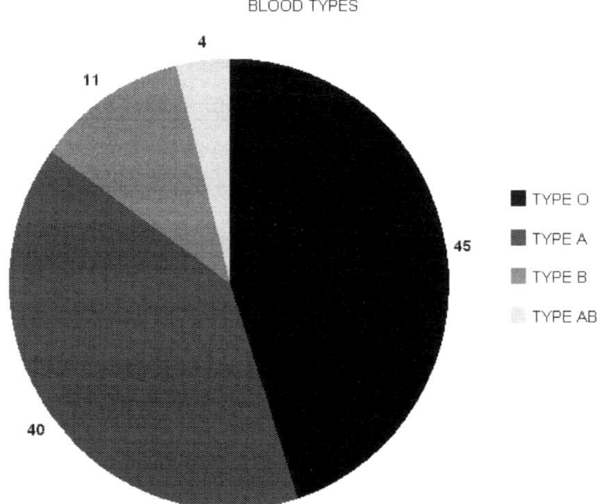


**25. Based on this pie chart, which of the following statements is true?**

a. More people have Type O blood than all other types combined.
b. More people have Type O blood than Types A and B combined.
c. More people have Types O and AB blood than A and B combined.
d. More people have Type O blood than Types A and AB combined.

*Refer to the following for question 26:*

It is important for students at all grade levels to be read aloud to daily at school. Teachers should read aloud for 20 minutes to a half hour and should choose books that encourage students' appreciation of literature, increase their vocabulary, and promote reading as an enjoyable activity. As the teacher reads aloud, he or she should encourage discussion of vocabulary words, story conflict, opinions of certain characters in the story, and predictions about what may happen next in the book.

**26. According to the passage, all of the following statements are true EXCEPT:**

a. Older students can still benefit from being read aloud to.
b. Student opinions are not as important as discussions about vocabulary words.
c. Predicting what will happen in a story is an important skill for all students.
d. Teachers should ask questions as they read.

*Refer to the following for question 27:*

There are several important rules regarding Five Oaks guests' vehicles. Please ensure you understand and abide by these regulations and indicate such by initializing and returning a copy of this sheet to the front office.

Parking tickets will be issued for those vehicles left in the main lot overnight. If you plan to spend the night at Five Oaks, please ensure you have registered your vehicle, secured and displayed a window label, and are parked in the side lot. We cannot be responsible for tickets issued by the city Police Department.

If you are returning to Five Oaks after 11:00 p.m., please use the four-digit pass code to enter the side parking lot. This code changes every 48 hours and should be kept confidential.

Thank you for your attention to these rules which are in effect for your safety and the safety of others at Five Oaks.

**27. According to the passage, which of the following is an example of going against regulations?**

a. Displaying a window label
b. Overnight parking in the main lot
c. Using the pass code
d. Registering a vehicle

## Writing

**28. "Everybody has ____ own copy of the book." Which word(s) correctly fill(s) in the blank?**

a. His or her
b. Their
c. Your
d. Our

**29. Which sentence has correct subject-verb agreement?**

a. Bart and Lisa takes the first turn.
b. Both of them takes the first turn.
c. Lisa or Marge takes the first turn.
d. Either of them take the first turn.

**30. Of the following sentences, which is in the present tense?**

a. Today we will take the test.
b. Yesterday we took the test.
c. We take this test each year.
d. We have taken many tests.

**31. Which of these is an example of the future tense?**

a. We will complete that by tomorrow.
b. We will have done it by next month.
c. We had finished before the deadline.
d. We were going to finish it next week.

**32. Which of these sentences uses the past tense of the verb?**

a. Teddy prepares a delicious gourmet meal.
b. Teddy prepared a delicious meal for us all.
c. Teddy is preparing a delicious meal for us.
d. Teddy has prepared for us this delicious meal.

**33. Of the following, which contains a verb in the present perfect tense?**

a. Danny said that he had already finished his homework.
b. Danny says that he has already finished his homework.
c. Danny says he will have finished his homework by then.
d. Danny says that he is finishing his homework right now.

**34. Which of the following has a present progressive verb tense?**

a. Joyce and Eric are heading up our new committee.
b. Joyce and Eric will be heading our new committee.
c. Joyce and Eric have headed up our new committee.
d. Joyce and Eric had been heading a new committee.

**35. Which version of this sentence uses the past perfect progressive verb tense?**

a. Manuel is improving his grades steadily so far this year.
b. Manuel was improving his grades steadily all last year.
c. Manuel has been improving his grades steadily all year.
d. Manuel had been improving his grades steadily all year.

**36. In English, which subject person, number, and verb tense always has a verb with an *-s* ending?**

a. First person, singular, present tense
b. Third person, plural, past tense
c. Second person, plural, present tense
d. Third person, singular, present tense

**37. In which choice does the reflexive pronoun agree with the noun it renames?**

a. Now it's every boy for themself.
b. It's now every girl for himself.
c. Now it's every group for itself.
d. It's now each team for themselves.

**38. Among these choices, which demonstrates pronoun-antecedent and subject-verb agreement?**

a. The one who should apologize is he, not she.
b. The person responsible for this task are you.
c. The people who have to do the job are them.
d. When asked who did it, Sylvia said it was her.

**39. In which sentence does the pronoun agree with its antecedent?**

a. The payment was divided between Ralph and I.
b. They gave identical payments to Ralph and me.
c. They divided a payment between he and Ralph.
d. The money was divided among they and Ralph.

**40. "They described their best attorney, which was my uncle." What is true about the relative pronoun?**

a. It should be "who."
b. It should be "that."
c. It should be "whom."
d. It is correctly "which."

**41. Which of the following sentences is correct?**

a. The house is sinking on it's foundation.
b. Simone says that the building is her's.
c. The family agrees the house is theirs.
d. If you want to fix it, its your job.

**42. Of the following, which version of the sentence uses demonstrative pronouns appropriately?**

a. This book here is better than that book here.
b. This book there is better than that book here.
c. This book there is better than that book there.
d. This book here is better than that book there.

**43. The student's reading skills were poor, but his writing skills were _____. What word correctly completes this sentence?**

a. worst
b. worse
c. worser
d. poorest

**44. "The hostess with the mostest" is a familiar American English expression. Though it was intended to create humor and a rhyme, what else is true about the word "mostest"?**

a. It is an acceptable superlative form outside of this expression.
b. It is incorrect because it is the superlative rather than the comparative form.
c. It is incorrect to use as the superlative because it is redundant.
d. It is superfluous, but it is acceptable outside of this expression.

**45. Which of the following is an example of a complete sentence?**

a. Let's go.
b. Let's go when the rain.
c. Let's go even though they say.
d. Let's go because all the other guests.

**46. Which of these choices is a sentence fragment?**

a. The city was beautiful.
b. With bright lights, the city was beautiful.
c. We visited the beautiful city with its bright lights.
d. The beautiful city we visited with all the bright lights.

**47. Of the following versions, which is an example of a run-on sentence?**

a. Jack loves to write he would write in every class if he could.
b. Jack loves to write; he would write in every class if he could.
c. Jack loves to write. He would write in every class if he could.
d. As Jack loves to write, he would write in each class if he could.

**48. Which of the following sentences is grammatically correct?**

a. We are going Tuesday won't you come with us?
b. We are sorry you can't attend we will miss you.
c. We will go on Tuesday; won't you come along?
d. We are sorry you cannot go, will bring pictures.

**49. The punctuation is correct in which of the following?**

a. They asked for permission, however, he refused.
b. They asked for permission; however, he refused.
c. They asked for permission, however; he refused.
d. They asked for permission, however he refused.

**50. Which of the following sentences contains correct standard capitalization?**

a. The Mayor and Councilmembers discussed a new ordinance regarding pedestrian traffic.
b. After the accident, Mayor Wells discussed a new ordinance with his councilmembers.
c. Concerned for the safety of citizens, mayor Wells and his councilmembers discussed a new ordinance.
d. Mayor Wells met with the Councilmembers to discuss a new ordinance for pedestrian safety.

**51. Which word is spelled incorrectly?**

a. Subtle
b. Ubiquitous
c. Pinnicle
d. Malicious

**52. Which of the following sentences contains correct standard capitalization?**

a. Johnny famously stated, "If it does not fit, you must acquit."
b. Johnny famously stated, "if it does not fit, you must acquit."
c. Johnny famously said that if it did not fit, "You must acquit."
d. Johnny famously stated need for acquittal "If it does not fit."

**53. With respect to capital letters, which phrase below is incorrect?**

a. draconian laws
b. herculean feat
c. quixotic behavior
d. german lullaby

**54. Among the following sentences, which spells the common word correctly for its context?**

a. "The name identifies county verses state government."
b. "The implications of acting verses waiting are unclear."
c. "The lengthy epic poem contains a great many verses."
d. "The Army verses Navy game was anticipated by fans."

## Mathematics

**55. What is the value of the underlined digit in 23,0<u>8</u>5?**

a. 8000
b. 800
c. 80
d. 8

**56. In the number 376.1, what is the hundreds digit?**

a. 7
b. 3
c. 1
d. 6

**57. What is 125,420 rounded to the nearest hundred?**

a. 400
b. 500
c. 125,000
d. 125,400

**58. How many inches are in 4 feet?**

a. 48
b. 36
c. 24
d. 12

**59. How many meters are equivalent to 336 millimeters?**

a. 336,000
b. 33,600
c. 3.36
d. 0.336

**60. The length of a rectangular room is 14.2 feet and the width is 9.6 feet. Using estimating, what is the minimum amount of carpeting that will completely cover the floor in this room?**

a. 135 $ft^2$
b. 140 $ft^2$
c. 143 $ft^2$
d. 148 $ft^2$

**61. A square has side lengths of 5.8 cm. Estimate the perimeter of the square to the nearest whole centimeter.**

a. 34 cm
b. 33 cm
c. 24 cm
d. 23 cm

**62. What is the sum of $12 + 18 + 14 + 16$?**

a. 40
b. 60
c. 59
d. 50

**63. Add $4,670,897 + 56,905 + 709,846$.**

a. 5,437,648
b. 5,437,638
c. 5,436,648
d. 4,437,648

**64. Ms. Robinson buys a coat that is originally marked $225. If she receives a $45 discount, what is the sale price of the coat?**

a. $190
b. $185
c. $170
d. $180

**65. Ms. Wise receives $5,695 in prize money after taxes. She deposits $1,200 in savings and purchases a vacation cruise package for $3,975. She donates the remaining amount to charity. How much does Ms. Wise donate to charity?**

a. $520
b. $515
c. $510
d. $505

**66. Chloe buys 3 CDs at $7 each and 4 t-shirts at $8 each. If she pays for these items with an $100 bill, how much money does she have left?**

a. $43
b. $57
c. $53
d. $47

**67. The enrollment of Lincoln High school is as follows: Freshmen 334, Sophomores 410, Juniors 312, and Seniors 345. What is the total enrollment?**

a. 1,491
b. 1,401
c. 1,301
d. 1.472

**68. Find $325 \times 1,000$.**

a. 3,250
b. 3,250,000
c. 32,500
d. 325,000

**69. A storage unit contains 3 pallets of 8 boxes. If each box contains 10 laptop computers, how many computers does the storage unit contain?**

a. 210 computers
b. 225 computers
c. 230 computers
d. 240 computers

**70. What is the remainder when 3500 is divided by 120?**

a. 20
b. 30
c. 40
d. 50

**71. Divide 864 by 24.**

a. 28
b. 26
c. 36
d. 46

**72. The Jewel Corporation has a profit of $156,168. If the profit is divided evenly among 324 employees, how much does each employee receive?**

a. $482
b. $582
c. $472
d. $478

**73. Mr. Miller bought a refrigerator for $2,160. He agreed to make 12 equal monthly payments. How much more than $100 will each payment be?**

a. $180
b. $160
c. $80
d. $60

**74. If it takes $1\frac{1}{2}$ teaspoons of sugar to make 1 cup of hot lemonade, how much is needed to make 16 cups of hot lemonade?**

a. 12 teaspoons
b. 24 teaspoons
c. 18 teaspoons
d. 28 teaspoons

**75. What is the product of $\frac{6}{11} \times \frac{11}{9}$?**

a. $\frac{1}{3}$
b. $\frac{2}{3}$
c. $\frac{2}{9}$
d. $\frac{4}{9}$

**76. Mr. Elliott bought 1.25 pounds of nails. If the cost is $4.08 per pound, what was the cost of the nails?**

a. $5.01
b. $5.10
c. $6.00
d. $6.10

**77. If the cost of hamburger is $1.39 per pound, what is the cost of 5 pounds of hamburger?**

a. $6.95
b. $5.95
c. $6.85
d. $6.55

**78. A survey of 200 high school students reveals that only 5% prefer strawberry ice cream over chocolate ice cream. How many students prefer strawberry ice cream?**

a. 20
b. 15
c. 10
d. 5

**79. Ms. Marejo paid $52 for a dress from the clearance rack. If the dress was 20% off, what was the list price?**

a. $65
b. $260
c. $62.40
d. $41.60

**80. Convert 125% to a decimal.**

a. 1.25
b. 12.5
c. 0.125
d. 0.00125

**81. Convert 3.25 to a mixed number.**

a. $2\frac{4}{5}$
b. $3\frac{1}{5}$
c. $3\frac{1}{4}$
d. $3\frac{1}{2}$

## Instructional Support

**82. An elementary school teacher assigns a teaching assistant to work with small groups of beginning reading students to help them learn irregular sight word spellings (e.g., is, are, were, the, who, what, know, etc.). Which instructional procedure would best meet this need?**

a. Reading words in context
b. Drilling for memorization
c. Relating texts to real lives
d. Picture-to-word matching

**83. To analyze the sequence of a story plot, which learning activity would most benefit a student with a predominantly visual learning style?**

a. Oral summary
b. Written outline
c. Manipulative(s)
d. Drawn timeline

**84. A class includes students with disabilities, gifted students, average students, and a variety of reading levels. To support reading, which type of instructional resources would afford the most benefits to the most students?**

a. Printed materials
b. Pictorial materials
c. Multimedia materials
d. Manipulative materials

**85. An ELL student from another country speaks excellent conversational English and has mastered the basics of reading written English, but has comprehension difficulties owing to insufficient knowledge of general English vocabulary. Which resource would be most helpful to this student?**

a. Desk dictionary
b. Word thesaurus
c. Textbook glossaries
d. Encyclopedia

**86. In a lesson for grades 3–8 on skimming nonfictional text for comprehension, which choice represents the best sequence of instruction?**

a. Explain how students can use skimming, define the goal for skimming the specific lesson text, conduct a think-aloud while modeling how to skim, collect student questions and feedback, have students practice, model using keywords in questions, get student questions and feedback, repeat modeling and student practice.
b. Conduct a think-aloud while modeling how to skim, repeat modeling and student practice, define the goal for skimming the specific lesson text, explain how students can use skimming, have students practice, collect student questions and feedback, repeat modeling and student practice, model using keywords in questions.
c. Model using keywords in questions, conduct a think-aloud while modeling how to skim, explain how students can use skimming, have students practice, repeat modeling and student practice, collect student questions and feedback, define the goal for skimming the specific lesson text, get student questions and feedback.
d. Define the goal for skimming the specific lesson text, model using keywords in questions, explain how students can use skimming, have students practice, collect student questions and feedback, conduct a think-aloud while modeling how to skim, repeat modeling and student practice, get student questions and feedback.

**87. A teacher has assigned reading of informational social studies and science texts to middle school students. To encourage them to think critically about their reading, as well as to model questioning skills, the teacher prompts students by asking open-ended questions. Which choice is a good example of such a question(s)?**

a. "What subject was covered in this text?"
b. "What are some facts? Some opinions?"
c. "Did you understand all of the reading?"
d. "Does the author give supporting data?"

**88. A teacher of a class with a wide range of backgrounds, reading levels, and reading skills wants to differentiate her lesson plans, instructional strategies, and assessment methods to meet every student's needs best. Which way of collecting information on their reading progress will best help her do this?**

a. A whole-class test
b. Current Lexile levels
c. Small-group projects
d. Individual observations

**89. During classroom instruction, a teacher conducted formative assessments aligned to state standards, finding all students demonstrate high comprehension rates with grade-level reading. But on the state reading test two months later, nearly half of the students scored below grade level in comprehension. This test used different texts, but all texts were grade-level. What is the most likely reason for this change?**

a. Assessment instruments used were different.
b. Each assessment used different sets of texts.
c. There was no ongoing formative assessment.
d. The summative assessment is always harder.

**90. During which component of the writing process should a student remove extraneous content, add missing necessary information, and rearrange the order of some paragraphs?**

a. Planning
b. Proofing
c. Drafting
d. Editing

**91. A student working on a composition is going through the entire document and correcting grammar, spelling, punctuation, and capitalization as needed. In which stage of the writing process should this student be?**

a. Proofreading a final draft
b. Editing an intermediate draft
c. Revising a first or rough draft
d. Proofreading the rough draft

**92. Students should find a focus before writing, and they can also improve their focus during revision. To guide revisions for reinforcing focus, teachers and students can pose questions. Which of these is not a good guiding question for this purpose?**

a. What is the most important point in your composition?
b. Does your composition keep focus on your main point?
c. Regardless of why, do you know what you write about?
d. Did you use ideas that do not reinforce the main point?

**93. Writing research identifies characteristics of "mature" writers to which writing students can aspire. Which of the following behaviors demonstrates one of these characteristics?**

a. Planning during writing from one sentence to another
b. Setting a goal during planning for direction and focus
c. Revising in spots as needed to give better information
d. Planning and revising as separate parts of the process

**94. Among the following technological resources, which would best support writing for students who cannot manually operate writing implements or computer keyboards but can read, hear, and speak?**

a. Speech-to-text computer software programs
b. Text-to-speech computer software programs
c. Communication boards or voice synthesizers
d. Large-print text and/or magnification devices

**95. Which of these would present the most difficulty for students to look up words in a standard dictionary?**

a. Not knowing the meanings of words
b. Not knowing words' pronunciations
c. Not knowing the spellings for words
d. Not knowing words' parts of speech

**96. The principal, faculty, and staff of a public school are interested in how their students' writing skills compare to those of other public-school students in the same grades nationwide. Which type of assessment would give them this information?**

a. A criterion-referenced test
b. A classroom writing test
c. A formative assessment
d. A norm-referenced test

**97. A 4th-grade teacher introduces the math topic of decimals to the class. Together they preview their textbook chapter on decimals. The teacher assigns small groups of students to generate questions to which they want answers. Which of the following examples is the least helpful question to guide them at this stage of their learning?**

a. "How are decimals important to us in our everyday lives?"
b. "How can decimals be whole numbers and also fractions?"
c. "In the number 467.912, which digit is in the hundredths?"
d. "Can we make fractions decimals, and decimals fractions?"

**98. Which statement is true about the arithmetic examples below?**

I. 375 ÷ 5 = 75
II. 5 × 75 = 375
III. 75 + 5 = 375
IV. 375 – 5 = 370

a. Sample III is incorrect and Sample II corrects it.
b. Sample I is incorrect and Sample IV corrects it.
c. Sample II is incorrect and Sample III corrects it.
d. Sample IV is incorrect and Sample III corrects it.

**99. A teaching assistant identifies a "teachable moment" when two kindergarten students are arguing about whose toy is bigger. Which resource can she provide in showing them how to settle the dispute objectively?**

a. Computer
b. Graph
c. Chart
d. Ruler

**100. To assess early math learning in young children, which is/are the most appropriate material(s)?**

a. Cookies or candies
b. Marbles or pennies
c. Simple worksheets
d. An arithmetic exam

# Answer Key and Explanations for Test #2

## Reading

**1. A:** The word *feeble* means weak, infirm, or unable to walk. It can refer to physical or mental frailty. However, when meaning *senile* (B), it is more commonly compounded to *feeble-minded*. The sentence is not referring to memory loss but to weakness in enforcing classroom management. Both *haphazard* (C) and *rare* (D) could fit the context of the sentence, but do not match the meaning of *feeble*.

**2. B:** The verb *to temper* means to moderate, tone down, or change, whether used literally such as "to temper glass or metal," or figuratively as in "to temper emotion with reason." Its meaning is closest to that of the adjective *temperate*, meaning moderate, such as a temperate climate or disposition, rather than the noun *temper* meaning the heat of anger (A); the noun *temper* meaning one's disposition (C), such as "she has an even temper"; or the adjective *temperamental*, meaning sensitive, moody, or irritable (D). The sentence is explaining that strictness is made more moderate, or balanced, by kindness.

**3. C:** The main idea that a teacher's classroom management style affects the classroom environment and success of teaching is stated in the last sentence of the first paragraph. The title (A) identifies the topic of classroom management but not the main idea of the four styles. The first sentence of the first paragraph (C) introduces the topic. The last sentence of the last paragraph (D) gives supporting details on one classroom management style.

**4. C:** The first and third paragraphs begin with a statement that introduces the topic of that paragraph. The second paragraph discusses the four classroom management styles and begins with the first one rather than introducing the topic, so the first sentence of each is not a topic sentence (A). Two paragraphs do have a topic sentence, not just a main idea, so choice B is incorrect. The topic sentences are not at the conclusion of each paragraph (D).

**5. D:** The first paragraph defines the classroom management styles but does not describe the results. The second paragraph gives examples of results ("[Students] learn to be responsible and take on leadership."). The third paragraph also gives examples ("students not only learn better but also grow better emotionally").

**6. C:** The first paragraph states that an Authoritarian teacher exhibits high control and low involvement, while a Permissive teacher has low control and low involvement. Authoritative and Indulgent teachers both have high levels of involvement.

**7. A:** The opening sentence is a good example of a topic sentence. It also introduces the piece. The second sentence (B) adds details to the first sentence. The final sentence (C) gives the thesis statement of the paragraph, but is not the topic sentence.

**8. D:** The first paragraph introduces the topic, briefly describing each of the four classroom management styles. The second paragraph goes into more detail on each style, describing the effect each has on the students and class environment. The final paragraph suggests which style is most effective for positive outcomes. This paragraph is more of an application of previous material than a summary of it (A). No true problem and solution are mentioned (B), and neither are a cause and effect (C).

**9. B:** A bar graph gives a clear visual depiction of how many teachers fall under each category, allowing the viewer to easily compare the four styles and see which ones are used most or least. A line graph (A) is best for showing how values change, which is not applicable for a one-time value. A scatter plot (C) shows each individual value, which is useful for tracking trends but makes it difficult to see how many teachers fall under each category since each teacher is listed separately. A Venn diagram (D) is useful for showing overlap between categories, but unless the teachers could be measured to exhibit a certain percentage of various styles, this graph could not be used here.

**10. C:** *Host* means a large number, though it can also mean one who entertains guests or an organism that supports another. This sentence is referring to the many opportunities afforded by technology, not to hospitality or biology (A). "Dearth" (B) is the opposite of the correct meaning, and "exclusive selection" cannot be inferred from the word or context.

**11. D:** This sentence refers to students' "research competence." While competence can include knowledge (B), here it is referring to skill or ability in researching. While *competence* and *compete* have similar etymology, this term is not referring to being victorious (A) or aggressive (C).

**12. A:** The opening sentence introduces the topic of technology in education and the fact that it has both pros and cons. The rest of the passage builds on this. The second sentence (B) expounds on the first. The second paragraph (C, D) deals with challenges of implementing technology, which is only part of the passage's subject.

**13. C:** This choice best restates the main idea. Choice (A) is not specific enough, making the general statement that technology has both pros and cons, but not mentioning that the passage is referring to technology use in schools or that the pros outweigh the cons. Choice (B) restates the main point of the second paragraph and choice (D) restates ideas from the third paragraph.

**14. D:** The first paragraph (A) introduces the topic, but does not summarize it. Most of the last paragraph (C) is on the topic of the benefits of technology, rather than summarizing the entire passage. Only the last sentence summarizes the two contrasting ideas (the pros and cons). Since there is a summary statement, choice B is incorrect.

**15. B:** The first paragraph introduces the subject. It mentions that there are "challenges" to implementing technology, but does not name them. The second paragraph is devoted to these challenges, and the final sentence of the third paragraph summarizes the subject, specifically mentioning two of the drawbacks. So, the second and third paragraphs both discuss the drawbacks.

**16. A:** The passage makes the argument that although technology has challenges, its benefits outweigh the challenges. This is a persuasive text, stating both sides of an issue and then indicating which is best. It is not confrontational (B) because it does not condemn anyone for holding the opposite opinion. It is not just informative (C), because it does not merely offer facts and allow the reader to draw his own opinion. And it is not concerned (D) because it does not have an emotional tone.

**17. D:** The final sentence sums up the selection, briefly restating the arguments for and against technology, and agrees with the pro side. Because an argument can be made for each side of the case, this is an opinion, although it is backed up by facts. Because it gives equal time to each side and uses factual information to fairly support each side, it is not biased.

**18. B:** The first paragraph introduces the subject, stating that there are two sides but not giving any details for either side. Based on the final sentence, which states that the pros of technology outweigh the cons, we can say that pro-technology is the main Argument and anti-technology (or the argument that the drawbacks outweigh the benefits) is the Counterargument. So, the second paragraph is the Counterargument since it focuses on the challenges of implementing technology. The third paragraph gives the Argument, stating reasons technology should be implemented in education, and ends with a Summary sentence that restates the arguments and gives a conclusion.

**19. C:** The last sentence states that Laurie was "an incorrigible tease." From this statement you can infer that Laurie was unruly or unmanageable. *Stoic* means not showing passion or emotion. *Taciturn* means silent. *Uncanny* means supernatural. There is nothing in the passage to imply he had any of these characteristics.

**20. C:** Point of view refers to the vantage point from which a story is written. First person uses the pronoun *I*. Second person uses the pronoun *you*. Third person uses the pronouns *he/she/they*. There is no fourth-person point of view. This passage was written in the third person.

**21. B:** The words *mysterious* and *important* used in the sentence help the reader deduce that Jo looked secretive. Jo did not look jubilant (joyful), disheveled (disarrayed), or angry.

**22. B:** In Week 1, the number of outbursts was 12; in Week 5, it was four. Because four is one-third of 12, the outbursts have decreased to one-third of what they were. They have not decreased by one-third of what they were (A), which would be a decrease of four, i.e., 12 – 4 = 8. If they had decreased by half of what they were, half of 12 is six, so 12 – 6 = 6. If they had decreased to half of what they were, they would also be six in Week 5.

**23. A:** The line graph shows an overall descending pattern, meaning the number of outbursts is decreasing weekly overall. However, the number increased from eight in Week 3 to 10 in Week 4 before resuming the pattern of decreasing. The line overall goes down, so the pattern is not increasing (B), (D). Multiple changes between Weeks 1 and 5 indicating instability (C) do not exist on this graph; there is only one change in Week 3, while all other weeks after Week 1 show decreases.

**24. C:** To find the average, first add all of the numbers of outbursts each week: 12 + 8 + 10 + 6 + 4 = 40. Then divide this sum by five weeks: 40 ÷ 5 = 8. So, 40 (A) is the sum of all outbursts over all five weeks, 12 (B) is the number of outbursts in Week 1, and 12 is also the largest number in any week shown. Four (D) is the number of outbursts in Week 5, and the smallest number in any week shown.

**25. D:** The chart shows 45% of people have Type O blood, so the other three types total 55%, making choice A incorrect. Choice B is incorrect because 40% have Type A and 11% have Type B blood, which sum to 51%. The portion of people with Type O or Type AB blood is 49%, so choice C is incorrect. However, the 44% total of people who have Type A or AB blood is less than the 45% of people that have Type O blood, which makes choice D correct.

**26. B:** The passage states that the teacher should encourage discussions about vocabulary words and students' opinions, meaning that they are of equal importance (B). Predictions about a story's plot (C) is also listed as an important topic teachers should lead students to discuss. According to the passage, teachers can ask questions to encourage these discussions as they read (D). The passage states that reading aloud to students is beneficial for students at any grade level, which includes older students (A).

**27. B:** In the second paragraph, the passage notes that parking tickets will be issued for vehicles left in the main lot overnight. Overnight guests are instructed to register their vehicles (D) and display a window label (A), so these actions do not violate regulations. The pass code is for guests who need to access Five Oaks after 11:00 p.m., so it is neither an instruction or against regulations (C).

## Writing

**28. A:** "Everybody" is singular and requires these singular pronouns to agree; "their" (B) and "our" (D) are plural. Although "your" (C) can be singular or plural, it would go with a plural subject like "All of you" or a singular subject like "One of you," but does not fit with "Everybody," which refers to the third person rather than the second (C) or first person (D). (Note: If "his or her" becomes stilted, make the subject plural, e.g., "All students have their own copies.")

**29. C:** Using *or* between two nouns, proper nouns, or pronouns indicates a singular subject and verb (takes). *And* indicates plural subjects and a plural verb (take), so choice A should be *take*, choice B should be *take*, choice C is correct, and choice D should be *takes*.

**30. C:** "We take" is the present tense of "to take" with a first-person plural subject. The predicate in choice (A) is in the future tense "will take." Future tense always uses auxiliary verb(s) "will," "will be __ing," etc. The past tense is "took" (B). "(We) have taken" (D) is the present perfect tense.

**31. A:** Future tense is generally indicated by an auxiliary verb like "will" plus the plain or uninflected form of the verb. Auxiliary verbs "will" and "have" plus the perfect form of the verb "done" (B) indicate the future perfect tense. Auxiliary verb plus past verb form "Had finished" (C) indicates the past perfect tense. Auxiliary plus participle "were going" (D) indicates the past progressive (aka past continuous) tense.

**32. B:** Sentence A uses the present tense of the verb "to prepare." Sentence B uses the past tense of this verb, so this is the correct choice for the question. Sentence C uses the present progressive tense (also called the present continuous tense). Sentence D uses the present perfect tense.

**33. B:** Choice A contains the past tense "said" and the past perfect "had... finished." The other choices all use "to say" in the present tense, "says." Choice B uses the present perfect tense of "to finish," "has finished." Choice C uses the future perfect tense, "will have finished." Choice D uses the present progressive (aka continuous) tense "is finishing."

**34. A:** This is an example of the present progressive (or present continuous) tense, indicating something that is currently ongoing. Option B is an example of the future progressive tense, indicating something that will be ongoing in the future. Option C is an example of the present perfect tense, indicating something that has occurred in the past before the present. Option D is an example of the past perfect progressive tense, indicating something ongoing in the past before something subsequent, also in the past.

**35. D:** Version A uses the present progressive tense ("is improving"). Version B uses the past progressive tense ("was improving"). Version C uses the present perfect progressive tense ("has been improving"). Version D uses the past perfect progressive tense ("had been improving").

**36. D:** A verb modifying a noun in the third person singular (a pronoun like he, she, it, or any other singular noun or other word) in the present tense is the only combination that always has an *-s* ending on the verb, e.g., is, has, does, goes, walks, likes, sees, thinks, feels, wakes, sleeps, etc. Examples with a regular verb are, of choice A, "I walk"; of choice B, "They walked"; and of (C), "You walk." Only choice D would be "She walks," "He walks," or "It walks."

**37. C:** The reflexive pronoun "itself" correctly renames the noun "group" by agreeing with its neutral gender. "Themself" is not a word (A), "himself" disagrees with the feminine gender "girl" (B), and "themselves" disagrees with the singular "team" (D).

**38. A:** Each of these pronouns agrees with the antecedent *one*, as each can replace that subject grammatically. In choice B, singular subject *person* and pronoun *you* agree, but the verb *are* disagrees with subject *person*, instead incorrectly agreeing with pronoun *you*. The third person plural pronoun to agree with "people... are" (C) is *they*, not *them*. Similarly, the third person feminine singular pronoun referring to Sylvia and agreeing with "it was" is *she*, not *her* (D).

**39. B:** To test pronoun-antecedent agreement when the pronoun is the object, make it the *only* object: since we would write, "They gave the payment to me," not "to I," we would not change the form just because the pronoun is compounded with another object, like Ralph (A). The same applies to "Ralph and him" or "him and Ralph," not "he and Ralph" (C); and to "Ralph and them" or "them and Ralph," not "they and Ralph" (D).

**40. A:** The correct relative pronoun to refer to "their best attorney" and "was my uncle" is "who." "That" (B) is used with nonrestrictive more than restrictive clauses, but both "that" and "which" are used with things whereas "who" is more appropriate with people. "Whom" (C) is only used as an object—direct (e.g., "Whom do you choose?") or indirect (e.g., "To whom did you give it?")—not a relative pronoun. Because choice A is correct, choice D is incorrect.

**41. C:** Possessive pronouns differ from possessive proper nouns in that, whereas both nouns and proper nouns take *–'s* endings when possessive (e.g., "the woman's hat," "the man's house," "Mary's hat," "Walter's house," etc.), pronouns do not. Hence, choice A should be written as *its foundation*, choice B should be written as *hers*, choice C is correctly written as *theirs*, and choice D should be written as *it's*.

**42. D:** Use the demonstrative pronoun *here* to refer to things closer at hand and *there* to refer to things farther away. Do not use *here* for both (A), *there* for both (C), or use each for the opposite meanings (B) of those identified.

**43. B:** The correct comparative modifier meaning more than bad is "worse." "Worst" (A) is the superlative, not the comparative, and is not used when comparing only two things. "Worser" (C) is not a real word: it is redundant because *-er* denotes more, but "worse" already means more bad. "Poorest" (D), like "worst," is the superlative form and inappropriate here.

**44. C:** In describing quantity (relative to words like *few*, *little*, *some*, *much*, *many*, etc.), the comparative word meaning "a greater amount or number" is *more*, and the superlative word meaning "the ultimate quantity" is *most*. Hence, *mostest* is redundant. It is not acceptable outside of this expression (A), nor acceptable despite being superfluous (D). It is the superlative form rather than comparative (B), but this does not make it incorrect.

**45. A:** Complete sentences can be brief as long as they contain a subject, a verb, and express a complete thought. Choice B is a sentence fragment with an incomplete dependent clause lacking a verb (e.g., "when the rain STOPS"). Choice C needs either a phrase or clause to complete "they say" (e.g., "we should not," "not to go"), or another verb replacing "say" (e.g., "refuse," "protest," "complain," "criticize," "laugh," "joke") needing no object. Choice D needs either a verb completing "guests" (e.g., "went," "are going," "will go," "are there"), or "of" inserted ("because OF all the other guests").

**46. D:** Choices A, B, and C are all complete sentences, as each has a subject and verb and expresses a complete thought. However, choice D has a subject (*city*) but no verb. Unlike in choice C, *we* and *visited* are not the subject and verb in choice D, but they modify *city* as does the rest ("with…"). To complete this fragment, the subject needs its own predicate (e.g., "The beautiful city we visited with all the bright lights was a popular destination" or "…had a large population," etc.).

**47. A:** This is an example of a run-on sentence, which combines two independent clauses without the necessary division of punctuation and/or a conjunction. This can be corrected by dividing the clauses with a semicolon (B), separating them with a period into two sentences (C), or making one clause dependent/subordinate by adding a subordinating conjunction and separating it from the independent clause with a comma (D). Alternatively, a comma plus a conjunction (e.g., ", and" or ", so") can also join these clauses.

**48. C:** This sentence correctly connects two independent clauses with a semicolon. The other choices are all run-on sentences. Option A can be corrected with a semicolon or period between "Tuesday" and "won't." Option B can use the same between "attend" and "we," or a comma plus conjunction "and." Option D needs either a period or semicolon plus "we" before "will."

**49. B:** When connecting two independent clauses using *however* as a conjunctive adverb, punctuate with a semicolon before *however* and a comma after it. Using a comma before *however* (A) incorrectly creates a comma splice. Choice C reverses the correct punctuation sequence. By omitting the comma after *however*, choice D alters the meaning: it reads as if they asked for permission no matter how he refused.

**50. B:** Neither *mayor* nor *councilmembers* are capitalized when used as a common noun, so choices A and D are incorrect. When used as a proper noun, *mayor* should be capitalized, so choice C is incorrect.

**51. C:** The correct spelling is "pinnacle." All of the other words are spelled correctly.

**52. A:** The first letter of the first word in a sentence should always be capitalized. This rule also applies to the first letter of the first word in any full quotation, regardless of whether it appears in the middle of another sentence. Hence choice B is incorrect. However, a partial quotation and/or one that continues the sentence containing it should not begin with a capital letter, so choices C and D are both incorrect.

**53. D:** Although adjectives derived from proper nouns are normally capitalized, choices A, B, and C here are exceptions: over time, these have become so commonly used that they no longer need to be capitalized, although it is still common to use capitalization. However, adjectives derived from proper nouns like country names, e.g., German (D), French, English, etc. are still capitalized at all times.

**54. C:** The spelling "verses" indicates the plural noun, singular "verse," meaning a line of poetry, song lyrics, or Biblical scripture. In sentences A, B, and D, the correct spelling should be "versus," meaning against, contrasting with, or opposing. Though both words originate from the same Latin source, their English meanings have evolved to be very different.

## Mathematics

**55. C:** The place value is assigned by the position of the digit. The places to the left of the decimal are ones, tens, hundreds, then thousands, respectively. Since the digit 8 is in the second place to the left of the implied decimal, it's in the tens place. The value of this digit is $8 \times 10$, which is 80.

**56. B:** The place value of a digit depends on its location in relation to the decimal point. The places to the left of the decimal are ones, tens, then hundreds, respectively. The places to the right of the decimal are tenths, hundredths, and thousandths, respectively. Since the digit 3 is in the third position to the left of the decimal point, its place value is hundreds.

**57. D:** The place value of a digit depends on its location in relation to the decimal point. The places to the left of the decimal are ones, tens, then hundreds, respectively. To round a number to a certain place value, look at the digit to the immediate right. If the digit to the right is 5 or more, round up by adding one followed by a zero. If the digit is less than five, round down by keeping the same digit followed by a zero. For this problem, the digit in the hundreds place is 4. The digit to its immediate right is 2. Since 2 is less than 5, round down. So, 125,420 rounded to the nearest hundred is 125,400.

**58. A:** Since 1 foot equals 12 inches, the conversion factor is $\frac{12\text{ in}}{1\text{ ft}}$. Multiply by the conversion factor.

$$4\text{ ft} \times \frac{12\text{ in}}{1\text{ ft}} = 48\text{ in}$$

Therefore, there are 48 inches in 4 feet.

**59. D:** Since 1 meter equals 1,000 millimeters, the conversion factor is 1,000. Since a millimeter is shorter than a meter, we divide by the conversion factor.

$$336\text{ mm} \times \frac{1\text{ m}}{1{,}000\text{ mm}} = 0.336\text{ m}$$

So, 336 millimeters is equal to 0.336 meters.

**60. B:** The area of the rectangular room equals the amount of carpeting needed. The area of a rectangle equals the product of the length and the width. The length of the room is approximately 14 feet, and the width of the room is approximately 10 feet. The area of this room is approximately 140 $\text{ft}^2$.

**61. C:** The perimeter of a square is found by the equation $p = 4s$, where $p$ represents the perimeter and $s$ represents the length of the sides. Since the question wants an estimation, all numbers should be approximated to the nearest whole number before calculations occur. That means the side length should be rounded to make calculations quick and easy. Thus, it is approximately 6 cm. The perimeter of this square is found by $p = 4(6) = 24$ cm. On the contrary, if the question wanted the final answer rounded to the nearest whole centimeter after completing normal calculations, the final answer would have varied. It is important to pay attention to what the question is asking and wanting.

**62. B:** The sum can be found by adding the digits in the ones column $(2 + 8 + 4 + 6 = 20)$, and then carrying the 2 to the tens column and adding the digits $(2 + 1 + 1 + 1 + 1 = 6)$. Then the sum is 60. Alternately, $12 + 18 = 30$ and $14 + 16 = 30$, so $30 + 30 = 60$.

**63. A:** The sum is found by adding the ones column $(7 + 5 + 6 = 18)$ and carrying the 1 to the tens column. Then add the tens column $(1 + 9 + 0 + 4 = 14)$ and carry the 1 to the hundreds column. Then add the hundreds column $(1 + 8 + 9 + 8 = 26)$ and carry the 2 to the thousands column. Then add the thousands column $(2 + 0 + 6 + 9 = 17)$ and carry the 1 to the ten thousands column. Then add the ten thousands column $(1 + 7 + 5 + 0 = 13)$ and carry the 1 to the hundred thousands column. Then add the hundred thousands column $(1 + 6 + 7 = 14)$ and carry the 1 to the millions columns. Then, add the millions column $(1 + 4 = 5)$. Pulling the digits all together in their proper places yields 5,437,648.

**64. D:** The sale price is equal to the difference between the original amount and the discount. The sale price equals $225 − $45 or $180.

**65. A:** The amount Ms. Wise donates to charity is equal difference between the original amount of prize money and the sum of the savings deposit and cost of the cruise package. Then, the amount she donates equals $5,695 − ($1,200 + $3,975) or $520.

**66. D:** The amount of money Chloe has left is equal to the difference between the amount of money she started with and the amount of money she spends. The amount she spends equals 3($7) + 4($8) or $53. The amount she has left equals $100 − $53 or $47.

**67. B:** The total enrollment is the sum of the enrollments of the individual classes. The enrollment is equal to $334 + 410 + 312 + 345 = 1{,}401$.

**68. D:** To multiply numbers ending in zero, first multiply the numbers ignoring the zeros and then add the zeros after the last digit of the product. Then $325 \times 1 = 325$ and adding the three zeros yields 325,000.

**69. D:** The number of computers in the storage unit is the product of the number of pallets, the number of boxes, and the number of computers in each box. The number of computers equals $3 \times 8 \times 10 = 24 \times 10$, or 240 computers.

**70. A:** Since $120 \times 29 = 3480$ and $120 \times 30 = 3600$ (which is more than 3500), the remainder is $3500 - 3480 = 20$.

**71. C:** To divide 864 by 24, the first step is to divide 86 by 24. Since $24 \times 3 = 72$, the divisor 24 goes into 86 three times. Then place the 72 under the 86 and subtract. Then $86 - 72 = 14$. Now bring down the 4, and determine how many times 24 goes into 144. Since $24 \times 6 = 144$, the divisor 24 goes into 144 six times. Then place the 144 under the 144 and subtract to get zero. This means that $864 \div 24 = 36$.

**72. A:** The amount of money each employee receives is equal to the quotient between $156,168 and 324. Then $156,168 ÷ 324, which is $482.

**73. C:** The amount of the monthly payment is the quotient of the cost divided by the number of payments. The payment equals $2160 ÷ 12 or $180. The payment of $180 is $80 over $100.

**74. B:** The amount of sugar needed is equal to the product of the number of cups of lemonade needed and the amount of sugar per cup. The amount of sugar needed is equal to $16 \times 1\frac{1}{2} = 16 \times \frac{3}{2} = 24$ teaspoons.

**75. B:** When multiplying fractions, first try to cancel factors in the numerators with factors in the denominators. Then multiply the numerators and denominators and reduce: $\frac{6}{11} \times \frac{11}{9} = \frac{2}{1} \times \frac{1}{3} = \frac{2}{3}$.

**76. B:** The cost of the nails is equal to the product of the pounds of nails and the cost per pound. The cost equals 1.25 × $4.08 or $5.10.

**77. A:** The cost of the hamburger is the product of the number of pounds and the cost per pound. The cost equals $1.39 × 5 or $6.95.

**78. C:** This question is basically asking, "What is 5% of 200?" Let *n* represent *what*, and replace the *of* with a multiplication symbol and the *is* with an equal sign. But first, we need to convert the 5% to a decimal. Remove the percent sign and move the decimal point two places to the left. Then we have $n = 0.05 \times 200 = 10$. This means that only 10 of the 200 students prefer strawberry ice cream over chocolate.

**79. A:** Since the dress was 20% off, $52 is 80% of the list price. Then, this question is asking, "$52 is 80% of what number?" Let *n* represent *what number*, and replace the *of* with a multiplication sign and the *is* with an equal sign. But first, we need to convert the 80% to a decimal. Remove the percent sign and move the decimal point two places to the left. Then we have $52 = 0.80 \times n$. To solve this equation, divide both sides by 0.80: $52 \div 0.80 = n$, so $n = 65$. Thus, the list price of the dress was $65.

**80. A:** To convert a percent to a decimal, remove the percent symbol and move the decimal point two places to the left. So 125% equals 1.25.

**81. C:** To convert a decimal to a fraction, move the decimal point two places to the right, place the number over 100, and simplify the fraction. Then 3.25 equals $3\frac{25}{100}$, which simplifies to $3\frac{1}{4}$.

## Instructional Support

**82. B:** Students cannot decode irregular words that do not follow phonics (letter-sound) rules. To recognize these on sight, children must simply memorize them; drilling is best. Reading words in context (A) is inappropriate for beginning readers who have not memorized these words. Relating text to real life (C) is important to reading instruction, but unrelated to learning irregular words. Pictures (D) help beginning readers, but most irregular words (see examples in the question) are function words and/or express abstract concepts, and cannot be pictured like concrete meanings (e.g., dog, cat, house, etc.)

**83. D:** Students with visual learning styles learn best from things they can see, e.g., videos, pictures, diagrams, drawings, etc. A timeline drawing shows plot sequence visually. An oral plot summary (A) would benefit students with auditory learning styles, who learn best from things they can hear. A written outline (B) would benefit students with verbal learning styles, who learn best from things they can read and write. Manipulatives (C) would benefit students with haptic (tactile) learning styles, who learn best from things they can touch, feel, move, and rearrange.

**84. C:** The more modalities and media the learning materials include, the more they can address a larger number of varied student needs. There are two reasons for this: (1) if one modality or medium is not effective for certain students, then another one will be; (2) presenting the same information redundantly and through different modalities makes learning more effective for all students than presenting it through only one (A), (B), (D).

**85. A:** A dictionary will help the student look up unfamiliar words encountered when reading. A thesaurus (B) provides synonyms and antonyms for given words, which would help students vary their word choice when writing, but would not help this student learn general English vocabulary for reading. Textbook glossaries (C) would help the student learn vocabulary and terminology specific to each text, but not general English vocabulary found in other reading. An encyclopedia (D) would provide extensive information about subject content, not vocabulary.

**86. A:** The best sequence is: explain skimming enables students to find text parts important to them and disregard others. Identify the goal for skimming the lesson's specific text. Model skimming, narrating with a think-aloud (e.g., "Let's look for this in the table of contents first," etc.). Collect students' questions and feedback. Invite students to practice locating information in a caption, diagram, graph, or under a heading. Model (with think-aloud) finding keywords in questions about text to guide skimming. Get student questions and feedback. Continue modeling and student practice until students demonstrate successful skimming for information.

**87. B:** This is a good example because it requires critical thinking for students to differentiate facts vs. opinions; it is also open-ended, allowing a variety of valid responses. Choice A requires only factual knowledge and a limited response range. Choice C can be answered yes or no, so not open-ended; to improve it, follow "no" responses with, "What did you not understand?" or" What questions do you have?" Choice D is also a yes or no question; it can be improved by following "yes" responses with, "How do the data support the author's viewpoint?"

**88. D:** Of the choices given, the best way to get information for differentiating instruction for individual students is through observations of individual students (D) with detailed observational notes of their specific reading needs and strengths. A whole-class test (A) will yield different individual student scores and even need and strength areas, but less information about specific students. Lexile levels (B), when available, help identify texts at suitable reading levels for each student rather than inform instructional differentiation. Small-group projects (C) yield group, not individual, student results.

**89. C:** Differences between assessment instruments (A), different (yet both grade-level) texts (B), and even the greater difficulty of standardized summative assessments than of classroom formative assessments (D) cannot explain such a significant discrepancy. The most likely cause is the two months between the teacher's classroom formative assessments and the state reading test: formative assessment must be ongoing to show current student status, which can change over time, so monitoring must be continuous.

**90. D:** The activities described are part of the editing component of the writing process. The planning (A) part occurs before the student starts writing and includes activities like brainstorming ideas, establishing focus, doing research, making outlines, etc. The drafting (C) component involves producing a rough draft before progressing to any editing actions. The proofing (B) or proofreading component involves checking and correcting all writing and typing mechanics in the final draft, after drafting and editing.

**91. A:** Proofreading to correct mechanics is the last step for a student before turning in a composition. Editing (B) does not involve proofreading, but rather entails removing, adding, changing, and rearranging content as needed to produce a logical, coherent, cohesive, unified piece. Revising a rough draft (C) is like editing. Proofreading is only done with the last draft, not the first or rough draft (D).

**92. C:** Good questions that teachers and students can use during writing revisions include identifying the most important point (A); whether the piece remains focused throughout on that most important point (B); and whether the student included ideas that detract from, weaken, or do not strengthen their central focus (D). Before and during writing, students should ask themselves not only what they write about, but moreover why they write about it (C).

**93. B:** Writing researchers find that "mature" writers do not plan during writing by letting one sentence dictate the next (A). They see their work as a whole, and plan and revise recursively, instead of only revising in certain places and/or concentrating on giving information (C) in a linear fashion. They plan and revise globally throughout the entire writing process (D). They focus their writing in part by setting a goal, so their planning and revising are then goal-directed (B).

**94. A:** Speech-to-text software programs enable students who cannot manually write or type but can speak to dictate compositions to computers and have these programs convert their spoken words to printed text. Text-to-speech software programs (B) would support students who can write and type but cannot speak. Communication boards and voice synthesizers (C) would support writing for students who cannot write, type, or speak. Large-print text and/or magnification devices (D) would support writing for students with impaired vision.

**95. C:** Students need not know every letter of the correct spelling of a word in order to look it up in a standard dictionary, but they must know the initial letter. For example, many Greek-derived words are spelled beginning with *ps-* but pronounced beginning with /s/; the "p" is silent. A few phonetic dictionaries, enabling lookup by pronunciation respelling, have been published to address this. Not knowing word meanings (A) is a perfect reason for looking them up in a regular dictionary, which will also provide their pronunciations (B) and parts of speech (D).

**96. D:** Norm-referenced tests are standardized, so the performance of all students in the nation or state is measured the same way. They refer to a norm, i.e., student scores are compared to the average scores of a normative sample of students as representative of most students in the country/state. Criterion-referenced tests (A) do not compare student scores to any such norm, but only against a preset performance criterion. Classroom writing tests (B) enable comparing among classmates, not with students nationwide. Formative assessments (C) typically only measure learning during instruction within a classroom.

**97. C:** Question A is good for meeting the standard of applying mathematics to real life. Question B is good for students to learn the conceptual relationship of decimals and fractions as different yet equivalent ways of expressing parts of a whole. Question D is good for students to learn how to convert fractions to decimals and vice versa. Question C is better asked by the teacher than by students—and not at this stage of their learning, but only after they understand place value.

**98. A:** Sample III uses the plus sign, but gives the product of multiplication instead of the sum of addition. Sample II corrects this error. Samples I, II, and IV are correct as they are (B), (C), (D). Samples I and II reverse each other by dividing (I) and multiplying (II) the same values. If Sample III were corrected, then Samples III and IV would reverse each other by adding (III) and subtracting (IV) the same values.

**99. D:** Young children tend to focus on only one attribute of objects to the exclusion of others—e.g., height but not width, number of pieces rather than overall size or amount, etc. A computer (A) is overkill; a graph (B) or chart (C) is irrelevant. By providing a ruler (D) and then showing them how to measure both toys, the assistant can teach the children how to use an objective measurement.

**100. B:** An arithmetic exam (D) is inappropriate to assess early math learning in young children, who may not even be able to write numbers or letters yet. Similarly, even very simple worksheets (C) are not developmentally appropriate. Familiar concrete objects are best for instructing and assessing abstract concepts with very young students. However, cookies or candies (A) are problematic as young children are likely to eat them. Marbles or pennies (B) are better for demonstrating and practicing adding, subtracting, comparing, etc.

# NYSTCE Practice Tests #3, #4 and #5

To take these additional NYSTCE practice tests, visit our online resources page:
**mometrix.com/resources719/nystceatas-34344**

# How to Overcome Test Anxiety

Just the thought of taking a test is enough to make most people a little nervous. A test is an important event that can have a long-term impact on your future, so it's important to take it seriously and it's natural to feel anxious about performing well. But just because anxiety is normal, that doesn't mean that it's helpful in test taking, or that you should simply accept it as part of your life. Anxiety can have a variety of effects. These effects can be mild, like making you feel slightly nervous, or severe, like blocking your ability to focus or remember even a simple detail.

If you experience test anxiety—whether severe or mild—it's important to know how to beat it. To discover this, first you need to understand what causes test anxiety.

## Causes of Test Anxiety

While we often think of anxiety as an uncontrollable emotional state, it can actually be caused by simple, practical things. One of the most common causes of test anxiety is that a person does not feel adequately prepared for their test. This feeling can be the result of many different issues such as poor study habits or lack of organization, but the most common culprit is time management. Starting to study too late, failing to organize your study time to cover all of the material, or being distracted while you study will mean that you're not well prepared for the test. This may lead to cramming the night before, which will cause you to be physically and mentally exhausted for the test. Poor time management also contributes to feelings of stress, fear, and hopelessness as you realize you are not well prepared but don't know what to do about it.

Other times, test anxiety is not related to your preparation for the test but comes from unresolved fear. This may be a past failure on a test, or poor performance on tests in general. It may come from comparing yourself to others who seem to be performing better or from the stress of living up to expectations. Anxiety may be driven by fears of the future—how failure on this test would affect your educational and career goals. These fears are often completely irrational, but they can still negatively impact your test performance.

## Elements of Test Anxiety

As mentioned earlier, test anxiety is considered to be an emotional state, but it has physical and mental components as well. Sometimes you may not even realize that you are suffering from test anxiety until you notice the physical symptoms. These can include trembling hands, rapid heartbeat, sweating, nausea, and tense muscles. Extreme anxiety may lead to fainting or vomiting. Obviously, any of these symptoms can have a negative impact on testing. It is important to recognize them as soon as they begin to occur so that you can address the problem before it damages your performance.

The mental components of test anxiety include trouble focusing and inability to remember learned information. During a test, your mind is on high alert, which can help you recall information and stay focused for an extended period of time. However, anxiety interferes with your mind's natural processes, causing you to blank out, even on the questions you know well. The strain of testing during anxiety makes it difficult to stay focused, especially on a test that may take several hours. Extreme anxiety can take a huge mental toll, making it difficult not only to recall test information but even to understand the test questions or pull your thoughts together.

## Effects of Test Anxiety

Test anxiety is like a disease—if left untreated, it will get progressively worse. Anxiety leads to poor performance, and this reinforces the feelings of fear and failure, which in turn lead to poor performances on subsequent tests. It can grow from a mild nervousness to a crippling condition. If allowed to progress, test anxiety can have a big impact on your schooling, and consequently on your future.

Test anxiety can spread to other parts of your life. Anxiety on tests can become anxiety in any stressful situation, and blanking on a test can turn into panicking in a job situation. But fortunately, you don't have to let anxiety rule your testing and determine your grades. There are a number of relatively simple steps you can take to move past anxiety and function normally on a test and in the rest of life.

## Physical Steps for Beating Test Anxiety

While test anxiety is a serious problem, the good news is that it can be overcome. It doesn't have to control your ability to think and remember information. While it may take time, you can begin taking steps today to beat anxiety.

Just as your first hint that you may be struggling with anxiety comes from the physical symptoms, the first step to treating it is also physical. Rest is crucial for having a clear, strong mind. If you are tired, it is much easier to give in to anxiety. But if you establish good sleep habits, your body and mind will be ready to perform optimally, without the strain of exhaustion. Additionally, sleeping well helps you to retain information better, so you're more likely to recall the answers when you see the test questions.

Getting good sleep means more than going to bed on time. It's important to allow your brain time to relax. Take study breaks from time to time so it doesn't get overworked, and don't study right before bed. Take time to rest your mind before trying to rest your body, or you may find it difficult to fall asleep.

Along with sleep, other aspects of physical health are important in preparing for a test. Good nutrition is vital for good brain function. Sugary foods and drinks may give a burst of energy but this burst is followed by a crash, both physically and emotionally. Instead, fuel your body with protein and vitamin-rich foods.

Also, drink plenty of water. Dehydration can lead to headaches and exhaustion, especially if your brain is already under stress from the rigors of the test. Particularly if your test is a long one, drink water during the breaks. And if possible, take an energy-boosting snack to eat between sections.

Along with sleep and diet, a third important part of physical health is exercise. Maintaining a steady workout schedule is helpful, but even taking 5-minute study breaks to walk can help get your blood pumping faster and clear your head. Exercise also releases endorphins, which contribute to a positive feeling and can help combat test anxiety.

When you nurture your physical health, you are also contributing to your mental health. If your body is healthy, your mind is much more likely to be healthy as well. So take time to rest, nourish your body with healthy food and water, and get moving as much as possible. Taking these physical steps will make you stronger and more able to take the mental steps necessary to overcome test anxiety.

## Mental Steps for Beating Test Anxiety

Working on the mental side of test anxiety can be more challenging, but as with the physical side, there are clear steps you can take to overcome it. As mentioned earlier, test anxiety often stems from lack of preparation, so the obvious solution is to prepare for the test. Effective studying may be the most important weapon you have for beating test anxiety, but you can and should employ several other mental tools to combat fear.

First, boost your confidence by reminding yourself of past success—tests or projects that you aced. If you're putting as much effort into preparing for this test as you did for those, there's no reason you should expect to fail here. Work hard to prepare; then trust your preparation.

Second, surround yourself with encouraging people. It can be helpful to find a study group, but be sure that the people you're around will encourage a positive attitude. If you spend time with others who are anxious or cynical, this will only contribute to your own anxiety. Look for others who are motivated to study hard from a desire to succeed, not from a fear of failure.

Third, reward yourself. A test is physically and mentally tiring, even without anxiety, and it can be helpful to have something to look forward to. Plan an activity following the test, regardless of the outcome, such as going to a movie or getting ice cream.

When you are taking the test, if you find yourself beginning to feel anxious, remind yourself that you know the material. Visualize successfully completing the test. Then take a few deep, relaxing breaths and return to it. Work through the questions carefully but with confidence, knowing that you are capable of succeeding.

Developing a healthy mental approach to test taking will also aid in other areas of life. Test anxiety affects more than just the actual test—it can be damaging to your mental health and even contribute to depression. It's important to beat test anxiety before it becomes a problem for more than testing.

## Study Strategy

Being prepared for the test is necessary to combat anxiety, but what does being prepared look like? You may study for hours on end and still not feel prepared. What you need is a strategy for test prep. The next few pages outline our recommended steps to help you plan out and conquer the challenge of preparation.

### Step 1: Scope Out the Test

Learn everything you can about the format (multiple choice, essay, etc.) and what will be on the test. Gather any study materials, course outlines, or sample exams that may be available. Not only will this help you to prepare, but knowing what to expect can help to alleviate test anxiety.

### Step 2: Map Out the Material

Look through the textbook or study guide and make note of how many chapters or sections it has. Then divide these over the time you have. For example, if a book has 15 chapters and you have five days to study, you need to cover three chapters each day. Even better, if you have the time, leave an extra day at the end for overall review after you have gone through the material in depth.

If time is limited, you may need to prioritize the material. Look through it and make note of which sections you think you already have a good grasp on, and which need review. While you are studying, skim quickly through the familiar sections and take more time on the challenging parts.

Write out your plan so you don't get lost as you go. Having a written plan also helps you feel more in control of the study, so anxiety is less likely to arise from feeling overwhelmed at the amount to cover.

### STEP 3: GATHER YOUR TOOLS

Decide what study method works best for you. Do you prefer to highlight in the book as you study and then go back over the highlighted portions? Or do you type out notes of the important information? Or is it helpful to make flashcards that you can carry with you? Assemble the pens, index cards, highlighters, post-it notes, and any other materials you may need so you won't be distracted by getting up to find things while you study.

If you're having a hard time retaining the information or organizing your notes, experiment with different methods. For example, try color-coding by subject with colored pens, highlighters, or post-it notes. If you learn better by hearing, try recording yourself reading your notes so you can listen while in the car, working out, or simply sitting at your desk. Ask a friend to quiz you from your flashcards, or try teaching someone the material to solidify it in your mind.

### STEP 4: CREATE YOUR ENVIRONMENT

It's important to avoid distractions while you study. This includes both the obvious distractions like visitors and the subtle distractions like an uncomfortable chair (or a too-comfortable couch that makes you want to fall asleep). Set up the best study environment possible: good lighting and a comfortable work area. If background music helps you focus, you may want to turn it on, but otherwise keep the room quiet. If you are using a computer to take notes, be sure you don't have any other windows open, especially applications like social media, games, or anything else that could distract you. Silence your phone and turn off notifications. Be sure to keep water close by so you stay hydrated while you study (but avoid unhealthy drinks and snacks).

Also, take into account the best time of day to study. Are you freshest first thing in the morning? Try to set aside some time then to work through the material. Is your mind clearer in the afternoon or evening? Schedule your study session then. Another method is to study at the same time of day that you will take the test, so that your brain gets used to working on the material at that time and will be ready to focus at test time.

### STEP 5: STUDY!

Once you have done all the study preparation, it's time to settle into the actual studying. Sit down, take a few moments to settle your mind so you can focus, and begin to follow your study plan. Don't give in to distractions or let yourself procrastinate. This is your time to prepare so you'll be ready to fearlessly approach the test. Make the most of the time and stay focused.

Of course, you don't want to burn out. If you study too long you may find that you're not retaining the information very well. Take regular study breaks. For example, taking five minutes out of every hour to walk briskly, breathing deeply and swinging your arms, can help your mind stay fresh.

As you get to the end of each chapter or section, it's a good idea to do a quick review. Remind yourself of what you learned and work on any difficult parts. When you feel that you've mastered the material, move on to the next part. At the end of your study session, briefly skim through your notes again.

But while review is helpful, cramming last minute is NOT. If at all possible, work ahead so that you won't need to fit all your study into the last day. Cramming overloads your brain with more information than it can process and retain, and your tired mind may struggle to recall even previously learned information when it is overwhelmed with last-minute study. Also, the urgent nature of cramming and the stress placed on your brain contribute to anxiety. You'll be more likely to go to the test feeling unprepared and having trouble thinking clearly.

So don't cram, and don't stay up late before the test, even just to review your notes at a leisurely pace. Your brain needs rest more than it needs to go over the information again. In fact, plan to finish your studies by noon or early afternoon the day before the test. Give your brain the rest of the day to relax or focus on other things, and get a good night's sleep. Then you will be fresh for the test and better able to recall what you've studied.

### Step 6: Take a Practice Test

Many courses offer sample tests, either online or in the study materials. This is an excellent resource to check whether you have mastered the material, as well as to prepare for the test format and environment.

Check the test format ahead of time: the number of questions, the type (multiple choice, free response, etc.), and the time limit. Then create a plan for working through them. For example, if you have 30 minutes to take a 60-question test, your limit is 30 seconds per question. Spend less time on the questions you know well so that you can take more time on the difficult ones.

If you have time to take several practice tests, take the first one open book, with no time limit. Work through the questions at your own pace and make sure you fully understand them. Gradually work up to taking a test under test conditions: sit at a desk with all study materials put away and set a timer. Pace yourself to make sure you finish the test with time to spare and go back to check your answers if you have time.

After each test, check your answers. On the questions you missed, be sure you understand why you missed them. Did you misread the question (tests can use tricky wording)? Did you forget the information? Or was it something you hadn't learned? Go back and study any shaky areas that the practice tests reveal.

Taking these tests not only helps with your grade, but also aids in combating test anxiety. If you're already used to the test conditions, you're less likely to worry about it, and working through tests until you're scoring well gives you a confidence boost. Go through the practice tests until you feel comfortable, and then you can go into the test knowing that you're ready for it.

## Test Tips

On test day, you should be confident, knowing that you've prepared well and are ready to answer the questions. But aside from preparation, there are several test day strategies you can employ to maximize your performance.

First, as stated before, get a good night's sleep the night before the test (and for several nights before that, if possible). Go into the test with a fresh, alert mind rather than staying up late to study.

Try not to change too much about your normal routine on the day of the test. It's important to eat a nutritious breakfast, but if you normally don't eat breakfast at all, consider eating just a protein bar. If you're a coffee drinker, go ahead and have your normal coffee. Just make sure you time it so that the caffeine doesn't wear off right in the middle of your test. Avoid sugary beverages, and drink enough water to stay hydrated but not so much that you need a restroom break 10 minutes into the test. If your test isn't first thing in the morning, consider going for a walk or doing a light workout before the test to get your blood flowing.

Allow yourself enough time to get ready, and leave for the test with plenty of time to spare so you won't have the anxiety of scrambling to arrive in time. Another reason to be early is to select a good seat. It's helpful to sit away from doors and windows, which can be distracting. Find a good seat, get out your supplies, and settle your mind before the test begins.

When the test begins, start by going over the instructions carefully, even if you already know what to expect. Make sure you avoid any careless mistakes by following the directions.

Then begin working through the questions, pacing yourself as you've practiced. If you're not sure on an answer, don't spend too much time on it, and don't let it shake your confidence. Either skip it and come back later, or eliminate as many wrong answers as possible and guess among the remaining ones. Don't dwell on these questions as you continue—put them out of your mind and focus on what lies ahead.

Be sure to read all of the answer choices, even if you're sure the first one is the right answer. Sometimes you'll find a better one if you keep reading. But don't second-guess yourself if you do immediately know the answer. Your gut instinct is usually right. Don't let test anxiety rob you of the information you know.

If you have time at the end of the test (and if the test format allows), go back and review your answers. Be cautious about changing any, since your first instinct tends to be correct, but make sure you didn't misread any of the questions or accidentally mark the wrong answer choice. Look over any you skipped and make an educated guess.

At the end, leave the test feeling confident. You've done your best, so don't waste time worrying about your performance or wishing you could change anything. Instead, celebrate the successful completion of this test. And finally, use this test to learn how to deal with anxiety even better next time.

**Review Video: Test Anxiety**
Visit mometrix.com/academy and enter code: 100340

## Important Qualification

Not all anxiety is created equal. If your test anxiety is causing major issues in your life beyond the classroom or testing center, or if you are experiencing troubling physical symptoms related to your anxiety, it may be a sign of a serious physiological or psychological condition. If this sounds like your situation, we strongly encourage you to seek professional help.

## Online Resources

Due to our efforts to try to keep this book to a manageable length, we've created a link that will give you access to all of your online resources:

**mometrix.com/resources719/nystceatas-29098**

# It's Your Moment, Let's Celebrate It!

**Share your story @mometrixtestpreparation**